The California Coast

A Traveler's Companion

DONALD B. NEUWIRTH AND JOHN J. OSBORN JR.

THE COUNTRYMAN PRESS
WOODSTOCK, VERMONT

Library of Congress Cataloging-in-Publication Data
Neuwirth, Donald B., 1946–
The California coast: a traveler's companion/Don Neuwirth and John J. Osborn, Jr.
p. cm.
Includes index.
ISBN 0-88150-395-9 (alk. paper)
1. Pacific Coast (Calif.)—Guidebooks. I. Osborn, John J., 1945–
II. Title
F868.P33N48 1998
917.94—dc21 97—47558
CIP

Cover photo of Diver's Cove, Laguna Beach © 1996, Michele Burgess/The Stock Market
Cover design by Seventeenth Street Studios
Text design by Seventeenth Street Studios
Maps by Eureka Cartography, © 1998 The Countryman Press

While the authors and publisher have made every attempt to make this guide accurate and up to date, things are bound to change, and we cannot take responsibility for any loss, injury, or inconvenience experienced by any traveler as a result of our information. We welcome updates, comments, and questions. Please address letters to *California Coast* Editor at the Vermont address below.

Published by The Countryman Press
PO Box 748
Woodstock, VT 05091-0748

Distributed by W.W. Norton & Company, Inc.
500 Fifth Avenue
New York, NY 10110

Printed in the United States of America
10 9 8 7 6 5 4 3 2 1

Dedicated to Rebecca S. Neuwirth and Meredith B. Osborn

Acknowledgments

Thanks and appreciation for their time and effort go to the following people who helped us with this project: Research associates Diane Duvall, Paul Kretkowski, Sherry Minkowski, and Becca Neuwirth; and photographers James Blank, Tom Mikkelsen, Leah Minkowski-Emkin, and Jan Rentzer. We would also like to thank all the helpful and inspirational people up and down the coast who let us interview them and tell their stories as our "coastal companions."

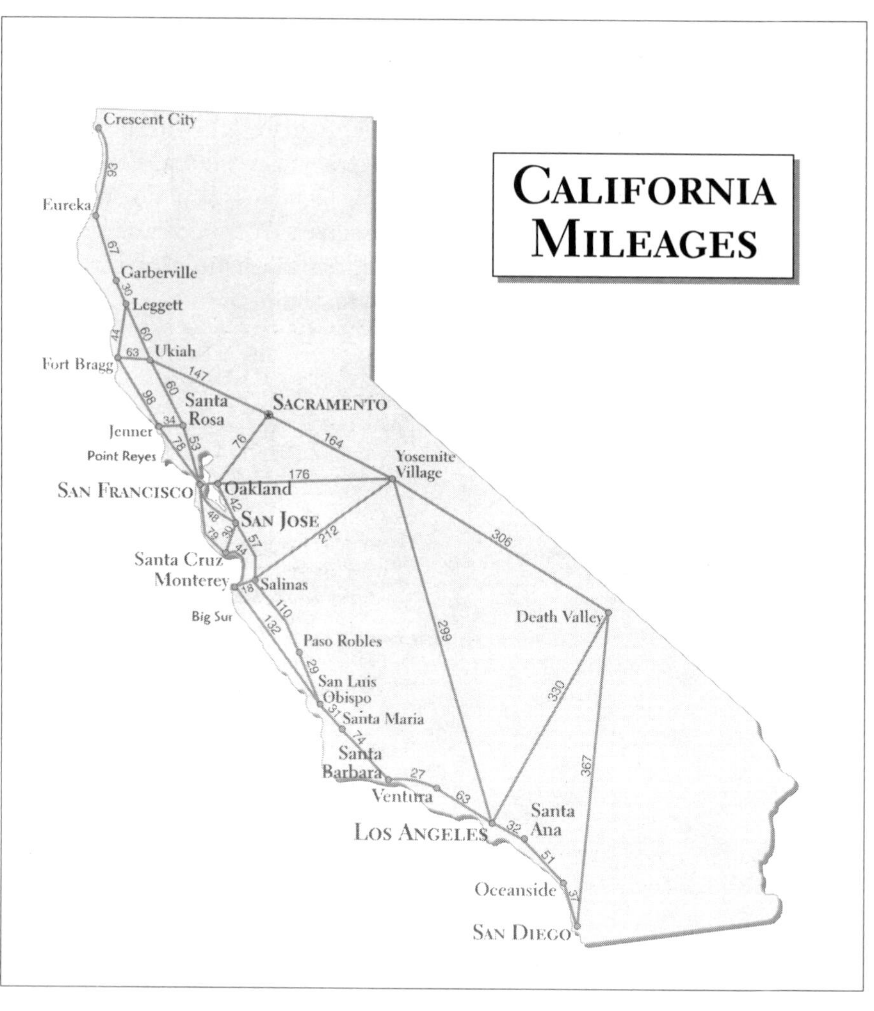
California Mileages
Crescent City
Eureka
Garberville
Leggett
Fort Bragg
Ukiah
Santa Rosa
Sacramento
Jenner
Point Reyes
Yosemite Village
San Francisco
Oakland
San Jose
Santa Cruz
Monterey
Salinas
Big Sur
Death Valley
Paso Robles
San Luis Obispo
Santa Maria
Santa Barbara
Ventura
Los Angeles
Santa Ana
Oceanside
San Diego

Contents

Foreword

THE "COAST" IS A STATE OF MIND and an image of a state. It is the shorthand psychic reference that much of the country uses for the state of California. It conjures up movie stars, Highway 1 twisting through the hills of Big Sur, surfers at Rincon Point, and *Baywatch* lifeguards on duty. The coast is a series of moods: the rugged poetry of Robinson Jeffers in Big Sur, the dark detective novels of Ross Macdonald set in Santa Barbara, the naturalistic tales of John Steinbeck on *Cannery Row*.

The coast is also a real place. It is schoolchildren exploring the tide pools at the James Fitzgerald Marine Reserve in San Mateo County and families hiking the coastal redwood hills of Del Norte Coast Redwoods State Park. It is swimming off Shell Beach in the warm water of Tomales Bay in Marin, or visiting the Monterey Aquarium. It is playing beach volleyball on Manhattan State Beach in Los Angeles and fishing off the Ocean Beach Pier in San Diego. It is visiting an art gallery in La Jolla in San Diego County, and riding a wonderful roller coaster on the Santa Cruz Boardwalk. Or the coast can be a quiet weekend at a bed & breakfast on the bluffs above Albion Cove in Mendocino or riding horseback along Ocean Beach in San Francisco.

The real coast is geologically complicated. Northern and southern California are polar opposites in the cultural mind, but the real northern and southern California meet at a real place: Point Conception in Santa Barbara County. Here the characteristic north–south Coast Ranges of northern California meet the east–west "transverse ranges" of southern California. To the north, all the way to the Oregon line, the coast is serrated, rugged, and often wild, where the shoulders of the Coast Ranges fall into the sea. To the south of Point Conception, the coast is forgiving, because wide valleys between east–west mountain ranges unfold gently to the beach.

The water also changes at Point Conception. The California Current sweeps down the northern coastline, bringing cold waters from Alaska. At Point Conception this current turns west and flows out to sea. In the south, the Southern California Countercurrent brings warm water north from Mexico. At Point Conception it, too, turns west.

Even the sand is different, north and south. Above Point Conception, dark sand from the north moves south with the current. Below the point, the countercurrent brings up ground quartz and feldspar from the hundreds of miles of uninhabited shores of the Baja coast to the beaches of southern California. Here, the beaches are white.

The real coast is also complicated in other ways, and easy generalizations, like these about northern and southern California, are always suspect. For the coast is also the story of the San Andreas fault and plate tectonics, which have combined to move sections of southern California north to San Francisco. And within some regions—Sonoma County, for example—the fault winds back and forth along the coastline, creating headlands, harbors, valleys, coves, pocket beaches, sea stacks, wetlands—a coastline that varies mile by mile.

In short, the real coast is diverse and complicated. A reliable, comprehensive guide can be a help.

We believe this is one of the most comprehensive guidebooks to the California coast ever written, but we have also tried to be helpful coastal companions. Thus, we have made value judgments, derived from our personal experience exploring and learning the coast.

The two of us learned the coast in two very different ways and believe our differences have helped us evaluate it. John Osborn was raised in California. He has camped on the coast as a child, surfed the coast as a teenager, and sailed down the coast as an adult. Today, he spends most weekends on the shore, finding adventures that will accommodate the wide variety of interests of his three children. Don Neuwirth is a native New Yorker, and was first exposed to coastal management while he worked his way through college as a lifeguard on Coney Island. As the California Coastal Commission's first Coastal Access Program manager, Don was responsible for opening up and developing dozens of new beach accessways and recreational facilities up and down the coast, helping to shape the experiences all of us have on the coast of California. As program manager, he also produced the first three editions of the *California Coastal Access Guide*, the first comprehensive explanation of coastal access. Later, as the head of the Marin Conservation Corps, Don was responsible for building coastal access facilities and trails in one of the most ecologically sensitive areas in the state. He knows the coast not only as a user but also as a planner and manager.

These personal experiences have given us strong feelings about what is good—and bad—on the coast. We both agree that certain places on the coast are not worth your time. However, rather than complain about these locations—a maximum security prison sited in a beautiful bay, for example—we have simply left them out. We have included every single place on the coast that we can honestly recommend. All of the usable, attractive locations are here. We cover beaches, lodging, restaurants, coastal museums, cultural attractions, camping locations—omitting only those places that we feel do not rate a visit. Additionally, we have presented all the secret places that we regard as ours especially.

At the same time, we acknowledge that things are constantly changing on the coast. If you find an error, or have an addition or comment for inclusion in the next edition, please let us know.

THE COASTS OF CALIFORNIA

We have emphasized six particular "coasts" of California. The first is the **Family Coast**—those locations offering special experiences that can be enjoyed by the whole family, as at the Monterey Aquarium. Sometimes these recommendations take the form of extended trips, in which it is possible to visit a variety of locations for a full-day or weekend outing.

Second, we feature the **Quiet Coast**. Many Californians use the coast as a sanctuary, a way to get away from major urban centers. Our Quiet Coast consists of isolated, hidden, and beautiful beaches, nature preserves, tide pools, and secluded bed & breakfast inns. (Even in the southern California urban corridor there are patches of Quiet Coast.)

Third, we explore the **Living Coast**, those areas that emphasize the animals, plants, and insects of the coast. This includes not only naturally occurring protected habitats, both on the coast itself and in adjacent underwater locations, but also arboretums and flower gardens.

Fourth, we note the **Sporting Coast**, explaining where to find skin diving, horseback riding, surfing, beach volleyball, fishing, swimming, and biking. After some soul searching, we have even included a spot where one can legally drive a dune buggy among lovely sand dunes.

Fifth, we have highlighted the **Cultural Coast**. Spanish missions, the Hearst Castle, art colonies, the Getty Museum, the Santa Cruz Surfing Museum, and many other places help to bring the history and culture of California into focus. The Cultural Coast includes California's diverse literary tradition as well.

Sixth, we provide the **Urban Coast**, areas where city and beach intermingle, as at the great urban beachfronts of Los Angeles and San Diego. Here are the beachfront shopping areas, often with unique boutiques, and noted restaurants overlooking the Pacific.

At the back of this book are comprehensive lists that break down the coast into these six divisions in order to help with trip planning. Within these larger designations, we highlight features that help make any visit to the coast go smoother, such as shopping areas.

Finally, we attempt to explain the coast of California through the people who live and work there. Thus, you will find sprinkled throughout the book stories about certain "coastal companions." These are ordinary people whose honest tales explain more about the real coast of California than our own research and words ever can.

We hope this book will also be an honest companion on your visits to the California coast.

How to Use This Book

THE CENTRAL SECTION of this guide is a south-to-north description of the coast. It is divided into two regions, northern and southern California. Each region has an introduction, followed by chapters giving detailed descriptions of each county. A locator map at the upper right corner of each page spread allows the reader to find each county quickly. Each county is broken down into sections describing shoreline facilities, other coastal attractions, and recommended places to eat and stay overnight. Each individual entry has a description, detailed directions, parking information, and any other relevant facts. We also include valuable natural and cultural background for each area. We evaluate the sites. We have included sources of additional information such as local independent bookshops, chambers of commerce, and tourist information centers.

EXPENSES

All entries provide an estimate of the admission or parking fees. These costs are always changing. Therefore, we cite a range of charges rather than an exact price, which is likely be inaccurate. Almost everything except admission fees is subject to state and local sales tax of approximately 8 percent.

Beaches, parks, and recreational facilities are still inexpensive; they cost less than $25 for day use. As fiscal austerity continues in the public sector and market pressures affect private facilities, entrance charges and parking fees are being collected for the first time or are increasing in cost. State and national parks are still bargains, charging $5–10 for day use. County and municipal facilities have comparable charges. Nonprofit environmental organizations own and administer many coastal facilities. They request a donation or charge a fee for tours or classes. Private beaches charge what the market will bear, often comparable to nearby public facilities.

Also inexpensive are most museums, aquariums, and cultural facilities. They charge from $5 to $15 for admission. Memberships are available for those who visit frequently or wish to support the institution. Amusement parks are rarely inexpensive; prices now approach $25 for an adult admission.

We consider any complete lunch or dinner (including tax and 15 percent tip) under $15 per person to be inexpensive. Moderate meals range from $15 to $30.

Meals above $30 we categorize as expensive. We have excluded most chain and fast-food restaurants. They are ubiquitous on the coast, and their marketing efforts don't need our help. Local and regional restaurants providing distinctive food and enjoyable atmosphere are included, and we have made an effort to list less expensive dining options, too.

Campsites and hostels are the only inexpensive lodgings on the coast. State, federal, county, and local campsites with full services range up to $25 per night. Hostels cost less than $15 per person per night for bare-bones facilities. Tent camping is cheaper, about $10 per site. Moderate hotels and inns cost $50 to $100 per night for double occupancy. Above $100 per night is considered expensive. We include listings in each category. Remember that there are occupancy taxes in many jurisdictions that can add 10 percent or more to your bill.

As noted in the introduction, the last section of this book, The Coasts of California, contains a series of lists describing the physical, cultural, and biological diversity, variety of recreational opportunities, and distinct communities of the coast. Each of the various "coasts"—sporting, cultural, family, and so on—is symbolized by an icon. The attractions listed are also indexed to the page in the county chapter in which their detailed description occurs.

KEY TO SYMBOLS USED IN THIS BOOK

These symbols flag entries that may be of particular interest.

quiet coast

living coast

sporting coast

cultural coast

urban coast

PART I

Southern California

IN SOUTHERN CALIFORNIA, the mountains run east to west. These are the transverse ranges. The largest are the Santa Monica, the San Gabriel, and the San Bernadino. Among the transverse ranges lie valleys that terminate at the beach. The largest of these broad, flat valleys is the Los Angeles.

Flowing up from the south, the Southern California Countercurrent brings warm Mexican water to southern California. Carried as sediment suspended in the warm sea are ground quartz and feldspar from the hundreds of miles of pristine beaches of the Baja coast. These "white sands" are distributed along the southern California beaches, renewing them.

The convergence of the wide east–west valleys, the warm waters of the countercurrent, and the unspoiled sand of the desolate Baja Peninsula combine to create the great white, wide beaches of southern California, perhaps the finest in the world.

The wide, flat valleys of southern California also create easy beach access that is unheard of in northern California. There, the coastal highway often hugs the side of steep cliffs; the beach is hundreds of feet below. Access is difficult. Local knowledge and a good guidebook are essential.

In the south, the coastal highway runs at sea level. Sometimes it runs on the beach itself. The ease of access has allowed the formation of wonderful city beaches: miles of wide white sand flanked by the highway and urban sprawl. Whatever its faults, the TV show *Baywatch* realistically portrays this aspect of the great southern California beaches.

Make no mistake about it: By and large, these *are* terrific beaches. But they are also full of people, lined by condos, malls, asphalt bike paths, and highways.

There are places here to get away from it all, and we describe them to you, but the large urban beaches of southern California are worthy in their own right: great multiuse jumbles of humanity, displaying and playing upon a precious and beautiful ribbon of white and blue.

The southern California beaches span five counties. Moving from south to north they are San Diego, Orange, Los Angeles, Ventura, and Santa Barbara.

San Diego, Orange, and Los Angeles Counties are all part of a single, homogeneous coastline, a huge hollow half-circle, the longest urban beachfront in the United States. Here, in an area from the Mexican border to the Los Angeles County line, wetlands, deltas, and low headlands hem miles of sandy beach, broken by the occasional jutting point—which often creates perfect surfing conditions.

To the north lies San Pedro Bay, broad and shallow, in the lee of the Palos Verdes headland. This bay contains the Port of Los Angeles, the largest port in the world. North of the headland is huge, gently curving Santa Monica Bay, an area of wide sandy beaches and intense urbanization. In the north of the bay, the coastline is more rugged and slightly less densely populated.

Santa Monica Bay terminates at Point Dume. Above the point, the coastline bulges slightly to the west where there is a large agricultural delta, formed by rivers, which makes up most of Ventura County. From Pitas Point in northern Ventura to Point Conception in Santa Barbara, the coast swings west. Protected by the Channel Islands, and with undulating, sandy shoreline, this long section of beach in Santa Barbara is one of the most pleasant in the state.

Point Conception marks the end of the southern California coastline. Here, the coast swings abruptly north; it is immediately wilder and less forgiving.

San Diego County
Riverside County
San Clemente
Camp Pendleton
San Onofre State Beach
Camp Pendleton Beach Access
Asistencia San Antonio de Pala
Agua Tibea Wilderness
Cleveland Nat'l For
San Luis Rey de Francia
Harbor Beach
Oceanside City Beach
South Oceanside Beach
Oceanside
Carlsbad
Carlsbad City Beach
South Carlsbad State Beach
Escondido
Cleveland
Beacon's Beach
Stone Steps Beach
Fellowship Hermitage Grounds
Encinitas
San Elijo State Beach
Cardiff-by-the-Sea
Rancho Santa Fe
Solana Beach
National
Tide Beach Park
Del Mar
Torrey Pines State Reserve
Black's Beach
Scripps Institute of Oceanography
La Jolla Beach
La Jolla
Pacific Beach
Pacific Ocean
Forest
Pine Creek Wilderness
Hauser Wilderness
San Diego
See San Diego detail map
Sweetwater Marsh National Wildlife Refuge
National City
Silver Strand State Beach
Chula Vista
Imperial Beach
Tijuana River Estuarine Research Reserve
Border Field State Park
Tijuana R.
Tijuana
Mexico
n
0 5 10 Miles
0 5 10 15 Kilometers

CHAPTER ONE

San Diego County

IN THE SOUTH OF SAN DIEGO COUNTY is a huge bay cut from the ancient delta of the San Diego River. This is the best natural harbor in southern California, and in all of the state only San Francisco rivals it. Just to the north another large bay, Mission Bay, is in the lee of La Jolla, a headland of steep cliffs. These sandstone cliffs are among the most remarkable in the state; deep caves and arches are notched into the cliff face both above and below the sea.

From La Jolla to the Orange County line, long sandy beaches run north. They are backed by coastal bluffs that vary in height. Along this coastline are many beaches, most of which are safe for swimming in the warm waters. At the northern end of the county is a huge Marine base, Camp Pendleton. Development has not taken place here. Elsewhere, the 74 miles of San Diego coastline form a chain of cities and villages that lie just to the east of the beaches below headland bluffs.

Near the Mexican border is Tijuana River Estuarine Research Reserve, a large, diverse, protected habitat that huge flocks of migrating birds use as a stopping ground. Just to the north of the reserve begin the suburbs of the city of San Diego and, farther north, the western edge of San Diego Bay. Running along this section of coast are many intensively used, beautiful beaches. Among the best are Coronado City Beach, Silver Strand State Beach, and Imperial Beach.

Just to the north of this chain of beaches, running to the San Diego Harbor entrance, is the large Coronado Naval Air Station. There is no beach access in this area, but across the harbor entrance lie the Point Loma Ecological Reserve and the Cabrillo National Monument. Both are on the tip of Point Loma. Here trails meander through bluffs, from which migrating whales are often seen; many of the trails lead to tide pools that are among the best in all of California.

To the north of San Diego Harbor you'll find the coastal city of Ocean Beach and the harbor of Mission Bay. In this area Sunset Cliffs Park provides an outstanding view of the coast. In Mission Bay is Sea World, the justly famous aquatic theme park. Running north, broad, unprotected, and heavily used Pacific Beach curves into the La Jolla headland. There are several excellent pocket beaches here, including Hermosa and Marine Street Beach. Sun Gold Point, also in this area, is rocky but has good tide pools. Near Point La Jolla, at the northern end of the headland, is the Coast Walk. The condition of the walk changes with storms and erosion and it can be dangerous, but it is also the best place from which to view the La Jolla cliffs and the deep caves cut into them.

As the La Jolla headland swings east, La Jolla Bay begins. Here is the Scripps Institution of Oceanography, its aquarium and museum open to the public. Excellent interpretive exhibits explain the Scripps Shoreline–Underwater Reserve. This preserve is part of three linked, protected underwater areas that extend from La Jolla north to the city of Del Mar. In this area is La Jolla Shores beach. The waves here are larger in the north than they are in the southern part of the beach. This is caused by the La Jolla Submarine Canyon. As the waves of the southern beach pass over the canyon, their energy is dissipated by the great depth of the sea.

Above La Jolla, the San Diego coast begins its gentle westward curve toward Orange County. At Torrey Pines State Reserve, the preserved coastline is honeycombed with walking trails. Many lead to viewpoints looking out to steep coastal cliffs and the remarkable caves cut into them. The ocean cliffs here reach a height of 350 feet; they are the tallest in southern California. Just above the reserve is beautiful Torrey Pines State Beach. Sandy and large, the beach is protected by giant sandstone cliffs.

Above Torrey Pines is the Del Mar region of the San Diego coast. Here a former delta was carved by the San Dieguito River. In the wide valley of this delta you'll find the city of Del Mar. Extending to the north are a series of towns—Solana Beach, Cardiff-by-the-Sea, Encinitas, and Leucadia. There are many beaches on the coast here, in the shadow of the towns huddled on the low bluffs above.

To the north is Batiquitos Lagoon, an ecological reserve and another important habitat for migrating birds. Above the lagoon are the oceanfront towns of Carlsbad and Oceanside. This is a delta area, created by the San Luis and Santa Margarita Rivers. Here, two linked harbors have been dredged, Oceanside Harbor and Camp Pendleton Boat Basin. The extensive jetties of these harbors have inhibited the flow of sand to the beaches directly to the south.

To the north of these harbors is the 11-mile-long western edge of Camp Pendleton Marine Base, where very wide, sandy beaches buffer the low cliffs of a sloping terrace. These extensive beaches are not the result of a littoral cell of flowing sand. Rather, they are caused in large part by a series of culverts that runs beneath the coastal San Diego Freeway, channeling sediment runoff down to the water's edge. This has created several of the largest and best beaches in southern California. Access to much of this beachfront is restricted, but to the north at San Onofre, near the Orange County border, are two exceptional linked beaches, San Onofre State Beaches north and south.

Beaches and Attractions

IN IMPERIAL BEACH

Border Field State Park This 2-mile stretch of sandy beach is backed by dunes and salt marshes. It is popular for swimming, clamming, and surf-fishing, although it is occasionally closed due to high releases from sewage plants to the south. Facilities include picnic areas, barbecue pits, and wheelchair-accessible rest rooms. There also are hiking and equestrian trails that crisscross the park's wetlands area, and visitors can rent horses. The Tijuana River Estuary within the park serves as habitat for rare plant and animal species. Visitors should note that, as this park is right on the Mexican border, there is a certain amount of excitement from time to time as the Border Patrol apprehends those attempting to enter the United States illegally. (For more excitement, the park is separated only by a fence from a Tijuana bullring.) Access is via the west end of Monument Road; for more information, call 619-575-3613.

National Estuarine Research Reserve ★ This reserve consists of 2531 acres of salt marsh, sandy beach, and dunes. The area includes the Tijuana Slough National Reserve Refuge and Border Field State Park (see above). Some areas are off-limits, including the sand dunes, while others are closed seasonally for nesting birds; fishing is allowed along the shoreline in open surf only. The visitors center lists trails and has rest rooms, exhibits, a small library, guided tours, and education programs. Rest rooms and some trails are wheelchair accessible. Access is via Highway 5 at Coronado Avenue. For more information, call 619-575-3613.

Imperial Beach/Imperial Beach Municipal Pier. This wide, sandy beach features swimming, bodysurfing, and surf-fishing. The annual US Open Sandcastle Competition takes place in July, attracting huge crowds. The Imperial Beach Municipal Pier has a landscaped plaza, fish-cleaning area, wheelchair-accessible rest rooms, and a café. The beach has lifeguards, rest rooms, and a shower. The beach was recently extended by dredging, and visitors should take care in swimming; the beach drops off sharply beyond the "added" portion. There is metered parking at the intersection of Evergreen and First Streets as well as well as on-street parking. Access is west of Ocean Lane from Carnation to Encanto Avenues. For more information, call the Imperial Beach Lifeguard Station at 619-423-8328.

©JAMES BLANK

Sand castle contest at Imperial Beach

IN CORONADO

Silver Strand State Beach This narrow, 2-mile strip of fluffy white sand fronts shallow, fairly calm water; it's used for swimming, surfing, clamming, surf-fishing, and catching grunion. There also are a lot of folks combing the beach for shells. Visitors also will find a calm-water swimming basin on the bay side, which is connected to the beach via pedestrian tunnels. Rest rooms are available near parking lots. There are also lifeguards, a ranger station with exhibits, picnic areas, fire pits, wheelchair-accessible rest rooms, and 125 campsites for RVs; there are fees for day and overnight use. Access is at 3500 Highway 75. For more information, call 619-435-5184.

Coronado Shores Beach. This good choice for surfing, fishing, and surf-fishing is located at the south end of the well-to-do community of Coronado Island (actually a peninsula). It is a northerly continuation of Silver Strand Beach (see above); there is also a promenade, running along the top of a seawall, with excellent views. Access is via the seaward side of Coronado Shores Condominiums on Highway 75. Parking for the seawall is at the end of Avenida de las Arenas. For more information, call Coronado Recreation Services at 619-522-7342.

Coronado City Beach. This is a wide, sandy beach running from the famed Hotel del Coronado to North Island Naval Air Station. It's used for swimming, surfing, and surf-fishing. Facilities include fire rings, a dog run, rest rooms, lifeguards, and a picnic area in **Sunset Park**, at the north end of Ocean Boulevard. For families, this is a good mix of beach and grassy knoll. Access is west of Ocean Boulevard. There is metered street parking; for more information, call 619-522-7342.

Centennial Park/Harbor View Park/Bay View Park On the bay side of Coronado Island, these parks feature wheelchair-accessible paths with good views of downtown San Diego. You can rent a bike, hang out at the beach, fish at the pier, or catch one of the frequent ferries to San Diego. Access is at 1st and Orange Streets; for more information, call the Coronado Chamber of Commerce at 619-435-9260.

IN CHULA VISTA

Chula Vista Launching Ramp. Visitors can set sail 6:30 AM–10:30 PM from this 10-lane, concrete boat-launch area, which features docks and a hoist. There's safe swimming here at the southern portion of San Diego Bay, as well as fishing and waterskiing. The kids can romp in the playground, and barbecue grills at the picnic area round out the picture. Note that swimming and skiing are not allowed in the launch area. Access is via the west end of Marina Way, off Marina Parkway. For more information, call 619-686-6227.

IN NATIONAL CITY

Sweetwater Marsh National Wildlife Refuge ★ To access this 316-acre refuge, which protects the largest salt marsh in San Diego Bay, visitors must catch the Nature Interpretive Center shuttle at the parking lot at the intersection of E Street and Bay Boulevard, or at the Chula Vista Visitors Center at E Street and I-5. Inside the refuge, walks are conducted by the interpretive center. The endangered California least tern, the California light-footed clapper rail, and the Belding's savannah sparrow are just a few of the 175 bird species that pass through here. Admission to the center is free; it's open 10 AM to 5 PM Tuesday–Sunday; do take a look at the natural history exhibits, aquariums, terrariums, and observation platforms. Access is via the east shore of San Diego Bay, in National City and in Chula Vista. For more information, call 619-422-2473.

IN THE SAN DIEGO AREA

To see the busy harbor, take a boat tour from **San Diego Harbor Excursions** (619-234-4111), 1050 North Harbor Drive. Inexpensive to moderate.

Seaport Village at Pacific Highway and Harbor Drive is a busy entertainment complex designed to look like a 19th-century seaport. Shops and galleries are found in a pleasing, parklike setting.

Horton Plaza is just inland at Broadway and G Street between 1st and 4th Avenues. A fairly typical urban shopping mall, Horton is done in a whimsical architectural style. Eclectic design and entertainment add interest to the shopping and eating experiences found there. Behind the plaza is the **Gaslamp District**, a large historic district featuring restored Victorian buildings. These commercial buildings formed San Diego's first business district, then became disreputable. Now revived, they're worth seeing on the stroll from Broadway and 6th Avenue to the waterfront.

The Museum of Contemporary Art (619-234-1001), 1001 Kettner Boulevard (at Kettner and Broadway), is worth a visit.

G Street Pier/Broadway Pier These piers are two great spots for fishing and enjoying San Diego Bay views. While waiting for a nibble on weekend afternoons, visitors can also tour any of several US Navy ships that tie up here. Access is west of N. Harbor Drive at the end of G Street. Access to Broadway Pier is via the west end of Broadway. For more information on ship tours, call 619-532-1431.

Maritime Museum This site features three historic ships, including a 125-year-old bark that used to make the London–New Zealand run. There is an admission fee. Access is west of Harbor Drive at the end of Ash Street. For more information, call 619-234-9153.

Embarcadero This centrally located bicycling and walking path runs along some of the most densely developed parts of San Diego's waterfront. Both the path and rest rooms are wheelchair accessible. There are also restaurants, fish markets, shops, and harbor excursion tours to be found along the way. Access is along Harbor Drive at the end of Hawthorne Street in San Diego's downtown. Many piers are open to the public, providing views of the working harbor. At the end of Kettner Drive is the **Embarcadero Marina Park**. It offers grassy picnic areas, ball fields and courts, and a fishing pier. Public rest rooms are available.

San Diego Zoo ★ This is the best zoo on the West Coast. It's worth a day visit (it's at 2920 Zoo Drive) to see hundreds of animals in realistic habitats. Admission fee charged. Call 619-234-3153 for more information.

IN POINT LOMA

Point Loma Ecological Reserve/Cabrillo National Monument ★ This is an underwater reserve on the western shore of Point Loma. Fishing is allowed, but only fin fish can be taken. The monument commemorates Juan Rodríguez Cabrillo's discovery of San Diego Bay; its attractions include a visitors center with exhibits, a gift shop, the Old Point Loma Lighthouse, and an overlook with a telescope useful for watching gray whales migrating December–March. There are also hiking trails, particularly the 1½-mile bayside trail, with some trails leading to tide pools. Access is via the south end of Cabrillo Drive. For more information, call 619-557-5450.

Commercial Basin. This busy marina houses primarily commercial vessels, but also comprises a sport-fishing service, three fishing piers, a fuel dock, launching ramp, marine railway, marine supplies, and boat sales and services. Whale-watching trips are offered December–March. Parking is available at Kettenburg Marine's parking areas after hours and at the public lots on Shelter Island Drive. Access is east of Rosecrans Street, north of Shelter Island Drive.

Shelter Island This complex of high-rise hotels and marinas built out into San Diego Bay provides safe protected beaches, trails, and boating facilities. Enter from Shelter Island Drive off Rosecrans near the airport. Rest rooms are available.

IN OCEAN BEACH

Sunset Cliffs Park Steep, eroded trails and stairways here lead to several beaches. Rough conditions make this the haunt of experienced divers and surfers only. There is a path along the cliffs that provides fabulous views of the coastline, but note that this path and others at Sunset Cliffs can be dangerous. Access is along Sunset Cliffs Boulevard, anywhere from Point Loma Avenue to Ladera Street.

Ocean Beach Municipal Fishing Pier. This is a T-shaped giant of 2100 feet located at the south end of Ocean Beach Park. Facilities include parking, wheelchair-accessible rest rooms, bait and tackle shops, and a fish-cleaning area. Visitors also can access a sandy beach from the pier, and there's good spectating of surfers a little way north at City Beach (see below). Access is via the end of Niagara Avenue. For more information, call 619-221-8901.

Ocean Beach Park. Just north of the Municipal Pier, this is an excellent surfing, swimming, and surf-fishing beach that also has tide pools and a picnic area. There are lifeguards, parking at Newport Street, outdoor showers, and wheelchair-accessible rest rooms. There is even a Dog Beach, where your canine can be off his leash during the day. Access is between the ends of Niagara Avenue and Voltaire Street. For more information, call 619-221-8901.

Ocean Beach City Beach This is a big family beach, or rather a series of pocket beaches and tide pools, good for sunbathing and surfing. Swimming, however, is hazardous because of rip currents and should be avoided despite the lifeguards. You get to a path that follows the shoreline by way of stairs at Santa Cruz, Bermuda, Orchard, and Narragansett Avenues. There is metered street and lot parking; access is between Ocean Beach Pier and the end of Pescadero Avenue. For more information, call the San Diego Coastline Parks Division at 619-221-8900.

IN MISSION BAY

Sea World ★ Enjoy excellent sea life exhibits in addition to the famous performing acts—worth a day's visit. It's located at Sea World Drive in Mission Bay. Call 619-226-3901 for more information.

Mission Bay beaches On this artificial bay, the beaches are small but safe, although water quality tends to be a problem at times. The bay is extensively developed with commercial recreational attractions. **De Anza Cove** and **Bonita Cove** are the best. These beaches are not as crowded as those at the ocean. You'll find good parking and facilities; rest rooms are available.

Mission Beach Park. Widened by sand dredging, this 3-mile-long strip runs the entire length of Ocean Front Walk. It has designated areas for surfing, swimming, and body-surfing, and visitors should pay attention to the lifeguards' continuously updated lists of water and tide conditions for safety. A paved promenade along the beach allows for jogging and all manner of wheeled transportation, including bicycles. Families who want to avoid rough water can try the Plunge public swimming pool, while thrill-seekers can take a swing at the recently restored Giant Dipper roller coaster. Access is west of Strand Way north of the Mission Bay entrance channel; there is lot parking. Call 619-221-8900 for further information.

IN PACIFIC BEACH

Pacific Beach Park/Palisades Park. These two northerly extensions of Mission Beach attract a lot of high school students, as well as college students from nearby La Jolla. The Crystal Pier is a good fishing spot here, and there are paved paths for pedestrians and bicyclists. Palisades Park has a grass picnic area. Access is west of Ocean Boulevard; there is lot parking. For more information, call 619-581-9927.

IN LA JOLLA

This community is world famous for surfing and shopping. The gentry gravitate toward the elegant shops and restaurants, and the kids enjoy the excellent surfing conditions.

Tourmaline Surfing Park This is one of the *grandes dames* of the San Diego surfing scene. Swimming is prohibited here, the better to give surfers a shot at the unusually large waves that break offshore. Skin diving and sea kayaking are allowed, though, and there are showers and rest rooms once you're back on land. There is lot parking. Access is west of La Jolla Boulevard at the end of Tourmaline Street; call the San Diego Lifeguard Service at 619-221-8901 for further information.

La Jolla Strand Park/Windansea Beach/Marine Street Beach These three beaches, together a mile long, see an enormous amount of surfing; they all are wide, alternately sandy and rocky, and host swimming, diving,

©JAMES BLANK

La Jolla

and fishing. Caution should be exercised in the large waves, though, and there are no lifeguards. Windansea is the beach Tom Wolfe wrote about in his classic *The Pump House Gang*, and 30 years later it's still a center of the surfing life. There is only street parking here; access is west of Neptune Place. Call 619-221-8901 for further information.

Scripps Institution of Oceanography ★ Here visitors will find a first-rate aquarium and museum complex, as well as a touch tide pool at the aquarium's entrance. Not only does Scripps have all different sorts of fish, but it also has some fine exhibits that explain tidal and wave action, the keys to understanding the California coast. Students' research projects are occasionally included in the exhibits, which invariably are fascinating to anyone interested in marine science. Access is via 8602 La Jolla Shores Drive; there is lot parking, and admission is free (although a small donation is suggested), making Scripps a real bargain. Call 619-534-3474 for more information.

Torrey Pines City Beach (aka Black's Beach) A steep path at the south end of Blackgold Road leads to good swimming and surf-fishing. The beach is sandy with eroded bluffs backing it up; visitors should note that this is a nude beach divided roughly into three parts: men only at the north end, coed in the middle, and nude surfers to the south. On-street parking is limited to 2 hours. The beach technically is the property of the University of California, and permission to use the path to get to it can be revoked by the owner. Access is via La Jolla Farms Road at Blackgold Road; there is limited free street parking. For more information, call 619-221-8901.

Torrey Pines City Park. The park overlooks the ocean with steep paths and stairs that lead down to the beach from the ends of the parking lot. This is a popular spot for hang gliding off the surrounding bluffs, and the park also has a radio-controlled model aircraft field. Pit toilets are available. Access is west of N. Torrey Pines Road, at the end of Torrey Pines Scenic Drive. For more information, call 619-221-8901.

Torrey Pines State Reserve/Torrey Pines State Reserve Extension ★ The Torrey pine is the world's rarest pine tree. Located on steep bluffs interspersed with deep ravines, the reserve is the only natural continental habitat for the these unusual trees. (The Torrey pine is otherwise found only on Santa Rosa Island, 175 miles northwest off Santa Barbara.) The finest stands of trees are located in the Torrey Pines Natural Preserve (a part of the State Reserve), but the nearby Los Penasquitos Marsh Natural Preserve hosts endangered bird species like the least tern and light-footed clapper rail. It is one of the few remaining salt marsh and lagoon areas in southern California, and a key feeding and nesting area for migratory birds. Visitors will have several opportunities to observe plants and animals while exploring the network of trails that lead to the beach. Interpretive programs and guided walks are offered on weekends and holidays. There is a day-use fee. The reserve extension has fabulous views of Los Penasquitos Reserve and the ocean from its trails leading through the extension. Sharp-eyed observers may see a black-shouldered kite or snowy plover. Parking is available off Del Mar Heights Road. Access is west of N. Torrey Pines Road, 2 miles north of Genessee Avenue. Access to the extension is west of I-5 off Del Mar Heights Road at Mar Scenic Drive. For more information on either site, call 619-755-2063.

Torrey Pines State Beach. This wide sandy beach stretches from Torrey Pines City Beach north to 6th Street. Beach access and parking are at the North Beach area. Visitors will find a lot of picnicking, swimming, surfing, surf-fishing, clamming, and skin diving here. The beach generally is more crowded and has coarser sand than at Black's Beach (in La Jolla; see above), but there is more clothing in evidence as well. The landscape at the southern end is a dramatic mix of beach, cliffs, and boulders that have fallen to the ocean. There are rest rooms, and lifeguards are on duty during the summer and on spring weekends. Dogs are not allowed on the beach. Parking is available at a fee lot until sunset. Access is at McGonigle Road, off Carmel Valley Road. For more information, call 619-755-2063.

IN DEL MAR

Del Mar City Beach. Located in the increasingly trendy village of Del Mar, this wide, coarse-sand beach fills up quickly on sunny weekends. Visitors can swim, surf, and surf-fish all along its length; there are outdoor showers and seasonal lifeguard service. Families like to come here, as well as students from nearby UC San Diego. There is off-street parking adjacent to the AMTRAK station near 15th Street, and some on-street metered parking. Access is across the AMTRAK tracks, west of Camino Del Mar, from 18th Street to Torrey Pines State Beach. For more information, call Del Mar Community Services at 619-755-1556.

IN SOLANA BEACH

Seascape Surf. A wooden stairway leads to this small but sandy beach; it's popular for surfing, skin diving, surf-fishing, swimming, and grunion-catching, and has nets for sand volleyball. There is free on-street parking. Access is via the stairway at 501 S. Sierra Avenue. For more information, call the Solana Beach Department of Marine Safety at 619-755-1569.

Fletcher Cove Park. A ramp leads you to a sandy beach where you'll find activities such as diving, swimming, surfing, surf-fishing, and grunion-catching. There are lifeguards on duty; the beach's north end is best for surfing, while the south end attracts beachcombers in search of shells. There are also basketball and shuffleboard courts, volleyball nets, picnic tables, and rest rooms. The beach is open 24 hours a day. Access is via 111 S. Sierra Avenue; for a 24-hour surf and weather report, call 619-755-1569.

Tide Beach Park. This small, sandy beach has lifeguards on duty during the summer; attractions include surfing, scuba diving, swimming, surf-fishing, and even spearfishing. Access to the beach is by a stairway leading down the bluff at Pacific Avenue and Solana Vista Drive. For more information, call the Solana Beach Department of Marine Safety at 619-755-1569.

IN CARDIFF-BY-THE-SEA

Cardiff State Beach/San Elijo State Beach. Cardiff is a wide, alternately sandy and rocky beach with good conditions for surf-fishing and surfing on its southern half and swimming on the northern half. Carry-on and soft-bottomed boats can be launched and landed on the north end of the beach, but that area is closed during the summer. You can also explore tide pools at the south end of the beach. Lifeguards patrol the beach year-round but are in the towers only during the summer. There is a fee parking lot; access is via Old Highway 101, directly west of San Elijo Lagoon. For more information, call 619-753-5091. **San Elijo State Beach** is a series of tide pools and sand located just north of Cardiff State Beach. The campground is on a bluff overlooking the beach and offers beautiful ocean views. There are 171 campsites, picnic tables, grills, showers, and beach equipment rentals. Call ahead for availability of these facilities. Access is via Old Highway 101 north of Chesterfield Drive. For more information, call 619-753-5091.

IN ENCINITAS

Swami's This is an excellent surfing beach reached via stairs from a small blufftop park. Surf-fishing, scuba diving, and swimming are popular here, but note that lifeguards are on duty only during the summer months. The park has wheelchair-accessible rest rooms and a picnic area with barbecue grills; outdoor showers are located near the base of the stairway. Parking is available. Access is west of Old Highway 101 (First Street), just south of Santa Fe Drive. For more information, call 619-633-2740.

Self-Realization Fellowship Hermitage Grounds This is a meditation area with blufftop gardens that afford stunning, wraparound views of the San Diego coast. Hours are Tuesday–Saturday 9 AM–5 PM. Visitors should be aware that this is not a public beach, and that commercial photography and swimming attire are prohibited. Access is at 215 K Street. For more information, call 619-753-2888.

Moonlight Beach. This sandy beach is good for surfing, swimming, and surf-fishing. Out of the water you'll find volleyball and tennis courts, beach equipment rentals, a snack bar, picnic tables, fire rings, rest rooms, and outdoor showers. It's a good family beach; a major drainage for the local sanitary district runs nearby (in the form of a cement culvert), but generally causes no problems. Parking lots are at 4th and C Streets and at the end of C Street. There is additional parking for vehicles carrying wheelchairs at 4th and B Streets. Lifeguard service is seasonal. Access is via 4th Street at the west end of B Street. For more information, call 619-633-2740.

Stone Steps Beach. A long stairway with a bench at the top leads to a very narrow sand-and-cobble beach. Stone Steps is popular for swimming, surfing, and surf-fishing, and lifeguards are on duty. Visitors can find free on-street parking

©JAMES BLANK

Moonlight State Beach in Encinitas

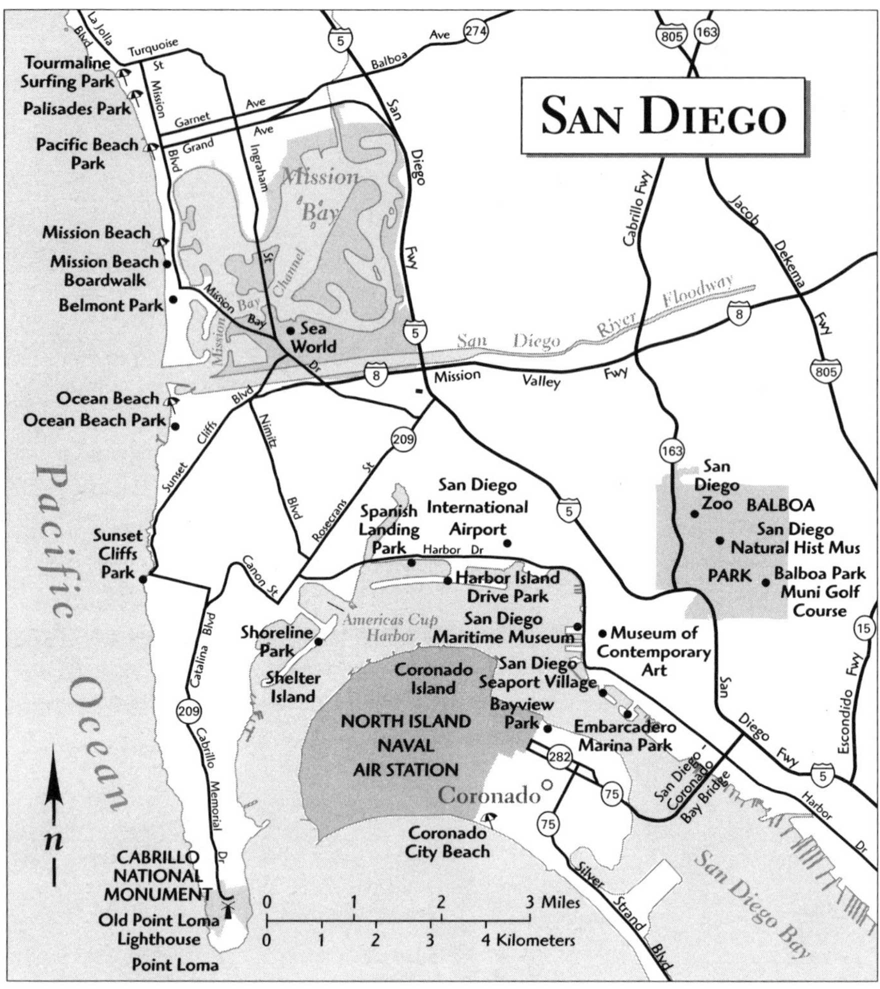

along Neptune Avenue. Access is via the west end of S. El Portal off Neptune Avenue. For more information, call 619-633-2740.

Encinitas Beach. Swimming and surf-fishing are the main activities at this narrow, sandy beach. To get there, walk south along the shore from Beacon's Beach or north from Stone Steps Beach. For more information, call 619-633-2740.

IN LEUCADIA

Beacon's Beach. Formerly a state beach, this stretch is now managed by the town of Leucadia. It consists of a small beach at the foot of yellow sandstone

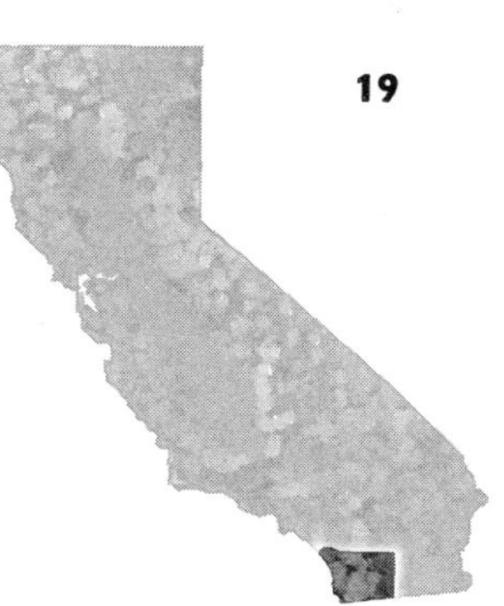

cliffs. Visitors can surf, swim, scuba dive, and surf-fish here, and there are lifeguards. Parking is available at the beach and at the end of Grandview Street; a wide dirt path leads to the beach. Access is at the west end of Leucadia Boulevard. For more information, call 619-633-2740.

IN CARLSBAD

South Carlsbad State Beach. This is a big, 4-mile-long, sand-and-cobble beach popular with surfers, who have to scramble over all sorts of debris to get to some larger-than-average waves. I-5 runs very close by the campgrounds, and there is an occasional problem with tar showing up on the beach, which has eroded some since the construction of Oceanside Harbor to the north. None of these factors keeps the beach and campgrounds from filling up quickly, though; campers should make reservations well in advance. There are more than 200 blufftop campsites that have hot showers, a self-service laundry, grocery, bait store, and beach equipment rentals. Day-use parking within the park is limited, but roadside parking is available along Carlsbad Boulevard at San Marcos Creek. There are day-use and camping fees. Access is west of Carlsbad Boulevard at Poinsettia Lane. For more information, call 760-438-3143. For camping reservations, call 1-800-444-7275.

Agua Hedionda Lagoon. This lagoon's calm waters make a popular swimming, fishing, and water-skiing spot for those looking to avoid the large waves off Carlsbad. A walkway leads from Cove Drive past a condominium development and out to views of the lagoon, and to a small sandy beach. There are also several walkways and paths along the blufftop, and a vista point off Park Drive west of Neblina Drive. Access is east and west of I-5, 1.4 miles south of the Civic Center in Carlsbad.

Carlsbad State Beach/Carlsbad City Beach. These two are essentially the same beach; bluffs overlook both sandy and rocky areas below, where visitors will see surfers, swimmers, sunbathers, surf-fishers, and scuba divers. The beaches offer rest rooms, benches, picnic tables, grassy areas, and overlooks along the bluff. Note that lifeguards are on duty only during the summer. Surfing at City Beach is restricted to the months of May–October. A paved pedestrian-only path at the state beach runs along the seawall with stairs leading up to viewing platforms. Access to Carlsbad State Beach is west of Carlsbad Boulevard, between Pacific and Elm Avenues. Access to City Beach is west of Ocean Street, between Pacific and Elm Avenues. For more information about either beach, call 760-438-3143.

IN OCEANSIDE

South Oceanside Beach (including Buccaneer Beach) This is a small, immaculate, sandy beach bordered by Buena Vista Lagoon to the south and the outlet of Loma Alta Creek to the north. It's good for surfing, relatively uncrowded, and lifeguards are on duty during the summer. Visitors can also swim. Along the blufftop is a park called the Strand, which features benches and picnic tables. Access is west of Pacific Street, between Morse and Eaton Streets. Buccaneer Beach is accessible via stairs in the 1500 block of Pacific Street, at the end of Cassidy Street and adjacent to 1639 Pacific Street. For more information, call the Oceanside Department of Harbors and Beaches at 619-966-4580.

Oceanside Pier. Another southern California giant, this pier measures more than 1900 feet long. It is lighted and patrolled, and includes a bait and tackle shop, restaurant, and rest rooms. No license is required to fish from the pier, and a motorized, wheelchair-accessible trolley runs from the pier gate to the pier's end. There is also a community center, and gym facilities that are open to the public for a small fee. There is a fee for parking. Access is at the west end of Pier View Way. For more information, call 619-966-4580.

Oceanside City Beach. Oceanside City Beach is a long, wide, sandy stretch popular for swimming, surfing, and surf-fishing. Facilities include covered picnic tables, barbecue grills, outdoor showers, and rest rooms. There are lifeguards, and a landscaped concrete path runs from Breakwater Way to the Oceanside Pier along the Strand. There are fee and free parking lots; access is along the Strand, between San Luis Rey River and Witherby Street. For more information, call 619-966-4580.

Harbor Beach. This is a wide, sandy beach augmented by dredging, and good for sunbathing, swimming, and surf- and rock-fishing. Facilities include wheelchair-accessible picnic areas, fire rings, and playground equipment, and lifeguards are on duty during the summer. There are campsites for self-contained RVs. Free parking is available. Access is at the corner of Harbor Drive South and Pacific Street. For more information, call 619-966-4580.

IN CAMP PENDLETON

Camp Pendleton Beach Access. Camp Pendleton, the Marine base, restricts access to this stretch of sand and surf to permits obtained via lottery. Even with a permit, visitors are limited to Las Pulgas (Red) Beach for surf-fishing and self-contained RV camping, with swimming and surfing prohibited even with a permit. Beach access permit applications are accepted only in November and drawings are held the first week in December; only 1,000 fee-based permits are selected each year. To apply, send a self-addressed, stamped postcard with your name and your immediate family members' names to: Director, Natural Resources Office, Marine Corps Base, Camp Pendleton, CA 92055. Access is west of I-5, at Las Pulgas Road. For more information, call 619-725-3360.

Bike path. This paved path (it has no formal name), primarily a former access road, runs west of I-5 from the south entrance of Camp Pendleton, north into Orange County and San Clemente. It's a very pleasant, safe ride along the bluffs of San Diego County's northernmost beaches. Bicyclists should not be rattled if they encounter a uniformed, armed Marine sitting in a booth in the middle of the road in the middle of nowhere, who may ask to see identification. The path exits Camp Pendleton into San Onofre State Beach Campground, crosses to the east side of I-5 at Cristianitos Road, and ends at Avenue del Presidente in San Clemente.

IN SAN ONOFRE

San Onofre State Beach South (aka Bluffs Beach). Located on bluffs punctuated by occasional ravines and canyons, this is a large campground with 221 tent and trailer spaces, as well as a group camp for up to 50 people. There are also rest rooms and showers. You'll find 26 tent spaces at the Echo Arch hike-in camp, which has no other facilities. This site is closed during the winter rainy season. The southern end of the beach is a very popular clothing-optional spot. For years there was a duel between the hardier nudists who wanted to bare it all a little farther south, on Camp Pendleton's beaches, and the security-conscious commandos who attempted to cite them. The nudists would flee back north onto state, rather than federal, property, and the game would start over again the next day. Things have relaxed a bit since then. There are fees for day use and camping. Several hiking trails lead from the campsite to the beach, providing panoramic views of the coastline and excellent vantage points for whale-watching. Leashed dogs are allowed. Access is southwest of I-5 (take the San Onofre exit), 2.5 miles south of Basilone Road. For more information, call 714-492-0802.

San Onofre State Beach North. This is a wide, sandy beach below the sandstone bluffs that characterize this last bit of San Diego coast. The beach is just north of the San Onofre Nuclear Generating Station, providing a remarkable picture of the contrast between the works of nature and those of man. This beach has several well-known surf spots; the famed Trestles Beach is 1.5 miles to the north and Surf Beach lies just to the south. A paved trail leads to Trestles from the parking lot at Cristianitos Road and El Camino Real. Surf Beach

Petty Officer Ron Pojar—Coast Guard Team Leader

■ Boats going in and out of the great harbors of San Diego—San Diego Bay in the south and Mission Bay above it—rely on a system of buoys. Going into these bays, or into any harbor in the United States, ships keep the red buoys to the right and the green buoys to the left. ("Red right returning" is the catch phrase that sailors learn as children. They also learn "the red ship left port," which means to keep the red buoy to the left, or "port," side of the boat when they are leaving a harbor.) Following these simple rules they avoid rocks, submerged wrecks, sandbars, and all the other countless hazards that lie under the water.

Buoys float on the water. Typically, they are in the shape of a bottle, that is, they taper up to a small top. This kind of buoy is called a nun. Another shape is called a can, which is just what it looks like. Underneath each buoy is a length of chain attached to a heavy weight that lies on the sea floor, keeping the buoy in place.

But even with the heavy weight, buoys do move: A strong tide, a slight change in an ocean current, or fierce waves will gradually shift them off position. Then the passage into the harbor can become treacherous.

Ron Pojar's father was a member of a Coast Guard ATON team. (ATON stands for Aids to Navigation.) Ron's father inspected the buoys, made sure they hadn't drifted off course, and, if they had, moved them back to their proper position. If the buoys had lights or whistles or bells, he inspected them and replaced any components that were not functioning correctly.

To know if a buoy was in its correct position, Ron's father used a sextant, the same instrument that Columbus and Magellan used. Working with a sextant involves taking a precise reading on the position of the sun from the deck of a moving boat and using that "fix" to deduce the buoy's correct position through complex mathematical calculations. Often it could take two hours or more to find out exactly where the buoy was and where it should be.

Following in the steps of his father, Ron Pojar is also in the Coast Guard and the leader of an ATON team in the San Diego area. He goes out each day and inspects the 66 important buoys that are his primary responsibility. Ron is also responsible for 50 secondary buoys, which are too large for Ron and his team to move with their moderately sized Coast Guard vessel. To move the secondary buoys, Ron calls in a huge Coast Guard buoy tender that can pull almost anything up off the ocean bed.

Unlike his father, Ron doesn't use a sextant to determine if a buoy is in its correct position. He uses a Global Positioning System, or GPS unit. These units communicate with satellites to give a sailor an exact, instantaneous position. They work in any kind of weather, and at night. Although all GPS units are accurate, the Coast Guard units are particularly good. Ron can always find the correct position of a buoy to within ten meters, and usually within two.

When Ron needs to service a buoy, he swings out a boom from his boat and catches the chain that leads from the buoy to the weight on the ocean floor. He uses a "chain stopper" to grip the chain, and then hauls it up with an electric motor. He cleans the buoy and chain if they need it or replaces the chain entirely if that's what's called for. Then he looks at the screen on his GPS unit and drives the buoy to the exact correct position.

Most of the buoys that Ron works with are "Nerf" buoys. They look the same as the buoys that Ron's father worked with—that is, they are shaped like nuns and cans. But they are built of a soft, spongy material that resembles the stuff used to make Nerf balls. When Ron's father was servicing buoys, they were made of steel or hard plastic, and if a ship hit one, it would "crack the shell." Then the buoy had to be replaced. The Nerf buoys don't crack; they absorb the blow. And even if a piece of one is broken off, the buoy maintains its integrity because the color goes all the way through the material. They are also much lighter than the steel buoys that Ron's father dealt with. The smallest Nerf buoys are so light that a Coast Guardsman can lift one out of the water with his bare hands.

Ron's ATON group is a three-person team, one of only two three-person ATON teams left in all the Coast Guard. When they go out, all three must be in the boat because it takes one person to drive and two to service the buoys. These three people are responsible for all the crucial buoys in the San Diego area, one of the busiest harbor systems on the California coast.

It seems incredible that only three people perform this job, and do so with such reliability and skill that San Diego Harbor is one of the safest in the world. The answer to this paradox is that although San Diego Harbor is important and busy, it does not have a large number of buoys because it does not have a river. San Francisco Bay, for example, is the terminus of the Sacramento River. The buoy system there winds through the Bay and goes miles upriver into the central valley, buoys marking all the twists and turns and the entrances to all the harbors and tributaries along the way. In San Francisco Bay, there are more than 500 buoys, while only 120 are needed in the San Diego area. (On the Snake River and the Columbia River, ATON teams have to service buoy systems that run from the coast into Idaho. There are more aids to navigation in the United States than in all the rest of the world.)

Ron considers keeping the buoys in good shape the greatest job in the world. He thinks of himself as working for the "knowledgeable mariner," making sure that the people who know what they are doing can leave port safely and come back home. He takes pride in the fact that he makes a daily difference in their lives; he calls what he does "preventative search and rescue."

Not too long ago, Ron's father called up to ask about GPS units. Ron's father likes to go fishing in a 16-foot boat. Sometimes it's foggy, which of course makes it difficult to know exactly where you are. (A sextant is useless in the fog.) He wanted to know if he should buy a GPS unit. Today, you can get a very reliable GPS unit for around $100, so small and light that one will fit into your pocket. Yet it will tell you exactly where you are at any particular time, will show you exactly the route you followed to get there, and will guide you right back home. Most of the units have a pointing device that you can bring up on their tiny display screens, so that even if you don't know anything about navigation, all you have to do is follow the arrow to get home. GPS units are useful for hikers as well as boaters—in fact, they are very useful for anyone who travels the California coast. Ron appreciated his father's sentimental attachment to the sextant, but he recommended that his father buy a GPS unit. ■

©JAMES BLANK

Hotel Del Coronado

is located farther south off Basilone Road. The entrance to Surf Beach and the parking lot are west of the road, and there is a wetland area at the mouth of San Mateo Creek. There are 160 campsites at the San Mateo Campground, east of the highway on Cristianitos Road. Wheelchair-accessible rest rooms can be found at Surf Beach. Access is southwest of I-5 at Basilone Road. Call 714-492-0802 for further information.

Lodging

IN IMPERIAL BEACH

The Seacoast Inn (619-424-5183; 1-800-732-2627), 800 Seacoast Drive. Moderate. This deluxe 38-room hotel is right on the beach. Facilities include a heated swimming pool and hot tub, and the beachside units have full kitchens. It's a very popular place, so make reservations for a summer stay at least a year in advance.

Hawaiian Gardens Suite-Hotel (619-429-5303), 1031 Imperial Beach Boulevard. Moderate. The hotel, which is located about 10 blocks from the beach, provides 65 studios and several suites. Rooms are spacious; extras include a pool, sauna, and clubhouse.

IN CORONADO

Hotel del Coronado (619-435-6611), 1500 Orange Avenue. Expensive. This is a place to stay just to be able to say you stayed here. It is massive, deluxe, famous, architecturally distinctive (mostly because it was built in 11 months without blueprints!), and right on the beach. And it's where Jack Lemmon realized he liked wearing women's clothes in *Some Like It Hot*. The Hotel Del, as locals call it, is the grande dame of southern California beach resorts and worth every penny for its location and the amenities it provides: gardens, acres of lawn, an Olympic-sized pool, 24-hour room service, a croquet green, and a birdcage elevator in the lobby.

Coronado Inn (619-435-4121; 1-800-598-6624), 266 Orange Avenue. Inexpensive. Near the ferry landing, downtown shops, and restaurants. Modest, clean rooms include refrigerators. This is the best deal in town.

Village Inn (691-435-9318), 1017 Park Place. Moderate. Near the main city beach, in the midst of the downtown shopping district, these are quaint, European-style accommodations. A common kitchen is available.

El Rancho Motel (619-435-2251), 370 Orange Avenue. Inexpensive. Busy, basic accommodations are provided without any charm, but it's a good value.

IN DOWNTOWN SAN DIEGO

Note: What is generally referred to as "the city of San Diego" is actually a series of well-defined neighborhoods or communities. These are, moving from south to north, Coronado, downtown San Diego (which is within San Diego Bay), Point Loma, the Old Town/Mission Bay/Ocean Beach/Pacific Beach area, and La Jolla. We have located our lodging and restaurants under our listings for these communities.

Harbor Hill Guest House (619-233-0638), 2330 Albatross Street. Moderate. This charming and elegant bed & breakfast has views to the bay.

U.S. Grant Hotel (619-232-3121 or 1-800-237-5029), 326 Broadway. Expensive. This elegant, 280-room hotel has been restored to turn-of-the-century style.

San Diego Hostel International (619-525-1531), 521 Market Street. Inexpensive. Located in downtown San Diego's Gaslamp Quarter, this hostel offers dorms, private rooms (some with TVs), and a common kitchen.

IN POINT LOMA

Elliott (Point Loma) International Youth Hostel (619-223-4778), 3790 Udall Street. Inexpensive. This centrally located hostel has room for about 75 people and provides a fully equipped kitchen. A deposit for the first night's lodgings may be required.

IN OLD TOWN/MISSION BAY/OCEAN BEACH/ PACIFIC BEACH

Ocean Villa Motel (619-224-3481), 5142 W. Point Loma Boulevard, San Diego. Moderate. This is a quiet, clean, modest choice.

San Diego Princess Resort (619-274-4630), 1404 W. Vacation Road, San Diego. Expensive. On an artificial island in the middle of Mission Bay, this luxury resort has its own beach surrounding individual units and multiple-unit buildings. Facilities include a pool, recreation courts, and meeting rooms. This is a low-key, elegant destination resort—quiet but near all the action.

Mission Bay Motel (619-483-6440), 4221 Mission Boulevard, San Diego. Inexpensive. Convenient location, basic rooms, and proximity to the beach make this a good choice for families.

Ocean Beach Motel (619-223-7191), 5080 Newport Avenue, San Diego. Inexpensive. A surfer motel, it's one step up from a hostel.

Ocean Park Inn (619-483-5858), 710 Grand Avenue, San Diego. Moderate. On the Pacific Beach Boardwalk, these pleasant rooms with balconies are convenient and near the pier and shops.

IN LA JOLLA

Colonial Inn (619-454-2181), 910 Prospect Street. Expensive. Classy hotel since 1913. Well-appointed rooms, pleasant grounds, and excellent service make this a splurge worth the price.

Summer House Inn (619-459-0261), 7955 La Jolla Shores Drive. Expensive. This high-rise hotel near the beach has all the amenities, ocean views, and great service.

The Empress Hotel of La Jolla (619-454-3001; 888-369-9900), 7766 Fay Avenue. Moderate–expensive. Near downtown and a ways from the beach, this hotel is nothing special, but provides adequate lodging in peak season when the pickings are slim.

Shell Beach Apartments & Motel (619-459-4306; 1-800-248-2683), 981 Coast Boulevard. Moderate. Friendly, shabby but genteel accommodations are centrally located. Large apartments are also available. Get a place with a view; it's worth the added cost.

La Jolla Cove Motel (619-459-2621; 1-800-248-2683), 1155 Coast Boulevard. Moderate. A modern motel, the main selling point is its location—almost on top of La Jolla Cove. Some rooms have balconies overlooking the ocean, and there is a heated swimming pool.

IN DEL MAR

Del Mar Motel on the Beach (619-755-1534), 1702 Coast Boulevard. Moderate. This clean, charming motel is right on the beach.

Best Western Stratford Inn (619-755-1501), 710 Camino Del Mar. Expensive. A quiet, well-designed hotel near the center of town.

L'Auberge Del Mar (619-259-1515), 1540 Camino Del Mar. Expensive. Very pricey spa. It's all here: facials, all kinds of baths, massages, and varieties of self-indulgences too numerous to mention here.

Les Artistes (619-755-4646), 944 Camino Del Mar. Expensive. You'll find barely adequate accommodations, tiny rooms, but hip decor. The Erte Room is worth a look if not a night. Noisy location.

IN NORTHERN SAN DIEGO COUNTY

Hotel Villa Mar (619-753-1267), 960 First Street, Encinitas. Moderate. Pleasant, clean rooms are near beach, restaurants, and shopping.

Countrydise Inn (619-944-0427), 1661 Villa Cardiff Drive, Cardiff-by-the-Sea. Moderate. This large hotel has a bed & breakfast feel.

La Costa Resort & Spa (619-438-9111), 2100 Costa del Mar Road, Carlsbad. Expensive. You'll find golf, pools, and tennis, but no beach. Luxury and pretense abound.

Surf Motel (619-729-7962), 3136 Carlsbad Boulevard, Carlsbad. Moderate. Convenient, a little noisy, this motel is okay for a night or two.

Ocean Palms Beach Resort (619-729-2493), 2950 Ocean Street, Carlsbad. Expensive. Across the street from the beach, this former apartment house offers warm, friendly service and adequate rooms.

Restaurants

IN IMPERIAL BEACH

Brendory's by the Sea (619-423-3991), 710 Seacoast Drive. Moderate. This is part of a regional restaurant chain specializing in "healthier" cuisine—salads, sandwiches, and grilled meats. It's a bit upscale for this part of the coast.

El Tapatio's (619-423-3443), 260 Palm Avenue. Inexpensive. This taco joint offers good, standard Mexican fare for a sit-down meal or takeout.

IN CHULA VISTA

La Bella Pizza Garden (619-426-8820), 373 3rd Avenue. Inexpensive. This simple Italian restaurant serves pizza, lasagna, veal, ravioli, and other pastas at bargain prices.

IN CORONADO

Peohe's (619-437-4474), 1201 First Street at the Ferry Landing Marketplace. Moderate. Get past the Hawaiian hoopla to find very good seafood with a great view of San Diego.

The Mexican Village (619-435-1822), 120 Orange Avenue. Inexpensive. This old-time local favorite serves Mexican classics and some modern dishes.

La Salsa! (619-435-7778), 1360 Orange Avenue. Inexpensive. Part of a regional chain of fast-food restaurants, you'll eat healthier Mexican food with a great selection of salsas.

Marius (619-435-3000), 2000 2nd Street in Le Meridien Hotel. Expensive. A formal, French-style restaurant, Marius features a multicourse menu. The excellent wine selection well matches the food.

Miguel's Cocina (619-437-4237), 1351 Orange Avenue in the El Cordova Hotel. Moderate. Excellent fish tacos, squid, and chicken dishes are served here.

IN DOWNTOWN SAN DIEGO

Ida Bailey's Restaurant (619-544-1886), 311 Island Avenue. Moderate. This restaurant serves a primarily American menu along the lines of roasts, chops, and steaks, and otherwise is notable for its previous life as a brothel.

Croce's Restaurant (619-233-4355), 802 5th Avenue. Moderate. This Gaslight-district restaurant is owned by the widow of the singer Jim Croce. The menu

runs the gamut from salads to pastas to fish, and there is a bar with live music just next door.

Anthony's Star of the Sea Room (619-232-7408), 1360 North Harbor Drive. Expensive. Formal attire required for an expensive and extensive seafood menu. The **Fish Grotto** (619-232-5103) next door is cheaper for fine fresh fish.

IN OCEAN BEACH

Hodad's (619-224-4623), 5010 Newport Avenue. Inexpensive. A relaxed, friendly surfer joint that advertises having the best—and some might say biggest—burgers in the world.

IN LA JOLLA

George's at the Cove (619-454-4244), 1250 Prospect Street. Expensive. A good complement to a stay at the La Jolla Cove Motel (see **Lodging**—"In La Jolla"), this restaurant also looks out on the Pacific, taking advantage of a glass-walled outdoor patio and gas lamps. The menu is primarily seafood but leans toward California cuisine.

Jose's Court Room (619-454-5655), 1037 Prospect Street. Moderate. This is a loud, festive Mexican restaurant and bar; but not for the kids at night. Out-of-town singles are welcome; food's okay.

IN DEL MAR

Fish Market (619-755-2277), 640 Via de la Valle. Moderate. Another great choice for fresh seafood of all types, located close to the famed Del Mar racetrack.

Cafe Del Mar (619-481-1133), 1247 Camino Del Mar. Moderate. Italian food in a more creative mode. Stick to the pasta.

IN NORTHERN SAN DIEGO COUNTY

Fidel's (619-755-5292), 607 Valley Avenue, Solana Beach. Moderate. Fidel's is a busy Mexican restaurant with standard fare.

Vinaka (619-720-7890), 300 Carlsbad Village Drive, Carlsbad. Inexpensive. A quirky coffeehouse, it serves sandwiches and desserts.

Johnny Mañana's (619-721-9999), 308 Mission Avenue, Oceanside. Inexpensive. Good Mexican food.

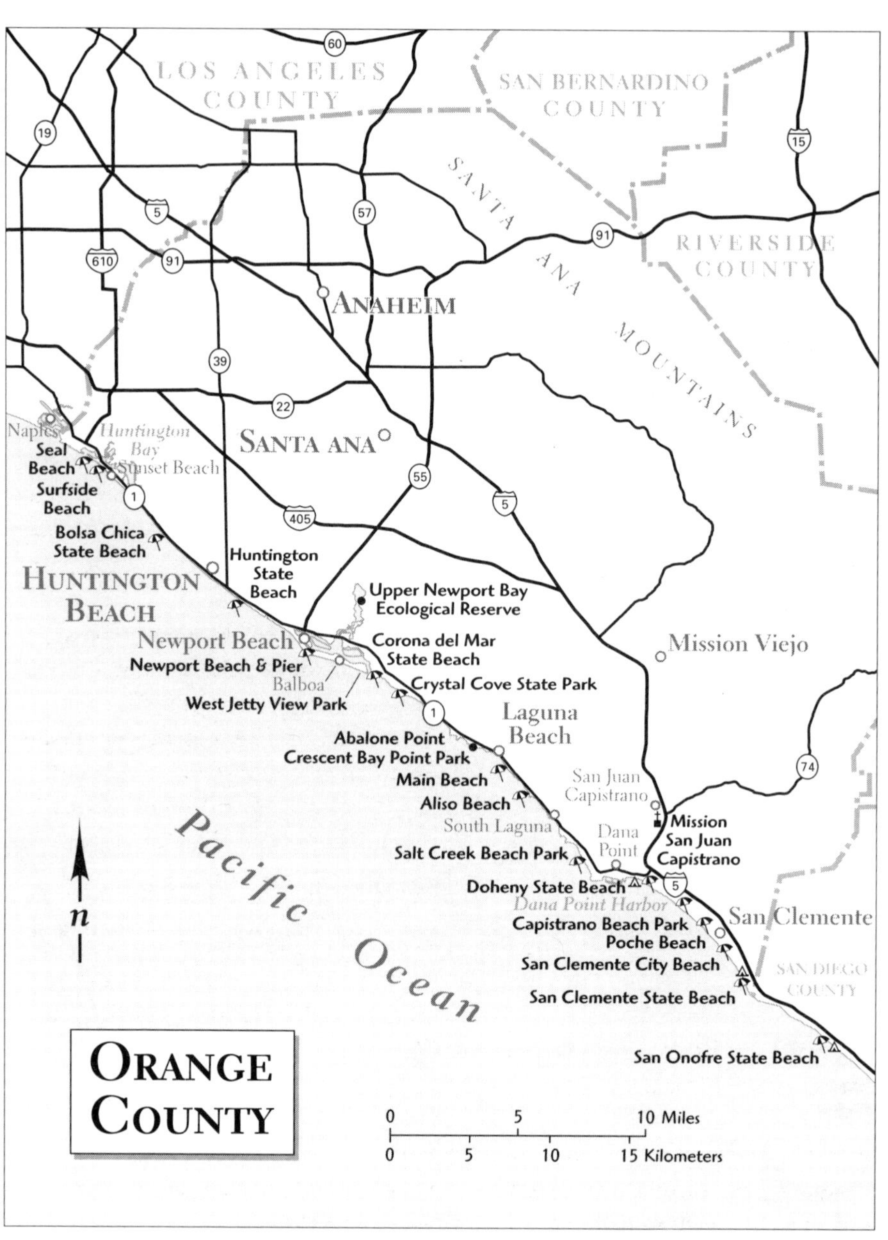
LOS ANGELES COUNTY
SAN BERNARDINO COUNTY
SANTA ANA MOUNTAINS
RIVERSIDE COUNTY
ANAHEIM
SANTA ANA
Naples
Huntington Bay
Seal Beach
Sunset Beach
Surfside Beach
Bolsa Chica State Beach
HUNTINGTON BEACH
Huntington State Beach
Upper Newport Bay Ecological Reserve
Newport Beach
Newport Beach & Pier
Corona del Mar State Beach
Balboa
Crystal Cove State Park
West Jetty View Park
Mission Viejo
Laguna Beach
Abalone Point
Crescent Bay Point Park
Main Beach
Aliso Beach
San Juan Capistrano
South Laguna
Mission San Juan Capistrano
Dana Point
Salt Creek Beach Park
Doheny State Beach
Dana Point Harbor
Capistrano Beach Park
San Clemente
Poche Beach
San Clemente City Beach
SAN DIEGO COUNTY
San Clemente State Beach
San Onofre State Beach
Pacific Ocean
n
ORANGE COUNTY
0 5 10 Miles
0 5 10 15 Kilometers

CHAPTER TWO

Orange County

ORANGE COUNTY RUNS FROM SOUTHEAST TO NORTHWEST, in a straight line from San Mateo Point, just south of San Clemente, to Seal Beach and the San Gabriel River at the Los Angeles County line. From San Mateo Point north to Corona del Mar, the coast is mostly cliffed, irregular, with many pocket beaches. These beautiful headlands, which back sandy beaches, are often set in isolated coves between the shoulders of hillside. The hills are part of the San Joaquins, which, in turn, are part of the Peninsular Ranges, a mountain range that extends down the coast into Baja California.

Above Corona del Mar, the coastline is backed by the southern section of the Los Angeles basin. Here are mile upon mile of wide sandy beach, often with low coastal mesas or filled wetlands to the east. Although highly developed, the coast here is beautiful.

The huge beaches of the northern half of Orange County are created by sand carried to the coast by two rivers, the San Gabriel at the county line and the Santa Ana at Huntington Beach. These rivers have now been channeled and their sand flow restricted. But the beaches also benefit by being in the San Pedro littoral cell, which is a pocket of coast along which prevailing waves and wind, here north to south, drive sand. The San Pedro "pocket" extends from Newport Beach in the south to Point Fermin in the north. At Newport Beach the sand flows into a large underwater canyon, Newport Canyon, which begins just off the beach's pier.

This forgiving, lovely coast, now dotted with expensive, exclusive residential communities, was developed first as an area for summer vacationers from Los Angeles to the north. A remnant of this earlier period is the Balboa Pavilion in Newport Beach at the end of the Pacific Electric Railway, once a dance hall and now a restaurant.

From the Orange/San Diego county border to Dana Point are miles of beaches. A railroad line runs close to the shore. The beach is often accessed by pedestrian overpasses and stairs, as at San Clemente City Beach. The coastal cliffs above the beach hold extensive suburban developments.

The coast from Dana Point north to Corona del Mar, with its cliffs, coves, and pocket beaches, is varied and beautiful. The coast is highly developed here, but the houses are scattered in a pleasing, colorful, Mediterranean mosaic. This is an expensive and often exclusive area, where access to the beach can involve a close association with privilege, as it does at lovely Salt Creek Beach, where the trail down to the water crosses the grounds of the Ritz-Carlton Hotel.

To the north of Dana Point, the city of Laguna Beach, set above sandy pocket beaches on low headlands, is a vibrant coastal village, though an expensive one. Known as an artists' colony, it has numerous galleries, shops, and restaurants. Just to the north of the city is a series of beautiful small beaches, accessed by stairways and ramps.

Between Laguna Beach and Newport is Crystal Cove State Park, one of the most scenic sections of the southern California coast. Here a wide and long sandy beach lies between the ocean and sandstone bluffs. Formerly ranch land, the park includes almost 3000 acres of the San Joaquin Hills. There are tide pools, good swimming, and surfing. Offshore is the Irvine Coast Marine Life Refuge, a protected ocean area where divers will find kelp forests teeming with fish. This beach is a family destination area.

Above Newport Beach lie Huntington Beach, Bolsa Chica State Beach, Sunset Beach, Surfside Beach, and Seal Beach. These beaches are at the edge of the Los Angeles basin—wide, sandy, forgiving, and popular with surfers. Except at Bolsa Chica, which is part of the Bolsa Chica Ecological Reserve, a protected wetland area, these beaches are backed by urban settings.

Beaches and Attractions

IN SAN CLEMENTE

Even many Californians associate San Clemente with just one thing: the western White House and the presidency of Richard M. Nixon. In fact, some of the most beautiful beaches in California are located within walking distance of the place Nixon returned to after his resignation, and stories abound of the former president walking the beach in a business suit and leather loafers, surrounded by tan and scantily clad sun-worshipers.

San Clemente State Beach. This southernmost beach in Orange County is narrow and sandy, backed by visibly eroding cliffs and fronted by some fairly hazardous stretches of ocean. It's located slightly south of "downtown" off Avenida Calafia. However, up above there are campsites, showers, and a snack bar. The beach's riptides and overall ruggedness discourage swimmers—especially kids—but it does feature some decent surfing, including year-round breaks toward the beach's north end. A steep but hikeable/bikeable asphalt trail leads down a ravine from the campsites. AMTRAK trains can be seen going by on the surf-threatened right-of-way above the beach. Parking fee. For more information, contact San Clemente State Beach at 714-492-3156.

San Clemente City Pier. The oceanfront of the city of San Clemente proper, the pier is located at the west end of Avenida del Mar. Popular for fishing, it has a bait and tackle shop and sinks for cleaning your catch. While waiting for a nibble on the line you can watch wet-suited surfers below on both sides of the pier. For more information, call 714-361-8219.

San Clemente City Beach More crowded and developed but more centrally located than the state beach (see above), this brown-sand beach is still recovering from the pounding it took during 1983's winter storms. Access is the same as for the City Pier. Blanketed with healthy-looking surfers, it's a good swimming beach and has lifeguards, showers, fire pits, and rest rooms. For beach information, call the San Clemente Department of Marine Safety at 714-361-8219.

IN SAN JUAN CAPISTRANO

Poche Beach. Along Camino Real north of San Clemente, Poche Beach is accessed via a stairway that starts on the inland side of the Pacific Coast Highway. It's relatively uncrowded and is a good surfing beach. There are no facilities, however.

Capistrano Beach Park Generally wider and gentler than San Clemente's beaches, here you'll find sparkling white sand, good swimming, and surfing, plus picnic areas, volleyball nets, outdoor basketball courts, and lifeguards—the whole southern California beach scene.

Doheny State Beach The surfing beach made legendary by the Beach Boys in "Surfin' Safari," this is a ¾-mile stretch of wide, white sand, ideal for both swimming and beginning surfing. The legendary surf of the 1960s is somewhat tamer due to construction of the jetty that forms the south end of Dana Point Harbor, just to the beach's north. Once out of the water, there's a 5-acre lawn with picnic tables for families to enjoy. It's all extremely beautiful and can get crowded during the summer, so be sure to arrive early. Camping costs $14-20/night; day parking is $5/vehicle. The beach also has a visitors center with interpretive displays, five aquariums, and a tidal "touch pool." Call Doheny State Beach, at 714-496-6171, for more information.

IN DANA POINT

Dana Point Harbor. This full-service marina also provides restaurants, recreational facilities, and parks. Call Harbor Patrol for more information at 714-248-2222.

Salt Creek Beach Park Accessed via Ritz-Carlton Drive off the Pacific Coast Highway in Dana Point, this is one beach where the access trail by itself is worth the walk. It has several benches along a bluff that offers views of gray whale migration routes, Catalina Island, and the southern Orange County coast. After taking one of several side pathways and stairways down to the beach, you'll find changing rooms, outdoor showers, rest rooms, fire pits, and a snack bar. It's a popular surfing spot, but there are other great reasons to visit, like hiking the several miles of nature trails that follow Salt Creek upstream. Though the sections of beach north and south of the Ritz-Carlton are all part of Salt Creek Park, the southern part is called Selva Beach. The parking lot is open 6 AM–midnight; for more information, contact Salt Creek Beach Park at 714-661-7013.

IN SOUTH LAGUNA

Aliso Beach County Park. This park is notable not only for its clean, coarse-sand beaches but also for the 620-foot-long Aliso Pier, which has actually won design awards for its upward slope and unique, diamond-shaped platform. The fishing is good; other features are good body-surfing conditions, lifeguards, picnic areas, volleyball nets, and a snack bar. Access is through the metered parking lot on the 31300 block of Pacific Coast Highway. Call the county's South Beaches Operation Office at 714-661-7013 for more information. Entrance fee.

IN LAGUNA BEACH

Thalia Street Pocket Beach. One of a series of small urban pocket beaches in Laguna Beach that lie to the south of Main Beach. As its name implies, this one is found at the end of Thalia Street. It's a good local surfing spot and is open to surfers year round. (It is one of the beaches in the area where one can surf all day long, even in the summer.) Older surfers favor it, many riding log boards. Other pocket beaches are found at the end of Brooks Street, Cress Street, and Saint Ann's Street. The Brooks Street beach is also a good surfing spot.

Main Beach Located in the absolute dead-center of the village of Laguna, the beach scene here rivals that of Venice Beach. You'll see swimming, volleyball, basketball, roller skating, and sunbathing at every hour of the day.

Crescent Bay Point Park. Accessible from the west end of Crescent Bay Drive in Laguna Beach, this is a green bluff overlooking a somewhat hazardous surfing and bodysurfing beach. There are lifeguards, but the swimming can be rough. The main draws for the nonsurfer are tide pools and the sea lions that gather on Seal Rock just offshore.

Crystal Cove State Park This is one of the true gems of the Orange County coast: a perfect, 3-mile-long beach located inside 2700 acres of undeveloped land in the San Joaquin Hills. Hiking trails and bike paths abound, sportfishing and camping are allowed, and there's great skin diving at the Irvine Coast Marine Life Refuge, an "underwater park," just off the beach. The beach tends to be lightly used on weekdays, making it perfect for vacationers seeking solitude. This combination of features and facilities makes for a great family beach. The park will eventually connect with another, slightly larger parcel of land to the south, with the result to be called the Irvine Coast Wilderness Park. Access is at three points along Pacific Coast Highway between Corona del Mar and Laguna Beach (from north to south): Reef

©JAMES BLANK

Laguna Beach

Point, Los Trancos, and Pelican Point. Los Trancos has the largest parking lot, on the east side of Pacific Coast Highway. Entrance fee. For more information, call Crystal Cove State Park at 714-494-3539.

IN CORONA DEL MAR

Little Corona del Mar Beach. A comfortably secluded cove features tide pools and reefs for good snorkeling, swimming, scuba diving, and general exploring. Sandstone bluffs above the beach show off the local sedimentary geology, and the Corona del Mar Tidepool Reserve organizes tours around the tide pools. Entrance is at the corner of Poppy Avenue and Ocean Boulevard. Free street parking and the lack of an access fee make this beach an all-around good deal. For more information, call the Newport Beach Conference and Visitors Bureau at 1-800-94-COAST.

Corona del Mar Beach. Sometimes called "Big" Corona del Mar Beach, this large, fluffy-sand beach is just east of the jetties that protect Newport Harbor's entrance. It's got all the classic California beach amenities: volleyball nets, equipment rentals, lifeguards, food concessions, outdoor showers, and fire pits. There are picnic tables on a nice landscaped lawn. Climbing the rocks at the beach's north end will net visitors a great view of Newport Harbor, albeit a

Corona del Mar

slightly guilty one because of signs warning against climbing the rocks. Closer to ground level are fine views of the harbor entrance and thousands of pleasure boats moving in and out. Because of its central location, though, it nearly always draws a crowd. Access is at Ocean Boulevard and Iris Avenue in Corona del Mar; entrance fee. Call Newport Beach Newport Beach Conference and Visitors Bureau at 1-800-94-COAST for more information.

IN BALBOA

West Jetty View Park. Located at the absolute bottom of Balboa Peninsula and just across the harbor entrance from Corona del Mar Beach, this is the site of the infamous "Wedge," reputed to hold the most fearsome bodysurfing in the world. Bottom conditions and the jetty itself combine to create waves up to 20 feet tall, and they break in such a way that surfing is out and only the most experienced bodysurfers will want to tackle a wave here. Access is via the south end of Channel Road in Balboa.

Balboa Beach/Balboa Pier The quintessential family beach, Balboa is a wide, sandy, swim-friendly strip with a remarkably intact dune structure. A long wooden pier juts out into the Pacific from the end of Main Street, and this is also the most crowded area of the beach. All the usual amenities, including lifeguards, are here, and the pier is just a short walk from many restaurants, markets, and the ferry to tiny Balboa Island within the harbor. On the bay side at about the level of Balboa Pier is Balboa Pavilion, which includes a restaurant, gift shop, offices of Catalina tour operators, boat rentals, and fishing licenses. Next to it is a small, permanent carnival called the Fun Zone, which features rides. It's crowded and the bars certainly can be rowdy, but overall it's a relaxed scene and a great place to bring the kids.

Back on the beach is the southern terminus of a concrete bike/walk pathway that extends north into Newport Beach. It's heavily used and a convenient, though winding, thoroughfare. (Take care when riding a bike on this path; blowing sand can make traction a problem.) There's also a playground for the kids and a lawn shaded by palm trees. Access is through the west end of most side streets in Balboa.

IN NEWPORT BEACH

Newport Beach/Newport Pier Another good choice for the family. Narrowing from south to north, this beach is "centered" at the elbow of the Balboa

©JAMES BLANK

Newport Beach

Peninsula, from which juts the Newport Pier between 20th and 21st Streets. Since this beach is so central, accessible, and surrounded by amenities, it is frequently very crowded. Good surfing can be had at the level of 18th, 24th, and 56th Streets; it is regulated by the lifeguards, who fly flags from towers along the beach. Access is all along the west side of Ocean Front in Newport. Parking is at metered spaces and at lots along Balboa Boulevard.

Upper Newport Bay State Ecological Reserve ★ Set snugly within Santa Ana, Newport Beach, and Irvine, this 200-acre plot is the largest estuary in southern California. It's also part of the so-called Pacific Flyway, the major West Coast migratory path for birds heading north and south. More than 200 species can be seen here, including the endangered light-footed clapper rail and Belding's savannah sparrow. The reserve's mudflats are bounded on the east by Backbay Drive, a narrow but drivable road at marsh level, making access from Newport Beach's Jamboree Road easy. There are also equestrian, hiking, and biking trails, and tours are available on the first and third Saturday of each month. No fee; for more information, call 714-640-6746.

Santa Ana River County Beach. A sandy strip that runs on either side of the mouth of the Santa Ana River, this is a reasonably uncrowded surf spot with no facilities, except that it does have a lifeguard. Access is at Seashore Drive between 61st and Summit Streets, and there is metered street parking.

IN HUNTINGTON BEACH

Huntington State Beach ★ Beginning just north of Santa Ana River Beach, Huntington State is a wide, 3-mile-long surfers' legend. (The nearby town of Huntington Beach is the "Surf City" of Jan and Dean's 1963 hit, although the town squabbles endlessly with Santa Cruz, California, over the title.) It's a veritable desert of soft sand and there's practically always safe swimming and great surfing to be had. There's a bike path paralleling the water and a 5-acre preserve for the endangered least tern. Also in the wildlife category is grunion-watching: Under certain lunar and tidal conditions, these creatures come out of the ocean to lay their eggs. Lifeguards, food concessions, outdoor showers, volleyball nets, and extensive ramps for wheelchair access complete the picture of a great beach for everyone. Access is along the west side of Pacific Coast Highway, from the Santa Ana River north to Beach Boulevard. There's an entrance fee of $5/vehicle. Call 714-536-1454 for more information.

Huntington City Beach/Huntington Pier Pretty much the center of California's surfing world for decades, this is the northerly continuation of Huntington State Beach and the site of numerous international surfing competitions. There's more flawless swimming and surfing, plus surfboard rentals and food concessions. The 1800-foot-long **Huntington Pier** was commandeered by the Army as an observation post and machine-gun emplacement during World War II. The only thing marring the view here is the line of oil derricks to the north; they seem to climb right out of the Pacific and onto shore. Beach access is west of Pacific Coast Highway, between Main Street and Beach Boulevard; there's a $6/vehicle entrance fee. There's camping, with a one-night limit during the summer. Call 714-536-5281 for more information.

Huntington Beach International Surf Museum (714-960-3483), a short walk away, claims to be the largest surfing museum in existence. Located at 5th Street and Olive Avenue, it's one of a number of such institutions that have sprung up in recent years, such as the **Surfing Walk of Fame** at the intersection of Main Street and the Pacific Coast Highway. The museum features a bust of Duke Kahanamoku, the Hawaiian surfer and Olympic swimmer credited with popularizing surfing in the mainland United States and a legend in his own right.

Huntington Harbor. Located east of the Pacific Coast Highway in Huntington Beach, this private small-craft harbor offers slips, moorings, and services for boaters. Also provided is a sheltered sandy beach, picnic tables, wheelchair-accessible rest rooms, and free parking. Commercial services are located off Pacific Coast Highway. For more information, call 714-840-1387.

Bolsa Chica State Beach Yet another beautiful northern Orange County beach, this one is 6 miles of fluffy sand. It's backed up by the Bolsa Chica Ecological Reserve (see below), a wetlands area bordered on the north by Huntington Harbor. During the summer, the surf here is gentler than it is on the more southerly Huntington beaches, making this a good choice for families and swimmers. It runs north from Main Street up to Warner Avenue along the Pacific Coast Highway. Parking is between Warner Avenue and Golden West Street, and costs $5/vehicle at various fee lots. For more information, call 714-846-3460.

Bolsa Chica Ecological Reserve ★ The Bolsa Chica preserve is 300 acres of state-owned wetlands in which live five endangered bird species: the clapper rail, peregrine falcon, savannah sparrow, California brown pelican, and California least tern. Bolsa Chica is also a valuable archaeological site because of the presence of many "cogged stones" used by pre-Columbian Indians in ceremonies. Tours of the reserve are given on the first Saturday of the month, October–March; call 714-897-7003 for more information. Access

©JAMES BLANK

Huntington Beach and pier

is via parking lots at Warner Avenue and the Pacific Coast Highway and across from the main Bolsa Chica Beach entrance.

Sunset Beach. This small public beach features lifeguards and volleyball nets, but little else. Access is via the end of Pacific Avenue; for more information, call the Orange County Harbors, Beaches, and Parks office at 714-723-4511.

Surfside Beach. This small beach is accessible only through a pedestrian/bike gateway into the private residential community of Surfside. No parking, motor vehicle access, lifeguard, or facilities.

IN SEAL BEACH

Seal Beach/Seal Beach Pier. The last town before crossing the San Gabriel River into Los Angeles County, Seal Beach is unusual in not having the Pacific Coast Highway run directly through its center. This has given it a small-town feel nearly unique in coastal Orange County and spares it most of the traffic running between Newport and Long Beach. Though the beach is long, fine, and sandy, the surf is erratic. Minor spills from the offshore oil pipelines and derricks create a mess, but it's usually cleaned up quickly by the oil companies or town bulldozers and volunteers. Swimming can be hazardous due to offshore currents and the large jetties framing the San Gabriel River, but there is also a large contingent of lifeguards on the beach. The 1885-foot pier was destroyed by storms in 1983 but the town quickly rebuilt it; an electric tram takes visitors from one end to the other. Fishing is popular here and the pier features fish-cleaning sinks. For beach information, call the Seal Beach Chamber of Commerce at 562-799-0179.

Seal Beach National Wildlife Refuge ★ Preserved as part of the US Naval Weapons Station, these 911 acres of wetlands are habitat to a variety of shorebirds and waterfowl, including the endangered least tern. Many species of animals and plants coexist with oil production and Navy activities.

Lodging

IN SAN CLEMENTE

San Clemente Holiday Inn Resort (714-361-3000), 111 S. Avenida de Estrella. Moderate. Although a chain hotel, its amenities beat many more-expensive lodgings in San Clemente proper—a heated pool, fitness center, sun deck, and spa, all within walking distance of the City Beach.

Paul Kretkowski–Biking the Coast

■ Usually, there is some kind of spiritual hunger that needs to be fed. Or some stranger inside your brain suddenly wakes up and makes herself known for the first time. Or maybe it's one of those depressing disconnections with your world—it just isn't the same anymore, you don't really care for it as you did, it's time to be somewhere else. Only, you aren't sure where someplace else is.

These are all good reasons to get on the bike and ride. Some people decide to go in the morning and they're on Highway 1 in the evening, heading down the coast.

Always it is down the coast, north to south. That is the flow of the prevailing wind, which makes the trip easier. Also, since you ride on the right, next to the ocean, the view is usually better. And finally, you are visible on the outside, highlighted against the sky, rather than in the shadows of a coastal ridge. This is the most important reason of all.

Paul Kretkowski rode Highway 1 down the coast in two stages, first going south from San Francisco to the Mexican border, and then taking the bus north to the Oregon border and going south to San Francisco. He was young, and the Gulf War had just ended. Even San Francisco in the springtime couldn't revive his spirits. Everywhere he looked, he saw nothing.

Paul is a methodical man. Before his journey, he bought a bike rack and saddlebags, which he filled with weights and telephone books to simulate his gear, and spent a month in training. In the mornings he pedaled his telephone books over the Golden Gate Bridge, into the hills of Marin County. He also got a complete series of US Geological Survey maps of the entire coast and Highway 1. (They would prove useless—the topographical details were accurate only in 200-foot increments, not enough detail for a slow-moving bike where every rise counts.) On March 19, he turned 24. On April Fool's Day, he took off.

His only flat tire in more than 1000 miles happened on his first day, just a mile out of San Francisco, on his way to Half Moon Bay. He was already beginning to hate weight by then, but at the first bike store he came to he bought a spare inner tube so that he wouldn't have to do the patch himself every time. Hating weight was one of the good things that happened to Paul on the trip—one of the ways that the bike changed his relationship to the material world and reconnected him to something more important. He got so that he was resentful of his small camera, and then resentful even of the batteries inside it—resentful of the weight of them.

He traveled with minimum essentials: sleeping bag, tent, two pairs of bike shorts, two T-shirts, sweats, a flimsy windbreaker, and sunglasses. No cans—not ever. Paul met a biker in Monterey with a full case of tuna cans in his saddlebags, and three liters of orange juice—too much weight. This guy had just been laid off his job at an advertising agency. He blew out his knees and had to turn back.

Biking in the spring, there were 12 hours of usable, bikeable daylight. You could blow through several miles in the morning and have half a day at the next campsite. Or you could take your time and admire the scenery. Biking makes you the actor in your life, instead of some "engineer in Detroit" and a speed limit sign that keeps you moving at between 50 and 65.

Paul moved down the coast like a hermit crab, carrying everything on his back, scuttling through a concrete jungle. He began to feel more relaxed, and much more patient.

Paul met retired professors and rail engineers. He met a guy who was a camel fanatic, just back from a camel bazaar in India, now biking the coast. In Mendocino he met a guy from Australia who was planning to charge down the coast, was going to do 90 miles a day. Two years later, Paul saw him in Marin County, still on his bike. Two years, only 300 miles? Biking the coast rearranges priorities.

It was still early in the season when Paul made his trip. The heavy bike traffic along the coast is in July and August, and Paul did his riding in April and May. He had been a little worried about the dangerous Big Sur coast. Paul had seen a picture of one of those twisting arrow signs at the start of the Big Sur coast that read NEXT SEVENTY-FOUR MILES. There was a biker in front of the sign, on his knees, praying. Big Sur proved uneventful for Paul. (The only things that gave him trouble were the RVs, swinging out behind the cars on the curves.)

One dangerous part of the coast is the beautiful, mostly level and straight road between Gualala and Sea Ranch. Here big tractor-trailers try to make up the time they lose on the curves of Mendocino. Another perilous section is Los Angeles. Paul was a purist, following Highway 1, the coast road, taking no detours. In the bowels of L.A., Highway 1 merges into Sepulveda Boulevard and ducks into a tunnel under the Los Angeles airport. The narrow tunnel seemed to carry all of L.A.'s rush-hour traffic, and one bicycle—Paul's—the rider screaming and praying for an exit.

Paul finished his trip on a foggy San Francisco afternoon. He had been planning to arrive in time to have lunch with a friend, but he didn't make the deadline. The change in plans didn't bother Paul a bit; he had dinner with the friend instead. Now Paul is a writer, putting his words on paper, just the way he pounded out the miles of the California coast, day by day. ■

San Clemente Inn (714-492-6103), 2600 Avenida del Presidente. Moderate. This inn operates as a hotel/condominium and features many apartment-style suites as well as shuffleboard courts, a pool, and a spa.

Beachcomber Motel (714-492-5457), 533 Avenida Victoria. Expensive. Right on the beach, this older motel shows the years, but a great location makes it a good choice.

Casa Tropicana (714-492-1234), 610 Avenida Victoria. Expensive. Each of the nine rooms plays out a different fantasy theme. A real getaway.

IN CAPISTRANO BEACH

Capistrano Seaside Inn (714-496-1399; 1-800-252-3224), 34862 Coast Highway. Moderate. Just across the highway from the beach. Pleasant rooms have fireplace, balcony, or patio.

IN DANA POINT

Ritz-Carlton Laguna Niguel (714-240-2000), 1 Ritz-Carlton Drive. Expensive. Luxury on the bluffs. Supurb service, great views, and fabulous facilities make this southern California's premier beach resort. Excellent on-site restaurants.

IN LAGUNA BEACH

Casa Laguna Inn (714-494-2996), 2510 S. Pacific Coast Highway. Expensive. Two miles south of Laguna's main beach, this inn consists of a central building and 19 outlying cottages in Mission and Spanish Revival styles. It features a swimming pool that overlooks the ocean, and the similarly located cottages are highly recommended.

Surf & Sand Hotel (714-497-4477), 1555 S. Coast Highway. Expensive. A three-year renovation and rooms directly above the beach make this hotel stand out. Spread over four buildings, the hotel nonetheless manages to supply lots of amenities: hair dryers, bathrobes, phones, and Godiva chocolates on the pillows.

Laguna Riviera (714-494-1196; 1-800-999-2089), 825 S. Coast Highway. Expensive. On the beach and close to the action. Rooms are well furnished; many have ocean views.

IN BALBOA

Balboa Inn (714-675-3412), 105 Main Street. Expensive. Once owned by basketball star Kareem Abdul-Jabbar, this historic hotel has a quiet lobby and shady courtyard, as well as room service. Each of the 16 rooms and eight suites is decorated differently; Abdul-Jabbar's old room, for example, features high ceilings and an extra-long bed.

IN NEWPORT BEACH

Newport Channel Inn (714-642-3030), 6030 W. Pacific Coast Highway. Moderate. A modest hotel across the Pacific Coast Highway from the town's northern beach, this motel features a good location and a friendly, knowledgeable staff.

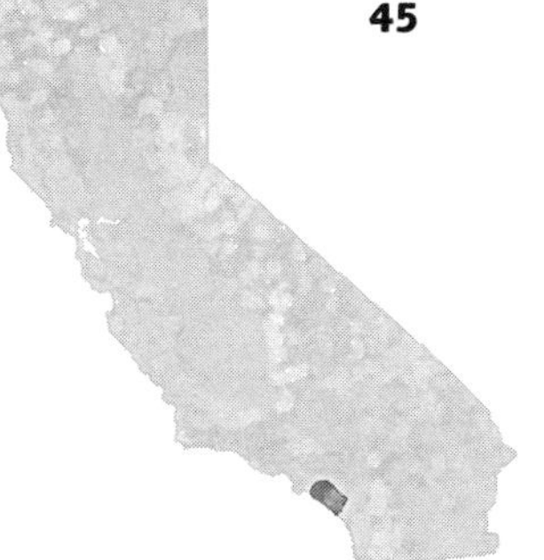

IN HUNTINGTON BEACH

Sunset Bed and Breakfast (562-592-1666), 16401 Pacific Coast Highway. Expensive. Right on the Coast Highway through Huntington Beach, this six-room B&B also has touches like ceiling fans and handcrafted wood fixtures.

IN SEAL BEACH

Seal Beach Inn and Gardens (562-493-2416), 212 5th Street. Expensive. A 60-year-old French Mediterranean inn with gardens containing dozens of types of flowers. Restored now to combine bed & breakfast coziness with hotel amenities like private baths in each room and an ironing board for guest use, the Seal Beach Inn also is littered with antiques and art. The kitchen serves breakfast 7:30–10 AM.

Restaurants

IN SAN CLEMENTE

Dave's Mexican Restaurant (714-492-7867), 1701 N. El Camino Real. Moderate. This is perhaps the best Mexican food in San Clemente. There's an emphasis on low-calorie, healthy fare.

Fatburger (714-492-9182), 1017 El Camino Real. Inexpensive. A local hangout, great food for the price.

Fisherman's Restaurants (714-498-6360), on San Clemente Pier. Moderate to expensive. The right side of the place is a bar with "bar food" including light salads and hamburgers. To the left is an excellent seafood restaurant. Both sides have unsurpassed views and are great places to watch the sunset. (Then go for a walk on the beach!)

Tina and Vince's (714-498-5156), 221 Del Mar. Inexpensive to moderate. This family-owned and -operated restaurant has wonderful pizza and excellent subs, among other things. Buy a picnic lunch here, and take it down the street to the beach.

Beach Garden Cafe (714-498-8145), 618 Avenida Victoria. Inexpensive. The Beach Garden serves simple fare (burgers, fish-and-chips) in a casual space—good for kids.

Tommy's (714-492-1353), 1409 S. El Camino Real. Inexpensive. Here you'll get classic American food, but it's not a designer diner. Family-style atmosphere.

IN SAN JUAN CAPISTRANO

El Adobe de Capistrano (714-493-1163), 31891 Camino Capistrano. Moderate. Notable for solid Mexican food and as Richard Nixon's favorite restaurant.

IN DANA POINT

Cafe Piazza (714-496-0992), 33585 Del Obispo. Inexpensive to moderate. Although located in the Albertson's strip mall, Cafe Piazza has a charming interior and excellent Italian food. A local favorite.

Lucy's El Patio Cafe (714-496-9074), Camino Capistrano (in the Capistrano Beach section of Dana Point). Inexpensive to moderate. Wonderful Mexican food. It has been owned by the same family for more than 30 years.

Chart House (714-493-1183), 34442 Street of the Green Lantern. Moderate to expensive. Yes, it's a chain, but it has an incredible view of the harbor, and to the south, Oceanside. The Mud Pie they serve up is pretty good too.

Traditions Tea Room (714-248-7660), 34241 Coast Highway. Moderate. They serve breakfast, lunch, and dinner, but what's really good here is the traditional English tea served every afternoon. It is on a par with that served at the Ritz-Carlton, but much less expensive. After tea, visit the antiques shop downstairs.

Peking Dragon Restaurant (714-493-9499), 34171 Pacific Coast Highway. Moderate. Excellent Chinese food.

Renaissance Cafe & Wine Bar (714-661-6003), 24701 Del Prado. Moderate. Good food. You can sit inside, but the outdoor patio with fireplace and live music is better.

Luciana's Ristorante (714-661-6500) 24312 Del Prado. Expensive to very expensive. Excellent Italian food.

Proud Mary's (714- 493-5853), located at the Dana Point sportfishing dock in the harbor. Inexpensive. Good for breakfast, when you can watch the fishing boats leaving as you eat. It's a local hangout.

J C Beans Coffee House and Espresso Bar (714-496-4700), 34114 Pacific Coast Highway. Inexpensive. There's a drive-through for coffee, but also a small indoor seating area. Favored by locals in the know.

Watercolors (714-661-5000), at the Dana Point Resort, 25135 Park Lantern. Moderate. Contemporary American cuisine from land and sea is prepared to be as good looking as it is good tasting. (Under renovation as this book goes to press.)

Harbor Grill (714-240-1416), 34499 Golden Lantern. Moderate. This local favorite offers excellent seafood; good views, also.

IN LAGUNA BEACH

The Five Feet Restaurant (714-497-4955), 320 Glenneyre Street. Very expensive. Flashy and elegant, with a changing, creative menu, Five Feet features inventive Chinese food. Aficionados—and there are many—drive from the distant reaches of Orange County to dine here (others feel it is overpriced).

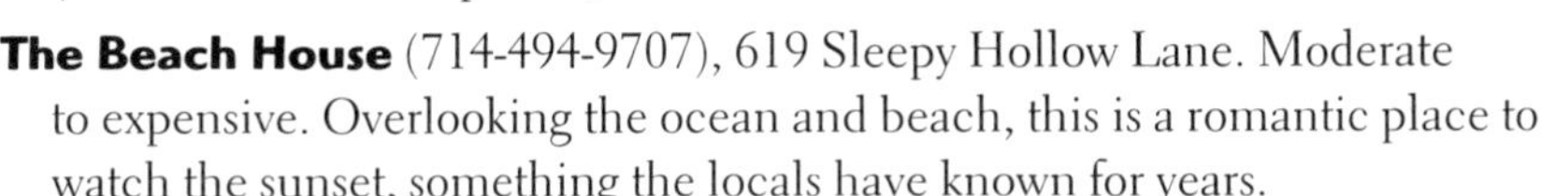

The Beach House (714-494-9707), 619 Sleepy Hollow Lane. Moderate to expensive. Overlooking the ocean and beach, this is a romantic place to watch the sunset, something the locals have known for years.

The White House (714-494-8088), 340 S. Coast Highway. Moderate to expensive. A Laguna Beach institution, the food is only okay, but there is great live music that differs night to night.

Partners Bistro (714-497-4441), 448 S. Coast Highway. Moderate to expensive. Very good Continental food in an intimate atmosphere.

The Cottage (714-494-3023), 308 N. Coast Highway. Moderate. Across from Heisler Park and the art museum, this is a Laguna Beach landmark that dates to the '30s. You can eat indoors or outdoors. The good American food and reasonable prices mean that you will often have to wait for a table. The wait is worth it.

Royal Hawaiian (714-494-8001), 331 N. Coast Highway. Moderate to expensive. This family-owned Polynesian restaurant serves excellent ribs. The atmosphere is dark and enticing.

Papa's Tacos (714-499-9822), 31618 S. Coast Highway. Inexpensive to moderate. A local hangout, this place serves a great lobster taco.

Penguin Cafe (714-494-1353), 981 S. Coast Highway. Inexpensive to moderate. You'll get excellent breakfasts and good lunches at this local favorite.

Sorrento Grill (714-494-8686), 370 Glenneyre Street. Expensive. Upscale, but serves excellent food. There's a martini bar.

Crystal Cove Shack (714-497-9666), 7408 Coast Highway. Inexpensive. Halfway between Laguna and Corona del Mar, the Shack has incredible views and serves shakes that are out of this world. (Try the peanut butter shake.) Also serves sandwiches.

Ti Amo's (714-4399-5350), 31727 Coast Highway. Expensive. Located on the ocean side of the highway with an enclosed patio and valet parking, its prices can be steep but the food is worth the price.

Bombay Duck and Indian Restaurant (714-497-7307), 229 Ocean Avenue. Inexpensive to moderate. A good basic Indian restaurant.

The Stand Natural Foods (714-494-8101), 238 Thalia. Inexpensive to moderate. All natural foods, no animal products. A local favorite with those who want to purify the body (and there are many).

Las Brisas (714-497-5977), 361 Cliff Drive. Moderate. A popular lunch and dinner spot done up in French Riviera style, its menu concentrates on seafood and Mexican fare. Sunsets a must.

Ruby's Autodiner (714-497-7829), 30622 S. Coast Highway. Inexpensive. This designer diner serves burgers; a good spot for kids.

Clares Seafood, Etc. (714-376-9283), 425 S. Coast Highway. Expensive. Inside the Hotel Laguna, offering beach views. You'll find excellent seafood and California cuisine here.

IN NEWPORT BEACH

The Crab Cooker (714-673-0100), 2200 Newport Boulevard. Inexpensive. Hard by Newport Pier, this bright red building boasts fresh, hook-and-line-caught fish and seafood, as well as big crowds and great atmosphere. It's a Newport tradition and always packed, but the owner provides postcards—and postage, if you mail the cards there—so you can write home while waiting. No reservations, no credit cards.

21 Oceanfront Restaurant (714-673-2100), 2100 W. Ocean Front. Expensive. Excellent seafood is on the menu, with good service in an elegant setting, across from the pier.

The Warehouse (714-673-4700), 3450 Via Oporto. Moderate. This restaurant does it all: lunch, dinner, weekday happy hours, and Sunday champagne buffet brunches, and all tables have views of Newport Harbor.

IN CORONA DEL MAR

Mayur (714-675-6622), 2931 E. Coast Highway. Moderate. Excellent Indian food, well served and with an authentic feel. Mayur serves lunch and dinner; dinner only on Saturdays.

IN BALBOA

Britta's Cafe (714-675-8146), 205 Main Street, Newport. Inexpensive. A casual restaurant frequented by locals, it's not fancy but, being attached to a gourmet kitchen shop, boasts its share of meat dishes, pastas, and sandwiches.

Ruby's (714-675-7829), 1 Balboa Pier, Balboa Isle. Inexpensive. Order burgers in a designer diner on the end of the pier. Limited menu with an unlimited view.

CHAPTER THREE

Los Angeles County

THE COASTLINE OF LOS ANGELES COUNTY is a huge, easterly curving bay set between two points: in the north, Point Dume, and in the south, Point Fermin, which is on a large headland, the Palos Verde Peninsula. This large bay is Santa Monica; to the south of it, beyond Point Fermin, lies a smaller bay, San Pedro, which has the largest man-made harbor in the world.

Santa Monica Bay is the coastal edge of the Los Angeles basin, a wide plain formed by rivers, most of which have been lost to the expansion of the city. The shape of the bay creates a littoral cell, or "pocket," a catch basin for sand traveling along the coast. The prevailing waves and wind, coming from the North Pacific, sweep into the bay, pushing sand along the shore. The Palos Verdes Headland, in the south, stops this flow, keeping it within the bay. The accumulation of sand has created the beautiful, legendary beaches of Los Angeles: Malaga Cove, Redondo, Hermosa, Manhattan, Venice, Topanga, Malibu, and Zuma.

At the southern end of Los Angeles County, in San Pedro Bay, lies the mouth of the Los Angeles River, which has been channeled into a canal. Here is the port of Long Beach, where the Queen Mary, the largest luxury liner in the world, is permanently berthed and operates as a tourist attraction. Just to the north, in the lee of Point Fermin and Palos Verdes, is Los Angeles Harbor, another huge man-made harbor. The close proximity of these two harbors, Los Angeles and Long Beach, forms a massive urban working harbor, the largest in the world, with a huge fishing fleet, shipyards, private marinas, and attractions such as Cabrillo Marine Aquarium and Whalers Wharf, a mock New England seaport from the 19th century.

Today's gigantic ports of Los Angeles and Long Beach are the result of more than a century of work, which has transformed the former estuary basin into a concrete maritime center with more than 28 miles of thriving commercial waterfront. Here you will find supertankers, container ships, shipyards, and dry docks, as well as a large fishing fleet with adjacent canning facilities.

These are true "coastal" ports, carved more out of the ocean than the land. The San Pedro Breakwater, at places more than 2 miles offshore, is a man-made granite seawall begun at the turn of the century. Large gates in the walls of the breakwater

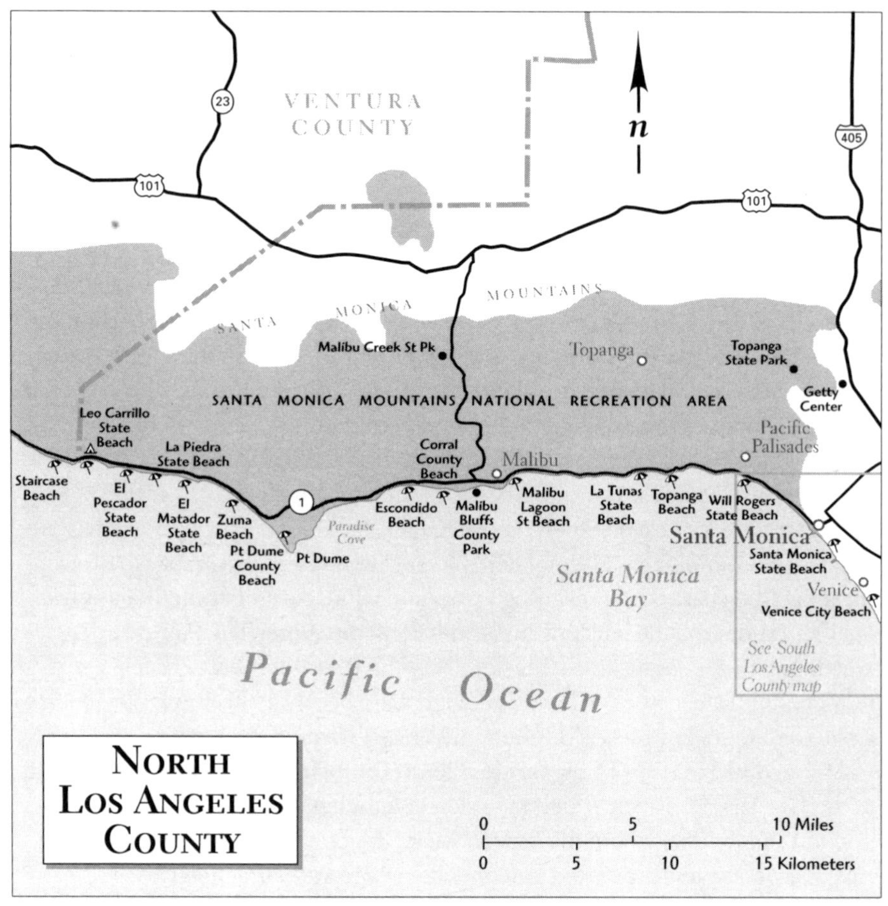

provide access to shipping traffic. The breakwater span protects both Los Angeles and Long Beach Harbors. Within its wall, the port occupies a huge, separate, calm marine environment, connected with, but cut off from, the ocean beyond.

In its unique way, the Port of Los Angeles provides a breathtaking experience that children particularly enjoy. The starting point for a tour of the port is the Cabrillo Marine Aquarium, which has interactive displays about Los Angeles marine life, as well as exhibits that describe the activities here. The nearby Los Angeles Maritime Museum, which occupies the old Municipal Ferry Building, continues the history of the port, with detailed exhibits that explain its construction. Combined with visits to Long Beach, this area is an important family destination as special in its own way as a trip to the rugged and isolated Big Sur coast.

The Palos Verdes Peninsula headland, which protects the two harbors to the south, is an area of active faults and landslides. Here is Palos Verdes Estates

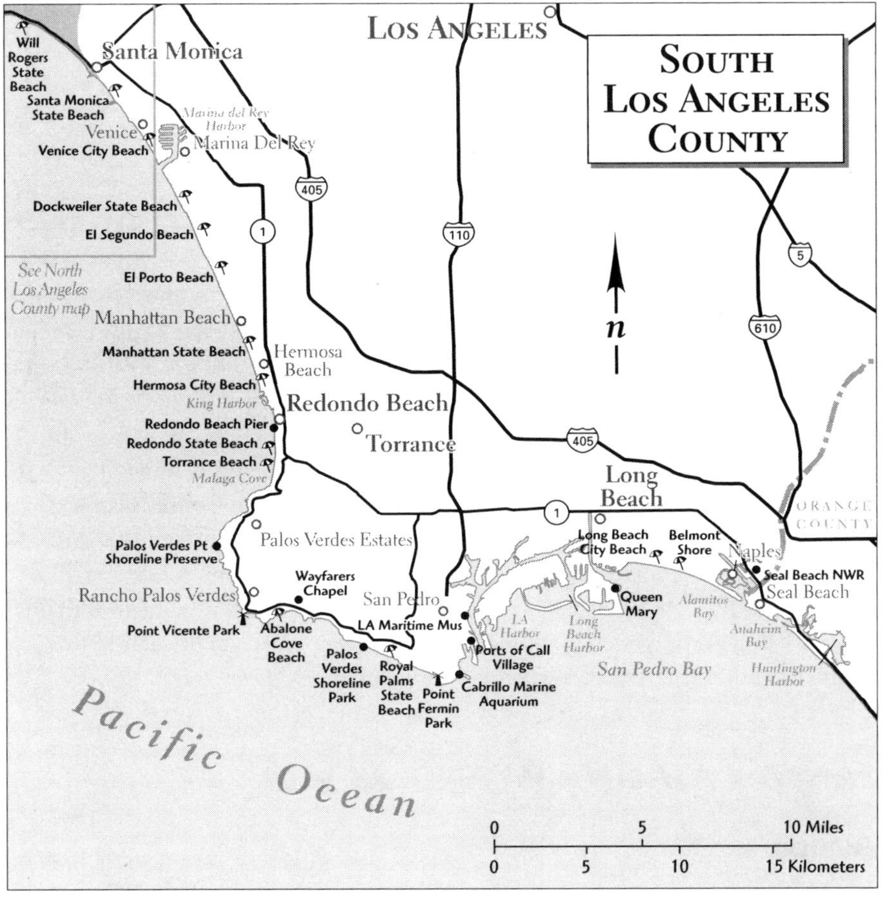

Shoreline Preserve, a park that has scenic views and dangerous paths to the rocky beaches below.

Around the headland, to the north, the great wide beaches of Los Angeles begin: Redondo and Hermosa, which are actually increasing in size today as the littoral pocket of Santa Monica Bay sweeps sand into them. Farther north are several more wide beaches: Manhattan, El Segundo, Dockweiler. These are forgiving, much used beaches. All have lifeguards and are safe for swimming.

Marina del Rey Harbor, just to the north of Dockweiler State Beach, is the largest man-made pleasure-boat harbor in the world. It is a forest of thousands of masts with walkways threading among them. To the north lie the crowded beach communities of Venice and Santa Monica. Santa Monica has the Santa Monica Pier, which boasts an amusement arcade, Ferris wheel, and famous carousel, used as a set in many movies and TV shows.

The wide beaches of Santa Monica and Venice are intensively used. (In 1985, Griggs and Savor, in *Living with the California Coast*, estimated that there was approximately ¼ inch of sandy beach, between Santa Monica and Dana Point in the south, for each person living in the Los Angeles area.) They are also safe, and with playgrounds, picnic areas, and attractions such as the Pier, they can be quite enjoyable for children.

North of Santa Monica State Beach, as the Los Angeles coast ends its arch at Point Dume, the coastline begins to become more rugged, unstable, and less populated. Here the Los Angeles basin terminates as the shoulders of the Santa Monica range arrive at the coast. Near the shore lies an active fault, the Malibu, which in 1971 during the San Fernando earthquake exploded in a hot-water plume off the Malibu Pier. Landslides and rockslides are common along Route 1. It is also a beautiful section of coastline. Here is the Malibu Beach Colony, built on a spit of land extending out from Malibu Creek, home to many people in film and TV. To the north, past Point Dume, is Zuma Beach County Park, the county's largest public beach and another legendary surfing area. With its many facilities, it is a good family destination. At the Los Angeles/Ventura county line is Leo Carrillo State Beach, the coastal edge of a 3000-acre park that extends into the mountains to the north. With caves, migrating gray whales, tide pools, and lifeguards, this is another excellent, and less crowded, Los Angeles family destination.

SANTA CATALINA ISLAND

Avalon

Seventy-six square miles in area, Santa Catalina is about 22 miles off the coast of Los Angeles County. Eighty-six percent of its land is managed by a foundation, the Santa Catalina Conservancy; the rest is given over to cattle ranching and private dwellings. The only town on the island is tiny Avalon, in the southeastern corner facing Los Angeles proper.

At the **Avalon Pier** visitors can book daytime or nighttime tours to a nearby cove packed with undersea life. Although the boats are glass bottomed, so no scuba gear is necessary, there are dive shops for rentals on the pier. Night tours during the summer may catch amazing phosphorescent flying fish in Catalina's waters.

Back on land, visitors can check out the **Wrigley Memorial and Botanical Garden,** which shows off cacti and several plant species native only to the island. It is open 8 AM–5 PM all year and is easily reached by foot or tram from Avalon. Admission is charged. Outdoors roam wild boar and turkey, mountain goats, foxes, and, oddly, bison, which were imported to the island for the filming of a 1920s Western.

Summer is the high season on Catalina, so plan accordingly for crowds. "Getting away from it all" to the island's undeveloped interior is tightly regulated;

you'll need a permit for hiking or biking more than a mile from town, available from the office of the **Santa Catalina Island Conservancy** on Claressa Avenue in Avalon; phone 310-510-1421 for more information. Alternatively, the conservancy runs four-wheel-drive tours of the island with good chances for seeing large wildlife. A range of island and water tours is also available from **Santa Catalina Island Company's Discovery Tour Center** at 310-510-2500, or **Catalina Adventure Tours,** 310-510-2888.

Other than that, there are very few cars on the island; the ferries don't take them, and residents' four-wheel drives and golf carts are the dominant mode of transport in "downtown" Avalon. Santa Catalina has numerous small permit campgrounds; call the conservancy (see above) for more information. The **Avalon Chamber of Commerce and Visitor's Information Center** (310-510-1520) on the pier can also help with tours and accommodations.

TRANSPORTATION ON CATALINA

Access to the island is via boats from Long Beach, San Pedro, and Newport Beach; they leave year-round several times a day, and tie up in Avalon Bay. **Catalina Cruises,** 320 Golden Shores Boulevard, Long Beach, offers twice-daily service between Long Beach and Avalon during the week and up to eight departures on weekends. Tickets are moderate in cost. The crossing takes about 2 hours. Reservations are recommended during the summer and weekends; call 562-436-5006 or 1-800-228-2546. **Catalina Express** at Berth 95 in San Pedro provides similar service from both San Pedro and Long Beach to Avalon and Two Harbors. Call 310-519-1212 or 1-800-618-5533. The fastest but most expensive way to Catalina is a 15-minute **helicopter ride** from Long Beach by the *Queen Mary* and from San Pedro at the Catalina terminal. Call 310-510-2525.

Visitors' cars are not allowed on Catalina, and residents can have theirs only by permit. But there are plenty of ways to see the island, and letting go of that dependence on The Automobile is part of Catalina's charm. Avalon is only 1 square mile, so walking is the easiest way to get around. While just a few streets are pedestrian-only, traffic is very light. Bicycles are one of the best ways to see the Avalon area, and they can be brought in on the cruise boats. Permits, however, must be obtained from the Santa Catalina Island Conservancy, 310-510-1421, for taking bikes into Catalina's interior. **Catalina Auto** at the corner of Metropole and Crescent (310-510-0111) rents beach cruisers for \$5/hour; mountain bikes run \$10/hour. At **Brown's Bikes,** 107 Pebbly Beach Road (310-510-0986), rates are inexpensive for single-speed bikes and 21-speed mountain bikes. It also has tandems, strollers, and wheelchairs available for rent.

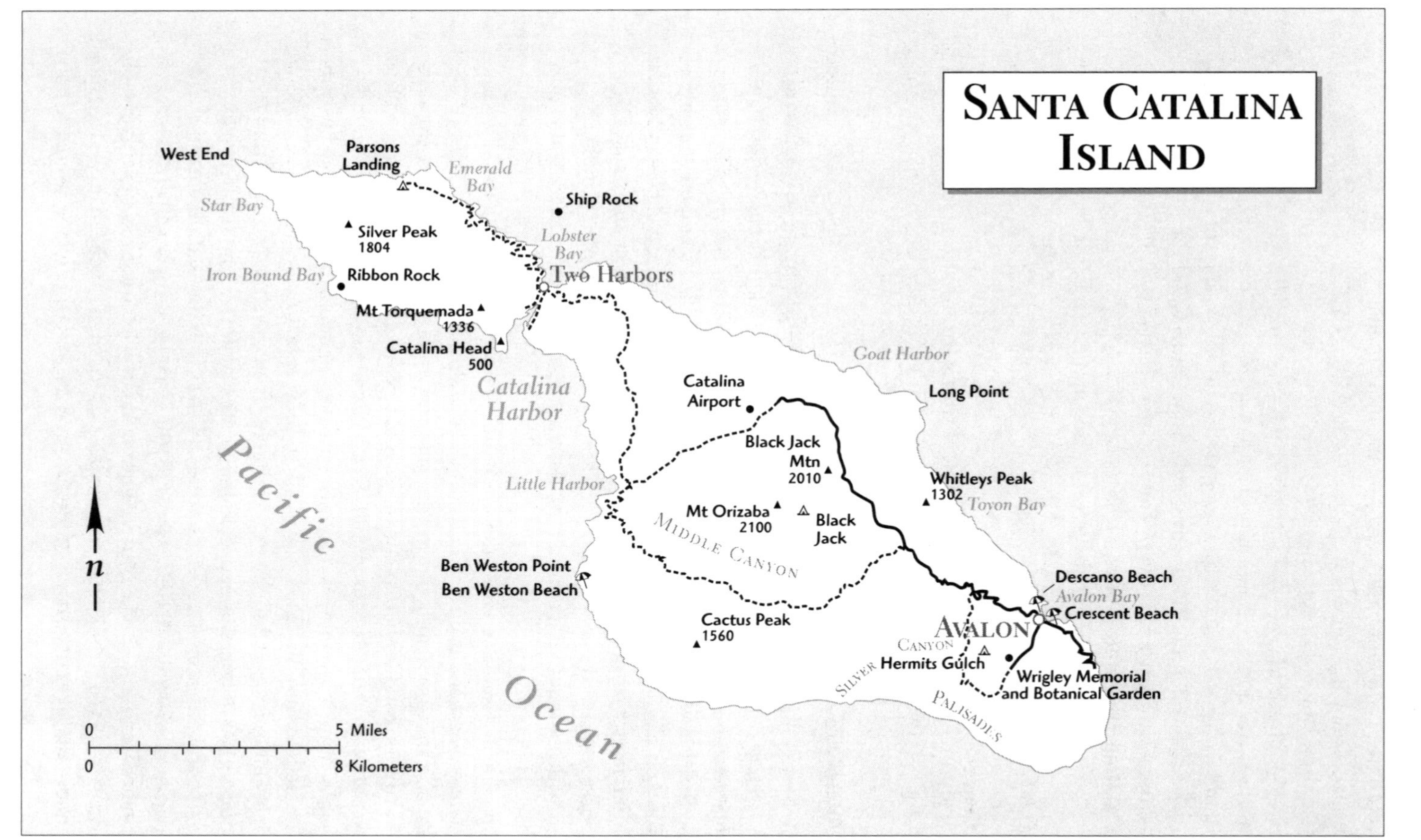
Santa Catalina Island
West End
Parsons Landing
Emerald Bay
Star Bay
Ship Rock
Silver Peak 1804
Lobster Bay
Iron Bound Bay
Ribbon Rock
Two Harbors
Mt Torquemada 1336
Catalina Head 500
Catalina Harbor
Goat Harbor
Catalina Airport
Long Point
Black Jack Mtn 2010
Pacific
Little Harbor
Whitleys Peak 1302
Mt Orizaba 2100
Black Jack
Toyon Bay
Middle Canyon
Ben Weston Point
Ben Weston Beach
Descanso Beach
Avalon Bay
Crescent Beach
Cactus Peak 1560
Avalon
Canyon
Silver
Hermits Gulch
Wrigley Memorial and Botanical Garden
Palisades
Ocean
n
0
5 Miles
0
8 Kilometers

Golf carts, a popular Catalina "car," are available at **Cartopia** for a moderate charge (cash or travelers' checks only, and you must be 25 or older). Call 310-510-2493. Also try **Island Rentals** (310-510-1456) at 125 Pebbly Beach Road. Its rates and rules are similar, but its minimum age is 21. For divers, **Argo Diving Service** offers a dive boat charter service. To make reservations, call 310-510-2208. Someone will meet you at your hotel or on the pier. If you need to rent equipment, **Catalina Divers' Supply** (310-510-0330) is right on the Green Pier.

CATALINA BEACHES AND ATTRACTIONS

Crescent Beach. A sandy, surf-free beach at the southern end of Avalon Bay, it tends to be crowded but has showers, lockers, rest rooms, and a lifeguard. Access is via Crescent Avenue at the Green Pleasure Pier. Call the conservancy for more information.

Avalon Bay. This tiny beach is immediately adjacent to the pier in the middle of Avalon Bay. It's crowded, but convenient for those who don't want to wander too far from Avalon's busy waterfront.

Descanso Beach. Just northwest of Avalon Bay, this private beach offers cabanas and snacks with the purchase of a day pass.

Casino This distinctive circular structure houses the **Catalina Island History Museum,** a theater, and a ballroom. Guided tours are available daily; call 310-510-7400.

TWO HARBORS

The only other developed area on the island, this town essentially consists of a small fishing pier, a few restaurants, a general store, and a boat harbor. It is at the narrowest point of the island's figure-8 outline.

Catalina's eastern and western landforms are linked by a ½-mile-wide strip rising no more than 50 feet above sea level. Two Harbors refers to Isthmus Cove to the north and Catalina Harbor to the south. This picturesque spot, used for filming such movies as *Mutiny on the Bounty, Treasure Island,* and *McHale's Navy,* offers good diving, snorkeling, fishing, waterskiing, and swimming. Hiking, naturalist and photo safaris, and camping are available through the **Camp and Cove Agency** (310-510-0303). Facilities at Two Harbors include a dive shop, snack bar and restaurant, fuel and dinghy docks, and boat rentals. Direct access from the mainland is by **Catalina Express** (310-519-1212) in San Pedro and Long Beach. There is ferry service from Avalon 12 miles away. If you're arriving by private boat, call the Cove and Camp Agency (see above) for the required landing card. Moorings are on a first-come, first-served basis.

Ben Weston Beach A small, sandy beach favored by locals, it's 11.5 miles south of Two Harbors on the west side of the island. The beach is pewter-colored, the waves are decent, and swimming is good when the tide is low. There are no facilities other than toilets, but it is secluded and thus a good place to escape the crowds. Access is via Middle Ranch Road, which was washed out in the January 1995 rains, so check ahead to see whether it's open.

CATALINA ISLAND CAMPING

Permits are required to hike, bike, or camp in the interior of Catalina, as are reservations for camping. Contact the Santa Catalina Island Conservancy at 125 Claressa Avenue, 310-510-1421, or the Cove and Camp Agency (310-510-0303) for reservations, permits, fees, and shuttle/shore boat access to Catalina's campgrounds.

Blackjack Campground. This 1500-foot-high campground is inland and about 9 miles northwest of Avalon, west of Old Stage Road. There are picnic tables and water at this walk-in campsite. There is also shuttle service from Avalon.

Hermit's Gulch Campground. Hermit's Gulch is an easy mile inland from Avalon. Although reservations are not required, they are recommended. The 55-site grounds have a camp store, picnic tables and barbecue grills, coin showers, and wheelchair-accessible rest rooms. Access is via Sumner Avenue through Avalon Canyon. Follow the AVALON CANYON ROAD signs.

Little Harbor Campground. On the west coast of Catalina, Little Harbor campground is on the site of an ancient Indian settlement, and it is also one of the most picturesque spots on the island. The 150-camper grounds, on a flat, sandy beach, have toilets, cold showers, picnic and barbecue facilities, fire pits, and phone. Access is a 6- to 8-mile hike from Two Harbors.

Parson's Landing Campground is on the northwest coast of the island near the beach. There are picnic tables, cooking areas with charcoal for sale, rest rooms, limited fresh water, and a ranger on duty. Parson's Landing can be reached by shore boat or a 7-mile hike from Two Harbors; there are also two moorings for private boats.

Little Fisherman's Cove Campground. This site is at the north shore of Two Harbors, right on the beach. There is a ranger on duty, and the grounds include tables, outdoor cold showers, fresh water, and firewood. Access is via shuttle from Avalon or by private boat.

CATALINA ISLAND LODGING

Zane Grey Hotel (310-510-0966), 199 Chimes Tower Road, Avalon. Expensive. Former home of the western novelist. Picturesque inn with great views.

Hotel Metropole (310-510-1884 or 800-541-8528), 205 Cresent Avenue, Avalon. Expensive. Ocean views, Jacuzzi, balconies, and all the amenities.

The Old Turner Inn (310-510-2236), 232 Catalina Avenue, Avalon. Expensive. A lovely bed & breakfast near the beach. Fine rooms are available. They rent bikes also.

CATALINA ISLAND RESTAURANTS

Cafe Metropole (310-510-0302), 107 Metropole Avenue, Avalon. Moderate. Great lunches at the scenic outdoor cafe.

Armstrong's Fish Market and Seafood Restaurant (310-510-0113), 306 Crescent Avenue, Avalon. Moderate. Offers pleasant seafood dining on the bay.

Avalon Seafood (310-510-0197), on the Green Pleasure Pier in Avalon. Moderate. Their fish-and-chips are excellent.

The Original Antonio's Pizzeria (310-510-0060), 114 Sumner Street, Avalon. Busy place, good Italian food. They deliver pizza throughout Avalon.

LEA MINKOWSKI-EMKIN

Offshore oil derricks disguised as a tropical island, Long Beach

LOS ANGELES ★

Beaches and Attractions

IN LONG BEACH

Long Beach is the southernmost coastal city in Los Angeles County. Its harbor is one of the busiest in the Pacific Rim. The Toyota Grand Prix runs through the city streets in mid-April, bringing the international race crowd. The Visitors Bureau is at One World Trade Center, Suite 300, Long Beach; call 562-436-3645 or 1-800-452-7829.

Long Beach City Beach This beach runs 4 miles from the end of Alamitos Peninsula just above the San Gabriel River, which marks the border with Orange County, to the eastern edge of Long Beach Harbor. Because of industry, offshore oil rigs, and the large volume of shipping that goes through the harbor, water quality here is not the best. Protection by the harbor complex and miles of offshore breakwaters make **City Beach** one of the safest swimming beaches in Los Angeles County, though. City Beach is wide, sandy, and backed by a flat area of Long Beach. The view offshore is of oil derricks named for dead astronauts, Island Grissom and Island White, for example. The beach offers lifeguards, sand volleyball courts, food concessions, outdoor showers, a paved bike path, wheelchair-accessible rest rooms, and fee and metered parking.

Alamitos Bay Beach. A narrow, protected area within Alamitos Bay, this is a safe, lifeguarded swimming beach. There is no surf within the bay, but the beach is sandy, conditions are ideal for windsurfing, and kayaks can be rented. The beach carries the nickname Horny Corners for the large number of buff, scantily clad, deeply tanned bodies roaming around or greasing up on towels. Parking is along Bay Shore Avenue (south of Second Street) and Ocean Boulevard. Call the Long Beach parks department (562-570-3100) or the Long Beach Sailing Center (562-570-1719) for more information.

Alamitos Peninsula, running southeast from 54th Place, buffers Alamitos Bay and forms the southern end of Long Beach City Beach. Walkways run along both the ocean and bay sides, and fee parking is available at the tip of the peninsula.

Belmont Shores, the middle portion of City Beach, runs between 39th and 54th Places. The northern portion runs west from Belmont Pier to 1st Place, below a bluff. Park at the end of Junipero Avenue to reach stairways to the beach at 2nd, 3rd, 5th, 8th, 9th, 10th, and 14th Places. Access to the entire Long Beach City Beach area is along Ocean Boulevard east of the harbor.

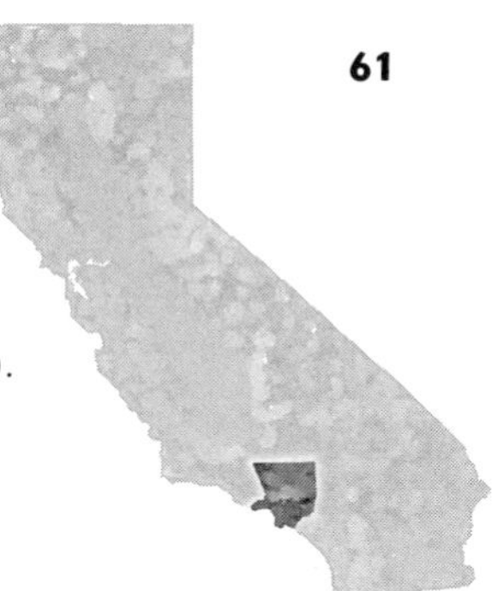

Belmont Pier, 1600 feet long and shaped like a T, bisects the beach at 39th Place. Open from dawn to dusk for fishing, it has a bait shop, snack bars, rest rooms, and nearby metered parking (at Termino Avenue). Sportfishing charters can be arranged (562-434-6781).

NAPLES

Lying just north of the peninsula, these three islands in the middle of Alamitos Bay are encircled almost entirely by a public walkway, affording views of the bay and canals. Naples is charming with its well-maintained, packed-together "cottages" along clean streets and sunny, narrow canals. Along the northern edge of the main island lies the end of Marine Park, where **Mother's Beach** offers swimming and grassy areas, lifeguards, volleyball, wheelchair-accessible rest rooms, and metered parking. Access to Naples is via 2nd Street either west off Pacific Coast Highway or east from Bay Shore Avenue.

Colorado Lagoon. Fed by seawater from nearby Marine Stadium, this wetlands area at Appian Way and 4th Street has a sand beach, lifeguards, playgrounds, barbecue grills, rest rooms, and metered parking.

Belmont Shore This busy shopping hub runs along 2nd Street from Bayshore Avenue to where 2nd becomes Livingston Drive just a few blocks above the beach. Despite four lanes of traffic, it has the inviting feel of a pedestrian mall. It features a wide range of restaurants, clothing and book stores, and artsy shops. Public parking is limited along the street, but more is available off Glendora Avenue.

Long Beach Museum of Art Located at 2300 E. Ocean Boulevard in Bluff Park above Long Beach City Beach, the museum features permanent and changing collections of modern and contemporary art, sculpture, photographs, video art, and a sculpture garden. Open Wednesday–Sunday 10–5, Friday to 8 PM. There is a modest admission fee, and food is available. call 562-439-2119 for more information.

Museum of Latin American Art (562-437-1689), 626 Alamitos Avenue (corner of 7th Street). This museum features changing exhibits of Latin American artists; a permanent collection is in the works. Open Wednesday–Saturday 11:30–7:30, Sunday noon–6. Admission fee for adults, and there is wheelchair-accessible parking in the free lot.

Bixby Park, along Ocean Boulevard at Cherry Avenue, offers a playground, picnic areas, benches, croquet and shuffleboard, wheelchair-accessible rest rooms, and open-air concerts. There is street parking and a tunnel underneath Ocean Boulevard that provides access to City Beach.

Shoreline Park at Shoreline Drive and Pine Avenue, off Ocean Boulevard, features an artificial lagoon, fishing, paths for bikers and walkers, picnic areas, wheelchair-accessible rest rooms, and parking. Call 562-570-3100. There is shopping, restaurants, and a restored carousel at the adjacent Shoreline Village.

Shoreline Marina provides more than 1500 boating slips, along with bike paths, rest rooms, and a park. Call 310-437-0375 for more information.

The *Queen Mary* The largest luxury liner of all time, the art deco *Queen* cruised the North Atlantic between 1934 and 1964. She is now permanently anchored in Long Beach Harbor as a floating hotel (see **Lodging**) and tourist site. Fireworks shows are scheduled Saturday evenings during the summer and on July 4. Guided and self-guided tours are available daily; admission is charged, with discounts for seniors, kids, and active military personnel. The *Queen Mary* is at 1126 Queens Highway. Access is over the Queensway Bridge from Shoreline Drive or at the end of the Long Beach Freeway (I-170). Parking charge depends on length of stay. Phone 562-435-3511 for more information.

JAN RENTZER

Queen Mary

Queens Marketplace Across from the *Queen Mary* is an attempt at a small, old-English–style village with a few deli and pizza-type food stands, a T-shirt shop, and an ice cream vendor. The high percentage of unoccupied shops and lack of variety make the marketplace somewhat uninviting. However, for those wanting just to view the *Queen Mary* without paying the entry fee, this is the only place for several miles to do that and get a drink or a quick bite to eat.

Mega-Bungee For the thrill seeker or the simply crazed, a 220-foot bungee plunge is available over the channel next to the *Queen Mary*. Open Wednesday–Sunday 10 AM–6 PM, this heart-stopper is expensive, with student and military discounts available. Ages 13 and up.

Port of Los Angeles San Pedro, Wilmington, and Terminal Island make up the Port of Los Angeles, one of the most extensive artificial deep-water ports in the world and home to the nation's largest commercial fishing and canning operations. After Long Beach Harbor, it is the largest commercial port on the West Coast. There are passenger and cargo terminals, shipyards, boat slips, marinas, and boating and fishing facilities on its 7500 acres. The center of the harbor area is Terminal Island. It can be reached from San Pedro via the Vincent Thomas Bridge, an enormous turquoise-green harbor landmark (50-cent toll for cars); from Wilmington via the Terminal Island Freeway (103); and from Long Beach over the Gerald Desmond Bridge. The best way to appreciate this vast harbor area is to drive over one of the bridges, pick a pier, and start exploring. Because it's so open, you can't get lost, but you'll get a feel for the magnitude of the marine enterprise here from the huge, hulking ships, the overwhelming stacks of containers piled high along the piers, and the towering gantry cranes used for on- and off-loading cargo vessels from all over the world.

IN WILMINGTON

Drum Barracks Civil War Museum This museum is all that is left of Camp Drum, a 7000-soldier Union Army base that helped keep California in the Union. It displays furniture, photographs, documents, an 1872 model naval Gatling gun, and other Civil War-era memorabilia. Located at 1052 Banning Boulevard, it is open Tuesday–Thursday, and Saturday and Sunday. Parking is free; a $2.50 donation is requested. Phone 310-548-7509 for more information.

General Phineas Banning Residence General Banning founded Wilmington in 1858 and was largely responsible for modernizing the original Los Angeles Harbor. The residence, at 401 E. M Street in Banning Park, is a mid-19th-century, restored Greek Revival built from Mendocino lumber with European marble and stained glass. Tours of the kitchen, family, and public rooms leave 12:30–2:30 Tuesday–Thursday, 12:30–3:30 Saturday and Sunday. A $2 donation is asked and there's street parking. Call 310-548-7777 for more information.

IN SAN PEDRO

Los Angeles Maritime Museum ★ This museum charts the harbor region's history since the 1840s in pictures and artifacts. There are scale models of the *Queen Mary* and the *Titanic*, the bridge deck of the Navy cruiser *Los Angeles*, and a promenade deck from which to view harbor activity. The museum, housed in a remodeled ferry building with much of the original operational gear intact, is in John S. Gibson Jr. Park, at Berth 84 off Harbor Boulevard at 6th Street. It is wheelchair accessible, open 10–5 (closed Monday), has free parking, and asks a donation. Phone 310-548-7618.

Ports o' Call Village and Whalers Wharf This tourist spot on the San Pedro (west) side of the main harbor channel replicates seaports and fishing villages from the 19th century. The village, Asian Center, and wharf have restaurants, shops, entertainment, and cruises with a Main Street, Disneyland, feel. There's a huge free parking lot, but on weekends it's very crowded. **Los Angeles Harbor Cruises** highlight harbor activities such as the yacht harbor, freighters, supertankers, cruise ships, and scrap yards as well as the Federal Prison, Angels Gate Lighthouse, Terminal Island, and Palos Verdes Peninsula. Cruises leave from the Village Boat House in Ports O'Call Village. Fares range up to $12 for a 2-hour cruise. Phone 310-831-0996. *Spirit Cruises*, also in the village, offers yacht, schooner, whale-watching, and dinner cruises. Phone 310-548-8080.

SS Lane Victory This merchant marine ship, built in 1945 and veteran of three wars, houses a museum and memorial to merchant marines buried at sea. It's at Berth 94 off Harbor Boulevard. The first 2 hours of parking are free. Phone 310-519-9545.

Cabrillo Beach ★ This alternately sandy and rocky beach straddles the San Pedro Breakwater; east of the breakwater it's protected, while to the west the beach is open to the Pacific. While the west end of Los Angeles Harbor may seem an unlikely location for a public beach, there is good swimming, diving, and surfing, as well as an increasing number of tide pools as you head west toward Point Fermin (see below). There are lifeguards, picnic tables, grills, showers, volleyball nets, a snack bar, wheelchair-accessible rest rooms, and a 24-hour boat-launch ramp. This is a major place to watch the grunion run, just after the highest tides from March through August. Access is via 40th

Street and Stephen M. White Drive; there is fee parking, and day-use fees are collected. Call 310-832-1179 for more information.

Cabrillo Fishing Pier. The 1000-foot-long fishing pier is connected to the Cabrillo Beach Breakwater. It has a bait and tackle shop and wheelchair-accessible rest rooms, and is open daily. There's fee parking. Call the City of Los Angeles Parks Department at 310-548-7643 or the Port of Los Angeles at 310-732-3522.

Cabrillo Marine Aquarium ★ This Frank Gehry-designed complex offers saltwater aquariums of native southern California sea life, hands-on tide pools, marine laboratories and displays, ship models, multimedia shows, whale-watching tours, and a gift shop. This especially kid-friendly facility is at 3720 Stephen M. White Drive. It's open noon–5 Tuesday–Friday and 10–5 on weekends, with free parking, wheelchair-accessible rest rooms, and a $1 donation asked of adults. Phone 310-548-7562 for more information. For museum-sponsored whale-watching tours, call 310-832-2676.

Fort McArthur Military Museum/Angel's Gate Park This museum above the beach at 3601 Gaffey is both an artillery brigade headquarters and a

JAN RENTZER

Point Fermin

Rim Fay–L.A. Lifeguard

■ In 1949 the construction of the Hyperion Sewage Treatment plant pushed extra sand onto the beaches of Santa Monica Bay. It was a hot summer, and there were lots of people on the beach. The extra sand extended the beach out into the ocean, and the waves crashed with extra force. More people, bigger waves—Rim Fay spent his second summer as a lifeguard pulling people out of the water all day long.

Rim was a good swimmer; he'd been on the team of Los Angeles City College. He was also vigilant and attentive. He often rescued people who were near other lifeguard stations. One, he remembers, was a young girl who'd waded into the surf and was swept out to sea by a riptide right next to another lifeguard who didn't see her.

Rim was learning that children in trouble are a special problem for lifeguards. Working alone in the Venice Beach lifeguard headquarters—a three-story building near the beach—handling the switchboard that communicates with the lifeguard stations, Rim suddenly saw trouble 400 yards away: a boy drowning in the surf, his mother jumping in to rescue him. Rim slid down the pole to the beach and jumped into a jeep. He roared past the lifeguard running to the rescue, and jumped into the riptide and found the boy. The other lifeguard rescued the mother.

The trouble with children is that their mothers, fathers, brothers, sisters, aunts, and uncles all jump into the surf to rescue them. One time, Rim saw seven people follow a child into a riptide, and every single one of these good-intentioned people had to be rescued.

PHOTO: TOM MIKKELSEN

park. Fort McArthur Military Reservation was a World War II training center and part of the West Coast line of defense. It is now a military museum, open Tuesday, Thursday, Saturday, and Sunday noon–5. Call 310-548-2631. The park has panoramic views of Point Fermin and the ocean. A pagoda houses the Friendship Bell, the Republic of Korea's gift in 1976 for the US Bicentennial. There are wheelchair-accessible rest rooms, a play area, basketball courts, a cultural center, and a public pool, open summers only. Call 310-548-7705 for park information, 310-548-7795 for the pool.

Point Fermin Park/Point Fermin National Wildlife Refuge ★ The park is 37 acres on a bluff that overlooks the Pacific and nearby Los Angeles Harbor. There are steep trails down to a rocky shoreline, and here visitors will find outstanding tidal pools at the base of dramatic cliffs. (*Note*: California and federal laws prohibit removing organisms from tidal pools, except where those species are designated "catchable" in fishing regulations.) The trails are via Barbar,

Another problem is boats coming too close too shore, getting into the surf line and flipping over. Once a party boat carrying eight people flipped on Rim's watch. Six of the passengers were rescued but two couldn't be found and drowned. In that incident, the father of a drowned girl sat vigil on the beach all week until his daughter's body washed up on shore. Another time, a man rented a boat in Newport Beach—and he didn't take an anchor or any lights. Rim found the boat while he was on night patrol in Playa Del Rey. There was no one in it.

Years went by. Rim looked around and realized that he was now the oldest active lifeguard in Los Angeles. He had rescued so many people that he had trouble remembering when and where the events had happened.

He was also developing a business diving for marine specimens, something he could do when he finally had to stop being a lifeguard. One afternoon, when Rim was going diving, he found an overturned Hobie Cat boat, four miles out at sea. There were two people clinging to it. Even when Rim was doing other things, he was still rescuing people.

By 1996, Rim had been a lifeguard in and around Los Angeles for almost half a century. In the early days, lifeguards had little training; they were high school dropouts—losers. Now they were serious professionals, college graduates, and they were disciplined, skilled swimmers. That's a good thing, because all the building on the Los Angeles coast has disturbed the original long, forgiving beaches. Now there are groins to trap sand, new harbors. Santa Monica Bay has become the most artificially disturbed marine environment in the world, Rim thought, with dangerous surges and back gullies where kids get trapped and swept into deep water.

In 1997, Rim decided to stop working as a lifeguard. He is 70 years old now, and spends six days a week on his growing marine specimen business, collecting sea urchins, tunicates (sea squirts), shrimps, mollusks, algae, crabs, and sponges. He just doesn't have the time. ■

Meyler, or Roxbury Street. The bluff at street level is a good place to watch migrating whales in season. There also are picnic tables, barbecue grills, and wheelchair-accessible rest rooms. Access is via Gaffey Street where it ends at Paseo del Mar; call the Los Angeles County Lifeguard Service at 310-832-1179 for more information.

Friendship County Regional Park. Just west of Western Avenue at 9th Street, this facility offers views of the harbor for picnickers. There are paved paths, and a playground and rest rooms at the adjacent **San Pedro Recreation Center.** It's open 8 AM–dusk.

Royal Palms State Beach. This boulder-strewn beach is at the base of sedimentary cliffs, now used primarily by surfers and tide poolers. It is the site of the former Royal Palms Hotel, which washed away in storms during the 1920s. The palm trees remain, however, and there are lifeguards during the summer as well as rest rooms. The bluff has a wheelchair-accessible lot with a ramp to

Catalina Avenue Shopping

■ If you're after shopping or browsing, head to the lovely four-block commercial strip on S. Catalina Avenue between Palos Verdes Boulevard and Avenue I at the south end of Redondo Beach. There is limited street parking on Catalina, and much more on the side streets. Shops include those selling southwestern art, antiques, holistic health care, and beachwear.

Coffee Cartel on the corner of Catalina and Elena sells coffees and teas, and has a juice bar and baked goods in the back. The front room has large sunny windows, inviting couches and tables, and shelves filled with a wide range of books to read or buy. There are also chess and backgammon sets. Outside there are more tables in a shaded garden that fronts Catalina. This is a lovely, quiet retreat from the beach hubbub.

Mixt, at 1722 S. Catalina Avenue, is another find. It sells handcrafted items including glass and tableware, lamps, fountains, candles and holders, clothing, and sculpture. Don't miss the garden—it's an imaginative and inventive shrine to "found art" with a planted iron bed frame and chairs, a dovecote, greenhouse, and sculpture. This is a most unusual and beautiful shop.

Sea and Sea Located at 1911 S. Catalina Avenue, this shop offers scuba equipment for sale and for rent, and gives lessons. Call 310-373-6355 for more information.

Marina Bike Rentals is at 505 N. Harbor Drive, next to the Cheesecake Factory. You can rent one-speed beach cruisers, mountain bikes, and tandems.

King Harbor At the southern border with Hermosa Beach, King Harbor nestles behind a long breakwater. More than 1400 small craft fill the three basins. There are fuel docks, marine supplies, slips, shops, charter boats, restaurants, and, in summer, a boat-launching ramp. Call the Harbor Patrol at 310-318-0632 for temporary berthing information, and 310-372-3566 for whale-watching boats (seasonal only). The **International Boardwalk,** a commercial and recreation area with restaurants, an amusement arcade, and souvenir shops, is in Basin No. 3.

E T Surfboards rents soft body-board-type surfboards (sorry, no wet suits) for $15/day with a credit card deposit. It is at 904 Aviation Boulevard just each of the Pacific Coast Highway; call 310-379-7660. For bikes, check out **Hermosa Cyclery,** 20 13th Street. It also has tandems. Call 310-376-2720. If you're looking for live entertainment, try **Lighthouse Cafe** at 30 Pier Avenue. Its musical offerings range from jazz to blues to R&B, from alternative to reggae to funk, with '70s and '80s dance music on Wednesdays. Call 310-372-6911. ■

rest rooms. Access is via Kay Fiorentino Drive near Paseo del Mar; there is a vehicle entrance fee. Call 310-832-1179 for more information.

Western Avenue which begins at Royal Palms State Beach, is one of the longest surface streets in Los Angeles. It curves through San Pedro and the border with Rancho Palos Verdes, then straightens out to run due north through Harbor City, Gardena, and central Los Angeles. After its more than 25-mile tour through L.A., it terminates at Los Feliz Boulevard beneath the Hollywood Hills.

IN PALOS VERDES ESTATES

Palos Verdes Peninsula Drive Palos Verdes Peninsula juts southwest into the Pacific at the south end of Santa Monica Bay. There is public access to its beaches (see below), but for those with less time, a 12-mile tour along Palos Verdes Drive between Western Avenue in San Pedro and Malaga Cove affords breathtaking views of the Pacific below the peninsula's chaparral- and mansion-covered bluffs. A bike path runs along Palos Verdes Drive as well.

Abalone Cove City Beach. Just west of the Portuguese Bend area on the southwest corner of Palos Verdes Peninsula, this is a rocky beach at the bottom of some impressive sedimentary bluffs. It's got gray sand, lots of tide pools, surfable waves, and a view of Santa Catalina Island. While it's probably inappropriate for swimming, there are picnic tables, chemical toilets, and lifeguards to be found. Wheelchair-accessible rest rooms are up on the bluff. Those who enjoy watching nature in action may want to walk or drive east to Portuguese Bend, a cliff area that is largely unstable and periodically threatens to throw everything built on it into the ocean. Access is via Palos Verdes Drive South at Narcissa Drive; call 310-372-2166 for more information. There is a $4/vehicle entrance fee.

Wayfarer's Chapel On a bluff overlooking the Pacific is the Frank Lloyd Wright-designed "Glass Church," built as a memorial to the Swedish theologian and mystic Emanuel Swedenborg. The tiny church is mostly glass in a wood-and-metal frame; climbing philodendrons inside and redwoods outside make this gem feel like a natural part of the gardens and grove in which it nestles. Located at 5755 Palos Verdes Drive South, it is open 9–5 daily with free, self-guided tours.

Marineland. This once pioneering and popular marine amusement park is now closed. However, there is free public parking 8:30 AM–4 PM on the grounds for beach access at 6600 Palos Verdes Drive South. Call 310-541-4566.

Point Vicente Park ★ This is 4 acres perched atop a bluff that overlooks the Pacific and the Point Vicente Lighthouse (which unfortunately is not open to the public). It features a paved trail, a whale-watching deck, and an interpretive center that has displays on the local ecology and natural history. The **Point Vicente Fishing Access** down a steep dirt path is just east of here, and has excellent surfing and diving opportunities. Access is via Palos Verdes Drive West, just south of Hawthorne Boulevard; there is a fee for the interpretive center. Call 310-377-5370.

Palos Verdes Estates Shoreline Preserve ★ This is an undeveloped city blufftop preserve with no facilities but lots of street parking. The preserve (nothing can be removed from the area) runs for 4.5 miles along the coast and includes overlooks, paths, and steep (dangerous) access to the beach below. There is surfing at Malaga and Bluff Coves and Lunada Bay. Access is along Palos Verdes Drive West in the Estates area of the peninsula.

Bluff Cove. The **overlook** for Bluff Cove is in the 1300 block of Paseo del Mar in the Estates. There is a dirt path headed south atop the bluff. To reach the cove just to the north, park on the street near 600 Paseo del Mar. The path beginning at Flat Rock Point leads to the rocky cove, tide pools, and surfing.

LEA MINKOWSKI-EMKIN

Redondo Beach

Malaga Cove, aka RAT (Right After Torrance), Beach. The northernmost point of the Palos Verdes coast, Malaga Cove has the only sand beach on the peninsula. There are tide pools to the south and sand volleyball courts, showers, lifeguards, and parking. Access is at Via Arroyo off Paseo del Mar; direct access to the southern tide pool and Haggerty's surfing area is via a path in the 500 block of Paseo del Mar at Vista Chino. Call 310-378-0383 for more information.

IN TORRANCE

Torrance County Beach. Torrance is wide and sandy with cement ramps leading down to it from fee parking lots above. There are lifeguards, outdoor showers, and wheelchair-accessible rest rooms. Here also is the southern end of the South Bay Bicycle Trail, which begins 20 miles away at Will Rogers State Beach. There's good surfing here as well, especially during winter's southern swells. Access is via a large parking lot on Paseo de la Playa; there is an entrance fee. The southern end can also be reached from Malaga Cove. Call 310-372-2166 for more information.

IN REDONDO BEACH

International Surf Festival This annual event sponsored by the Los Angeles County Department of Beaches is held in the Redondo/Manhattan/Hermosa Beach cities, usually in early August. You can choose from surfing and body-surfing contests, helicopter rescue demonstrations, beach runs, lifeguard runs, volleyball, and other beach and surf activities. The free local newspaper, the *Easy Reader*, prints a schedule of events, or call the Redondo Beach Visitors Bureau at 1-800-282-0333.

Redondo County Beach. The northerly continuation of Torrance County Beach, this is a wider, sandier stretch used for swimming and surfing, and while popular is still somewhat less crowded than neighboring Hermosa and Manhattan Beaches. There are lifeguards, showers, a bike path, and sand volleyball courts. This is the beginning of the series of beaches, leading to Venice, that practically define southern California coastal culture. Access is via metered street parking along Esplanade; the center of the beach is at approximately Torrance Boulevard. There is a day-use fee. Call 310-372-2166 for more information.

Blufftop Walkway. Above Redondo State Beach is a walkway paralleling the coast just west of the Esplanade. It runs for about 1 mile from Knob Hill Avenue in the south to Harbor Drive, with stairways connecting it to the Esplanade and the beach bike path. Metered parking is available.

Redondo Beach Piers. Redondo Beach is a fisherman's delight, with three major structures featuring some of the best fishing in southern California. From south to north, they are the Monstad Pier, Redondo Beach Municipal (Horseshoe) Pier, and Redondo Sportfishing Pier. The piers all are in a developed area of Redondo Beach and surrounded by restaurants, walking paths, the South Bay Bicycle Trail along Catalina Avenue, and numerous shops. Immediately adjacent to Redondo Pier is the International Boardwalk, with typical seaside shops and eating places. On the 4th of July, the Redondo Pier is one of the best places for watching fireworks. (Personal use of fireworks is banned in Los Angeles County.) Access to Monstad and Redondo Beach Municipal Piers are via the foot of Torrance Boulevard; access to Redondo Sportfishing is west of Harbor Drive just north of Harbor Basin No. 3. Monstad and Redondo Sportfishing are open 24 hours. A huge public parking lot for the pier is just off Catalina at Pacific.

Seaside Lagoon A good choice for those who like swimming in big spaces but don't want to worry about waves and riptides—particularly families with children—this is a 2½-acre saltwater lagoon located between Harbor Basins Nos. 2 and 3. It's open from Memorial Day to about Labor Day and has picnic tables and volleyball courts. Seaside charges a fee for access; it's located at 200 Portofino Way. For more information, call 310-318-0681.

IN HERMOSA BEACH

Hermosa City Beach/Hermosa Pier Wide enough that it's nearly impossible to overcrowd, Hermosa is 2 miles of extremely white sand roughly centered on a 900-foot-long pier. Swimming, fishing, and surfing all are highly recommended, though nearby Redondo Harbor reduces waves to a level that's good for beginners. The beach here was deeded to the city with the stipulation that it never be developed, making Hermosa something special among southern California beaches. It features sand volleyball courts, swing sets, lifeguards, showers, and rest rooms. Hermosa City Beach is bordered on the east by the Strand, a pedestrian walkway running its entire length, and by Pier Avenue, which has lots of interesting stores. Fishing is good from the pier, which has a bait and tackle shop, rest rooms, and a snack bar. The beach is beautiful and well maintained; the only major problem here is scarce parking. Access is all along the Strand in Hermosa Beach; call

310-372-2166 for beach information, **Hermosa Sportfishing** at 310-372-2124 for pier information.

IN MANHATTAN BEACH

Manhattan County Beach/Manhattan Beach Municipal Pier. Manhattan Beach's portion of the South Bay coast, this is another white, sandy, very wide beach backed by a seawall and fronted by numerous beach volleyball nets. It includes El Porto Beach; the water here is occasionally rough, but there are many lifeguards as well. The *playa* is surrounded by residential Manhattan Beach, which features many restaurants and lots of nonfranchise retail stores. The Municipal Pier is 900 feet long and bisects the beach; it features a bait and tackle shop. For more information, call 310-372-2166.

Roundhouse Marine Studies Lab and Aquarium ★ At the end of the pier is the Roundhouse Marine Studies Lab and Aquarium, offering local sea life and touch tanks with, among other animals, live sharks. It is open Monday–Friday 3 PM–sunset; weekends 10 AM–sunset; there is no charge but they ask for donations, their only funding source. Call 310-379-8117 for more information. Three blocks in from the beach, at 1116 Manhattan Avenue, is **Fun Bunns Beach Rentals.** They rent (and sell) everything for the beach: volleyballs, surfboards, body boards, bikes, in-line skates and roller skates, chairs, and umbrellas, for starters. Call 310-372-8500 for rates. Beach access is west of the Strand, and the pier is on Manhattan Beach Boulevard; there is metered street and lot parking, and an access fee is charged. Call 310-372-2166 for more information.

Parque Culiacan. Just north of Manhattan State Beach is a blufftop, grassy park with metered parking, wheelchair-accessible rest rooms, basketball court, and paved beach access. It's at 26th Street and Manhattan Avenue.

El Porto Beach. Just north of, and technically part of, Manhattan County Beach, this beach is accessed via the west end of 45th Street. Its facilities include lifeguards, volleyball nets, outdoor showers, swings, bike racks, and wheelchair-accessible rest rooms. This beach can be something of a scene, though, and louder than one might like. An access fee is charged; call 310-372-2166 for more information.

IN EL SEGUNDO/PLAYA DEL REY

Dockweiler State Beach/El Segundo Beach. Measuring 6 miles long, Dockweiler (and its subsidiary El Segundo) stretches from El Porto Beach north to

Marina del Rey, a continuation of the sand strip that began in Palos Verdes. It is another wide, sandy beauty (and made even wider by dredging), which unfortunately is located near an industrial area and the Hyperion Sewage Treatment Plant, as well as beneath the takeoff path for Los Angeles International Airport. This beach just south of Marina del Rey has 117 spaces for RVs only, with rest rooms, full hookups, and sewage disposal facilities. Call 310-322-4951 for reservations and fees. Access is off Vista del Mar Boulevard and Grand Avenue. There's practically never a crowding problem on beaches this big; there are beach volleyball nets, lifeguards, and access to the South Bay Bicycle Trail, and surfing is decent at El Segundo. Access to El Segundo is via the west end of Grand Avenue in the town of El Segundo; for Dockweiler, access is west from Vista del Mar Boulevard but mainly on the Pacific Coast Highway at Imperial Boulevard.

Del Rey Lagoon Park. Sandwiched between Dockweiler Beach and Ballona Creek by Marina Del Rey, this 13-acre park has no swimming but offers a playground, barbecue and picnic facilities, basketball courts, and a grassy area surrounding the lagoon. Access is at 6660 Esplanade, Playa Del Rey, where there is street parking. You can also park along the creek or, for the beach area to the south, at Pacific Avenue and 62nd Place.

IN MARINA DEL REY

Marina Del Rey Harbor This high-traffic harbor is the world's largest man-made facility of its kind, home to more than 6000 small pleasure craft. There are boat slips, marine supplies, fuel, sportfishing charters, yacht clubs, shops, hotels, and restaurants. Basin H has public docking space with showers, rest rooms, water, and electricity; assignments are made at the Community Building in adjacent Burton Chace Park. The **Marina Visitors Information Center** is at 4701 Admiralty Way at Mindanao Way; call 310-305-9545.

Fisherman's Village This tourist spot features restaurants and snack stands, shops, art galleries, boat rentals, fishing licenses and supplies, and hourly harbor cruises, all in a New England fishing village setting. Validated fee parking is available. The village is located in Basin H on Fiji Way. Call 310-823-5411 for village information; 310-301-6000 for harbor cruises.

Burton Chace County Park/Audrey E. Austin Jr. Memorial Park. Burton Chace Park is the site of two popular annual marina events, the boat show in early June and the Christmas Boat Parade on the second Saturday of December. This is also a good spot to view the marina's Fourth of July fireworks show. The park offers transient boat docks, an observation deck, snacks, a place to clean fish, and wheelchair-accessible rest rooms. Picnic shelters for groups are available on Saturdays, only by reservation; call 310-305-9595. The park, with its sweeping harbor views, is at the north edge of Basin H at the end of Mindanao Way. Parking is free only during daytime hours on weekdays.

Admiralty Park, just north of Basin F, runs along Admiralty Way between Lincoln Boulevard and Washington Street. The grass strip, in view of the harbor, has a 1-mile running course and an exercise course. Fee parking is available. This small park lies at the north shore of the entrance channel at the south end of Pacific Avenue. There are paved walkways, benches, and piers from which to watch the traffic flowing in and out of the marina, places to fish, and access to both the Ballona Lagoon Walkway and the south end of Venice Beach (see below). There is metered parking.

Promenade Walkway/Ballona Lagoon Walkway. The Promenade Walkway runs along the northern end of the marina, from Palaway Way around Basin E to near the fire station on Admiralty Way. It can also be reached through the Ritz-Carlton Hotel on Admiralty. It is open 6 AM–9 PM. The **Ballona Lagoon Walkway** is an unpaved path on the east side of the lagoon. It is accessible from Audrey E. Austin Jr. Memorial Park, from a pedestrian bridge at Lighthouse Street, and from a number of streets in the Silver Strand residential area.

Mother's Beach (aka Marina del Rey Public Swimming Beach) High up in a corner of the gigantic Marina del Rey Harbor, Mother's is aptly named for its protected conditions; no waves intrude, the beach is lifeguarded, and swimming is safe. There are also volleyball nets and sheltered picnic tables, and conditions are good for windsurfing. There is wheelchair access to the water via a paved ramp, and wheelchairs are available free for use in the water. The only drawback here is that the water quality in the harbor varies with the amount of boat traffic—and thus the amount of fuel and bilgewater—going in and out. Access is via Panay Way, at the end of Basin D. Call 310-305-9545 for more information.

Marina Del Rey Bike Path The bike path circles the harbor area and connects with the South Bay Bicycle Trail at both ends, forming part of the continuous path from Torrance County Beach in the south to Will Rogers State Beach in the north.

IN VENICE

Venice Beach The Godzilla of the southern California beach scene, Venice is the outgrowth of the dreams of tobacco millionaire Abbot Kinney, who wanted to re-create the Italian Venice in California. Though most of his canals have long since been filled in, people still flock to Venice Beach to witness an unending panorama of human diversity.

The beach itself begins just north of Marina Del Rey Harbor and continues to Santa Monica Pier 2 miles farther up, just beyond Pico Boulevard. It is wide, sandy, and in spots planted with palm trees; like Dockweiler, it is augmented with dredged sand. The beach is good for sunbathing, swimming, and diving, but is generally underused because of Venice's reputation for craziness and theft—and the fact that many use the beach's sands as a sort of catbox. **Venice Pier** is currently closed to the public.

A curving, 0.7-mile-long concrete **boardwalk** cuts through the most dense portion of Venice's beachfront, and here weekend visitors can—and will—be endlessly distracted by all manner of performers, preachers, sunbathers, in-line skaters, and weightlifters. You can get your fortune told, your back massaged, your portrait chalked, and your politics and eating habits debated. Don't miss the infamous chain saw-juggling act. And do keep a hand on your purse or wallet. The crowds can be very thick and not altogether benign. There is also great spectating at the blacktop basketball courts, whose games are famously high level, with even an occasional pro or two picking up. There's also **Muscle Beach** near 18th Avenue, with its all-day displays of weightlifting and exhibitionism. An enormous number of retail and restaurants line **Ocean Front Walk**,

©JAMES BLANK

Santa Monica Pier

which runs the entire length of the beach from Ozone Avenue to Washington Street. The most ubiquitous items for sale are beachwear, sunglasses, incense, and jewelry.

Beach access is via the major east–west streets in town: Washington Street, Venice Boulevard, Rose Avenue, Windward Avenue, and Park Boulevard, as well as from Ocean Front Walk. There are outdoor showers and wheelchair-accessible rest rooms. Parking, especially on weekends, is problematic. There aren't enough spaces for all the visitors to the human circus and the beach. If you're lucky, you'll find street parking on the main thoroughfares or one of the tiny side streets; pay attention to the parking signs, as regulations are strictly enforced. There is an inexpensive lot at a local elementary school on Main Street. The entrance is at Clubhouse Avenue. Other pay lots are sprinkled throughout the area. For more information, call the Los Angeles County Lifeguard Service at 310-577-5700.

Rentals on the Beach has three locations in Venice, at 3001, 2100, and 300 Ocean Front Walk. It rents a wide range of beach stuff, including bikes, tandems, three-wheeled fun bikes, in-line skates, boogie boards, umbrellas, and chairs. Call 310-821-9047 for 2-hour special rates and prices for other rentals.

IN SANTA MONICA

Santa Monica State Beach/Santa Monica Municipal Pier Santa Monica is a gem, a wide, sandy beach backed by beautiful but slightly unstable bluffs; these become steadily more rugged as you head north toward Will Rogers State Beach (see **In Pacific Palisades**). Santa Monica is much more heavily used than Venice Beach, and attracts largely middle-class families from all over Los Angeles. There are lifeguards, good swimming, and mild surfing, along with plenty of volleyball nets. **The pier** is a collection of delightful old-fashioned amusements, including a few newly installed thrill rides, a huge Ferris wheel, video-game arcades, skee-ball, a famous old carousel, bumper cars, rocking horses, gift shops, basketball shoots and other games, and the usual selection of carnival foods: hot dogs, burgers, cotton candy, and the like. **The Ash Grove,** a '50s and '60s folk music mecca, reopened on the pier when its West Hollywood location closed down. There are wheelchair-accessible rest rooms and beach access on both the north and south sides. It's all great fun on a remarkably long-lived wooden pier, which is old enough to need care after every winter storm. Access is to the west of the Pacific Coast Highway and especially at its intersections with Pico, Wilshire, and Santa Monica Boulevards. There are fee parking lots and metered street parking; for more information, call the Los Angeles County Lifeguard Service at 310-577-5700.

Main Street, Ocean Park, Santa Monica Ocean Park is the southernmost section of Santa Monica, lying just above Venice Beach. Main Street is a busy, upscale commercial strip running between Rose Avenue and Ocean Park Boulevard. A mix of locals, more-inland Los Angelenos, and tourists, Main Street invites slow walking, a wide range of culinary appetites, and people-watching. Along with the usual Gap, Armani A/X, and Starbucks are independent bookstores, a kite shop, boutiques, and outdoor cafés. There's minimal parking on Main, but public lots are found west of Main on, among other streets, Ashland and Hill. Just south of Rose, on Main Street, catch the **Chiat/Day Advertising Agency building,** designed by Frank Gehry. It's an eye-opener. And don't miss the clown in drag on the corner of Rose and Main. To the north, the **California Heritage Museum** at 2612 Main Street features restored rooms from the 1890s through the 1930s, as well as changing exhibits of California history and culture. It's open Wednesday–Saturday 11–4, Sunday noon–4; admission is charged, with senior and kids' discounts. Call 310-392-8537 for more information.

Farmer's Market. This is one of the best farmer's markets in Los Angeles. There are organic and nonorganic fruits and vegetables, cut flowers, plants, herbs, jams, honeys, and other products at outdoor stands, sold by those who grow or make their wares. It's great for picking up picnic food or just as a reminder that what we eat comes from somewhere else before it gets to the supermarkets. The market runs along Arizona Avenue between Ocean Avenue and 4th Street, Wednesday 9–3 and Saturday 9–noon. Find metered street or public parking structures. Call 310-319-6263.

Third Street Promenade Three blocks in from the bluffs above Santa Monica Beach is one of the few places in Los Angeles where the locals (from all parts of the L.A. basin) congregate to eat, shop, walk, and people-watch. The promenade runs along 3rd Street between Broadway on the south and Wilshire Boulevard to the north. The area was once a dying retail enclave of small shops and service businesses with street parking. It is now an inviting pedestrian strip with a mix of chains and one-of-a-kind clothing, shoe, art, book, and other shops, and restaurants to fit every budget. The promenade offers fountains, animal topiaries, and lots of places to sit and watch the world walk by. Limited metered parking is available on nearby streets; municipal parking structures are sprinkled throughout the area, including 2nd Street between Arizona and Wilshire; the first 3 hours are free. **Santa Monica Place,** designed by Frank Gehry, is an interesting mall below Broadway at the south end of the promenade. It also has parking.

Spokes N Stuff at 1715 Oceanfront Boardwalk, just behind Loew's Hotel, rents beach cruisers and mountain bikes. Call 310-395-4748. It also rents from its shop at the Jamaica Bay Inn in Marina Del Rey at 4175 Admiralty Way.

Bergamot Station. This 6-acre cultural center houses 20 art galleries featuring sculpture, photography, functional art, and contemporary paintings. Performing arts theaters are scheduled to open in 1998. Located just off 26th Street near Olympic Boulevard at 2525 Michigan Avenue, Bergamot boasts food establishments, plenty of free parking, and free admission. It's open Tuesday–Friday 10–5, Saturday 11–5. Call 310-453-7535.

Museum of Flying This gem of a museum features a collection of more than 30 vintage aircraft, wonderfully displayed in a multistory structure that feels like an old airplane hangar. There's also an interactive flight area and a fabulous collection of model airplanes. Donald Douglas built the first DC-3 on this site. The museum is at 2772 Donald Douglas Street; access is at 28th Street at Ocean Park Boulevard. It's open Tuesday–Sunday 10–5; admission is charged, with senior and kids' discounts, and there is plenty of parking. Call 310-392-8822 for more information.

Angel's Attic. Angel's Attic is a collection of antique dolls, toys, dollhouses, and miniatures in a restored Victorian residence at 516 Colorado Avenue. It's open Thursday–Sunday 12:30–4:30; closed the first week in September. Parking is on the street; admission is charged, with senior and kids' discounts. Call 310-394-8331.

Palisades Park. On the bluffs above Santa Monica Beach is a popular grassy park with benches, shuffleboard, rest rooms, and a camera obscura at the Senior Recreation Center on Ocean Boulevard. Call 310-454-1412. Access to the beach is via bike and footpaths over Pacific Coast Highway below. The park fronts Ocean Boulevard from Adelaide Drive to Colorado Avenue. The Visitors Assistance Stand is at Arizona Street and Ocean Boulevard.

J. Paul Getty Center. 1200 Getty Center Drive, Brentwood. Parking fee charged, reservations required (310-440-7300). Admission to the museum is free. Hours: Saturday and Sunday, 10–6, Tuesday and Wednesday 11–7, Thursday and Friday 11–9. Closed Mondays and holidays. The original Getty museum, which is right on the coast, recently closed for renovations and will not open again until 2001. In the meantime, the new Getty Museum is worth a visit; although not strictly speaking a coastal attraction, from its hilltop location there are splendid views of the coastline. More than a single museum, the new Getty is a complex of six related buildings occupying a ridge in the Santa Monica Mountains, perched above Brentwood and the San Diego Freeway. It is large enough to warrant an entire day's visit. Architecture critics have praised the new museum for the abundant natural light in its display rooms (the *L.A. Times* hailed its "gorgeous clarity of illuminated space"); the sunsets from its hilltop location are particularly striking.

IN PACIFIC PALISADES

Will Rogers State Beach. This wide, sandy beach several miles long is backed by the cliffs of Pacific Palisades, a community originally settled by Methodists. Now it is the home of people who are serious about the beach life. This also is the northern terminus of the South Bay Bicycle Trail, which runs 20 miles south to Torrance County Beach (see **In Torrance**). There are lifeguards, volleyball nets, outdoor showers, snack bars, and wheelchair-accessible rest rooms; swimming and diving are good, and surfing is too in the area near Sunset Boulevard. Access is via the 16000 block of Pacific Coast Highway, although the parking lot runs the beach's entire length. There is a modest vehicle fee for parking and access. Call 310-455-2465 for more information.

Will Rogers State Historic Park This was the ranch of Will Rogers, the noted cowboy humorist; now it is a 186-acre park. It features hiking and equestrian trails, mountain biking on fire roads, and a 12-minute film on Rogers's life at the park visitors center (Rogers's former house). The hiking trails are planted with eucalyptus and chaparral and offer great views of the Pacific as they wind upward; they also connect with the adjacent Topanga Canyon State Park (see **In Malibu**). There are polo matches here on the weekends. *Note:* The visitors center is open only on weekends, and dogs are not allowed in the park. Access is at 14253 Sunset Boulevard; there is a fee for parking. Call 310-454-8212 for more information.

Temescal Canyon Park/Temescal Gateway Park. Across Pacific Coast Highway from Will Rogers State Beach, Temescal Canyon Road winds uphill toward Pacific Palisades. Temescal Canyon Park (Lower Temescal) runs along both sides of the road and has playground facilities, dirt paths, picnic areas, and rest rooms. There is free street parking. At the end of Temescal Canyon Road across Sunset Boulevard is Temescal Gateway Park, through which trails lead to the Santa Monica Mountains National Recreation Area (see below). There are parking and wheelchair-accessible rest rooms. Bikes and fires are not allowed. Call 310-456-7049 for more information.

Self-Realization Friendship Lake Shrine This tranquil spot has long been a spiritual oasis away from the commotion of Los Angeles. The 10-acre site includes a bird sanctuary, lake, sunken garden, monuments representing the world's five major religions, a museum, and an outdoor temple, home of the Gandhi World Peace Memorial. Call 310-454-4114 for more information.

Santa Monica Mountains National Recreation Area (SMMNRA) The umbrella designation for a series of parks mostly high above the ocean, this transverse (east–west) mountain range runs from Oxnard to Los Angeles, covering roughly 150,000 acres between the coast and Highway 101, and not incidentally forming the northwest physical boundary of the Los Angeles basin in the process. It hosts oak, sage, and chaparral, as well as rare golden eagles and an increasing number of mountain lions. The park has summits reaching to 3000 feet and features numerous hiking trails. There are ranger-led hikes in many of the SMMNRA's subparks; write to the park service for a free calendar of upcoming events (see below). There are plans for a 55-mile-long Backbone Trail, which will connect the various parts of the area from Will Rogers State Historic Park to Point Mugu. The park also includes more than 50 miles of beaches from Santa Monica to Point Mugu. Vehicle access is primarily along Mulholland Drive and Mulholland Highway, which follow the Santa Monica Mountains' crest from urban northern Los Angeles to west of Malibu. Scenic canyon and crestline drives through the region include Topanga Canyon Boulevard, Malibu Canyon Road/Las Virgenes Road, Kanan Dume Road, and Latigo Canyon Road. Great coastal panoramas can be enjoyed from Saddle Peak and Tuna Canyon Roads; Corral Canyon Road offers typical mountain and canyon views. Write to the National Park Service at 30401 Agoura Road, Suite 100, Agoura Hills, CA 91301, or call 818-597-9192, for further information.

IN MALIBU

Topanga State Beach. A narrow, mile-long, somewhat rocky beach east of Malibu proper, it's backed by Topanga Canyon, the highway, and eroding bluffs, and is located at the mouth of Topanga Creek. It's good for surfing, but serious swimming here is not recommended due to submerged rocks. There are lifeguards, though, and wheelchair-accessible rest rooms and a picnic area. Access is via the 18500 block of Pacific Coast Highway; there is an entrance fee. Call 310-451-2906 for more information.

Las Tunas State Beach. This beach is the outlet for Tuna Canyon and its associated bluffs, which are much in evidence since the canyon occasionally ejects boulders onto buildings and the highway. There are lifeguards and surfing here, and also a good deal of surf-fishing. Swimming can be treacherous because of rusted metal groins in the water. Access is via the 19400 block of

Bank Wright–California Surfing

■ Surfing in California had always been a local thing—you needed local knowledge to know where to catch a wave—but in the '70s, something strange began to happen on the beaches: Suddenly there were *new* people on the waves.

In northern California, there were bleached-blond yahoos from L.A., and in the south there were white-skinned, wet-suited long-boarders from northern California. Surfing had changed: Provincial local surfers suddenly got the urge to travel.

They were doing so in significant numbers, and what's more, everyone seemed to know where to catch a wave.

This sudden intermingling of southern and northern California surfers goes a long way toward explaining the particular phenomenon of California surfing culture—a state of mind and music that is not indigenous to any single part of the state but draws on many influences.

Spontaneous cultural explosions—like the Great Awakening in 16th-century New England, or the California surfing culture of the '70s—are usually explained in sociological terms, as if they existed because they fulfilled an unmet need in a particular population. But there are always practical explanations as well: California surfing culture happened because of people like Bank Wright.

In the late '60s, Bank Wright was 21, out of the Army reserves, and had just returned from three years surfing the big waves in Hawaii. When he was in Hawaii, Bank had written a short guide explaining where to catch the best waves in the Islands. Now, living again at his parents' house in Hermosa Beach, casting about for something to do, Bank decided he would write a surfing guide for the entire state of California.

Bank loaded his wet suit, surfboard, cameras, and notebooks into a battered GMC van and started surfing at the Mexican line. He surfed through San Diego and up into L.A. Every Friday night he loaded the wet suit, surfboard, and cameras into the van and headed to the next section of coast. Weekend by weekend, he moved on—surfing through Ventura County, then surfing on through Monterey. Every time he found a surfable break, Bank took pictures, documented the conditions, and surfed the spot himself.

A year into the project, Bank was nearing San Francisco, so far north that he was outside the known territory of L.A. surfers. He was discovering breaks that had never been surfed before—and also finding small groups of northern California surfers who were eager to talk to him and find out what it was really like on the fabled big breaks to the south.

Bank managed to be in the right place at the right time. Just north of the city of Santa Cruz, for example, Bank saw a break off Pilar Point with monstrous waves, bigger than the huge ones he'd ridden in Hawaii. He could tell that the waves here wouldn't break all year long, that you had to be there at the right time, as he was. There was no one surfing these deadly walls. Bank wasn't even sure it was possible to ride them.

Bank took his pictures and wrote up his description, the first ever of a break known today as Mavericks, the ultimate California big wave, one of those spots that, like Everest, draw the adventurous from all over the world. (Mark Foo, a legendary Hawaiian surfer who heard Mavericks was breaking, flew in from Hawaii in the morning and by afternoon was dead. Foo's story would become one of the central events in Daniel Duane's brilliant surfing book, *Caught Inside—A Surfer's Year on the California Coast.*)

Bank surfed Ocean Beach in San Francisco: "Three miles of beach peaks. Steep and super strong in winter. Breaks all year, 2–12 feet. Medium tide best. Rarely surfed by locals." He drove across the Golden Gate Bridge into Marin and surfed Point Reyes: "Massive winter peaks off tip of point"; Drake's Bay: "Breaks on all swells but south is best"; and Stinson: "Shape changes daily."

Now Bank was surfing spots that had never before seen a surfboard. He was surfing all alone, in 40-degree water, testing waves, taking pictures, documenting every wave he saw. He went up north of the Russian River and surfed Mote Creek: "Owner doesn't mind visitors." He went on and surfed dangerous Point Arena: "Steep, hooking takeoff followed by a thick right shoulder."

The water was really cold now, but he was finding incredible waves that no one had ridden and friendly locals who were amazed to find a guy from Los Angeles out there with a surfboard in the middle of winter! "The people are mellow," Bank wrote of northern California. "Theirs is a simple life—close to the land. Surfers traveling north should try and leave their city habits at home . . . remember, it's super cold, so be prepared."

Two years into his quest, Bank was getting near the Oregon border—here the "locals" didn't even know what a surfboard was. Finally, he crossed over into Oregon and surfed Brooking: "Long peeling lines off a central peak. Breaks ⅛ mile out. Waves are soft and easy breaking. Fast and tubular across an inside reef." Then he turned his van around and headed home, back to Hermosa Beach.

Bank developed his photographs, turned his notes into text, and, with his father's help (Bank's dad was a printer, another stroke of luck), self-published his journal.

He called it *Surfing California.* It contained exacting, accurate, pinpoint descriptions of every surfable spot in the state, each with a good picture showing the break. The book had clarity because of the limited nature of its theme. Page after page featured pictures of waves. Looking at the pictures, reading the accompanying text, was a tutorial on how to study waves, how to spot the minute differences that make each wave individual, each break a unique creation. With his hundreds of pictures of waves, each individually described, Bank had unintentionally created not just a specialized guidebook, but also one of the great teaching tools for the California surfer.

After Bank had his book printed, he loaded the van again and went up the coast, leaving copies of *Surfing California* on consignment in every surf shop he could find. It was 1973 and Bank Wright was 23. In the next few years, armed with Bank Wright's book, thousands of California surfers took off to surf the waves he had described.

Bank Wright is in his 50s now. He still drives up and down the California coast, taking pictures, making notes in his journal, surfing, leaving copies of *Surfing California* in surf shops. You can order *Surfing California* directly from Bank at 213-379-9321. You can talk to him, too; he answers the telephone himself. ■

©JAMES BLANK

Malibu

Pacific Coast Highway; parking, surprisingly, is free. Call 310-455-2465 for more information.

Beach access. Between Las Tunas and Malibu Lagoon State Beaches off Malibu Road are public stairways providing access to the beach fronting private property; do not trespass. County garbage cans mark the sites. The first stairway is about 1 mile west of Las Tunas; the next is about 3 miles farther. **Zonker Harris Accessway** is adjacent to a restaurant in Malibu and is marked by a sign. Just past Surfrider, Malibu Road makes a beachward loop off Pacific Coast Highway. Five stairways, at 25118, 24714, 24602, 24434, and 24318 Malibu Road, provide access to the beach. Look for county-maintained garbage cans. Again, access is through private property, so stick to the public beach areas only. The stairways are closed between dusk and dawn.

J. Paul Getty Villa Modeled after a Roman villa, perhaps the best feature of the museum is the building itself. The ornamental gardens with sculpture and reflecting pools, the inlaid tile walks, the fountains, the progression through the colonnade to the entrance, provide a vivid vision of what it must have been like to be a wealthy Roman. Highlights of the museum's collection are pieces of Greek and Roman art. The museum is at 179885 Pacific Coast Highway. 310-450-7300. Closed now for renovations, the Villa is scheduled to reopen in 2001.

Malibu Lagoon State Beach. This beach encompasses the **Malibu Pier, Malibu Lagoon,** and **Surfrider Beach.** Malibu Lagoon itself is a brackish, occasionally contaminated outlet for Malibu Creek that no one should swim in. Walking through the wetlands surrounding it is a good idea, though, as there is a salt marsh containing both marine and shore birds. Picnic facilities and wheelchair-accessible rest rooms are available. The **Malibu Lagoon Museum** at the west end of Surfrider is open Wednesday–Saturday 11–3. Surfrider Beach has small but famously steady waves that break gently enough to make for long, long rides. The beach is somewhat crowded on sunny days—it's in Malibu proper—but there's great people-watching and a good family environment. To the landward side there are fabulous homes of the stars and the simply wealthy; toward the sea is white sand populated by innumerable southern California beachgoers, volleyball players, and surfers. There are rest rooms, showers, and lifeguards at 2300 Pacific Coast Highway. Access is via parking north of Malibu Pier; there is limited free street parking, but the fee parking lots are a better bet due to crowding. Call 310-457-9891 for more information.

Topanga State Park. Thirty-five miles of trails and fire roads lace this state park west of Topanga Canyon. There are meadows, woodlands, campsites, and a stream in these beautiful 10,000 acres, with sweeping views from atop Eagle Rock. Bikes are allowed on the fire roads only, and dogs and fires are not permitted anywhere within the park. The entrance is at 20825 Entrada Road off Topanga Canyon Boulevard. This park has walk-in and equestrian campsites with drinking water. There is a day-use fee; call 310-455-2465 for more information.

Malibu Creek State Park This 5000-acre park, where the classic movie *M*A*S*H* was filmed, includes hiking and horse trails, a self-guided Braille trail, a freshwater marsh, woodlands, canyons, waterfalls, camping sites, and a lake. There are also barbecue pits, wheelchair-accessible rest rooms, and a visitors center. There are 62 sites at this facility, which has solar pay showers; there are no hookups. The park is at 28754 Mulholland Drive west of Malibu Canyon Road. Access is off Malibu Canyon Road/Las Virgenes Road between Mulholland and Pacific Coast Highway, at Yerba Buena Road. Call 818-880-0367 or 1-800-444-7275 for camping reservations and more information.

Tapia Park. Part of Malibu Creek State Park, this 94.5-acre park along Malibu Creek has hiking and horse trails and picnic areas with barbecue grills. There is fee parking and wheelchair-accessible rest rooms. Bikes are prohibited, and dogs are not allowed on trails. Call 818-880-0367.

Paramount Ranch. Several miles inland and set back in the hills, Paramount Ranch's main draw is its **Old Western Town,** which is used for filming movies. There is also a nature trail running up Coyote Canyon, hiking and equestrian trails, and picnic areas. Access is via Cornell Road at Mulholland Highway, about 2.5 miles south of Highway 101.

Circle X Ranch in the Santa Monica Mountains National Recreation Area has two backpacking campgrounds with chemical toilets. The park has more than 30 miles of hiking trails. Access is off Yerba Buena Road, about 5.5 miles north of Highway 1. Call 818-597-9192 for more information. Other SMMNRA sites include **Cold Creek Canyon Preserve, Stunt Ranch, Solstice Canyon, Castro Crest, Calabasas Peak, Peter Strauss Ranch,** and **Rocky Oaks**.

Malibu Bluffs County Park Just below Pacific Coast Highway is a small park providing grassy picnic facilities, wheelchair-accessible rest rooms, a playing field, and free parking. The beach-access stairway can be reached from the park via a dirt path; it's about a 1½-mile walk. Enter the park where Malibu Canyon Road meets the Pacific Coast Highway. Pepperdine University looms on the hills above the highway. Call 310-317-1364 for more information.

Corral County Beach. This narrow, sandy strip has a lifeguard only during the high season. There is decent diving and surfing. Parking is limited to the road. Call 310-457-9891 for more information.

Paradise Cove Paradise Cove is a private fee beach for swimming and exploring only; no surfing is allowed, and fishing is permitted only from the pier. There is wheelchair-accessible parking, a restaurant and snack bar (summer only), and fee parking. It closes at sunset. For more information, call 310-457-2511.

Point Dume County Beach. Essentially a southerly continuation of Zuma Beach (see below), Point Dume is a little more isolated and backed by sandstone cliffs. In fact, there is a walk from the road of about a mile, but it's worth it: From the beach you can see the entire Los Angeles coast lined up to the south, as well as Santa Catalina Island standing offshore. This is a good beach for people who want Zuma's dramatic scenery with fewer people. It's an excellent beach for swimming, surfing, and diving, and there are tide pools for the invertebrate-minded. There also is a nude beach just east of Point Dume at Pirate's Cove; this is accessible via an informal trail over the Point Dume Headlands. Point Dume has rest rooms, lifeguards, and showers. Access is via the south end of Westward Beach Road (off Route 1) in Malibu, on the north side of Point Dume. There is a vehicle fee; call 310-457-9891 for more information.

Point Dume Whale-Watch ★ Above the beach is a whale-watching site with benches and panoramic ocean views. Access is via a stairway next to the restaurant at Westward Beach and Birdview Roads.

Zuma Beach County Park As rugged as Point Dume but more accessible from the road, Zuma is the largest county-owned beach in Los Angeles, with 4 miles of beachfront. It's everything visitors might want: long, wide, sandy, and backed by dramatic cliffs and canyons. It's a big family beach, with folks driving in from Ventura County and the San Fernando Valley to take advantage of this beautiful spot. The beach slopes up sharply from the breakwater, making Zuma a textbook candidate for rip currents, so some caution should be exercised in swimming and surfing. There is a large lifeguard contingent here, though, as well as swings, rest rooms, showers, volleyball courts, and food vendors. Access is via any of eight parking lots, particularly on the 30000 block of Pacific Coast Highway, about 6 miles west of Malibu. There is a parking fee.

Broad Beach. Access to Broad Beach is at stairways located at 31344 and 31200 Broad Beach Road, a loop off Pacific Coast Highway; street parking is scarce. Don't trespass on the private property on either side of the stairways. This area is open between sunrise and sunset.

Western Malibu beaches This heading includes **El Matador State Beach, La Piedra State Beach, El Pescador State Beach,** and **Nicholas Canyon County Beach.** These are small, sandy beaches—none larger than Nicholas, at 23 acres—between Zuma and Leo Carrillo, and all are backed by bluffs. They tend to be fairly uncrowded, as access is from dirt trails or stairways down from parking lots along Pacific Coast Highway. Nicholas Canyon is known informally as a nude beach, but the authorities like to discourage sunbathing in the buff. All these sandy stretches are beautiful and have lifeguards, but offer minimal facilities otherwise, meaning that there are pit toilets. Access is via Pacific Coast Highway at various points in the 32000s; Nicholas is 1 mile south of Leo Carrillo State Beach. Look for the COASTAL ACCESS signs. There is a vehicle fee for these beaches. Call 818-880-0350 for information on El Matador State Beach. These beaches are scenic getaways that open long stretches of shoreline for walks in either direction. Highly recommended.

Leo Carrillo State Beach This beach fronts a 3000-acre park at the extreme western tip of Los Angeles County, and actually is the last stop before Ventura County. There's more than a mile of coarse, brown-sand beach centered roughly on Sequit Point, and hiking and camping in the canyon upland from the beach. Swimming and surfing conditions are good, although waves crash hard and there can be strong winds coming around Sequit Point. The point has sea caves and a natural tunnel. There are lifeguards, pay showers, fire pits, and nature trails. Rockier parts of the shore offer ample tide pooling, and migrating whales are visible offshore November–May. Access is via the 36000 block of Pacific Coast Highway, about 1 mile south of the Ventura county line. There is a vehicle parking/access fee. A large campground has 127 tent and vehicle sites both on the beach and inland; 32 sites on the beach can accommodate RVs under 8 feet in height. There are pay hot showers, wheelchair-accessible rest rooms, a camp store, fire pits, and barbecue grills. A visitors center is open weekends. Access is at 36000 Pacific Coast Highway, just east of the Los Angeles–Ventura county line. Call 818-880-0350 for more information on this popular campground.

Lodging

IN LONG BEACH

The Hotel Queen Mary (562-435-3511), 1126 Queens Way (Pier J). Moderate. This hotel is composed of 365 of the ship's original staterooms, some of which are notably small and have only small portholes for light. Visitors will see an enormous amount of original art deco detail on the ship; also, there are elaborate dioramas re-creating shipboard life during the *Queen Mary*'s time, the Queen's Marketplace for shopping and eating, and a playland for children.

The Breakers (562-432-6700), 1501 Ocean Avenue. Expensive. A small motel, it is noted mainly for being a quiet place to stay in an otherwise rambunctious area.

IN SAN PEDRO

San Pedro Hostel International (310-831-8109), 3601 S. Gaffey Street. Inexpensive. This 40-bed facility has a full kitchen, laundry, and library. It's located in Angels Gate Park and open 7 AM–midnight daily. Entrance to the park is at 930 Paseo del Mar.

Sunrise Hotel (310-548-1080), 525 S. Harbor Boulevard. Moderate. You'll find basic accommodations, but with harbor views. A pool and Jacuzzi are available.

IN REDONDO BEACH

Palos Verdes Inn (310-316-4211), 1700 S. Pacific Coast Highway. Expensive. This is a spa with all the amenities, only three blocks from the beach. It offers several good restaurants.

Portofino Hotel and Yacht Club (310-379-8481), 260 Portofino Way. Expensive. Near the harbor, this is an adequate alternative to the hotel chains.

IN HERMOSA BEACH

Sea Sprite Ocean Front Motel (310-376-6933), 1016 Strand. Moderate. Basic accommodations right on the beach. Rooms and cottages are also available; views and pool on the second floor.

Hotel Hermosa (310-318-6000), 2515 Pacific Coast Highway. Expensive. Half a dozen blocks from the beach, this hotel has pools, pleasant grounds, and newer rooms.

IN MANHATTAN BEACH

Sea View Inn at the Beach (310-545-1504), 3400 Highland Avenue. Moderate. A small hotel with just nine units, its proximity to the beach makes up for its size. It's been remodeled recently, and has a swimming pool. A good combination of comfort, price, and location.

IN MARINA DEL REY

Marina Hostel (310-301-3983), 2915 Yale Avenue. Inexpensive. Near the marina, off Washington Boulevard, this small, 20-bed facility has a kitchen, laundry, and lockers. It's open 24 hours a day year-round.

IN VENICE

Hostel California (310-305-0250), 2221 Lincoln Boulevard, Venice. Inexpensive. Located a few blocks north of Venice Boulevard, it has 26 beds, three private rooms, a kitchen, laundry, and showers. Open all year; reservations are needed for the busy summer months. The beach is a 15-minute walk.

IN SANTA MONICA

Hostelling International Los Angeles (310-393-9913), 1436 2nd Street. Inexpensive. This is a large facility, accommodating 200 guests two blocks from the Santa Monica Pier. This wheelchair-accessible hostel has a lounge, kitchen, library, laundry, locked storage area, and lockers. It is open 7–10:30 AM and 12:30 PM–midnight.

Hotel Oceana (800-777-0758), 849 Ocean Avenue, Santa Monica. Expensive. Tony yet family friendly. All 63 suites have kitchenettes. Newly remodeled with pool.

Shangri-La Hotel (310-394-2791), 1301 Ocean Avenue. Expensive. This is an art deco landmark, very L.A. and very nice. Near the pier and across the street from the beach.

Belle Bleu Inn (310-393-2363), 1670 Ocean Avenue. Moderate. Although the rooms have seen better days, they are clean and adequate.

The Bayside (310-396-6000), 2001 Ocean Avenue. Moderate. Basic accommodations are here on the quieter end of Ocean Avenue.

Channel Road Inn (310-459-1920), 219 W. Channel Road. Expensive. Just a block from the beach, this quaint 14-room bed & breakfast offers a lot of frills: bubble baths, hot tub, flowers in the guest rooms, a big complimentary breakfast, and even bicycles that guests can use to ride around Santa Monica.

IN MALIBU

Casa Malibu (310-456-2219; 1-800-831-0858), 22752 Pacific Coast Highway. Expensive. On a private beach, the second-story rooms have excellent views.

Malibu Country Inn (310-457-9622), 6506 Westward Beach Road. Expensive. Near Point Dume State Beach, but back from the shoreline, the inn features pleasant grounds and private patios.

Malibu Beach Inn (310-456-6444), 22878 Pacific Coast Highway. Expensive. Forty-seven rooms in three stories right on the beach. Each room has beamed ceilings, and only sliding glass doors separate visitors from the sounds of the surf. A breakfast buffet is complimentary, and the inn can arrange delivery from nearby restaurants. *Note:* There's a minimum 2-night stay on summer weekends.

Topanga Ranch Motel (310-456-5486; 1-800-200-0019), 18711 Pacific Coast Highway. Moderate. This is a 1920s-era complex of 30 cottages, each of which shows its age in varying ways, but which overall are kept in good repair. Some cottages have kitchens; the complex is located across Pacific Coast Highway from the beach.

Malibu Beach RV Park (310-456-6052), 25801 Pacific Coast Highway. Inexpensive. This facility on the landward side of the highway has 120 hookups and 50 tent sites, a coin laundry, picnic and barbecue facilities, showers, propane, a spa, and wheelchair-accessible rest rooms.

Restaurants

IN LONG BEACH

Belmont Brewing Company (310-433-3891), 25 39th Place. Moderate. One of the older brewery-restaurants in the area, Belmont features a host of pale and amber ales, seasonal beers, and a porter called Long Beach Crude. The menu's got pasta, seafood, and gourmet pizza. Shoot for a seat on the patio; it overlooks the ocean.

Joe Joost's (310-439-5446), 2803 E. Anaheim Avenue. Inexpensive. This is no fashionable brewpub. It's the real thing—a southern California beer joint. The Joe's Special sausage sandwich and the pretzels and cold tap beer are justly famous.

IN SAN PEDRO

Twenty-Second Street Landing Seafood Grill & Bar (310-548-4400), 141 W. 22nd Street. Expensive. Good seafood dishes served with a view of the harbor. Choose from a large selection of fresh local catch.

Madeo Ristorante (310-521-5333), 2800 Via Cabrillo Marina. Expensive. A local Italian favorite; stick to the pastas.

IN REDONDO BEACH

Catalina Cantina Cafe (310-791-5440), 1701 S. Catalina Avenue. Moderate. Serves "Nuevo Latino" Mexican food and features live music of all types Sunday, 3–7 PM.

H.T. Grill/Village Bistro (310-316-6658), 1710 S. Catalina. Moderate. Serves salads, pasta, pizza, fish, and steaks, as well as breakfast on weekends.

Redondo Beach Brewing Co. (310-316-8477), 1814 S. Catalina. Moderate. A microbrewery currently producing almost a dozen varieties including a pilsner, lager, red, and peach. Its fare includes pizza, pasta, 10 salads, and weekly specials.

IN MARINA DEL REY

Cheesecake Factory (310-306-3344), 4142 Via Marina. Inexpensive. Though part of a chain, this restaurant redeems itself immediately by the size of both its menu and its portions. It has nearly everything, including jambalaya, seafood, pasta, and salads, plus, of course, cheesecake. Overlooks the marina.

Aunt Kizzy's Back Porch (310-578-1005), 4325 Glencoe Avenue. Moderate. A soul food restaurant in the Villa Marina Shopping Center. Fried chicken with all the fixings is the best bet.

Coffee Roaster Cafe (310-305-7147), 552 Washington Boulevard. Inexpensive. A good local hangout for excellent coffee and sweets, this café serves decent full meals as well.

IN VENICE

Sidewalk Cafe (310-399-5547), 1401 Ocean Front Walk. Inexpensive. This literary café with bookstore is in the heart of the action on the walkway. Outdoor seating lets you watch the scene.

Hal's Bar & Grill (310-396-3105), 1349 Abbot Kinney Boulevard. Expensive. Seafood is recommended at this arty, sophisticated restaurant.

IN SANTA MONICA

Pedals (310-458-0030), 1 West Pico Boulevard (in Shutters on the Beach Hotel). Moderate to expensive. The beach is the backdrop here. The menu includes fresh fish, bread, pasta, and meats served before a large wood fireplace; with luck, only sliding glass doors will separate you from the Pacific. Great breakfasts.

Broadway Bar and Grill (310-393-4211), 1460 3rd Street Promenade at Broadway. Moderate. This classic American bar and grill is right on the city's main drag and serves chicken, fish, and steaks. It also has tables outdoors, so you can watch Santa Monica go by.

Chaya Venice (310-396-1179), 110 Navy, at the corner of Main Street. Expensive. An elegant international seafood restaurant under a Japanese chef. There is also a full sushi bar. Valet and self-parking under the building.

Schatzi on Main (310-399-4800), 3110 Main Street. Expensive. Action-movie hero Arnold Schwarzenegger is the proprietor. It serves typical California cuisine. Valet parking is available at night, and underground parking is around the corner on Marine.

Chinois on Main (310-392-9025), 2709 Main Street. Expensive. Wolfgang Puck serves nouvelle California food with an Asian twist; the fish dishes, in particular, are excellent. For the single diner or a couple, seating at the

counter in the back gives a firsthand view of the open kitchen, an evening's fascinating entertainment in itself. Chinois has valet parking and requires reservations well in advance.

Wolfgang Puck Express (310-576-4770), 1315 3rd Street. Promenade. Inexpensive. The People's Puck, where the famous chef serves excellent pizza, pasta, and salads for just plain folk. No attitude, just good food.

IN MALIBU

Granita (310-456-0488), Pacific Coast Highway and Webb Way in the Malibu Colony Plaza. Expensive. Wolfgang Puck's elegant water fantasy-themed restaurant serves his unique cuisine, mainly seafood and meats as well as his signature pizzas. Reserve early for the weekends. Lunch Wednesday–Sunday; dinner every night.

Monroe's of Malibu (310-457-5521), 6800 Westward Beach Road. Expensive. Monroe's features excellent steaks and seafood, but the Indian food is outstanding.

Malibu Fish & Seafood (310-456-3430), 25653 Pacific Coast Highway. Moderate. Here you'll get good fresh seafood at fair prices for Malibu.

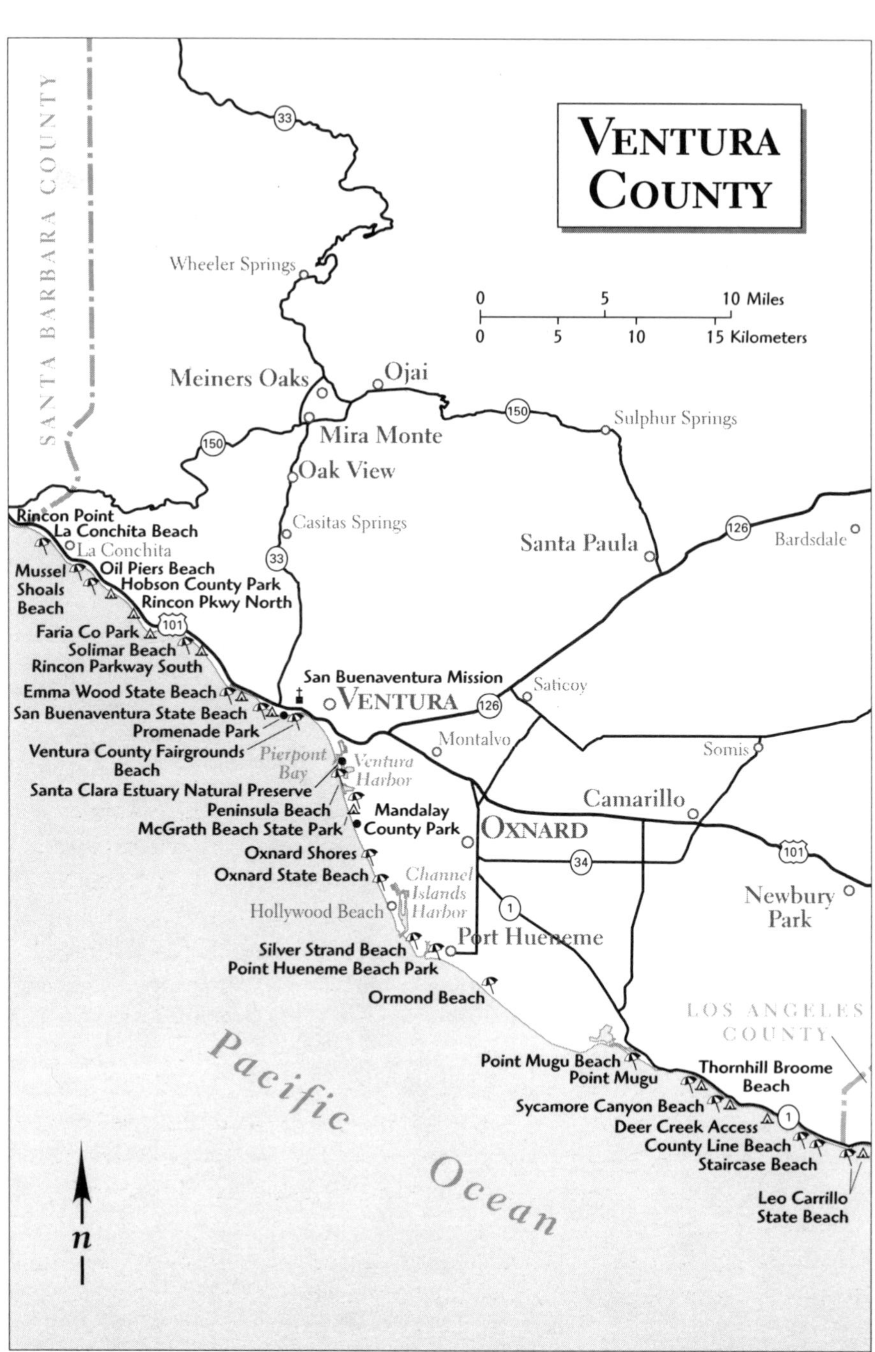

Ventura County
0
5
10 Miles
0
5
10
15 Kilometers
SANTA BARBARA COUNTY
Wheeler Springs
Meiners Oaks
Ojai
Mira Monte
Oak View
Sulphur Springs
Casitas Springs
Santa Paula
Bardsdale
Rincon Point
La Conchita Beach
La Conchita
Mussel Shoals Beach
Oil Piers Beach
Hobson County Park
Rincon Pkwy North
Faria Co Park
Solimar Beach
Rincon Parkway South
Emma Wood State Beach
San Buenaventura State Beach
Promenade Park
Ventura County Fairgrounds Beach
Santa Clara Estuary Natural Preserve
Peninsula Beach
McGrath Beach State Park
San Buenaventura Mission
Ventura
Saticoy
Montalvo
Somis
Pierpont Bay
Ventura Harbor
Mandalay County Park
Camarillo
Oxnard
Oxnard Shores
Oxnard State Beach
Channel Islands Harbor
Hollywood Beach
Newbury Park
Port Hueneme
Silver Strand Beach
Point Hueneme Beach Park
Ormond Beach
Pacific Ocean
LOS ANGELES COUNTY
Point Mugu Beach
Point Mugu
Thornhill Broome Beach
Sycamore Canyon Beach
Deer Creek Access
County Line Beach
Staircase Beach
Leo Carrillo State Beach
n

CHAPTER FOUR

Ventura County

FORTY-THREE MILES LONG, Ventura County is framed, in the north and south, by two transverse ranges, which run from east to west. These ranges are, in the south, the Santa Monica Mountains and, in the north, the Santa Ynez. Between them, the Ventura coast spills outward to the west in the gentle curve of a large fertile floodplain, the Oxnard. In the floodplain lie three connected cities that form a single urban beach area. They are Port Hueneme (say *Why-nee-mee*), Oxnard, and Ventura.

The Ventura River runs along the southern edge of the Santa Ynez Mountains. In the south, the larger Santa Clara River divides the city of Ventura from the city of Oxnard. The sediment carried from these rivers has created a valley of rich soil. Even along its coastline, Ventura has an agricultural tone.

At the Ventura–Los Angeles county line in the south, Leo Carrillo State Beach, which begins in Los Angeles County, runs north along the coast. Here the highway, Route 101/1, runs along the coastline from the county line just above Malibu to the naval base at Point Mugu, where the floodplain begins. Then the road curves inland through Ventura's linked cities.

Where the road begins its swing inland is Point Mugu State Park. Within Mugu lies one of the most beautiful beaches on all the coast, Sycamore Cove, and the related, inland park, Sycamore Canyon. Like many of the best beaches in California, Sycamore Canyon was an important Native American site, here Chumash. A meandering canyon swings through groves of stately trees; the path then goes through low dunes to the wide, gentle, white-sand beach protected by rocky points in the north and south. Often dolphin herd fish through the waters of the cove. The lovely trail runs up the canyon for 7 miles, where in season there are abundant wildflowers and monarch butterflies.

The beauty of Sycamore Cove is well known, but between Leo Carrillo at the county line and Mugu are many other "pocket" beaches, visible and accessible from the highway. Here, it is easy to find a secluded cove if Sycamore Canyon is crowded.

In the floodplain north of Mugu, the coastal highway runs through the urban Hueneme/Oxnard/Ventura area, loses itself in downtown Oxnard as it becomes

Oxnard Boulevard, and emerges again at the coast at the north end of the city of Ventura. These three coastal cities have a long history as small ports, from which the agricultural produce of the Oxnard plain was shipped south to Los Angeles. The pier in Hueneme Beach Park is the successor to one of the first piers built along the California coast, opening up the inland agricultural area to trade.

The beaches in this area are urban, with an innocent, small-town feeling. Many are wide and sandy. This urban beachfront is more friendly than that of Santa Barbara to the north or Los Angeles to the south; it's also less expensive.

Northern Ventura runs from the Ventura River to the Santa Barbara–Ventura county line. Here, Route 101/1 is close to the beachfront. Small rivers and streams once flowed through beautiful valleys and canyons—Padre Juan Canyon, Javon Canyon, Madrania Canyon. Unfortunately, these rivers and streams have been channeled and tamed. Now, the silt and rock that nourished the beaches have disappeared, and the wide sandy shores that existed 30 years ago are gone. Campsites at Hobson County Park, which once were located on the top of sand dunes, are now within the tide line. Within a few years, they will be gone as well.

The residents of small beach towns—Sea Cliff, Mussel Shoals, La Conchita—fight over access with tourists, beachgoers, and surfers but the beaches are now rocky. The sand is gone. Often the waves lap against, and erode, the foundations of the highway itself.

All that remain are the waves. For surfers, that is enough. In northern Ventura, at the terminus of the Santa Ynez range and at the dividing line between Ventura and Santa Barbara Counties, lies rocky Rincon Point. South of the point, the coast turns sharply to the northeast. Waves traveling the Pacific circle are sliced off by the point, forming "machine-perfect rights," as Bank Wright described them. Rincon breaks in all conditions. It is one of the best surfing spots in the world and a legend within the California surfing community.

Beaches and Attractions

Leo Carrillo State Beach North (Staircase Beach). This is the Ventura extension of the beach described in the "Los Angeles County" section. It is less developed than the southern half. Parking is at a public lot at the state park ranger's residence at 40000 Pacific Coast Highway. There is additional parking at 0.2 miles and 0.5 miles south of the ranger's residence. Signs are on the highway, and the ranger's residence is easily visible from the road. No camping or fires are allowed. There are vista points off the highway; rest rooms are near the ranger's residence.

County Line Beach (Yerba Buena Beach). This is an undeveloped beach directly off Highway 1. The highway tracks the beach in this area—off-road

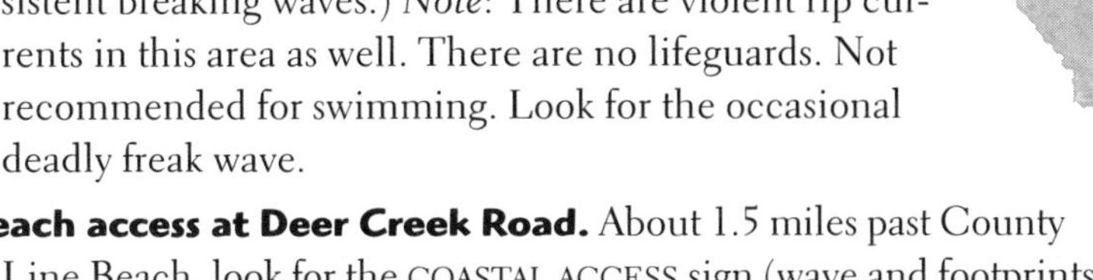

parking is by the side of the road. You will see the cars of surfers because here the surf breaks in all weather. (There are reefs offshore, which create consistent breaking waves.) *Note*: There are violent rip currents in this area as well. There are no lifeguards. Not recommended for swimming. Look for the occasional deadly freak wave.

Beach access at Deer Creek Road. About 1.5 miles past County Line Beach, look for the COASTAL ACCESS sign (wave and footprints) marking a stairway to the beach.

Point Mugu State Park covers 13,000 acres from the southern Ventura County coastline into the Santa Monica Mountains. There are miles of hiking trails and campsites both in the mountains and at the beach. The park is under the Department of Parks and Recreation; for more information, call 818-880-0350. **Sycamore Cove Beach, Sycamore Canyon, Thornhill Broome Beach,** and **La Jolla Valley** are part of Point Mugu State Park.

Sycamore Cove Beach/Sycamore Canyon (a destination beach) Just north of Leo Carrillo Beach and part of the state park system, it is clearly marked. This is one of the loveliest beaches in southern California, wide and

DON NEUWIRTH

Sycamore Cove Beach

DON NEUWIRTH

Sycamore Canyon Campground

sandy. Sycamore trees form the backdrop, which includes spectacular views of the Santa Monica Mountains. Schools of dolphins favor this beach, which was a major Chumash Indian settlement. Its beauty makes it a major destination point; advance reservations are necessary most of the year if you wish to camp on the beach. There are 55 picturesque, primitive drive-in campsites at the Sycamore Canyon Campground in Point Mugu State Park. This is the trailhead for the park, which provides miles of inland hiking through the Santa Monica Mountains. A fee parking lot is on the ocean side of Pacific Coast Highway. Camping fee. Call for reservations: 1-800-444-7275.

Thornhill Broome Beach (aka La Jolla Beach). The entrance, 1½ miles north of Sycamore Canyon, is clearly marked. Numerous pocket beaches are situated both above and below the official entrance. You may park off the highway and find your own way to many secluded areas. Although this series of beaches does not have the natural beauty of Sycamore, it is still highly recommended. Like Sycamore, advance reservations are needed if you want to camp. There are lifeguards, rest rooms, showers, picnic tables, and 102 campsites for tents and RVs. Dogs are allowed, but only on leashes. For reservations, call 1-800-444-7275. For beach information, call Department of Parks and Recreation at 818-880-0350.

Point Mugu Beach The entrance is 7 miles southeast of Port Hueneme along Highway 1 between spectacular Point Mugu Rock and the Navy firing range. This beach is small. The wildlife is beautiful, but most of it is off limits. It lies on the southern edge of the large Mugu Lagoon and the Navy Pacific Missile Test Center. Access is restricted, but there is surfing on the crescent beach behind Point Mugu Rock. Just south, in an area known to surfers as **Super Tubes**, western swells break in front of a huge seawall. There are rock formations offshore. This surf does not break regularly, but when it does, it produces dangerously large, Hawaiian-style waves. When breaking, expert surfers will be riding Super Tubes. They are close enough to the seawall to make that one of the best viewing locations. Aside from the occasional super surf, it probably makes sense to pass up Mugu Beach for one of the better beaches just a few miles east. There is an entrance fee to Point Mugu Beach, or use the limited but free roadside parking. Access hours are 9 AM–sunset.

Mugu Beach to Channel Islands Harbor. From Mugu Lagoon north to Ormond Beach, the coast belongs to the Navy: It is the Point Mugu Pacific Missile Range. Just above the range lies Ormond Beach, the first of Ventura County's urban beaches.

DON NEUWIRTH

Point Mugu and beach

IN PORT HUENEME

Ormond Beach. To reach Ormond Beach, exit Highway 1 at Hueneme Road and head west through farmland, warehouses, and industrial complexes. Turn left at Perkins Road and continue to the parking lot at the end of the road. There is a path and footbridge leading to a wide and sandy beach with dunes. There is no fee, but also no rest rooms or lifeguard at this little-used beach.

Port Hueneme Beach Park/Hueneme Beach Pier. Heavily used, there are lifeguards, wheelchair-accessible rest rooms, showers, picnic tables, fire rings, and playground equipment. The park is the site of the Hueneme Beach Pier—1240 feet long and built of warm, weathered wood. Pier lovers consider it a gem because the original pier at this spot was one of the first built on the coast. It provides excellent views of the ocean—and also of industrial Hueneme and the power plant with red and white smokestacks near Point Mugu. You can rent fishing poles on the pier and there are many places to get junk food. Parking is in a metered lot. The conventional wisdom, given in numerous travel guides, is that this beach is large enough to escape the unattractive industrial setting behind it. The truth is that it is windblown and drab. It is right off the harbor, with industrial buildings and condos to the south that abut the beach. Far nicer is Bubbling Springs Park (see below). Access to the beach is along Surfside and Ocean View Drives, which are bisected by the end of Ventura Road, off Hueneme Road.

Bubbling Springs Park. This long, narrow greenbelt snakes its way inland from near the beach. Facilities include a playground, picnic tables, fire pits, and a 1.5-mile bike path. There are no rest rooms. Park in free lots off Park Avenue at the Community Center or at Ventura and Bard Roads.

Silver Strand Beach. Just south of the mouth of Channel Islands Harbor, this city-run beach has acceptable surfing and fishing, but not much else. There are lifeguards in summer. An old shipwreck, the *SS La Jenelle*, forms a fishing jetty. Do not climb on the jetty, which is slippery and dangerous. The main access point is a parking lot at the foot of San Nicholas Avenue, where there are also rest rooms. From Channel Islands Boulevard, turn left onto Victoria Avenue, then left again onto Ocean Drive to the Sawtelle Avenue access.

IN OXNARD

Channel Islands Harbor Channel Islands Harbor offers boat ramps, fuel docks, berths, hoists, and boat-trailer parking. Along the interior western perimeter is **Channel Islands Beach Park**, with bike and walking paths, rest rooms, outdoor showers, grassy picnic areas, and a beach with summer-only lifeguards. This is a narrow strip beach that fronts a busy, working harbor. It can be a pleasant stroll. At various places, there may be lifeguards and rest rooms. If you happen to find yourself in the Oxnard area with small children, this can be a pleasant spot to spend an afternoon. From the beach, the harbor traffic is busy and interesting. The entrance is located at San Nicolas and Ocean Streets. There is free street parking all along the area. Contact the Oxnard Department of Parks and Facilities at 805-985-6621. The beach area is accessible at the corner of Victoria and Anacapa Avenues. Call the harbormaster office at 805-382-3007 for information about boating facilities.

Ventura County Maritime Museum Within the harbor at 2731 S. Victoria Avenue, just beyond Channel Islands Boulevard, this museum houses artwork tracing maritime history from ancient times to the present, as well as a collection of ship's models. There is also a rotating exhibition of local artwork with marine themes. The museum is open daily 11–5; donations requested. Call 805-984-6260.

Peninsula Park lies near the tip of the peninsula jutting south into the harbor. There are tennis courts, a grassy picnic area with cooking grills, a boat dock, a sandy playground, rest rooms, and free parking. Access is at the southern end of Peninsula Road.

Hollywood Beach. This beach lies on the ocean side of the peninsula forming Channel Islands Harbor. There are rest rooms, outdoor showers, and summer-only lifeguards. Nets are available for beach volleyball. Access is via the ends of streets bisecting Ocean Drive (Los Altos, La Brea, etc.). Park in the small lot at Ocean Drive and La Brea Street.

Oxnard Beach Park. This is a 62-acre park with a sandy beach as well as a dune trail system, bike and pedestrian path, picnic areas with tables and grills, and wheelchair-accessible rest rooms. There is fee parking. Access is just west of Harbor Boulevard between Beach Way and Falkirk Avenue. Call the Oxnard Department of Parks and Facilities at 805-385-7950 for more information.

Beach bike path A paved bike path begins at Oxnard State Beach and winds its way north through San Buenaventura Beach and Promenade Park, along the beach side of the Ventura County Fairgrounds, then east along the Ventura River, down Main Street, and ending near Highway 101's southbound entrance ramp by Emma Woods State Beach, just east of the railroad tracks.

Beach access at Oxnard Shores. Oxnard Shores is a housing development west of Mandalay Beach Road and Capri Way between W. 5th Street and Amalfi Way. Nine unmarked public beach accessways lie between residential parcels. There are also two public beaches in Oxnard Shores. The southernmost is at Neptune Square (a small picnic area with tables and playground); toward the northern end of the development, look for access between Channel Way and W. 5th Street.

Carnegie Art Museum For a short trip inland, the Carnegie Art Museum at 4th and C Streets has a permanent collection of works by 20th-century California artists. There are also fine and decorative arts and photography exhibits, and works by local artists. Access to the museum is off 5th Street, a major Oxnard east–west thoroughfare. Take 5th east from Harbor Boulevard near Mandalay Beach; or from the harbor area, take Channel Islands Boulevard east to any of the major north–south routes: Victoria Avenue, Patterson Road, or Ventura Road, then go right on 5th. C Street is along the west side of Plaza Park. The museum is open Thursday and Saturday 10–5, Friday 11–6, and Sunday 1–5; admission is charged, with senior and student discounts. Call 805-385-8157 for more information.

Ventura County Gulls Wings Children's Museum About a block from the Carnegie Art Museum at 418 W. 4th Street is a hands-on children's museum with puppet theater, a medical room with anatomical models and equipment, a farmer's market, an optical illusions room, a career costume center with stage and video equipment, a campground, a geological room with fossils, and computers. Open Wednesday–Saturday 1–5. Special events are scheduled Saturday at 2. Admission fee is charged; those under 2 are free. Call 805-483-3005 for more information.

Mandalay County Park. This is an undeveloped area of beach and dunes, reached from the end of W. 5th Street to the south. The Mandalay Generating Station lies just to the north. Do not trespass in this private area.

McGrath State Beach. McGrath has 174 sites for tents and RVs. You can reserve by calling 1-800-444-7275, and, especially during the summer, reservations are necessary. The tent sites are excellent, as park tent siting goes, protected and semiprivate. There's 2 miles of broad beach, beautiful but often windy. On the beach between Oxnard and the Santa Clara River is a fine hiking/nature trail through the river estuary system and large, excellent dunes. *Note:* Surfers avoid McGrath when waves are above 2–3 feet. This is an indication of the beach's inherent danger. The sand shifts, and there are extremely strong currents. Lifeguards are on duty during the summer (on weekends only during spring and fall), and there are wheelchair-accessible rest rooms. Parking and day-use fees. Call 805-654-4610 for more information.

Santa Clara Estuary Natural Preserve ★ The Santa Clara River empties into the Pacific through marshlands at the border between Oxnard and Ventura.

This wildlife area is a great place to bird-watch. Access is from McGrath State Beach to the south or Peninsula Park to the north.

Peninsula Beach. On the ocean side of the southern peninsula forming Ventura Harbor, this sandy beach is partially protected by breakwaters. There is a play area with rest rooms, limited paved parking at the north end of Spinnaker Drive, and undeveloped parking to the south.

IN VENTURA

Ventura Harbor This large inland harbor has northern and southern marinas, charter boats, sailboat rentals, fuel docks, bait and tackle shops, a free launching ramp, and wheelchair-accessible rest rooms. Parking for both cars and boat trailers is off Anchors Way Drive near the boat ramp. The harbor lies west of Harbor Boulevard. For access to the southern peninsula, turn

DON NEUWIRTH

McGrath State Beach

DON NEUWIRTH

San Buenaventura State Beach

west off Olivas Park Drive (which becomes Spinnaker Drive in the harbor area). The northern peninsula is off Peninsula Avenue or Pierpont Boulevard. Call 805-642-8538 for harbor information.

The harbor is a jumping-off point for a visit to the **Channel Islands. The Channel Islands National Park Headquarters and Visitor Center** is at 1901 Spinnaker Drive on the southern peninsula. It is open 8:30 AM–4:30 PM daily. Half-day, full-day, and overnight environmental tours of the islands are available from Island Packer Tours, 1867 Spinnaker Drive. Call 805-642-1393.

Olivas Adobe Historical Park Less than 2 miles inland from the harbor at 4200 Olivas Park Drive is a Monterey-style adobe residence built in 1847 by Raymundo Olivas. The home and outbuildings contain furnishings, handcrafts, and relics of the California adobe and rancho era. There are also herb and rose gardens. The grounds are open daily 10–4, the house Saturday and Sunday only, 10–4; there are guided tours, and they're free. Call 805-644-4346.

Marina Park On the northern peninsula of the harbor, Marina Park has playground facilities, a short bike path, basketball courts, picnic sites, a boat dock, and access to the beach. The Ventura City Parks and Recreation

Department offers sailing classes. Marina Park is at the south end of Pierpont Boulevard. Call 805-652-4550 for more information.

San Buenaventura State Beach This wide, sandy beach runs for nearly 2 miles from Marina Park to the Ventura Pier to the north. Breakwaters provide for good swimming. There are lifeguards during the summer (weekends only during spring and fall), picnic areas with fire pits, volleyball standards, outdoor showers, dressing rooms, wheelchair-accessible rest rooms, and a snack bar. A bike path runs along the edge of the beach, starting at the main entrance off San Pedro Street at Pierpont Boulevard. There is a parking fee if you enter here. Access is also from the Ventura Pier, along Harbor Boulevard between the pier and San Pedro Street, and from the ends of 24 streets running east–west off Pierpoint Boulevard, including Seaward Avenue, an exit off Highway 101.

E. Main Street, Ventura The eastern end of Main Street is only a few blocks from the beach. It offers any number of attractions as well as a slow-paced place to walk, shop, and dine. This is not your upscale, chain-store promenade, but more reminiscent of a 1950s outdoor shopping area. There are bookstores, antiques and vintage-clothing shops, a 1960s-style head shop, and cafés, with plenty of street and side-street parking.

Albinger Archaeological Museum This interesting museum is located just west of Ventura Avenue at 113 E. Main. It houses a collection of artifacts, some 3500 years old, excavated from a site next to the San Buenaventura Mission. There are displays of the California coastal Chumash Indians from approximately A.D. 1500, and an earlier Indian culture from around 1600 B.C. Artifacts from the mission era, including part of its original foundation and an earth oven, can be seen at the dig site. The museum is open Wednesday–Sunday 10–4, and it's free.

Ventura County Museum of History and Art This fine museum is across the street from the Archaeological Museum, at 100 E. Main. Its collection documents the successive Native American, Hispanic, and pioneer cultures in the county. There is also a research library and changing art and history exhibits. Open Tuesday–Sunday 10–5; admission fee is charged, and those under 16 with an adult are free.

San Buenaventura Mission This mission, founded in 1782 and finished 27 years later, has a restored church still in regular use, a museum of Chumash Indian and mission relics, and a school (not accessible to the public). It is located at 225 E. Main Street, and the entrance is just east of the mission through a gift shop. Hours are Monday–Saturday 10–5, Sunday 10–4, and admission fee is minimal. Call 805-648-4496.

Ventura Pier. The 1700-foot-long Ventura Pier marks the northern end of San Buenaventura Beach and provides a panoramic view of the sweeping coastline to the south. There is a restaurant and snack bar, wheelchair-accessible rest rooms, and a bait shop. Park at the beach entrance.

Promenade Park. Just west of the pier is a long and narrow beachfront park with paved walking and bike paths, volleyball standards, benches and tables, playground facilities, and ramps to the beach. Park at Surfer's Point (see below) or in the lot on the west side of the pier.

Surfer's Point Good waves have made this a favorite Ventura County surfing spot. There's a sandy beach, outdoor showers, wheelchair-accessible rest rooms, and parking. Surfer's Point is at the end of Figueroa Street.

Ventura County Fairgrounds Beach. This mostly rocky beach along the west bank of the Ventura River has only a narrow sandy area. It's accessible from Surfer's Point to the east; there are no facilities.

Seaside Wilderness Park ★ Just over the Ventura River is a sandy and rocky beach backed by a stand of Monterey pines and palm trees. There are also dunes at this bird-watching area. Park at Emma Woods State Beach to the north; access is a ¾-mile walk along the beach side of the railroad tracks.

Emma Woods State Park. This is the first beach in Ventura North; the beach is limited, however. Camping is directly on the beach, which is good, but at certain campsites the beach is so eroded that waves come up to the tents. Use this as a stopping place. Access is just north of Ventura, before the turnoff for Old Rincon Highway. The park is administered by the state: Contact Emma Woods State Beach at 805-654-4936. It has lifeguards, rest rooms, showers, picnic tables, and barbecue grills. There are two camping locations at Emma Woods. To the south is the **Ventura River Group Camp** with four 30-person sites, rest rooms, stoves, tables, cold outdoor showers, and a small facility for biking and hiking campers. The sites are ¼ mile from the south end of Emma Woods State Beach. To the north are 61 individual campsites and two group sites adjacent to the beach. Access to Emma Woods Beach is at the south end of Old Pacific Coast Highway, north of W. Main Street. Fees are $10 and up per night. Call 1-800-444-7275 for reservations.

Rincon Parkway South. The interlocking beaches are just north of Emma Woods State Park—parking is alongside the highway. There are 103 sites for recreational vehicles in designated locations south of Solimar Beach (see below). These camping spots are easily visible from the road. A stairway south of Solimar Beach leads to the beach. Rung ladders in the seawall can be used to reach the beach at low tide. There is a fee, but reservations are not needed. For more information call 805-654-3951.

Solimar Beach Five miles north of Ventura, just above the Rincon Parkway South, this public beach fronts the small, private beach community of Solimar. The paths are just to the north and south of the town. Not recommended: Access rights are unclear, and the beach completely disappears at high tide, which leaves the seawall holding (for now) the highway. The surfing, however, is excellent.

Faria County Park and Beach The campground here is serviceable but not beautiful. It rests on rocks, and the strip of sand that forms the beach is eroding. The main activity here, as at Solimar, is surfing, which is excellent. Stairs provide access to the sand beach. There are rest rooms, showers, picnic tables, and fire pits. Camping and parking fees are charged. At Pitas Point west (actually south) of Highway 101 and about 7 miles northwest of Ventura, Faria Point has 40 tent and trailer campsites with tables and fire pits, wheelchair-accessible rest rooms, showers, and a concession stand. The sites are just up from the beach. Fees are cheaper here than at state park campgrounds. It's best to make reservations for this popular site; call 805-654-3951.

Rincon Parkway North to La Conchita Beach This is a string of surfing beaches, listed in order from Rincon Parkway North to La Conchita Beach. Highway 101 runs right along the beach through this stretch. Often, only a seawall keeps the waves off the road. The first is **Rincon Parkway North,** a strip beach; parking is along the road and access is through rung ladders set in the seawall. Beach access is at low tide only. Rincon Parkway North is about 1 mile north of Pitas Point, just off Highway 101. There are 112 sites for self-contained RVs on a first-come, first-served basis only. Call 805-654-3951 for more information. The next beach is **Hobson County Park**, which is to the south of the small town of Seacliff. There are picnic and barbecue facilities, showers, a concession stand, and wheelchair-accessible rest rooms. Entrance and camping fees are charged. Call 805-654-3951 for more information and to make reservations. **Oil Piers Beach** is to the north of Seacliff. There is roadside parking. Four long oil piers, one disguised as a tropical isle, lead out to drilling platforms. These piers have no public access. There is excellent surfing, which is the only worthwhile activity here. **Mussel Shoals Beach** is a sandy public beach in the small town of Mussel Shoals. Parking is on the old highway along the beach. Access is at the west end of Ocean Avenue and the north end of Breakers Way, but access rights are unclear. The beach itself is administered by the Ventura

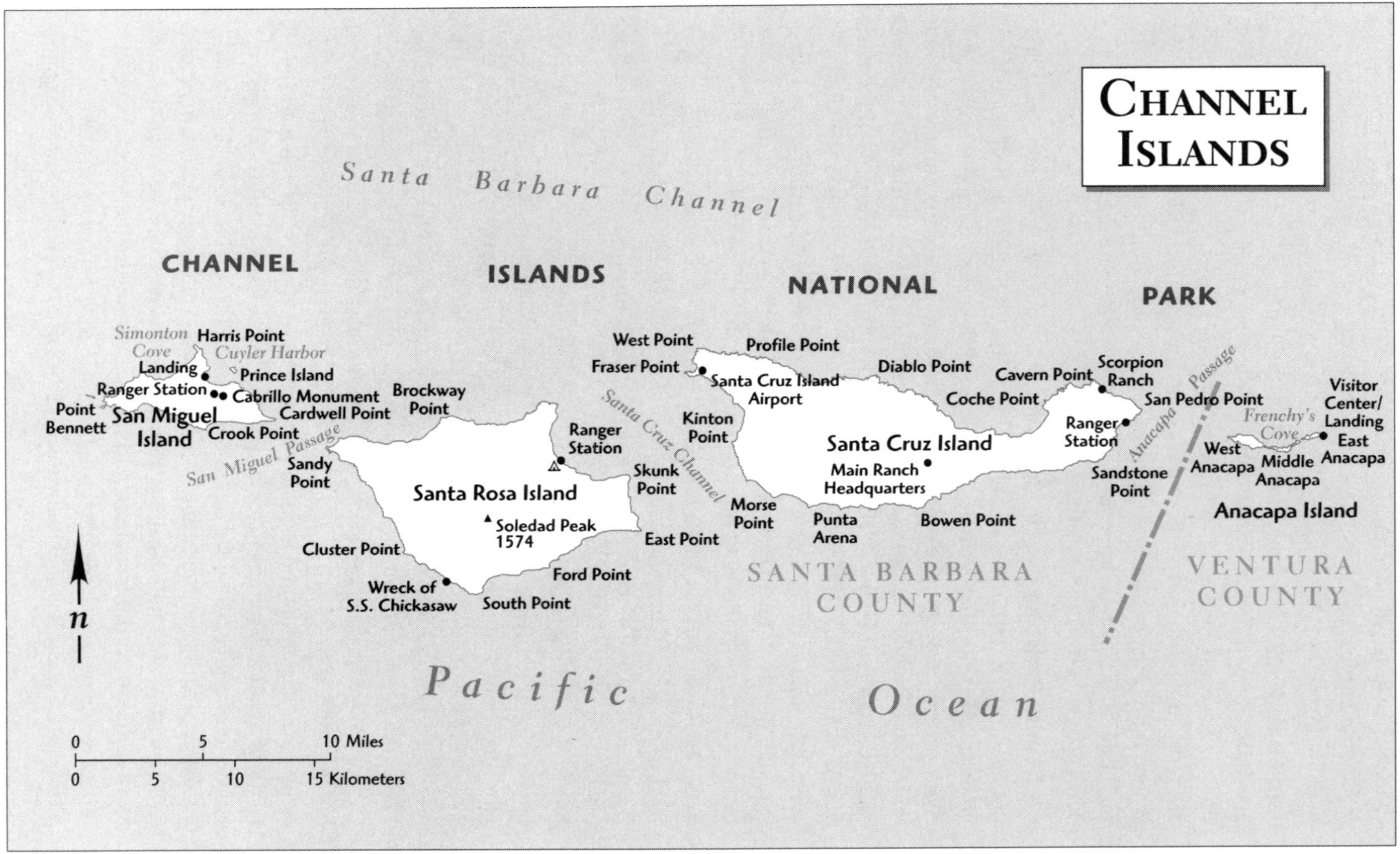

Channel Islands

Santa Barbara Channel

CHANNEL ISLANDS NATIONAL PARK

Simonton Cove
Harris Point
Cuyler Harbor
Landing
Prince Island
Ranger Station
Cabrillo Monument
Point Bennett
San Miguel Island
Cardwell Point
Crook Point
Brockway Point
San Miguel Passage
Sandy Point
Santa Rosa Island
Ranger Station
Soledad Peak 1574
Cluster Point
Wreck of S.S. Chickasaw
South Point
Ford Point
East Point
Skunk Point
Santa Cruz Channel
West Point
Fraser Point
Santa Cruz Island Airport
Profile Point
Kinton Point
Morse Point
Punta Arena
Santa Cruz Island
Main Ranch Headquarters
Diablo Point
Coche Point
Bowen Point
Cavern Point
Scorpion Ranch
Ranger Station
Sandstone Point
San Pedro Point
Anacapa Passage
Frenchy's Cove
West Anacapa
Middle Anacapa
East Anacapa
Visitor Center/ Landing
Anacapa Island
SANTA BARBARA COUNTY
VENTURA COUNTY
Pacific Ocean
n
0 5 10 Miles
0 5 10 15 Kilometers

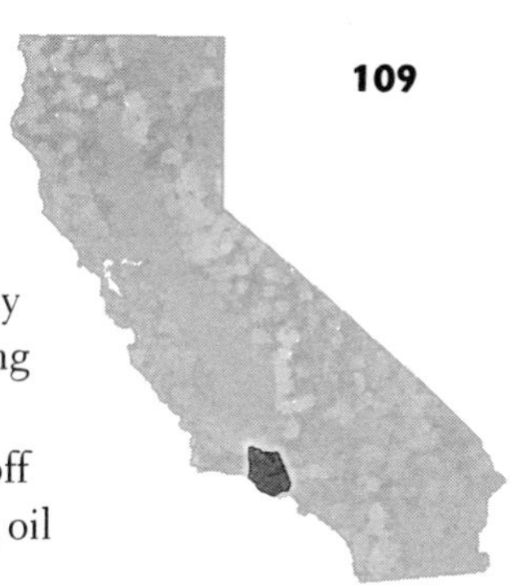

County Department of Parks and Recreation (VCDPR). **La Conchita Beach** is just above the town of Mussel Shoals. This small beach also is run by the VCDPR; call 805-654-3951. There is some parking alongside the highway. Access to the beach is down a rocky seawall. The only reason to visit here is to surf off **La Conchita Point,** which is marred by another long oil platform and pier.

Rincon Point and Rincon Point Surfer Park (a destination beach)
The beach at Rincon is rocky and unpleasant. The shoreline—also rocky—is hazardous, particularly at high tide. However, the surf is spectacular, perhaps the best on the coast, and mentioned in the Beach Boys' "Surfin' U.S.A." Rincon Point has three separate surf breaks. Bring binoculars to see some of the best surf, and surfers, in the United States. Well worth an afternoon—this is the beach equivalent of getting free tickets to a professional baseball game. First Point is the western- and northernmost point, containing the classic "machine-perfect" right lines. Second Point is where the coastline begins to curve inward into a shallow, small bay to the north of the first point. Third Point, or The Indicator, is the outermost break of Rincon Point. It contains the biggest surf at Rincon, though not the best. The best access point at Rincon is the Rincon Point Surfer Park—a parking lot to the south of Rincon Beach County Park, adjacent to Highway 101 and its southbound entrance ramp. There is also access at Rincon Beach County Park, which is at the southern end of Santa Barbara County, at the county line. There is a free parking lot, overlook, picnic table, and access to the beach by stairway, which runs down the cliff to the beach. The park is 500 yards north of Rincon Point itself. For more information, contact the Santa Barbara County Department of Parks and Recreation (SBCDPR) at 805-568-2460.

CHANNEL ISLANDS ★

The Channel Islands are composed of eight islands: four grouped in the north, which are part of Santa Barbara County along with a more southerly island, Santa Barbara; and three in the south, two of which—San Nicolas and San Clemente—are US Military Reservations. The third southern island is Santa Catalina, which is part of Los Angeles County and is discussed in that section.

Ordinarily, when people refer to the Channel Islands they are talking about the northern Islands: San Miguel, Santa Rosa, Santa Cruz, Anacapa, and the small southerly island, Santa Barbara. These islands exist in their natural state.

Together, they make up the **Channel Islands National Marine Sanctuary,** which extends for a mile around each island.

Santa Rosa, Anacapa, and Santa Barbara are run by the National Park Service. San Miguel is under the authority of US Navy. And Santa Cruz is privately owned, though The Nature Conservancy controls most of it. Regardless of the management or ownership, all are wild and rugged. It is possible to visit all the islands, and to camp on San Miguel, Anacapa, and Santa Barbara. The camping conditions are primitive on each of these islands, and permission to camp must be arranged well ahead of time. Permits to camp on San Miguel, Anacapa, and Santa Barbara are obtained from **Channel Islands National Park** (805-658-5700).

Though it can take time to arrange a camping trip, especially during the summer, it is well worth it. Tide-pooling is excellent. There are seals and sea lions. The vistas seem unchanged and unmarked by human hand. But remember that though these islands are beautiful, this is a wild and often unforgiving place. There are no real beaches to speak of. The shore at most places is rock and often marked by cliffs.

It is also possible to take day trips to the Channel Islands. The trip to Santa Rosa from Ventura takes about three and a half hours. These can be arranged through **Island Packer Tours** (805-642-1393), 1867 Spinnaker Drive, Ventura. Next door to Island Packer is the **Channel Islands National Park Headquarters** (805-658-5700), 1901 Spinnaker Drive, Ventura. The Park Headquarters has informative displays explaining the geology of the islands and the marine life around them.

Trips to Santa Cruz Island are conducted by **The Nature Conservancy** (805-962-9111), 213 Stearns Wharf, Santa Barbara. Santa Cruz, 24 miles long, is the largest of the Channel Islands, and perhaps the most diverse. In the center of the island is a lovely valley.

Small Anacapa Island, which is closest to the mainland, comprises three closely related islands, West, Middle, and East. On East Anacapa, it is possible to camp for 14 days at a time. Though an extended camping trip on a remote island, in primitive conditions, is not for everyone, such an expedition is one of the great nature experiences possible on the California coast. Twice a year, in January and March, gray whales pass Anacapa. At all times, there are seals, seal lions, and excellent birding.

Lodging

The south Ventura Coast, largely state park, has no restaurants or accommodations. Ventura/Oxnard/Port Hueneme, an urban area, is the nearest place to stay on the coast. Though none of the accommodations is especially notable, several are more than adequate. All of them are moderately priced. Also consider checking out Ojai (see below).

Mandalay Beach Resort (805-984-2500; 1-800-362-2779), 2101 Mandalay Beach Road, Oxnard. Expensive. Here is beachfront luxury with full amenities, including Jacuzzis in every room.

Inn on the Beach (805-652-2000), 1175 S. Seaward Avenue, Ventura. Moderate. This highly recommended beachfront hotel is unassuming but clean and convenient.

The Shores Motel at the Beach (805-643-9600), 1059 S. Seaward Avenue, Ventura. Moderate. A block off the beach, this motel is a little noisy, but well run and clean.

La Mer Gaestehaus (805-643-3600), 411 Poli Street, Ventura. Expensive. A good place to stay in Ventura, this hotel is near the ocean and overlooks the Pacific. This is a Cape Cod-style hotel, easily recognized from a distance because the innkeeper, Gisela Baida, originally from Germany, flies the flags of many different countries from her front porch. There are five guest rooms, each with private entrance, and each is decorated to reflect a different European country. All have private bath. As Ventura hotels go, this is expensive, though nothing like staying in Ojai (see sidebar).

Excursion to Ojai

■ Coastal Ventura County has few hotels or restaurants that make any of the recommended lists of the more discriminating California guides. Inland, the city of Ojai is a well-known resort destination, about 20 minutes from the Ventura/Oxnard area. Exit Highway 101 onto Highway 33. **The Ojai Valley Inn** (805-646-5511) at the end of Country Club Drive is an expensive resort with acres of lush grounds, a fitness center, and all the amenities, such as wood-burning fireplaces, well-stocked bars, and personal bathrobes. There is golf and tennis, and the inn has two good restaurants.

Wheeler Hot Springs, 16825 Marcopa Highway, is a moderately priced day resort. There are rustic baths with private hot tubs. The adjoining restaurant is well run. Inexpensive package deals, involving lunch or dinner with hot tub and bath, are a good deal. There are no overnight accommodations.

Ojai also has **L'Auberge** (805-646-2288), 314 El Paseo, an excellent restaurant featuring French country cooking. Less expensive, and favored by local residents, is **The Ranch House** (805-646-2360), S. Lomita and Besant. This is a garden restaurant that bakes its own bread, makes its own desserts, and has a good wine list. ■

Harbortown Marina Resort (805-658-1212), 1050 Schooner Drive, Ventura. Expensive. A "four-star resort" a block from the beach, close by the marina. Designed by the Frank Loyd Wright Foundation, there are ocean views from many rooms, a heated swimming pool, tennis courts, spa, nearby golf. A good restaurant, **Alexander's**, is in the hotel.

Pierpoint Inn (805-643-6144), 550 Sanjon Road, Ventura, is a local favorite with nice grounds and a small-town feel. The inn includes a decent restaurant.

Holiday Inn Ventura Beach Resort (805-648-7731), 450 E. Harbor Boulevard, and **Doubletree Hotel** (805-643-6000), 2055 Harbor Boulevard, are two chain hotels that will do fine in a pinch.

Restaurants

Capistrano's (805-984-2569), 2101 Mandalay Beach Road, at the Mandalay Beach Resort, Oxnard. Moderate. Traditional French cuisine is augmented by seafood specialties.

Sal's Mexican Food (805-483-9015), 1450 S. Oxnard Boulevard, Oxnard. Inexpensive. Enjoy hearty Mexican fare in this local favorite.

The Lobster Trap (805-985-6361), 3605 Peninsula Road, Oxnard. Moderate. Located in the Casa Sirena Resort, it offers local seafood and fresh Maine lobster. Try the scalone, a puree made of scallops and abalone.

Pastabilities (805-648-1462), 185 E. Santa Clara, Ventura. Inexpensive. Pick your own combination of pasta and sauces. Pizza and other entrées also served. Kids will enjoy this spot.

The Greek (805-650-5350), 1583 Spinnaker Drive, Ventura Harbor Village, Ventura. Moderate. Traditional Greek food such as moussaka and kabobs are well prepared. Harbor views enhance the dining.

Franky's Place (805-648-6282), 456 E. Main, Ventura. Moderate. Franky's is put together as a rococo-designed art gallery that serves decent food. Natural and vegetarian sandwiches are served for lunch daily; open for dinner only on Friday and Saturday.

Duke's Griddle and Grill (805-653-0707), 1124 S. Seaward Avenue, Ventura. Inexpensive. Sawdust on the floor, pool tables, and a classic surfer scene make this spot worth looking for. Good greasy burgers, fried seafood, Mexican and Japanese food provide sustenance to beachgoers; indoor and outdoor seating. Takeout available. Public parking; the lot is at the end of the street.

Seaside Johnny's (805-652-1095), 1140 S. Seaward Avenue. Moderate. Seaside Johnny's offers slightly more upscale seafood and burgers with good salads. Indoor and outdoor seating available. Breakfast, lunch, and dinner are served daily.

Pierpont Inn (805-643-6144), 550 Sanjon Road. Moderate. This is a local favorite: family owned since 1928, with ocean views. Located in the hotel.

Santa Clara House (805-643-3264), 211 E. Santa Clara Street, Ventura. Moderate. Enjoyable meals are served in a 1914 vintage building. Seafood, chicken, and steaks are prepared on an oakwood grill.

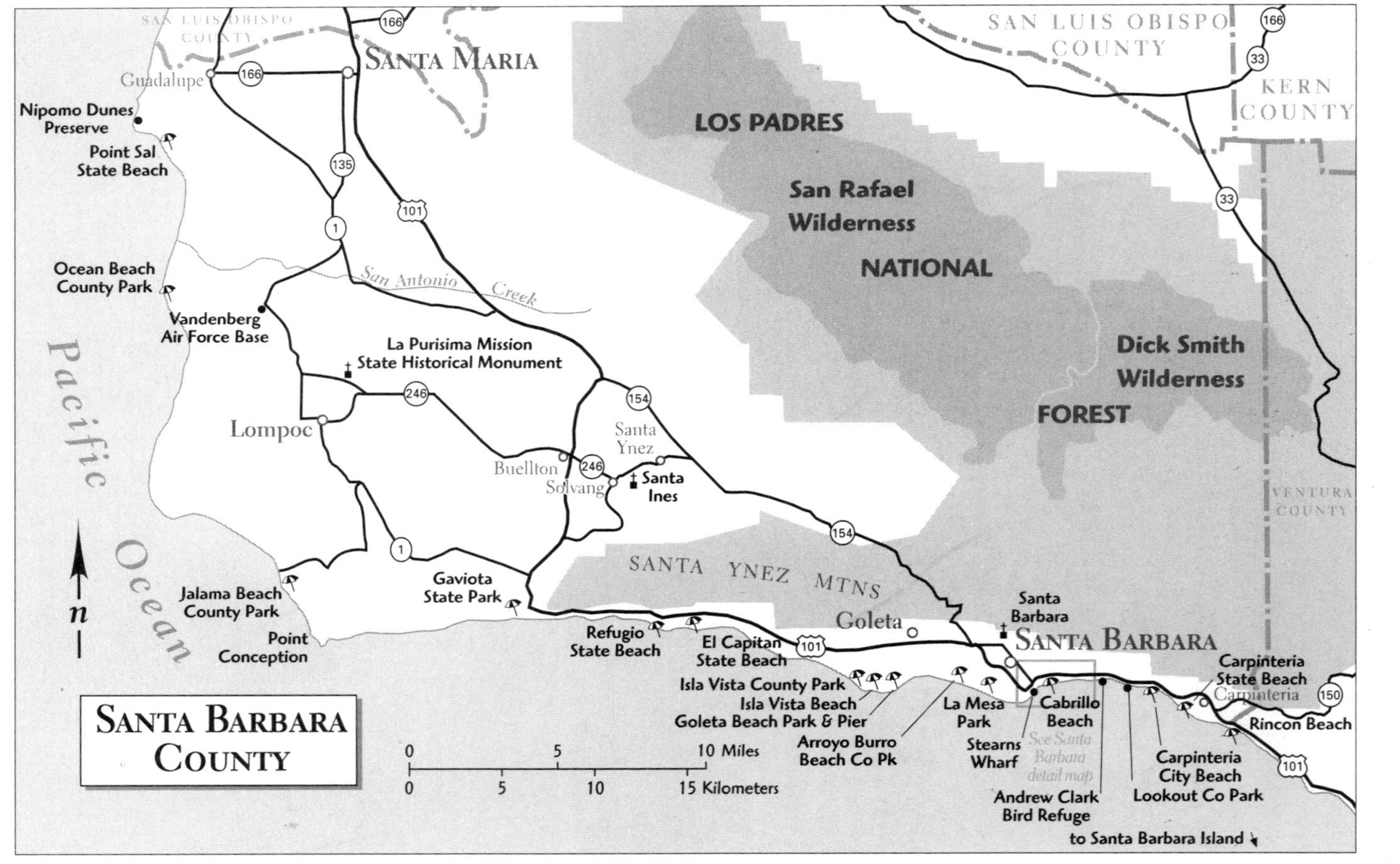

Santa Barbara County
San Luis Obispo County
Kern County
Ventura County
Santa Maria
Guadalupe
Nipomo Dunes Preserve
Point Sal State Beach
Ocean Beach County Park
Vandenberg Air Force Base
La Purisima Mission State Historical Monument
Lompoc
Buellton
Solvang
Santa Ynez
Santa Ines
San Antonio Creek
Los Padres
San Rafael Wilderness
National
Dick Smith Wilderness
Forest
Santa Ynez Mtns
Goleta
Santa Barbara
Santa Barbara
Carpinteria
Pacific Ocean
Jalama Beach County Park
Point Conception
Gaviota State Park
Refugio State Beach
El Capitan State Beach
Isla Vista County Park
Isla Vista Beach
Goleta Beach Park & Pier
Arroyo Burro Beach Co Pk
La Mesa Park
Stearns Wharf
See Santa Barbara detail map
Cabrillo Beach
Andrew Clark Bird Refuge
Carpinteria City Beach
Lookout Co Park
Carpinteria State Beach
Rincon Beach
to Santa Barbara Island
n
0
5
10 Miles
0
5
10
15 Kilometers
1
101
135
154
166
246
33
150

CHAPTER FIVE

Santa Barbara County

SANTA BARBARA IS TWO COASTS that meet at Point Conception. To the south of this famous point lies one of the great beachfronts of southern California. It is a long, dense, but carefully planned urban beach running from Carpinteria in the south to Santa Barbara and then on to Gaviota in the north. Northern Santa Barbara County and the true northern coast of California begin at Point Conception. The coastal ranges begin here—a continuous coastal wall that goes to the Oregon border.

Southern Santa Barbara is a sloping hillside, facing south, that sinks down to an underwater valley between two of the transverse ranges, the Santa Ynez, at the coastline, and the Santa Monica, of which the Channel Islands are a part.

Here, the waves and wind at the water's edge have carved out a shelf in the mountainside. This narrow shelf—at its greatest width, only 2½ miles—is the structure for the famous forgiving beaches of southern Santa Barbara, a 40-mile stretch running east and west from Rincon Point to Point Conception.

Often the beaches here are backed by bluffs, sometimes 200 feet high. These bluffs form a natural screen; although the southern Santa Barbara coast is an urban beachfront, the natural screen creates quiet sections of beach.

Where rivers have cut down the bluffs, the Chumash Indians established settlements. Access to the ocean was easy, fresh water was available, the land was flat and rich. Now the urban centers of Santa Barbara County reside in these places—the cities of Santa Barbara, Carpinteria, Goleta, and Gaviota.

The Channel Islands—the peaks of the Santa Monica range itself rise from the ocean to form them—provide a natural barrier to ocean waves. Warm waters from the south are funneled into this section. The conditions are perfect for swimming, sea kayaks, and paddleboards. It is also an excellent area in which to learn to surf, though more advanced surfers will want more tubular wave patterns.

Despite the visible oil-drilling platforms offshore, conservationists have been active in Santa Barbara. This is an area of carefully tended shoreline parks; lofty palm trees; and Spanish-style, red-roofed bathhouses.

North of Point Conception, where the shore swings 90 degrees to face north, the coastline is following the edge of the great Pacific Plate. Here, the mountains of the south coastal range have been shoved up like a barrier against the sea. Steep shoulders of the coastal range fall in great cliffs and crags. The waves of these beaches are tricky, treacherous; the water is colder. The views are spectacular. Access to the beach can depend on a good map and guidebook—it is often difficult to tell private property from state land.

Through northern Santa Barbara, a series of great points line this section of the coast: Government Point, Conception, Arguello, Purisima. All these are well-known landmarks to sailors, who navigate warily around them.

Given its pivotal position at the great turn of the coast, Santa Barbara County is an excellent staging ground for extended sight-seeing trips. The Malibu beaches, Getty Center, and Hearst Castle are all within day-trip range.

Of the possible places to stay, Carpinteria is the best, particularly for families with small children. The beach is delightful, the water is warm. West of a low headland to the north lies an offshore reef. The reef calms the incoming waves much as a breakwater does. Two results are that sand accumulates here and the water is calm and safe for swimming. Condominiums can be rented at reasonable rates. There are many options all along the well-populated Santa Barbara southern coast.

DON NEUWIRTH

Palm Park from Stearns Wharf

The city of Santa Barbara itself is another attractive place to stay—though it can be expensive. The harbor here is man-made—Palm Park, Sterns Wharf, West Beach constitute a pleasant bay walk. The Channel Islands can be visited from here through The Nature Conservancy (805-962-9111).

Beaches and Attractions

Rincon Point (See the Rincon listing under "Ventura County.") This hard beach formed by rocks washed down from Rincon Creek creates a reeflike substructure creating a near perfect wave pattern. This is a legendary surfing beach—and not for beginners. Not for swimmers, either.

Carpinteria State Beach This beach was an important Chumash site. Carpinteria Creek, small and attractive, goes through the middle of the park, creating a tidal lagoon around which the Chumash lived. Here, they built wooden canoes—*tomols*—which they used to visit the Channel Islands. Portola visited the site in 1769. There were 38 dwellings and 300 residents. He called the town La Carpinteria, or "the carpenter shop," because of the boatbuilding activities. Why did the Chumash choose this site? The protected beach is ideal for launching the boats they built. The tidal lagoon is still a beautiful spot, attracting fish and clams. But the area has another attraction: oil. Deposits of tar are endemic to this area—note the offshore oil platforms. The Chumash used the tar to caulk their boats.

South of the beach lie areas used by indigenous surfers but generally scorned by visiting surfers, who, rightly, spend their time at Rincon, only 2 miles to the south. Although Carpinteria is not prime surfing territory, it is one of the best swimming and wading beaches in the county. The beach is more than 80 acres, with a mile-long beachfront. There are rest rooms, picnic areas, fire pits, and 262 campsites. Some are wheelchair accessible. The park includes a display about the Chumash Indians. Contact Carpinteria State Beach for more information, 805-684-2811. Make reservations by calling 1-800-444-7275. Access is from the end of Palm Avenue. There is an entrance fee.

Carpinteria City Beach This is a small, good urban beach and an excellent place to bring small children. The offshore reef acts as a breakwater. Just to the west of the beach is the Carpinteria Marsh—a nesting ground for many coastal bird species. The beach is located within the city of Carpinteria, at the end of Linden Avenue. (The three main city roads that are useful in order to reach the beach are Ash, Lindon, and Palm.) There is a metered parking lot and lifeguards. For more information, call Carpinteria Community Services at 805-684-5405, ext. 449.

City of Carpinteria This is a small coastal city in transition. Located on one of the safest, most beautiful of California's beaches, it abuts private walled communities to the north, and is on the verge of becoming another La Jolla—private, expensive, inaccessible. Still, for now, it remains a relaxed, unpretentious beach community of the best kind. There are few hotels here, and none of substance. However, it is possible to rent condominiums near the beach. This can be a great vacation for families, particularly those with young children, as the city beach, and the adjoining state beach, is particularly safe. Moreover, Capinteria is only 10 miles from Santa Barbara to the north and within striking distance of the coastal museums of Malibu. It is even possible to use Carpinteria as the starting point for a day trip to Hearst Castle. We highly recommend this town—particularly as a family destination for northern Californians wanting to explore the south. At the same time, we recognize that our enthusiasm will contribute to the inevitable change that is sweeping this beautiful area. (See our notes on renting condominiums under **Lodging**.) Numerous creeks flow through Carpinteria. It is built at the south end of a marsh area; the marsh makes the area an important birding site. Gated communities are slowly destroying this important environmental area. *Note*: Just

DON NEUWIRTH

Carpinteria State Beach

west of Carpinteria is Santa Claus Lane, a block of small shops and toy stores. At **Toyland**—3821 Santa Claus Lane, 805-684-3515—your mail will be postmarked SANTA CLAUS, CALIFORNIA.

Loon Point We recommend this only for adventurous beach visitors. You are going through private land. Remember, however, that the lay of the land often defeats property rights, as it does here. The creek bed will take you to the beach. There you will find a wondrous breeding area for monarch butterflies. Out to sea, you will spot kelp beds that stretch a mile offshore. This area is accessible by parking on the shoulder of Route 101/1 and following the creek next to Toro Canyon Road. Park near the clearly marked turnoff for Toro Canyon Road. The creek bed is next to the road. Climb down into the creek bed, and follow the stream to the ocean.

Lookout County Park. There is a blufftop area with picnic sites, playground. Below is a small, attractive beach. There is a free parking lot. In the summer, there are lifeguards. Access is at the terminus of Lookout Park Road in Summerland, a small town 6 miles southeast of Santa Barbara and directly above Carpinteria. Call the Santa Barbara County Department of Parks and Recreation at 805-568-2460 for more information.

Montecito beaches. Montecito is a small town at the edge of Santa Barbara. Channel Drive is just off Highway 101, in Montecito, and it takes you along the shoreline of the city. Just to the southern end of Channel Drive, where the road curves back toward Highway 101, there is a beachfront area, accessible by three staircases. One is located at the end of Butterfly Lane, at the midpoint of Channel Drive. Farther west there are two stairways in front of the Biltmore Hotel. Access is also possible by merely walking through the Biltmore Hotel, or through the Miramar Resort Hotel, which is next door. Then walk west along the beach. Another good access point is a trail and ramp at the end of Eucalyptus Road, which marks the western end of this beach. It is approximately ½ mile west of Channel Island Road. There is a parking lot at the end of the short road, and a trail leads to the beach. This beachfront area is often uncrowded. Between the hotels, the beachfront is public, but it has no facilities.

Andree Clark Bird Refuge/Zoo/Dwight Murphy Field ★ Located between Montecito and the urban Santa Barbara beaches, this is a large, enclosed saltwater marsh. There is a bike path around the southern side. To the west of the refuge is **A. Child's Estate Zoo** and park, which includes a children's train ride. Further west is a park used for softball and soccer.

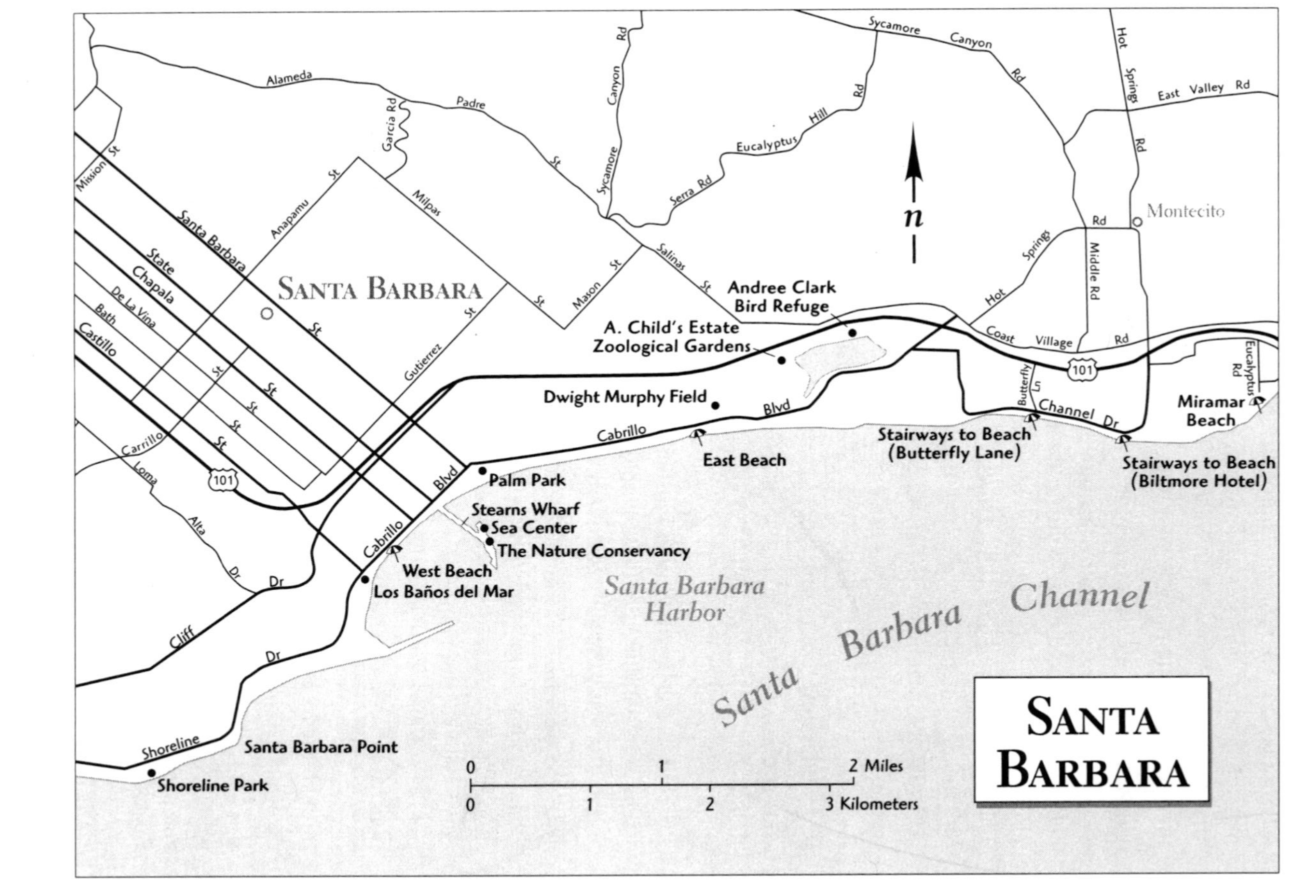

Santa Barbara
Santa Barbara
Montecito
Andree Clark
Bird Refuge
A. Child's Estate
Zoological Gardens
Dwight Murphy Field
East Beach
Stairways to Beach
(Butterfly Lane)
Stairways to Beach
(Biltmore Hotel)
Miramar
Beach
Palm Park
Stearns Wharf
Sea Center
The Nature Conservancy
West Beach
Los Baños del Mar
Santa Barbara
Harbor
Santa Barbara Channel
Santa Barbara Point
Shoreline Park
0
1
2 Miles
0
1
2
3 Kilometers
n
Alameda
Padre St
Garcia Rd
Mission St
Santa Barbara St
State St
Chapala St
De La Vina St
Bath St
Castillo St
Anapamu St
Milpas St
Gutierrez St
Mason St
Salinas St
Sycamore Canyon Rd
Eucalyptus Hill Rd
Serra Rd
Hot Springs Rd
East Valley Rd
Middle Rd
Coast Village Rd
Butterfly Ln
Channel Dr
Eucalyptus Rd
Cabrillo Blvd
Carrillo
Loma Alta Dr
Cliff Dr
Shoreline Dr
101

East Beach/West Beach/Palm Park/Stearns Wharf. The well-maintained urban beachfront of Santa Barbara is divided at its center by Stearns Wharf. Built in 1876 in order to unload coastal trading ships, the wharf was rebuilt in 1981 and now forms the eastern end of Santa Barbara Harbor, all of which is man-made. This is a substantial wharf—1500 feet long—that has interrupted the natural flow of sand along the beachfront. To the east of the wharf is East Beach. To the west is—obviously, given the configuration of the coast here—West Beach. Both have metered lot and street parking, lifeguards, rest rooms, picnic areas, and grills. East Beach has showers and the **Cabrillo Arts Center**, which offers shows, lectures, and movies (805-962-8956 for more information). West Beach has a municipal swimming pool, **Los Banos Del Mar**. Both East and West Beaches are calm. Tall palm trees run along the shoreline, as does a bike path. The beaches are clean, well tended, and patrolled by lifeguards. Contact the Santa Barbara City Department of Parks and Recreation for more information on West Beach, 805-564-5418, and 805-897-2680 for information on East Beach.

City of Santa Barbara beachfront The city of Santa Barbara has been a hotbed for environmentalists, among them the wonderful detective writer Ross Macdonald. It shows in one of the best—if not liveliest—urban beachfronts in California. Most of the city front is accessible from a highway set back from beach parks. It's called Shoreline Drive in western Santa Barbara, E. Cabrillo in the east. Shoreline Park, in the west, extends from the highway across a grassy bluff and onto the beach below (reached by staircases). The blufftop has picnic areas, overlooks, and children's play areas. To the west, Chase Palm Park has a wide beach, grassy areas, palm trees, and picnic tables. It also hosts cultural events. Elsewhere, the shorefront has pocket parks and beaches that flow into each other.

DON NEUWIRTH

Sculpture at the foot of Stearns Wharf

Plaza Del Mar. This 5-acre urban park has a view of the harbor, bandstand (summertime concerts), and picnic area. It's just west of Santa Barbara Harbor, on Shoreline Drive.

Leadbetter Beach Located just to the west of the Santa Barbara Harbor, this is a wide, sandy beach. Park at the harbor or the metered lot off Shoreline Drive. Snack food is available, and there is a picnic area. There are lifeguards and rest rooms. This beach has a soft break, excellent for beginning surfers.

Shoreline Park. Just to the west of Leadbetter Park, between the sea and Shoreline Drive, this is an excellent urban beachfront area, less crowded than East or West Beach to the south. The beach lies below a bluff. On the bluff, carefully tended grassy areas are used for kite flying and picnics. Stairs here lead down to the beach itself, which is sandy.

La Mesa Park. Just west of Shoreline Park, this is a playground on the bluff above the beach. Park on adjacent streets.

Mesa Lane Stairs lies just west of La Mesa Park, at the end of Mesa Lane. Take Cliff Drive to Mesa Lane. Park on the street, then take the steep stairway to the beach. It's a favorite of local surfers, but the surf can be tricky, and there are rocks. Hiking along the beach, however, is excellent. Tall cliffs provide protection and give a feeling of isolation. This is one of the best ribbon beaches in California, and the locals know it and use it.

Arroyo Burro Beach County Park has lifeguards, rest rooms, picnic areas, a restaurant, and fire pits. There is a protected stream habitat area here. The beach itself is wide and sandy—and very popular. It is located 2 miles northwest of Santa Barbara, on Cliff Drive. For more information, contact the Santa Barbara County Department of Parks and Recreation at 805-568-2460.

More Mesa. This is a destination beach for nude sunbathers. It can also become extremely crowded. Paradoxically, this area is an important Chugash Indian site, and an impressive birding site as well. Access can be tricky. Take the Turnpike Road exit from Highway 101. Go south to Hollister Avenue, then left. Take a right on Puente Drive, right on Vieja Drive, then left on Mockingbird Lane. At the end of the lane, take the footpath ½ mile to the beach.

Goleta Beach County Park Just to the southeast of Goleta Point, the home of the University of California at Santa Barbara, lies Goleta Beach County Park. This is a 29-acre park with large expanses of grass, picnic areas, snacks, and a fishing pier. There is also a boat hoist. Behind the park, there is a wetland slough, which has good bird-watching. The beach here is wide and sandy, the water is safe for swimming, and lifeguards are on duty. This beach is preferred by families and is often crowded. For more information, call the Santa Barbara County Department of Parks and Recreation at 805-568-2460.

The park has a moderately priced, attractive restaurant, the Beachside Bar Cafe.

City of Goleta. Just to the northwest of Santa Barbara, Goleta is a college town, home of the University of California at Santa Barbara. The main campus is at Goleta Point; the "west" campus is at Coal Oil Point. Between them is a wide, sandy beach, with some rocks in places. There are cliffs and bluffs behind the beach.

Goleta Pier. At 1450 feet long and north of Santa Barbara, Goleta Pier is a long arrow pointing south toward the Channel Islands. This pier is quieter than Stearns Wharf in Santa Barbara; rural areas lie to the north, where the Santa Barbara airport also is located. However, this is an urban pier. Sportfishing boats, boat and sailboat rentals, tackle shops, and a restaurant line the beginnings of the pier. As you move along, the fishermen (and fisherchildren) predominate. The pier is located at Goleta Beach, off Sandspit Road, which is reached via Ward Memorial Drive.

Isla Vista Beach and County Park. This beach is the sandy, calm area between Goleta Point and Coal Oil Point. Access is by stairway from the blufftop, at the terminus of Camino Majorca, Camino del Sur, and Camino Pescadero. At the end of El Embarcadero, there is a paved ramp. Park on the street. Though the beach is beautiful, and less crowded than at Goleta County Park, it is also more dangerous; swim with caution. Call the Isla Vista Recreation and Parks Department, 805-968-2017, for more information.

El Capitan State Beach marks the southern boundary of a 15-mile stretch of classic Santa Barbara coast—it runs from west to east and has high cliffs protected by sandy beaches. In this area, Highway 101 runs close to the shoreline. Access to the beach is by stairway. As in the rest of this region, the bluffs provide meadows for walking and areas for camping. There are 142 campsites. Try to reserve site #75. It is nearest the ocean. Food is available at the camp store, as are basic sundries. There is a small point jutting out here, called El Capitan Point, which produces a classic point break. Right tubes peel off and spit for miles. This is one of the longest tubes on the coast. Because there are rocks in the point area, surfing here isn't for the inexperienced, but on the beach to the east the surf is small and the bottom sandy, making it a good place for beginners. It is also a good place for surf-casting. Access to El Capitan is off Highway 101, just to the west of the town of Naples, and is clearly marked. Call Gaviota State Park at 805-968-1033 for more information; reservations can be made by calling 1-800-444-7275.

Refugio State Beach Three miles to the west of El Capitan State Beach, this is a continuation of the same stretch of high bluffs and beautiful Santa

DON NEUWIRTH

Gaviota State Beach

Barbara beach. There is a hiking trail and a bike trail on the bluff connecting the two parks. There are lifeguards in summer, rest rooms, showers, picnic tables, and 85 campsites for tents and RVs. Refugio is smaller than El Capitan, and its beach is narrow, often rocky. There are some active, interesting tide pools. Refugio Creek runs through the park, creating an attractive freshwater pool at the beach. While the central portion of the beach does not have bluffs—the stream has cut them away—to the east and west, the high bluffs have banana palms. Swimming here is reasonably safe, but not completely without risk. Watch out for tidal currents moving east–west along the shoreline. Access is clearly marked, off Highway 101. Make reservations by calling 1-800-444-7275. Call Gaviota State Park, at 805-968-3294, for more information.

Gaviota State Park Here, Highway 101 turns north, away from the beach. Gaviota marks the end of the east–west stretch of beach-bluff area that began with El Capitan. Gaviota is a varied beach, which is usual where a stream enters. There is good fishing and surfing, and beachcombing is excellent on both sides of the stream. To the north, there are turnouts at San

Onofre and Vista Del Mar. These, both part of Gaviota, are nude beaches. Because of its range of activities—the hiking, the good swimming, the beachcombing—Gaviota can be an excellent place to camp for a family, but a reservation is an absolute necessity. Gaviota has 54 tent and RV campsites, picnic tables, showers, and a store. The inland section of the park contains more than 2776 acres. It also adjoins the **Los Padres National Forest**. (For access to the wilderness hiking inland section of the park, take 101 north, go right at Highway 1, then turn right at the first stop sign. There is a dirt parking lot. The trail here leads to a small hot spring—lukewarm but pleasant. It continues on for 11 miles to Gaviota Peak. This 2458-foot hill provides striking vistas of the coastline and into Los Padres National Park.) Call Gaviota State Park, 805-968-3294, for more information.

Jalama Beach County Park Jalama is a beautiful beach in a beautiful setting: Sand dunes and bluffs, without intrusive housing, stretch to the north and south. Beyond them are rolling, soft hills and, farther in the distance, the Coastal Range. To the south is Point Conception, the dividing line between northern and southern California. Jalama Creek empties into a small wetland, which in turn empties into the ocean. The beach at the park is ½ mile long; the campsite is 28 acres. You can hike the beach to both the north and south of the park. To the north lies Vandenberg Air Force Base, which allows unlimited public access for 1½ miles. To the south, it is possible to reach Point Conception itself, though the going can be rugged, and at times dangerous. As noted in the introduction, beach access was successfully fought by those living on "estates" carved from the former Hollister Ranch. They do not welcome visitors, though of course it is perfectly legal to walk down the beach. The problem is that the beachfront contains high cliffs. At high tide, a hiker can be stranded. Even at low tide, it is necessary to bushwhack, at times, along rotting seawalls and old railroad tracks. There is a lifeguard station and lighthouse at Point Conception, but they are not particularly useful to beachgoers. Despite these difficulties, a visit to Point Conception is worth it. The lighthouse, in its isolated setting, is striking.

Jalama Beach is just north of Point Conception—take the Jalama Beach Road turnoff; the beach is 10 miles on. There is an entrance fee. There are rest rooms, picnic sites, and a small store. *Note*: There are also 120 campsites for tents and RVs. Fees to camp are charged, and camping reservations are not accepted. For information, call Jalama Beach County Park, 805-736-6316.

Vandenberg Air Force Base Beach From Purisima Point south for 3 miles, there are trails along the blufftop and paths leading down the cliffs to

Naomi Schwartz—Oil

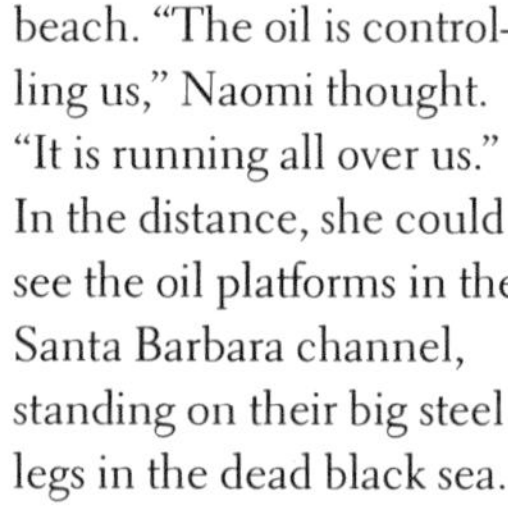

■ Naomi woke up smelling tar. It was a thick, powerful smell. She gathered up her children and walked down the long driveway to the street, thinking they must be paving it, but when she got to the road, no one was working on it. Some of her neighbors were standing around, trying to figure it out. Finally someone came along and told them there was an oil spill on the beach. Naomi was incredulous; she was a mile from the beach, and it smelled like they were paving just down her driveway. She walked back to the house, put the kids in the car, and drove to the beach.

Naomi was a housewife with four small children. The two older boys were just learning to surf. Santa Barbara's beautiful beaches were like an extension of her house—what you did with small children was take them to the beach, which was their playground.

Today the beach was black. Dead birds littered it. Nothing moved. There were no waves. The water was black, too. "There has been an assault on this beautiful place," Naomi thought. "The ocean is dead." There were some officials standing around, but nothing was being done to fix the beach. "The oil is controlling us," Naomi thought. "It is running all over us." In the distance, she could see the oil platforms in the Santa Barbara channel, standing on their big steel legs in the dead black sea.

When Naomi got home, she felt at loose ends. She wanted to do something, but what? The sight of the black beach left her damaged; she felt mutilated. Eight or nine months went by before anyone could use the beach again. For all the technology that was supposed to clean up after a spill, it turned out that the only way to get rid of the oil was to rake straw over it, then pick up the oil-soaked straw. Even that didn't do much. The spill just had to run its course.

She "sat with the spill for a while," Naomi remembers, thinking she had to do something but unsure what that might be. Other people were trying to start a

---

pocket beaches. Come early in the day, since access is limited to 50 people a day; a game warden supplies passes. (He's at building 13401 at the base.)

Ocean Beach County Park ★ Ocean Beach is part of a beautiful 15-mile-long north–south crescent of beaches lying between Point Arguello and Purisima Point. Here at the park, the beach runs along the access to the Santa Ynez River. Park in the well-maintained lot at the end of Ocean Avenue. A short trail leads under a railroad trestle to the beach. Like other beaches at river edges, there is a substantial wetland here, which attracts many species of birds. There are also dunes. The beach itself is wide and sandy, and the entire

commission that would take charge of the California coast, do something that might prevent oil spills and other problems so more damage could be avoided. The legislature wouldn't pass the bill, so they started a referendum drive. Naomi got involved in Santa Barbara, soliciting signatures on petitions.

Naomi had high hopes for the new Coastal Commission, created when Proposition 20 passed, but the people whom the governor appointed to it were the same people who had opposed the measure. In response, up and down the coast, people began forming "Coast Watch" committees to monitor the Coastal Commission, to go to meetings, to present the facts to the public.

Naomi was appointed the spokeswoman of the Santa Barbara Coast Watch Committee. Soon it expanded to include San Luis Obispo and Ventura Counties. Going to meetings, studying, Naomi soon became an expert on coastal erosion, septic tanks, French drains—and oil. Local "advisory" coastal commissions were set up to aid the big state commission. Naomi was appointed to one. She was the first woman appointed to the South Central Regional Commission.

She was also one of the best prepared—that was a huge eye-opener. She actually knew more than most of the "experts" who were testifying. In 1976, Naomi was appointed to the state Coastal Commission. She served as chairperson through 1982, when the wheels turned again in Sacramento.

In 1992, one of the incumbent supervisors of Santa Barbara County ran for Congress, leaving the supervisor's seat open. Naomi ran for it. She is now in her second term.

The same big oil platforms are still pumping the same oil from the Santa Barbara channel, but there hasn't been a serious oil spill in Santa Barbara since the big one in 1969 (500 barrels of oil spilled from Platform Irene in September 1997). They say it is much safer now. The technology has improved, they say. Naomi says that straw, and a man or woman raking it, is still the only way to clean the beach.

Note: The California State Coastal Commission published, and has periodically updated, the excellent *California Coastal Access Guide*, a list of the public access points along the coast. (University of California Press, $17.95). ■

---

park is 28 acres. Access is from Highway 135, which goes west from Highway 101 at Los Alamos; from Highway 246, which goes west from Highway 101 at Buellton; or from the Cabrillo Highway, which leaves Highway 101 shortly after it leaves the coast and turns north.

Point Sal State Beach (a destination beach) If you can get there—the road is often difficult—this is a beautiful hidden beach. Shielded by Point Sal, the stretch of coast here is wild and spectacular. There are no facilities; the water around the point is dangerous with unpredictable currents. It is beautiful, though, and still worth the trip. There is a hiking trail—approximately 5 miles long, leading from the beach, up steep trails and along the blufftop. Don't attempt the trail with small children. Even adults may have trouble. This untamed, beautiful beach lies at the end of Brown Road, which you reach via Highway 1, just to the south of Guadalupe Street and the Santa Maria River. The 8-mile road is unpaved, and sometimes unpassable. The entrance is clearly marked. Park in a dirt area at the end of the road. Access to the beach is via a steep dirt path. Just to the north lies Point Sal, where steep bluffs rise out of the sea off a sandy beach. Contact the Channel Coast District Office, California Department of Parks and Recreation, 1933 Cliff Drive, Suite 27, Santa Barbara 93101; 805-899-1400.

Guadalupe-Nipomo Dunes Preserve ★ (formerly Rancho Guadalupe County Park). Owned by The Nature Conservancy, Guadalupe lies at the terminus of the Santa Maria River, which divides Santa Barbara from San Luis Obispo County. Left in its natural state, this is a beautiful county park, noted for its huge sand dunes, including Mussel Rock, which rises to 450 feet and is the highest dune in California. This is a varied area—wetlands at the entrance to the river, backed by rolling sand dunes. It is possible to find your own secluded nook here; but it is also possible to find that the beach has been closed due to windblown drifts of sand, as impenetrable as a Sierra snowstorm. For more information about the preserve and guided tours, call The Nature Conservancy at 805-541-8735.

Lodging

The southern coast of Santa Barbara County has varied lodging and lots of it. Some of the best California beach hotels are in the city of Santa Barbara. There are famous resorts only slightly inland. Northern Santa Barbara County has almost no facilities. Indeed, it has few towns. For general information on hotels in southern Santa Barbara, contact **Santa Barbara Hotspots**, 36 State Street, 1-800-292-2222.

We recommend the Carpinteria area for families with children. As discussed, the beach here is excellent for them. Information about Carpinteria condominiums can be found from **Hotspots**, above, which also has information about condominium rentals in Santa Barbara itself. Three condominium developments in Carpinteria are: **Condominium Shores**, 805-684-3570; **Salamar Sands**, 805-684-5613; and **Sunset Shores**, 805-684-3682. Be sure to get specific information on the condominium you are renting: Ask if it faces the beach (preferred) and how far it is from the beach (you want to be close enough to walk). Price varies with the season.

The following list of our recommended hotels begins at the southern boundary of Santa Barbara County and works its way up the coast.

Eugenia Motel (805-684-4416), 5277 Carpinteria Avenue, Carpinteria. Moderate. A pleasant, clean 10-room motel—half the rooms have kitchens, ask for one. No pool or special facilities.

La Casa del Sol Motel (805-684-4307), 5585 Carpinteria Avenue, Carpinteria. Moderate. Offers pleasant but modest rooms, some with kitchens. There's a small but adequate pool.

Miramar Hotel (805-969-2203; 1-800-322-6983), 1555 S. Jameson Lane, Montecito. Moderate. Located on the beach, off Highway 101, you can get a room on the road for a moderate price, and then enjoy the rest of the 15-acre resort. Highly recommended for those on a limited budget.

Four Seasons Biltmore (805-969-2261), 1260 Channel Drive, Santa Barbara. Expensive. The Biltmore is incredibly pricey—but it's also one of the best hotels in California. It is a Spanish-style resort, located on the shoreline, with a nightclub/health club/resort complex. Most rooms have a private balcony looking at the ocean. Frankly, we'd rather camp, but you should at least go to the Biltmore to admire the architecture and enjoy a drink at the piano bar.

Hotel State Street (805-966-6586), 121 State Street, Santa Barbara. Moderate. One of the few funky yet acceptable hotels left in town. Free breakfast.

Secret Garden Inn (805-687-2300), 1908 Bath Street, Santa Barbara. Expensive. This is a beautiful, craftsman-style bed & breakfast with nine rooms, all with private bath.

Bath Street Inn (805-682-9680), 1720 Bath Street, Santa Barbara. Expensive. This beautiful Queen Anne Victorian bed & breakfast is moderately expensive, but quiet and stately. The complimentary breakfast is excellent.

The Upham (805-962-0058), 1404 De la Vina Street, Santa Barbara. Expensive. The restored Victorian hotel has cottages around a pleasant garden. It's two blocks off State Street in a quiet residential area. Highly recommended.

Beach House Inn (805-966-1126), 320 W. Yanonali Street, Santa Barbara. Moderate. Two blocks from the beach, this modest spot is clean and convenient.

Days Inn (805-963-9772), 116 Castillo Street, Santa Barbara. Moderate. Just a block from the beach, this motel has a small spa.

San Ysidro Ranch (805-969-5046; 1-800-368-6788), 900 San Ysidro Lane, Montecito. Expensive. This resort has 44 cottages in the hills above the beaches of town. Some rooms have private outdoor spas, some have wonderful views of the coast and mountains. There is tennis, a heated pool, and horseback riding.

Restaurants

Santa Barbara is a resort city and thus has some of the finest restaurants in southern California. Following are some of the best, ranging from inexpensive to outrageously pricey.

Brown Pelican (805-687-4550), 2981½ Cliff Drive, Arroyo Burro Beach Park. Inexpensive. This homey restaurant is a good deal. Try the sandwiches.

Harbor Restaurant (805-963-3311), 210 Stearns Wharf. Moderate. This is a good seafood restaurant right on the wharf.

Santa Barbara Shellfish Company (805-963-4415), 230 Stearns Wharf. Inexpensive. Takeout with picnic tables and excellent fresh seafood are served on Stearns Wharf.

Original Enterprise Fish Co. (805-962-3313), 225 State Street. Moderate. This bustling seafood emporium has fresh fish, attentive service, and a good oyster bar.

Galanga Thai Restaurant (805-899-3199), 507 State Street. Moderate. You'll find authentic Thai cuisine here, including many vegetarian dishes. Closed Wednesdays.

Joe's Cafe (805-966-4638), 536 State Street. Inexpensive. An old-fashioned local landmark. The deer and moose heads impart a certain hunting-lodge note. The food is good. This is the oldest restaurant in Santa Barbara, and one of the best deals.

El Encanto Restaurant (805-687-5000; 1-800-346-7039), 1900 Lasuen Road. Moderate. Good food with a wonderful view of the ocean. This is highly recommended—a great value.

Oyster's (805-962-9888), 9 W. Victoria Street. Moderate. This small, intimate restaurant has an outdoor patio.

Sojourner Cafe (805-965-7922), 134 E. Cañon Street. Moderate. An excellent coffeehouse that serves lunch and dinner, it's a local hangout.

Bay Cafe (805-963-2215), 131 Anacapa Street. Expensive. Located next to the Santa Barbara fish market, it offers excellent seafood. Often crowded, reservations are necessary.

La Super-Rica (805-963-4940), 622 N. Milpas. Inexpensive. Enjoy great Mexican food in a no-frills setting or take it out. No credit cards.

Louie's (805-963-7003), 1404 De La Vina Street, in the Upham Hotel. Moderate. Excellent pasta, seafood, and salads—eat on the porch, then walk through the hotel to enjoy the gardens.

Wine Cask Restaurant and Wine Bar (805-966-9463), 813 Anacapa Street. Moderate. Set in a pleasant courtyard, surrounded by tasteful shops, the restaurant serves light meals. The wine list is excellent.

PART II

Northern California

THE MOUNTAINS OF THE COASTAL RANGES trend in a south–north direction from Santa Barbara to the Oregon border. The San Andreas fault line, from San Francisco to northern Mendocino, winds north with the coastal mountains, sometimes crossing the range, sometimes running parallel. The relationship of the fault to the coastal range explains some of the variety of the northern coast.

At Point Conception in Santa Barbara County, there is an abrupt change in the coastline. Here it swings north. The ridge of a long mountain range begins its journey north. A series of important points jut into the sea above Point Conception. Between steep hillsides, there are small pocket beaches.

Above Santa Barbara County, several long, shallow bays are carved into the coast, at San Luis, Morro, Monterey, Half Moon, and Shelter Cove. Within these bays are ridges of the Coast Ranges, but also areas of low bluffs and, in front of them, long stretches of sandy beach.

Through this entire area the San Andreas fault is inland, but now near Mussel Rock, in northern San Mateo County near the San Francisco county line, the fault meets the coast and swings out to sea. It never swings far, however, and to the north of the Golden Gate, at Bolinas Point on the Point Reyes Peninsula, it touches land again. Between Mussel Rock and Bolinas lies the entrance to San Francisco Bay, and just to the north, the Marin Headlands, one of the great parklands of the California coast.

North of San Francisco from Bolinas to Bodega Bay, the fault slices through a large headland—Point Reyes—carving a valley and a long inlet, Tomales Bay. This area contains the Point Reyes Peninsula, a granite block that has been carried north along the fault line from Santa Barbara. The Point Reyes Peninsula has northern California's greatest beaches and some of its most beautiful parkland.

From Bodega Bay north to Point Arena, the San Andreas continues to run inland, parallel to the coast. Here it is closer to the coast—within a couple of miles—and it runs straight, carving out a long valley. At Alder Creek, 12 miles north of Point Arena, the fault swings out to sea and never again crosses the California coast. But from Point Arena north to Cape Vizcaino, 10 miles to the north of Westport, it is farther offshore. Along this stretch of coast—the Mendocino area—marine terraces are particularly in evidence. These are old beaches flattened by wave action and then raised above sea level by the uplift of the coastal range, rising against the knife edge of the offshore fault. The headlands here, and the coves carved by many rivers, are noted for their beauty.

At Cape Vizcaino, the marine terraces end and the high mountain wall of a particularly rugged section of the coastal range begins, which Highway 1 turns east to avoid. This change in coastline may be caused by the terminus of the fault at Cape Mendocino, 30 miles to the north. No one is sure. Highway 1 returns to the sea to the north, at Eureka. The area it avoids—called the lost coast—is impenetrable to all but the most hardy backpackers.

Highway 1 returns here in the delta formed by the Eel River—a wide tidal floodplain of bays and marshland. To the north, running to the border with Oregon, is parkland and coastal redwood forest. The forest stretches down the hills to the beach itself here—there are no marine terraces to carry the highway. Thus the road threads through the hills, sometimes lost in the forest, sometimes running near shore.

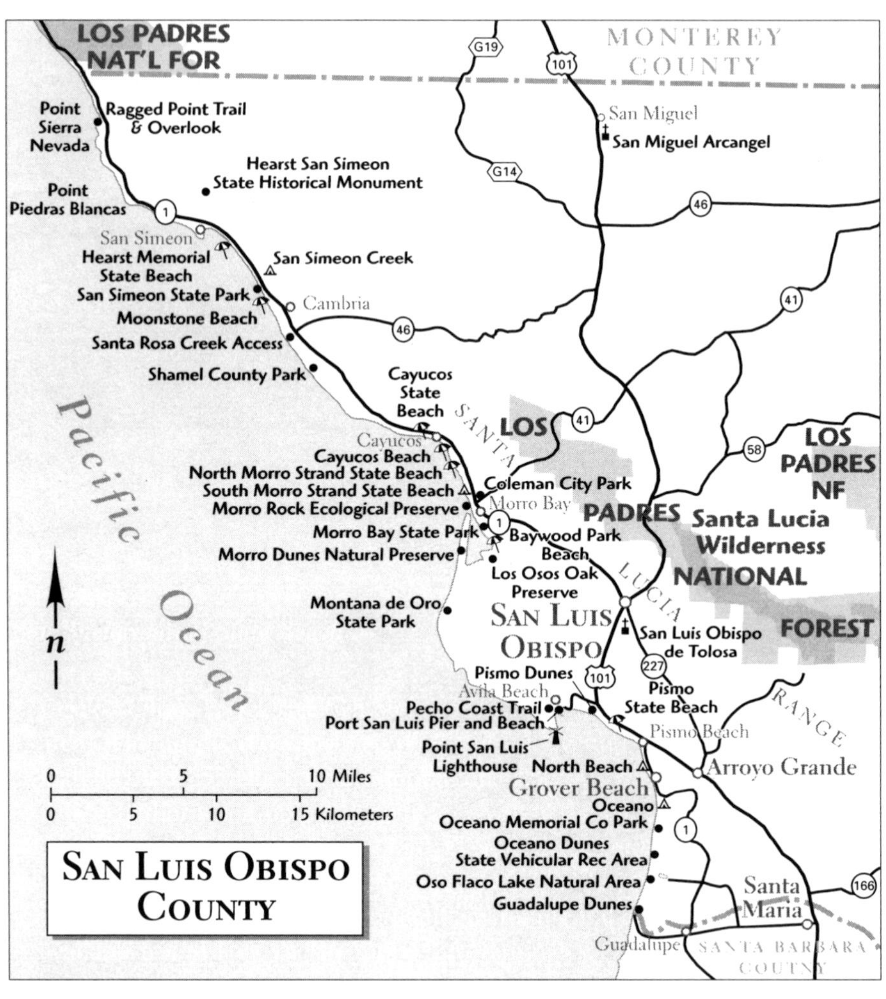

LOS PADRES NAT'L FOR
MONTEREY COUNTY
Point Sierra Nevada
Ragged Point Trail & Overlook
San Miguel
San Miguel Arcangel
Hearst San Simeon State Historical Monument
Point Piedras Blancas
San Simeon
Hearst Memorial State Beach
San Simeon Creek
San Simeon State Park
Cambria
Moonstone Beach
Santa Rosa Creek Access
Shamel County Park
Cayucos State Beach
Pacific Ocean
Cayucos
Cayucos Beach
North Morro Strand State Beach
South Morro Strand State Beach
Morro Rock Ecological Preserve
Coleman City Park
Morro Bay
Morro Bay State Park
Baywood Park Beach
Morro Dunes Natural Preserve
Los Osos Oak Preserve
LOS PADRES NATIONAL FOREST
SANTA LUCIA RANGE
LOS PADRES NF
Santa Lucia Wilderness
Montana de Oro State Park
SAN LUIS OBISPO
San Luis Obispo de Tolosa
Pismo Dunes
Avila Beach
Pismo State Beach
Pecho Coast Trail
Port San Luis Pier and Beach
Pismo Beach
Point San Luis Lighthouse
North Beach
Arroyo Grande
Grover Beach
Oceano
Oceano Memorial Co Park
Oceano Dunes State Vehicular Rec Area
Oso Flaco Lake Natural Area
Santa Maria
Guadalupe Dunes
Guadalupe
SANTA BARBARA COUNTY
n
0 5 10 Miles
0 5 10 15 Kilometers
SAN LUIS OBISPO COUNTY

CHAPTER SIX

San Luis Obispo County

SAN LUIS OBISPO COUNTY contains two large sculpted bays, San Luis Obispo Bay and Estero Bay. To their north lies the southern end of the Big Sur wilderness—and San Simeon, William Randolph Hearst's great coastal castle.

San Luis Obispo and Estero Bays are semicircles in the lee of the points for which they are named, Point San Luis and Point Estero. Like so many other California bays, they provide no protection from ocean waves.

The southern boundary of San Luis Obispo County lies at the Santa Maria River. Above the river entrance, a huge stretch of sand dunes has formed along the coast of San Luis Obispo Bay. These are the Nipomo Dunes. Much of this area is public parkland. The Oso Flaco Lake Natural Area, Oceano Dunes Vehicular Recreation Area, and the Pismo Dunes Preserve contain one of the largest sand dune habitats in the West. Here are miles of dune and the beach grass that stabilizes it. Much of the vegetation is exotic European beach grass, first introduced to North America in 1969 and now the dominant grass on the California coast—it has migrated down from San Francisco, where it was introduced, by way of the coastal waves and currents. The heavy, vertical fencelike face of the taller dunes is a reflection of this grass's ability to stabilize the flow of sand through the dunes. Little is left of the native Pacific beach grass—the only large area of this less invasive grass is found on the Point Reyes National Seashore and at the Lanphere-Christensen Dune Reserve near Arcata.

In the northern end of San Luis Bay lie Pismo Beach and the adjacent city of Pismo, which take their name from the pismo clam, more of which are found in this area than on any other section of the California coast. Intense clamming has reduced the once thriving pismo clam colonies, but at low tide they can still be dug. The city of Pismo is a low-key, unspoiled, pleasant place to stay while exploring the beach and dunes to the south.

To the north is Montana de Oro State Park, which includes Point Buchon. The park contains more than 8400 acres and miles of hiking trails, many of which lead to scenic bluffs with a fine view of the ocean. This beautiful and extensive park is often overlooked by visitors.

Just to the north is Morro Bay, an important fishing harbor with a small, sometimes dangerous entrance next to Morro Rock, a 576-foot majestic volcanic rock, now a preserve for the peregrine falcon. The small city of Morro Bay has the friendly, unpretentious flavor of a working port—it can be an excellent staging area for a family trip that explores San Simeon in the north and dune preserves in the south.

The northern end of this unassuming, often beautiful area of the coast is paradoxically the home of an immense baronial mansion, Hearst's San Simeon, designed by Julia Morgan, one of California's most notable architects. Morgan incorporated a portion of Hearst's huge art collection into the building, which became a grandiose Mediterranean hilltop village of linked houses, baroque grottoes, and pergolas. Aside from Disneyland, San Simeon is the most visited attraction in California.

Beaches and Attractions

Guadalupe Dunes ★ (805-343-2455), north of Mussel Rock and the Santa Maria River; south of Pismo Beach, Oceano. Stretching from Oso Flaco Lake to the Santa Maria River, this 6000-acre expanse of dunes lies at the seaward end of the Santa Maria floodplain. Look for Coreopsis Hill, where giant versions (up to 8 feet) of this sunny flower bloom February–April. Rambling dunes abound, including the 450-foot-high Mussel Rock, which ranks as the highest dune on the West Coast. Wildlife observers will want to bring binoculars, because this location attracts a bird population made up of almost 200 species, some of which are endangered. Be prepared for road closures due to shifting sands. There is a nude beach at the end of Oso Flaco Lake Road, but you have to walk across 4 miles of sand dunes to get there, so you are not likely to come across it unless you really want to.

Oceano Dunes Vehicular Recreation Area. (1-800-444-7275). Running from Oso Flaco to Grover City and covering more than 850 acres, this is the only area in California where it is legal to drive on the beach. Of course, there are restrictions. Beach driving in street-legal cars is allowed only between Oceano's Grand Avenue and milepost 2, and is limited to the firmly packed strip of sand near the tide's edge. For this reason, low tide is a prerequisite to this type of excursion. All-terrain vehicles (ATVs) and off-highway vehicles (OHVs) are permitted to venture beyond milepost 2 for approximately 3 miles southward, as well as in designated dune areas, provided that the wildlife protection rules are followed. Auto access to the dunes and beach is from the ramps at the ends of Grand Avenue in Grover City and Pier Avenue in Oceano. The speed limit for all vehicles is 15 mph. There is a day-use fee;

open 8 AM–11 PM. Rest rooms are provided, but there is no lifeguard on duty. Tent camping is allowed in the dune area, at specified locations. *Note*: While as many as 500 camping permits can be given out at any one time, reservations may still be necessary. Camping fees are charged. Call 1-800-444-7275 for reservations.

Beginning at Arroyo Grande Creek and stretching 1½ miles south and ¾ mile inland, the **Pismo Dunes Preserve area** is off-limits to vehicles. This, of course, makes it a deservedly popular hiking spot, since the spectacularly huge dunes here are sculpted by wind and footprints, and not by giant knobby tires.

Oso Flaco Lake Natural Area ★ is a beautiful, little-used, 75-acre lake and wetlands preserve set within the Oceano Dunes Vehicular Recreation Area, at the south end of Pismo Dunes. Oso Flaco is Spanish for "lean bear," a name bestowed by Portola when his soldiers killed a grizzly bear here in 1769. The namesake "lean" bear was more than 10 feet tall and weighed almost 400 pounds. These interconnected coastal lakes lie within beautiful sand dunes, which are frosted with wild beach-strawberry plants, as well as gooseberry and silverweed. The lakes' edges are nesting grounds for bird life, which makes them good places to look for herons, ducks, and even the endangered California least tern. To get there from Highway 1, proceed to about 4 miles north of the Santa Barbara County line, then take Oso Flaco Lake Road west to its end, about 3 miles. Trails and rest rooms are wheelchair accessible.

Pismo State Beach and **"The Five Cities"** (805-489-1869; 805-489-2684 for a recording). The city of Pismo Beach and its four related communities form one urban area tucked into the lee of Point San Luis to the north. (The five cities are Pismo, Arroyo Grande, Oceano, Grover City, and Shell Beach.) This charming area lies 90 miles north of Santa Barbara, distance enough to have protected the community against overuse, so it retains its small-town flavor. It has been either ignored or disparaged by most experts on the California coast—it has been called "an unattractive congeries of mobile homes and beach rental stands." While this may have summed up a certain aspect of the town 10 or 20 years ago, it is not an apt description today. The beach itself is part of the expansive **Nipomo Dunes**, and runs along the coast from the foot of Wilmar Street in the city of Pismo Beach to the edge of the county, which is marked by the Santa Maria River. There are many access points. Look for the following streets, which will take you to paths or stairways to the beach: Wilmar Street, Wadsworth Avenue (eight volleyball courts here), Main Street, Stimson Avenue, Ocean View Avenue, Park Avenue, Addie Street, La Sage Drive, Grand Avenue, Pier Avenue, McCarthy Street, Juanita Street, Gray Street, Surf Street, York Street, and Utah Street.

Oceano Memorial County Park is an overnight camping area with 64 sites southwest of Mendel Drive and Pier Avenue in Oceano. Some of the campsites have trailer hookups. For day use, a grassy park with picnic sites, playground, and access to the **Oceano Lagoon** is located west of Norswing Drive and north of Mendel Drive.

Callender Dunes lie just west of the town of Oceano. Look for dune mint, Indian paintbrush, and the scattered remnants of a Depression-era bohemian driftwood village, said to have been buried over time by the sand.

Pismo State Beach Oceano Campground. East of Pismo Beach and west of Oceano Lagoon on Roosevelt Drive, this site provides 82 campsites with stoves and tables, 42 of which have trailer hookups. Only one is wheelchair accessible. There are rest rooms and showers. A hiking trail begins at the eastern side of the campground, and extends around the lagoon. There are also primitive campsites along the beach, beginning ¾ mile south of Arroyo Grande Creek. For information, call 805-489-1869 or 805-489-2684; for camping reservations, call 1-800-444-7275.

Pismo State Beach North Beach Campground is on S. Dolliver Street, south of Addie Street in Pismo Beach. Its 103 campsites with stoves and tables are just 300 yards from the ocean, over the sand dunes and through the eucalyptus groves. Meadow Creek runs along the southern boundary of the campground. Beginning at a spot just off Dolliver Street and passing through a monarch butterfly preserve is a trail that extends along the creek and leads down to the beach. A trailer sanitation station is located near the entry kiosk. South of the campground off Grand Avenue is La Sage Golf Course, which is open to the public. Call 805-489-1869 or 805-489-2684; for camping reservations, call 1-800-444-7275.

©JAMES BLANK

Pismo Beach and pier

Pismo Coast Village RV Resort, adjacent to Pismo Beach, at 165 S. Dolliver Street, provides 400 RV sites with full hookups, laundry facilities, a store, and a pool. Call 805-773-1811.

Pismo Beach Pier. Situated in the middle of Pismo Beach at the end of Pomeroy and Hinds Avenues, this 1250-foot-long pier is illuminated at night, and has wheelchair access. At the north end of the parking lot are stairs leading to a wide, sandy beach area. At the left of the parking lot is a wheelchair-access road. A concession stand, bait sales, and fishing equipment rentals can all be found on the pier, and there are shops and restaurants nearby. Surfing is allowed only to the south of the pier.

Beach Access. There is a rocky pocket beach at 2555 Price Street, adjacent to the Shore Cliff Lodge and Motel, just north of Pismo Beach. Public access is through the wooden gate at the parking lot, then down a metal circular stairway.

Margo Dodd City Park can be found by taking Ocean Boulevard from Windward Avenue to Cliff Avenue in Pismo Beach. Just southward, there is a grassy blufftop park with a view of the ocean. Facilities include a gazebo, picnic tables, and benches. Park in the dirt areas west of Seaview Avenue and south of Cliff Avenue. Use extreme caution on the bluffs, which are highly eroded. At the end of Pier Avenue, there is a stairway leading to a rocky beach below. Rest rooms are available.

Ocean City Park is another grassy park set on the bluffs directly over the ocean. Take Ocean Boulevard from Vista Del Mar to Capistrano Avenue to find benches, bike racks, picnic tables, and a short concrete walkway. Access to the sandy beach and tide pools below is by stairways and the end of Vista Del Mar Avenue between Cuyama and Morro Avenues, and at the ends of Morro and Palomar Avenues. Also in Pismo Beach, at the southwest corner of Naomi Avenue and Seacliff Drive where it meets Park Place, a gravel path leads to a public walkway that will take you to a **viewing pavilion** at the top of the bluff. Benches are provided. **Memory Park**, another grassy blufftop viewing area equipped with benches, runs along the seaward edge of Seacliff Drive in Pismo Beach.

Spyglass City Park is at the southwest intersection of Spyglass Drive and Solano Road, in Pismo Beach. The bluffs here are highly eroded, so use extreme caution. Playground equipment, wheelchair-accessible picnic tables, and bike racks are available. A pathway at the northwest corner of Seacliff Drive provides additional access to the bluffs. Another trail leads down to a rocky shore and tide-pool area.

Avila State Beach. Take Highway 101 to Avila Road, then to Front Street, which will lead to this protected white sandy beach 5 miles north of Pismo Beach. It's equipped with showers, rest rooms, a playground, and volleyball standards. To the south, there is a public fishing pier with fish-cleaning facilities. During spring and summer, swimming is good, and lifeguards are on duty. This small, warm beach draws a college crowd, resulting in a relaxed and friendly atmosphere around town.

Cave Landing (aka Mallagh Landing). About ¼ mile east of Avila Beach off Cave Landing Road is a rock that juts out 150 feet into the water to form a natural pier. The Chumash Indians once fished from the rock, and buried their dead in the shallow caves of the east-facing cliffs. Just on the other side of this outcropping is a clothing-optional beach, known as **Pirate's Cove.**

Port San Luis Pier and Beach (from Highway 101, take Avila Road to Harford Drive and continue to the beach). A steam railroad was built between San Luis Obispo and the bay in 1867, eventually connecting to a wharf that was completed in 1873. During the wharf's short-lived heyday, steamships arrived several times per week, each carrying as many as 90 passengers and up to 200 tons of freight. In 1878, a seismic sea wave destroyed the structure. The port was revitalized in the 1940s as a result of the oil extraction operations in the Santa Maria River basin to the south, and became a major West Coast oil port during the war. The area is now a sport- and commercial fishing center where crab, bottom fish, and abalone make up the bulk of the catch. The 1320-foot pier is equipped with boat hoists, a fuel dock, boat trailer parking, and limited moorings for visitors. Rest rooms, lifeguards, and showers are available. Fees are charged for boat launching and storage; party fishing boats can be chartered. At nighttime, the full length of the pier is illuminated. Driving onto the pier is generally not allowed, but exceptions are made to accommodate the needs of the disabled. Two stairways lead to a small sandy beach at the foot of the seawall that runs between Port San Luis and the Union Oil Pier.

Pecho Memorial Coast Trail Harford Drive, Avila Beach. Above Port San Luis is a 3.7-mile trail that passes Port San Luis Lighthouse on the way up the coastal terrace to Montana de Oro State Park. Access is limited because the land is part of PG&E's Diablo Canyon reserve. Open only through docent-led tours. Make reservations with The Nature Conservancy, 805-541-8735. The views are worth the hassle.

Port San Luis Lighthouse This is one of seven West Coast lighthouses that were designed from a single plan. Built of redwood, the Victorian structure was completed in 1890 at a cost of $50,000. The intricate millwork was done on Mare Island in San Francisco Bay, then sent down the coast for assembly on-site. The Fresnel lens was transported from France in pieces by four separate vessels, to ensure that the entire lens could not be lost in a single shipwreck. When the heavy crystal prisms arrived in Port San Luis, they were hauled by mules up the rocky point to the site of the lighthouse. The port was a busy whaling station at the time the lighthouse was built, and the light was fueled by a plentiful supply of whale oil. These days, the Coast Guard uses an automated system for both the beacon and the nearby foghorn.

Laguna Lake Park ★ on Madonna Road off Highway 101, south of San Luis Obispo. This 150-acre park provides the setting for one of the few remaining natural lakes in the county. People come here to fish and windsurf. Campsites and picnic spots are also available. This is a good spot for birding, since the lake is a nesting ground for herons, rails, and grebes and a winter stopover for a variety of migrating ducks.

Mission San Luis Obispo de Tolosa 782 Monterey Street, San Luis Obispo. The fifth mission to be built in Alta California, this one is reputed to be the first to use red-tiled roofs to fireproof against the Indians' flaming arrows. It was founded in 1772 by Father Serra. The present structure was not completed until 1794, replacing original buildings that had been constructed of saplings, tules, adobe, and tar. Almost 800 Chumash Indians lived at or

Avila

Rene Avant—Coast Ranger

■ Rene Avant grew up as a "park brat," the son of a state park ranger. During the 1950s and '60s, the state park system still moved its rangers around in order to expose them to many different parks and environments, to make them well rounded. (It gave up the practice in the '70s and '80s because it was so expensive to move whole households.) Growing up, Rene went all over California, living in some of the most beautiful places in the state, in parks such as Torrey Pines, Calaveras Big Trees, Silver Strand, San Clemente, Fort Ross, and Salt Point.

One day in the '60s, Rene's father took him on a trip to Montana De Oro, a state park in San Luis Obispo County. On the trip, Rene's father said that Montana De Oro was the place where he wanted to live.

The park is even better now, 30 years after Rene visited with his father. Montana De Oro was originally in private hands, used for ranching and hunting. Over three decades it has recovered to its natural state; native wildflowers have spread over the meadows, badgers and coyotes have come back, and finally, even mountain lions have returned.

Now Rene is in his early 50s and a park ranger just like his father. He has a lot of seniority, possibly more than any other active ranger. (Seniority is how park assignments are chosen these days.) Able to get assigned to almost any park, Rene has chosen to live in Montana De Oro for 20 years. When he tells you that it's the best park in California for a ranger to live, and possibly the best park in California period, it's advice worth listening to.

A good place for a ranger to live and a good park for the general public to visit are not necessarily one and the same. A ranger has to determine whether the park is one in which he can do his job well and whether it provides a good environment for raising a family.

Montana De Oro is a big park, with an incredible variety of micro-environments. Within its more than 9000 acres, the park has 7 miles of beautiful coastline, ranging from dunes to sandy beach to steep cliffs. Much of the coast is marine headlands, below which are productive tide pools. The park stretches back from the beach into a wilderness area that runs from coastal meadow to forest to the steep slopes of Allen Peak. There are miles of hiking and horse trails and campsites for equestrians,

hikers, and car campers. Two active streams are known for their steelhead runs, and the land is home to birds and animals of all kinds—squirrels and mountain lions, sea gulls and snowy plovers.

Much of the time, only one ranger is responsible for all this: Rene Avant. You might think that this would be too much of a job, but there are features to Montana De Oro that make it possible for a single ranger like Rene to run this big park. Most important is access. Only one road leads into the park; everyone who enters has to leave the same way he came. (Once some bank robbers escaping down the coast highway turned into the park looking for a short cut. They were caught.) Rene can keep track of who goes in and out. He also has two excellent horses, Chip and Charley, who have been at the park as long as he has—20 years—and know the backwoods trails by heart.

Another benefit for a ranger is that the park offers diverse work. Like all rangers, Rene's work is determined by the park itself. For example, if the protected snowy plover is nesting, Rene may spend his time making sure they are left alone. Or if people are hiking in the backcountry, he may find himself riding Chip or Charley to help them out. Because the park is so close to a city, Rene sometimes leads schoolchildren on interpretive nature walks. Or he may find himself policing a camp site, making a DUI arrest, or dealing with a "273.5," which is the police code for spousal abuse. (Rene says that the stress of getting packed up for a camping trip sometimes brings out the worst in people.) Rene never knows exactly what he's going to do when he gets up in the morning. That's part of the excitement of a great park like Montana De Oro.

Another benefit that appeals to a ranger is that although the park is a great wilderness, the ranger's house is close to civilization. Rene has lived in state parks where it was possible to go shopping only once a month, because the nearest store was so far away. But Montana De Oro is only 15 minutes from great shopping in San Louis Obispo. Moreover, the park is halfway between the cultural centers of Los Angeles and San Francisco.

These are concerns specific to a ranger. A regular visitor to the park will find surfing, sea kayaking, hang gliding, horseback riding, hiking, mountain biking, tide-pooling, and surf casting along the park's 7 miles of coastline (steelhead fishing is not allowed).

Moreover, though the beauty of Montana De Oro is no secret, it is easy to find solitude, even on a summer weekend. Go a mile down a hiking trail heading east away from the beach, and the chances are you'll see no one else the entire day. Hike a half-mile up the beach, and the same thing happens.

We asked Rene for some recommendations of great things to do in Montana De Oro. He said to hike the Bluff Trail on the south side of Spooner's Cove. To the north, you can see Piedras Blancas. If it's cold, he suggests the Coon Creek Trail, at the south end of the park. In 3 miles, you cross seven or eight pretty bridges as you walk into a pristine natural area and a bishop pine forest. Finally, he recommends a five-mile hike along the sand spit where there are lovely dunes; if you walk north, you're likely not to see anyone. ■

near the mission in 1798; by 1859 the few who had remained succumbed to a cholera epidemic. In 1875, a New England–style wooden belfry was added, and wooden siding and shingles were attached to the outside of the building. These remained until 1933, when the embellishments were finally removed, and the mission was restored to its original appearance.

San Luis Obispo (chamber of commerce: 805-781-2777), Highway 1, 14 miles southeast of Morro Bay. This small, comfortable town sits in a valley 2000 feet below the Santa Lucia Mountains, and provides a friendly, interesting crossroads for beach-seekers. It has its own theater, opera, and symphony companies, a Mozart Festival, and art galleries. Over 40 wineries and vineyards are located in the San Luis Obispo Valley. The town of San Luis Obispo developed around the mission. By the 1840s and '50s, it had become a merchandising and marketing center for the ranchos in the surrounding territory. Between 1884 and 1894, the Southern Pacific Railroad brought 2000 Chinese people to the town to excavate the eight tunnels through Cuesta Pass. On a walking tour of the streets surrounding Mission Plaza, you can visit the Ah Louis store, which served as a countinghouse, bank, and post office for this early Chinese population. The tour also includes stops at the **County Historical Museum** and the **Murray Adobe**.

Los Osos Valley, Los Osos Valley Road from Morro Bay to San Luis Obispo. Early Spanish explorers named the area for los osos—"the bears"—most likely because there were once so many California grizzlies living here. In the early 1800s, the valley was used for cattle grazing as part of the 32,000-acre Rancho Canada de los Osos y Pecho y Islay. The northern edge of the valley is rimmed by a 20-million-year-old chain of volcanic peaks, which runs from Islay Hill southeast of San Luis Obispo to Morro Rock and several submerged peaks beyond.

Los Osos Oaks State Preserve ★ south of Los Osos Valley Road at Palomino Drive in Los Osos. Two miles of marked trails wind through an ancient grove of California live oaks, some of which are estimated to be from 600 to 800 years old. There are vista points along the way, overlooking Los Osos Valley and the Santa Lucia Mountains. Shell fragments and traces of charcoal are reminders that this land was once home to the Chumash Indians. Los Osos Creek, a perennial stream, marks the eastern edge of the preserve, and is shaded by sycamore, laurel, willow, and cottonwood trees. Freshwater fish live here, including the riffle sculpin and prickly sculpin. Throughout the park, wildlife abounds, and you will probably see some adorable or fascinating creature while hiking. You may or may not see the equally abundant rattlesnakes and poison oak, so be alert and stick to the trails.

Montana de Oro State Park Three miles south of San Luis Obispo on Highway 101, take the Los Osos/Baywood Park exit and drive 12 miles west on Los Osos Valley Road, which becomes Pecho Valley Road. Then take Pecho Valley Road to the park entrance. Golden poppies, wild mustard, and monarch butterflies converge in this park named Mountain of Gold by early Spanish explorers. Covering about 9000 acres of land, including 7 miles of coastline, Montano de Oro also encompasses sand dunes, jagged, cliffs, coves, caves, and reefs. An entrance fee is charged at the gate, and varies depending on whether and where you will be camping. Although parking and wheelchair-accessible rest rooms are provided, there is no potable water within the park, so be sure to bring something to drink.

Fifty miles of trails provide ample opportunity to explore the varied beauty of this landscape, some of which are available for equestrian use. The Hazard Canyon Trail, 1.5 miles south of the park entrance, is a ¼-mile-long path through the eucalyptus groves where the butterflies nest October–March. There are several trails leading to vista points along the blufftop; they begin along the road between the park office and Coon Creek to the south.

Along the rocky shore, people come to fish, scuba dive, and tide-pool. However, these beaches are rather untamed, with rough salt-and-pepper sand punctuated by rocky outcroppings and sea caves, and pounded by strong surf. The smoothest, calmest beach is at **Spooner's Cove**, where there is a nice crescent of sand, picnic tables, and a parking area. Across from Spooner's Cove is the old Spooner Ranch House, which is now used as park headquarters. Some intrepid surfers venture through the woods to the small beach at **Hazard Cove**; this is not recommended, since the area is aptly named for its dangerous surf. The Hazard Canyon Reef begins offshore at the north end of the park and extends south for more than 9 miles. It is a thriving sea-life ecosystem, providing a home for over 90 fish species, 100 species of algae, and other animals including sea stars, abalone, crabs, and hydroids, to name just a few. **Corallina Cove** sits at the southern end of the park, and can be reached by following a trail along the bluff from the parking area. Nude sunbathers favor the beach area about 1 mile south of Montana de Oro's main public beach.

East of the ranger's station above the Spooner's Cove beach and day-use parking area, there are 50 campsites with tables and stoves. Four environmental campsites are available. There is also a special equestrian camping area about ¼ mile south of the park entrance on Pecho Valley Road. It contains two sites, each of which is limited to 25 horses and 12 vehicles. The equestrian camps are available by reservation only. A fee is required for all camping. For reservations, call 1-800-444-7275. For park information, call 805-528-0513.

Morro Dunes Natural Preserve ★ on the ocean side of Morro Bay. This is a popular destination for bird-watching and clam digging. Some choose to fish. The spit itself is 3 miles long, and is flanked by 85-foot-high dunes. Tiny gray and white snowy plovers nest here, laying their eggs in the pebbly sand. South of the spit is a small preserve for the endangered Morro Bay kangaroo rat. There are a couple of ways to access this coastal area. One is by motorboat taxi, which departs from the Embarcadero Road marina in Morro Bay. Another is by way of a dirt road that can be found just off Pecho Valley Road, a half mile south of its junction with Los Osos (four-wheel-drive vehicles are probably required for this route). Finally, there is a hiking trail at the Shark Inlet parking lot.

Morro Bay Accessway, at the north end of Doris Avenue, north of Mitchell Drive, Cuesta-by-the-Sea. At this location is a 40-foot-wide dirt path leading to a popular birding area on Morro Bay. On-street parking is limited. The legal status of this accessway is in dispute—this passage may not be public. Take Avila Road to **See Canyon Road** for a scenic back road route to Morro Bay.

Baywood Park Beach, west of Pasadena Drive between Santa Ysabel Avenue and Baywood Way, Baywood Park. From the small parking area on Pasadena Drive, a path leads to a sandy beach area with picnic tables and benches. The Morro Bay mudflats are accessible from the beach when the tide is low. The intertidal areas provide essential forage for thousands of migrating waterfowl, and extensive and diverse habitats attract many bird species, particularly over the winter. There are also many types of clams in the mudflats, including gaper clams, razor clams, and pismo clams.

Morro Bay State Park ★ southwest of Highway 1 at South Bay Boulevard, Morro Bay. With more than 1500 acres of salt marsh, sandy beach, wetlands, and other terrain within its boundaries, Morro Bay State Park offers a wide variety of activities and experiences. Entrances to this area are found 1 mile south of Highway 1 on South Bay Boulevard and at the south end of Main Street in Morro Bay. Trails from White Point traverse the volcanic Black Mountain, the extensive marshlands of Chorro Delta, the Chorro Creek Estuary, and several archaeological sites. The park provides sweeping views of Morro Bay and the southern mudflats at the mouth of Los Osos Creek. The best vantage points are from the peak of Black Mountain and from the **Museum of Natural History** at White Point. Open daily 10 AM–5 PM, the museum, which is wheelchair accessible, provides exhibits on the wildlife, ecology, and Native American history of the surrounding area.

Just south of the park's entrance there is a protected heron rookery. While visitors are not allowed to enter here, there is plenty to observe from the road. Herons nest in the tops of the eucalyptus trees January– August. Call 805-772-7434 for more information.

To the north of the museum there is a small cartop boat-launch ramp and a path to the beach. Rest rooms and a dock with berths are to the south. There is a 135-unit campground with tables and stoves. Twenty of the sites have hookups for electricity and water, and laundry tubs and showers are available. Two group camps are reserved for parties of 30 or 50, and require advance booking. Some of the campsites are wheelchair accessible. There are fees for both overnight and day use of this park. For campground reservations, call 1-800-444-7275.

Sweet Springs Marsh, accessible from Ramona Street in Morro Bay. This 25-acre wetland with two freshwater ponds sits upland of a saltwater marsh along the bay. Monarch butterflies spend the winter in the eucalyptus trees in this area.

City of Morro Bay, 12.5 miles northwest of San Luis Obispo. In 1870, this town was established around two wharves, which existed for the export of local dairy and ranch products. Schooners brought redwoods from Santa Cruz County. By the turn of the century, vacationers began to come to the village to camp on the beach. It wasn't until the 1940s that Morro Bay began to develop its contemporary identity as an important fishing center. Due to a sharp decline in the abalone population, the town no longer retains its status as the heart of the abalone-harvesting industry, and only one processing plant operates in the area. Still, the fishing out of Morro Bay is good, counting halibut, sole, rockfish, lingcod, salmon, and albacore among the regular catches.

There are four public piers on Morro Bay. **The North T-Pier** stretches for 190 feet and accommodates fishing boats, dockside fishermen, and crab trappers. There is public parking west of the Embarcadero. Rest rooms are wheelchair accessible. Restaurants, a bait and tackle shop, fish-loading facilities, and a public shower are located on the pier or close by. Coast Guard boats are berthed at the north pier, and are usually open for tours. (Call 805-772-1293 for an appointment.) **The South T-Pier** is equipped with slips and moorings for both commercial and pleasure boats, and is a likely spot for chartering a vessel for ocean fishing. **Dune and Embarcadero Pier** is the third, and it provides benches and picnic tables. The 50-foot-long **Second Street Pier**, at the south end of Second Street in Baywood Park, is a great place to take in the view, as well as a favorite location for anglers, who catch northern anchovy, lingcod, and black perch. To the east is a cypress grove with benches. There is also public access to the bay at the south end of First Street.

All of Morro Bay's streets along the Embarcadero between Beach and Anchor end at the bayshore. There is also a series of variously equipped parks along this stretch of road. At the south end of the Embarcadero is **Tidelands Park**. A two-lane boat ramp with two docks sits adjacent to this park's small picnic area, which has wheelchair-accessible rest rooms at the south end of the parking lot. Mooring of boats at ramps and buoys is not allowed. There is a fish-cleaning station near the ramps, and there are parking spaces for boat trailers. From the west end of Morro Bay Boulevard at Front and Embarcadero, a stairway leads down to the petite **Centennial Park**, which affords benches, a shuffleboard court, and a giant chessboard. At the end of Front Street you will find parking and wheelchair-accessible rest rooms. **Dunes Street Bluff and Park** is located one block north of Harbor Street on the Embarcadero, adjacent to Morro Bay. It is a small, grassy park area with tables and benches, a deck for fishing and sight-seeing, and a small boat dock with slips. To the west of Coleman Drive and the Embarcadero is **Coleman City Park**, an area with playground equipment, picnic tables, fire rings, and rest rooms. Head north for access to the sand dunes and Morro Strand. A small, protected sandy beach lies to the south. Call 805-772-6278 for more information about these parks.

©JAMES BLANK

Morro Bay and beach

Morro Rock Ecological Preserve ★ at the west end of Coleman Drive, Morro Bay. Standing 576 feet high, Morro Rock is the northernmost above-water member of a chain of volcanic peaks beginning near the city of San Luis Obispo. Beginning in 1880, more than a million tons of stone were quarried from Morro Rock over a period of 89 years. The location achieved protected status in 1969, when all quarrying was halted to preserve the habitat of the peregrine falcon. It remains a state ecological preserve for the still-endangered peregrine, and therefore you may access the rock only visually—no climbing or other encroachment is allowed. Fishing, hiking, and parking around the base are permitted. A large parking area and rest rooms are located to the northeast of the rock. *Note*: The breakwater on the southwest side can be hazardous—watch for heavy surf. To the north of the rock there is a small protected beach, but parking here is limited.

Atascadero State Beach (aka Morro Strand State Beach, South)

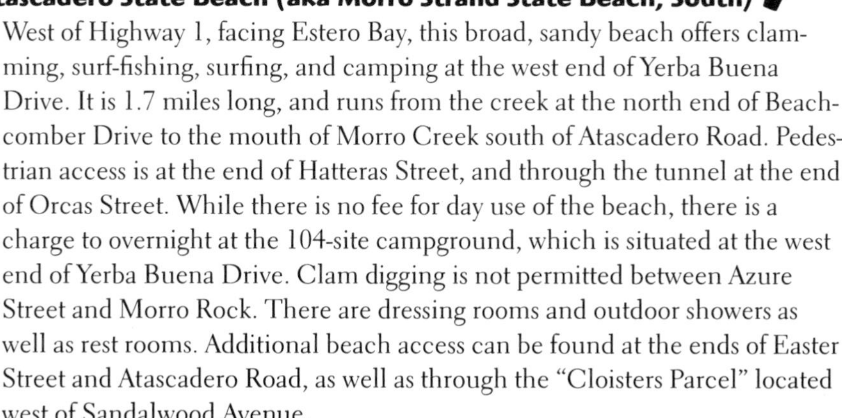

West of Highway 1, facing Estero Bay, this broad, sandy beach offers clamming, surf-fishing, surfing, and camping at the west end of Yerba Buena Drive. It is 1.7 miles long, and runs from the creek at the north end of Beachcomber Drive to the mouth of Morro Creek south of Atascadero Road. Pedestrian access is at the end of Hatteras Street, and through the tunnel at the end of Orcas Street. While there is no fee for day use of the beach, there is a charge to overnight at the 104-site campground, which is situated at the west end of Yerba Buena Drive. Clam digging is not permitted between Azure Street and Morro Rock. There are dressing rooms and outdoor showers as well as rest rooms. Additional beach access can be found at the ends of Easter Street and Atascadero Road, as well as through the "Cloisters Parcel" located west of Sandalwood Avenue.

Morro Strand State Beach (North). West of Studio Drive, 24th Street to Chaney Avenue, Cayucos. A long, skinny, sandy beach stretching almost 2 miles along Estero Bay, from 24th Street to the south end of Studio Drive, this is a good place for beachcombing, clamming, and fishing, just 1 mile north of Morro Bay. Camping and RV sites (without hookups) require a fee. A paved parking lot, rest rooms, and picnic tables are located at the end of 24th Street, and there is additional unpaved parking space at the north end of Studio Drive. Access to the beach is by stairs and paths along Studio Drive, 200 feet north of Juanita Avenue, and at the ends of Coronado, Mayer, Mannix, and Cody Avenues. The park entrance is along Yerba Buena Street. Restaurants and groceries are nearby in Morro Bay. Call 805-772-7434 for more information about these beaches, south and north.

Cayucos Beach, along Pacific Avenue between 1st and 22nd Streets, Cayucos. The town of Cayucos was a dairy farming center when it was founded in 1875. During the early 1900s, the present-day Veterans Memorial Building housed an abalone-drying enterprise. The abalones were shipped to San Francisco and Japan at a rate of about 3 tons per year. The existing Cayucos Pier replaced an earlier, 940-foot version that was built in 1875 by Capt. James Cass. Back then, the pier was a regular stop for the ships of the Pacific Steamship Company. Just a block east of the pier entrance, Captain Cass's Victorian home still stands. Flanked by private property on both sides, there are nine stairways marked PUBLIC BEACHWALK along Pacific Avenue between 1st and 22nd Streets leading to the sandy beach below. Facilities include rest rooms and picnic areas.

Cayucos State Beach is west of N. Ocean Drive between Cayucos Road and E Street, Cayucos. This beach has a popular, wheelchair-accessible fishing pier that is lit at night. Group barbecue and picnic facilities are located in the patio area adjacent to the Veteran's Memorial Building. (See Cayucos Beach, above.) Parking is along Ocean Front Road, and in the lot next to the patio area. Rest rooms are available. Reservations for the picnic and barbecue facilities can be made by calling the County General Services Department at 805-781-5219.

Cambria. Historically, this town has drawn sustenance from copper and quicksilver mining, as well as from farm-related trade and activity. Minerals, dairy products, and cattle hides were loaded onto schooners in San Simeon Bay until 1874, when William Leffingwell built a pier in the cove at Cambria. In 1894, the coastal shipping trade ended when a rail line connected the town of Cambria to San Luis Obispo. Still, the town remained fairly isolated until the completion of the coastal highway in 1937.

On a tree-lined ridge at the top of Hillcrest Drive (off Main Street) sits an unusual residence, now a California Historical Landmark. Built by local contractor Art Beal, or "Captain Nitwit," the several-story home is made of cement and decorated with embedded found objects, such as seashells, pieces of glass, beer cans, and auto parts. Paths crisscross the surrounding terraced hillside.

There is a series of accessways to the sandy beach and rocky shore in the Cambria Pines area along Sherwood Drive at the ends of Wedgewood, Castle, Harvey, and Lampton Streets. There is also a park at the end of Lampton Street. From Highway 1, take Ardath Drive to Sherwood Drive.

Shamel County Park is located at Windsor Boulevard and Nottingham Drive. Parking and beach access are at the northern edge of the park, which offers a playground, a grassy playing field, rest rooms, and fire pits. A swimming pool is open during the summer months only.

Santa Rosa Creek can be accessed west of Highway 1 near the south end of Moonstone Beach Drive. A parking area and benches are adjacent to the ocean. To get to the Santa Rosa Creek marshlands, proceed to the south of the parking lot. There are hiking trails that run northward along the bluffs, overlooking the rocky shoreline and tide pools.

Leffingwell Landing is also found along Moonstone Beach Drive, ¼ mile south of its intersection with Highway 1. North of the parking lot stands a cypress grove that shades picnic tables. This is a good location for spotting sea otters, since they frequent the rocky tide-pool areas just offshore and to the south, part of the California Sea Otter Game Refuge. There are wheelchair-accessible rest rooms here, as well as a ramp for cartop boat launching, and fishing areas. A path and stairs lead down to the beach. Hiking trails extend northward along the bluffs to the **Moonstone Beach Drive Vista Point**, which provides a view of the Moonstone Beach area of San Simeon State Beach. *Note*: These bluffs are highly eroded, and caution is warranted when hiking along the coastside trails to the south of the parking area.

San Simeon, on Highway 1 at San Simeon Road. This coastal village was a whaling station before it was purchased in 1865 by George Hearst, who promptly constructed a wharf, a store, warehouses, and a pier so that ranching and mining products could be exported more efficiently. The Sebastian General Store, established in 1873, has changed very little over the years, and offers a glimpse of the history of this tiny port town.

In and surrounding San Simeon, there are many ways to see and experience the beach. At the corner of Cliff Drive and San Simeon Avenue, there is access to a sandy cove beach by way of a public path along the north bank of Arroyo del Padre Juan Creek. On-street parking can be found near where the path begins, directly south of the Cavalier Inn, which is located west of Highway 1 and Hearst Avenue. More beach access is available at the west end of Pico Avenue, just south of Pico Creek, where there are benches looking out over the coast and a short stairway leading to a sandy beach. There are also five vista-point parking lots providing ocean views along Highway 1, the first at 3 miles south of San Simeon Road, and the last at 3.5 miles north of the town of San Simeon.

San Simeon State Beach (805-927-2035; 1-800-444-7275) West of Highway 1 and Moonstone Beach Drive, this wide and sandy state beach runs from San Simeon Creek to Santa Rosa Creek. Its 500-acre campground lies east of the highway off San Simeon Creek Road, and provides 201 campsites (some with wheelchair access), rest rooms, a bicycle and hiker group site, a trailer sanitation station, and an overflow trailer camp to the south of San Simeon Creek. The creek itself is accessible by short trails that begin at the lower campground. To cross the creek, proceed to its east end, where there is a footbridge. There is a camping fee, and reservations (1-800-444-7275) are recommended in summer.

Also south of San Simeon Creek is **Moonstone Beach**, named for the milky white agates that can be found in the sand. Vernal pools of collected winter rainfall appear in this area in the late spring, gradually developing into concentric rings of color as the water evaporates and the native plants cycle into bloom. At the southwest corner of the campground, there is a short path that leads under the Highway 1 San Simeon Creek Overpass to the beach.

William R. Hearst Memorial State Beach (805-927-2020), west of Highway 1 on San Simeon Road, San Simeon. This 8-acre park has a 1000-foot-long fishing pier, picnic facilities, and a protected beach. Located directly below Hearst Castle, this calm and sunny location is an excellent spot for swimming, as it is protected from wind and heavy surf by scenic San Simeon Point. A clothing-optional section known as the nude cove is past a group of pilings at the edge of the park. You can rent fishing equipment and charter boats at the west end of the main parking lot. There is a set of picnic tables in a beautiful eucalyptus grove north of the pier, and another in the grassy area near the park entrance. Some fire pits are available. Additional parking can be found to the north of the eucalyptus grove. There are also stairways and paths to the beach located at the Pico Avenue cul-de-sac just south of Pico Creek, and along the north bank of Arroyo del Padre Juan Creek. The park is open from 8 AM (earlier in the summer) to sunset, and is equipped with rest rooms. A parking fee is charged.

Hearst San Simeon State Historical Monument (Hearst Castle) east of Highway 1 on San Simeon Road. This 123-acre state monument is part of what was once the private estate of William Randolph Hearst. Located within 235,000 acres of private Hearst Ranch holdings, it is now open to the public, with daily tours approximately 8:20 AM–3 PM. There are extended hours during the summer months; no tours are held on Thanksgiving, Christmas, and New Year's Day.

William Randolph Hearst was the only child of George and Phoebe Apperson Hearst, and inherited a fortune in mining and real estate holdings, as well as a radio and newspaper empire, when his mother died. La Cuesta Encantada is the famous estate, or "castle," that sits atop a 1500-foot hill overlooking the Pacific. This palatial dwelling was built over the course of 30 years, beginning in 1919, and was designed by the famous architect Julia Morgan with significant input from Hearst. The lives of both of them are highlighted in exhibits at the visitors center at the bottom of the hill.

The main house, or La Casa Grande, has 115 rooms, and is flanked by three spacious guest houses. Although the general theme of the building has a Mediterranean feel, a unique combination of styles composes the overall design and defies all facile attempts at definition. Hearst used his estate as an entertainment center for the rich and powerful, and showcased his immense art collection and private exotic zoo to great effect. Portions of these collections remain at the estate, and there is still a small menagerie representing some of the rare animal species once gathered by Hearst. The expansive, beautifully landscaped gardens are embellished with pools, fountains, and statuary.

The only way to visit the estate is by taking one (or more) of five different tours of the grounds. Recommended for first-time visitors, Tour 1 leads visitors through the gardens and one guest house as well as through the ground floor of the main house, where a Hearst home movie is shown in the theater room. Tour 2 explores the upper floors of the main building, including Mr. Hearst's private quarters, his study, the guest rooms and library, and the kitchen. Tour 3 covers the north wing of the main building, one of the guest houses, and the garden. Guests who choose this tour also watch a documentary about the construction of the grounds. Tour 4 spends more time in the gardens, but also includes the wine cellar, the Neptune pool dressing rooms, and two levels of the largest guest house. All of these daytime tours include visits to both pools and last approximately 1¾ hours. The evening tour features a living history of the 1930s and covers highlights of the entire estate. All tours leave by shuttle bus from the visitors parking lot, which is located just off Highway 1. Wear comfortable shoes; considerable stair-climbing is involved. Tour 1 is the easiest, with only 150 steps to manage. Only the first three tours are offered year-round. Tour 4 is available only April–October, and the evening tours take place March–May and September–December. Smoking is restricted. Rest rooms are available. Wheelchair access is available by bus, and requires a 10-day advance reservation; call 805-927-2020. There are entrance fees, and reservations for the tours are highly recommended; call 1-800-444-4445.

Piedras Blancas Lighthouse on Point Piedras Blancas. Originally the site of a lookout for the purpose of spotting approaching whales, the lighthouse was built here in 1874. The Fresnel lens and iron lantern house are no longer on-site; they were removed in 1949 and are now on display in the nearby town of Cambria. The lighthouse grounds are currently used by the US Fish and Wildlife Service for the study of sea otters, and are therefore not open to the public.

Point Piedras Blancas, west of Highway 1, 7 miles south of Ragged Point. The "white rocks" at the point are a favorite hangout for sea lions, harbor seals, and cormorants. The surrounding coastal land was once home to a small population of Salinan Indians, who made camp along the bluffs during the winter, then traveled inland a few miles to gather food during the summer.

Point Sierra Nevada, west of Highway 1, 3.5 miles south of Ragged Point. Just south of the point, the Arroyo de la Cruz empties into the ocean. West of the highway is a small freshwater marsh, which is frequented by a variety of bird life.

Ragged Point Trail and Overlook is 15 miles north of San Simeon, west of the Ragged Point Inn and north of the Ragged Point peninsula. This grassy blufftop terrace provides scenic views of surf-washed rocks and beaches directly below, and of the Big Sur coast to the north. A steep switchback trail leads past a waterfall to a small sandy beach and rocky shore. Taking abalone from this location is prohibited. Parking and rest rooms are available.

Lodging

IN ARROYO GRANDE

Best Western Casa Grande Inn (805-481-7398), 850 Oak Park Road. Moderate. Just 2 miles from the Pismo Dunes beaches, this inn offers amenities including a pool, spa, gym, and game room.

Crystal Rose Inn (805-481-5566), 789 Valley Road. Expensive. You can see the sand dunes from the upper floor of this ornate, century-old Victorian home, which is painted in four shades of pink. A bountiful rose garden supplies each of the guest rooms with fragrant bouquets. Five rooms, two cottages, and four suites, all of which are nonsmoking, are furnished with carved mahogany, rosewood, and oak antiques. A parlor and sitting room offer games, jigsaw puzzles, a grand piano, and a fireplace. On weekends, there is a 2-night minimum stay. Breakfast and dinner are included. When the inn is full, meals are served in the restaurant, which is also open to nonguests. Otherwise, the upstairs dining room is used. The inn is surrounded by farmland, with the coast just 1 mile away, as the crow flies. "Not appropriate" for children under 16. Pets are not allowed.

IN PISMO BEACH

Best Western Shore Cliff Lodge (805-773-4671), 2555 Price Street. Moderate to expensive. The grounds here are an added attraction to this well-tended hotel, which provides a heated pool, lighted tennis courts, and a restaurant. The building sits on a high bluff, from which a stairway leads to a sandy cove. Two-bedroom suites and spacious rooms with ocean views and/or efficiency kitchens are available.

The Sandcastle Inn (805-773-2422), 100 Stimson Avenue. Expensive. For those who love the seacoast, the location of this hotel-condominium can't be surpassed: It is directly on the beach. Each plush guest room comes with a balcony, and continental breakfast is included in the room rate. The pier is within easy walking distance.

The Sea Crest Resort Motel (805-773-4608), 2241 Price Street. Moderate. Cliffside in the northern part of town, this 160-room motel combines dramatic views with reasonable prices. A heated pool is available. A few of the units have two bedrooms. A steep wooden stairway provides access to the sand below.

IN SHELL BEACH

The Cliffs at Shell Beach (1-805-773-5000 or in California: 1-800-826-7827), 2757 Shell Beach Road. Expensive. This five-story blue and white resort sits on a bluff overlooking the beach below and the ocean beyond. With 166 rooms and 27 suites, the Cliffs presents a wide assortment of amenities in an environment that combines luxury and informality. The decor ranges from tropical in the restaurant and lounge, to white and light in the lobby, to more traditional English and French in the guest rooms. Suites have white marble baths, Jacuzzi tubs, and ocean-view balconies. The resort offers complimentary valet parking, a fitness center, beauty salon, gift shop, conference rooms, catering, room service, and a bell staff. The pool and spa areas are adorned with an island waterfall theme. There is music and dancing nightly in the lounge. Children under 12 are free. Nonsmoking rooms are available.

IN AVILA

The Inn at Avila Beach (805-595-2300), 256 Front Street. Moderate. Plain, clean, and reasonably priced, this motel has a direct view of the beach. Most rooms are equipped with kitchens.

IN MORRO BAY

Best Western Tradewinds (805-772-7376), 225 Beach Street. Moderate. This perfectly adequate motel is the closest lodging to Morro Rock. Just one block from the waterfront, it offers 24 rooms, each with coffeemaker, TV, and refrigerator.

The Inn at Morro Bay (805-772-5651), 60 State Park Road. Expensive. This is a romantic, luxurious place to stay, set back from the main strip of shops and restaurants in Morro Bay. It can be found just inside the boundaries of Morro Bay State Park, on the bay. The 96 suite-sized guest rooms are thoughtfully designed and equipped, with gas fireplaces, water-view decks, and cathedral ceilings. The shaded grounds are nicely landscaped, and a pool is available.

The Harbor House Inn (805-772-2711), 1095 Main Street. Moderate. This well-kept, reasonably priced lodging is within easy walking distance of the waterfront. All rooms are equipped with coffeemaker and cable TV.

El Morro Lodge (805-772-5633), 1206 Main Street. Moderate. Comfortable and nicely maintained, this Spanish-style inn provides easy access to the bay at a very reasonable price. The 27 rooms are spacious, and most have balconies. Fireplaces are available in some rooms. The penthouse suite has a whirlpool, fireplace, and private sun deck.

Embarcadero Inn (805-772-2700; 1-800-292-7625), 456 Embarcadero Road. Expensive. Tastefully decorated rooms have plenty of space. Some also come with fireplace, wet bar, microwave, and balcony. Right on the Embarcadero, you're in the middle of Morro Bay's restaurant and shopping district.

Gray's Inn & Gallery (805-772-3911), 561 Embarcadero. Expensive. There are only three rooms in this unique inn on Morro Bay's waterfront. The rooms are behind or above the art gallery, also operated by the owner. Each room has a good-sized patio overlooking the harbor, providing remarkable sea views.

Blue Sail Inn (805-772-7132; 805-772-2766), 851 Market Avenue. Moderate. The rooms are modern, comfortable, and tastefully decorated in cool pastels. Restaurants, shopping, and beaches are only a few blocks away. Most rooms come with a view of the harbor and Morro Bay.

La Serena Inn (805-772-5665; 1-800-248-1511), 990 Morro Avenue. Moderate. The spacious rooms are decorated in earth tones. Some have a striking view of Morro Rock. The restaurants and shops of the Embarcadero are a 5-minute walk, and Morro Rock Beach is a short drive.

IN CAYUCOS

The Beachwalker Inn (805-995-2133), 501 S. Ocean Avenue. Moderate. The Beachwalker is an uncomplicated, two-story, 24-room lodging located just one block from the beach. Ocean views, fireplaces, and kitchenettes are available. All rooms have coffeemaker and cable TV.

IN CAMBRIA

Blue Whale Inn (805-927-4647), 6736 Moonstone Beach Drive. Expensive. Situated directly across from the ocean at the northern end of town, the Blue Whale is a six-suite inn, uniquely designed so that each spacious guest room has an open view of the water. The centrally located common room is comfortably furnished, and its windows offer panoramic coastal views. A garden set with stone walkways, benches, and waterways creates the visual foreground for these sweeping seascapes. Canopy beds, fireplaces, and skylights adorn the suites. The large tiled bathrooms are illuminated by garden-view windows. Breakfast is included in the room rate. Smoking is permitted only outside.

The Fog Catcher Inn (805-927-1400; 1-800-425-4121 for reservations only), 6400 Moonstone Beach Drive. Moderate to expensive. Designed to look like a group of quaint old English cottages, the romantically aged appearance of this shingled inn belies its youth. It is a new and spacious building, holding 60 guest rooms and suites equipped with fireplace, microwave, TV/VCR, and honor bar. Some rooms have ocean views, including the special bridal suite. The most spacious suite includes two private bedrooms, a large sleeping loft, a living room, and a dining area. All guests have access to a pool and hot tub. Full breakfast is included in the room fee.

Ollalieberrie Inn (805-927-3222), 2476 Main Street. Moderate. Cambria's first "chemist" lived in this now fully restored Greek Revival bed & breakfast inn, which is one of the few remaining historic buildings in town. Now, a century-old tree, cottage gardens, and caring proprietors welcome visitors. Each of the six guest rooms has a queen- or king-sized bed, private bath (although some are detached), and freshly supplied bathrobes. Color schemes range from forest green and burgundy to pale pastels, while furniture choices include antique-style brass and iron beds, lace-adorned canopies, and maple burl bedroom sets. Set on the banks of Santa Rosa Creek, this inn's location provides immediate access to town, which is just half a block away. Full breakfast and afternoon hors d'oeuvres with wine are provided. Three to four weeks' advance reservation is recommended, and a first-night's lodging deposit is required. A romantic getaway; children are discouraged.

The J. Patrick House (805-927-3812), 2990 Burton Drive. Moderate. This warm, woodsy, log-cabin-style inn can be found in a fragrant pine grove just 6 miles south of the Hearst estate. While the furnishings are of a simple and unpretentious American country style, the spirit of this lodging is undoubtedly Irish. The eight rooms are named for Irish counties, and all are adorned with private bath, queen or king bed, and fireplace. Behind the main house is a colorful garden. Continental breakfast is served 7:30–9:30 on the sun porch. Enjoy wine and hors d'oeuvres each afternoon in the living room area. Also look for the nightly appearance of a plateful of chocolate chip cookies in the kitchen pantry. Reservations should be made 3 to 6 weeks in advance.

Beach House (805-927-3136), 6360 Moonstone Beach Drive. Expensive. Seven rooms with private baths sit in this modern, angular blue house. Tall windows open to let in the sounds of the surf. This inn provides nice touches of hospitality by lending bicycles and umbrellas, and by offering wine and cheese in the evening. Equipped with binoculars and a telescope, a viewing deck on the second floor takes advantage of a spectacular ocean view. Decorated in white wicker and seashell shades of plum, blue, and gray, the guest rooms are in both the main three-story house and the backyard bungalow; all have cable TV. Books, games, and rocking chairs are provided in the common areas. Full breakfast is included. Smoking is not allowed.

Sea Otter Inn (805-927-5888), 6656 Moonstone Beach Drive. Moderate. All rooms here have gas fireplace, coffeemaker, refrigerator, and TV with VCR (videos are available for rent at the front desk). Some have whirlpools. The inn sits directly across from the beach, and has a pool.

Best Western Fireside Inn (805-927-8661), 6700 Moonstone Beach Drive. Moderate. Also across from the beach, this well-priced inn offers 46 spacious guest rooms on a single story. Some rooms have gas fireplaces—all have refrigerators and cable TV. Both a pool and spa are available to guests.

Sand Pebbles Inn (805-927-5600), 6252 Moonstone Beach Drive. Expensive. With its French country decor and canopy beds, this is among the most inviting of the ocean-view inns along Moonstone Beach Drive. A complimentary continental breakfast and afternoon tea are served in the tearoom. Each of the spacious rooms is equipped with a fireplace, refrigerator, hair dryer, and TV.

San Simeon Pines (805-927-4648), 5 miles south of San Simeon, near Cambria, at Moonstone Beach. Moderate. Set in the pines and cypress, with an easy stroll to Moonstone Beach, this is a casual resort for families or adults. Large rooms have high sloping ceilings, some with fireplaces. Mementos of the area's past accent the lobby and tree-shaded lawns—brands from Hearst Ranch, whalebones set along a pathway, an old quicksilver-mining cart, and a climb-aboard tractor. Clubs are loaned for the practice par-three golf course; there's a solar-heated pool and complimentary coffee. Although some rooms are by the freeway, they are virtually soundproof and are landscaped for privacy.

IN SAN SIMEON

San Simeon Lodge (805-927-4601), 9520 Castillo Drive. Moderate. Built in 1958, the year in which the state acquired the Hearst estate, this was the first motel in the area. The lodge offers 61 rooms on two levels, and a heated pool.

Best Western Cavalier Inn (805-927-4688), 9415 Hearst Drive. Moderate to expensive. This is the only oceanfront motel in town, and provides fireplaces and balconies along with direct access to 900 feet of coastline.

Best Western Courtesy Inn (805-927-4691), 9450 Castillo Drive. Moderate. This inn offers an indoor pool and spa, as well as tennis courts.

California Seacoast Lodge (805-927-3878), 9215 Hearst Drive. Moderate to expensive. Some of these bed & breakfast–style rooms have ocean views, gas fireplaces, and/or whirlpool tubs. There is a small pool available, and all rooms have a refrigerator.

Motel 6 San Simeon (805-927-8691), 9070 Castillo Drive. Moderate. Clean and convenient, this 100-room motel offers a heated pool and coin-operated laundry facilities.

Restaurants

IN PISMO BEACH

The Shore Cliff Restaurant (805-773-4671), 2555 Price Street. Moderate. This clifftop restaurant, located in the Best Western Shore Cliff Lodge, serves fresh seafood, well prepared. The eating area is designed to make the most of the panoramic view.

IN SHELL BEACH

Sea Cliffs Restaurant (805-773-3555), 2757 Shell Beach Road. Inexpensive. Some say that the best fine dining in town is available at this restaurant. It serves fresh, tasty seafood, most of which is mesquite grilled.

IN MORRO BAY

The Cannery (805-772-4426), 235 Main Street. Moderate. This relatively new franchise restaurant remains open at all hours.

Otter Rock Cafe (805-772-1420), 885 Embarcadero. Inexpensive. The food here is fast and fried, but good. You can eat at a table overlooking the water.

The Harbor Hut (805-772-2255), 1205 Embarcadero. Moderate. Opening in 1948, this was the first waterfront restaurant in town. The menu focuses on fresh seafood, prepared in a variety of ways.

The Great American Fish Co. (805-772-4407), 1185 Embarcadero. Moderate. An old reliable restaurant owned and operated by longtime local residents, this is another place to come and eat the catch of the day.

Bob's Seafood (805-772-8473), 833 Embarcadero. Inexpensive. Seafood here is prepared in many different ways, including Cajun-style. Bob also serves breakfast until noon, accommodating late-sleeping vacationers and those who can't resist a long morning walk on the beach.

Harada Japanese Restaurant and Sushi Bar (805-772-1410), 630 Embarcadero. Moderate. For seafood lovers who are interested in moving beyond grilled salmon, poached halibut, and sautéed scallops, there's sushi. At the sushi bar you can treat your taste buds to such undeniably oceanic flavors as sea urchin, octopus, and flying fish roe. For those who prefer more familiar, less raw eating, your sushi chef will be happy to prepare the very tame California Roll, a combination of boiled crab, avocado, and sticky rice wrapped up in nori, a type of dried seaweed with a very mild, nutty flavor. Unagi, or broiled sea eel, is another delicious, fully cooked sushi option. Of course, the restaurant also offers an entire menu of nonsushi meals, such as tempura and teriyaki.

Carla's Country Kitchen (805-772-9051), 213 Beach Street. Inexpensive. This is apparently *the* place for breakfast, with a selection of hearty, tasty scrambled egg dishes.

IN AVILA BEACH

The Olde Port Inn Restaurant (805-595-2515), End of Third Pier. Moderate. For fresh seafood, this place is hard to beat, since it prepares fish as it arrives from the boats.

IN CAYUCOS

Sea Shanty (805-995-3272), 296 S. Ocean Avenue. Inexpensive. Open 7 days a week, this restaurant posts its daily fresh-fish specials.

IN CAMBRIA

Brambles Dinner House (805-927-4716), 4005 Burton Drive. Moderate. Named for the brambles that practically engulf the surrounding property, this is an old-fashioned English dinner house. The quaint premises were built in 1874 and are now decorated with china-patterned wallpaper and heavy red drapes. The menu is basically American, with a selection of cheesecake and ice cream desserts to finish.

Sea Chest Restaurant (805-927-4514), 6216 Moonstone Beach Drive. Moderate. This is a good place for a satisfying meal of bread and Alaskan crab legs; the portions here are generous.

The Moonstone Beach Bar and Grill (805-927-3859), 6550 Moonstone Beach Drive. Moderate. The menu offers a variety of selections, the most popular of which is the seafood pasta.

Ian's (805-927-8649), 2150 Center Street. Inexpensive. Relaxed, romantic spot featuring California cuisine in a restored Victorian house. Dinners nightly, weekend lunches, and Sunday brunch.

Robin's (805-927-5007), 4095 Burton Drive. Inexpensive. Exotic furnishings and plants decorate the restaurant and match the eclectic international food. Take-out orders for excellent picnics. Lunch and dinner.

IN SAN SIMEON

San Simeon Restaurant (805-927-4604), 9520 Castillo Drive. Moderate. Legend has it that William Randolph Hearst himself ate here occasionally, probably because it used to be the only restaurant in town. The dining room, which adjoins the San Simeon Lodge, is full of San Simeon memorabilia, and offers standard American fare.

Europa (805-927-3087), 9240 Castillo Drive. Moderate. A nice alternative to the "more is better" theme of some of the local eateries, the internationally flavored menu at this restaurant will suit many tastes, whether craving beef, seafood, or pasta.

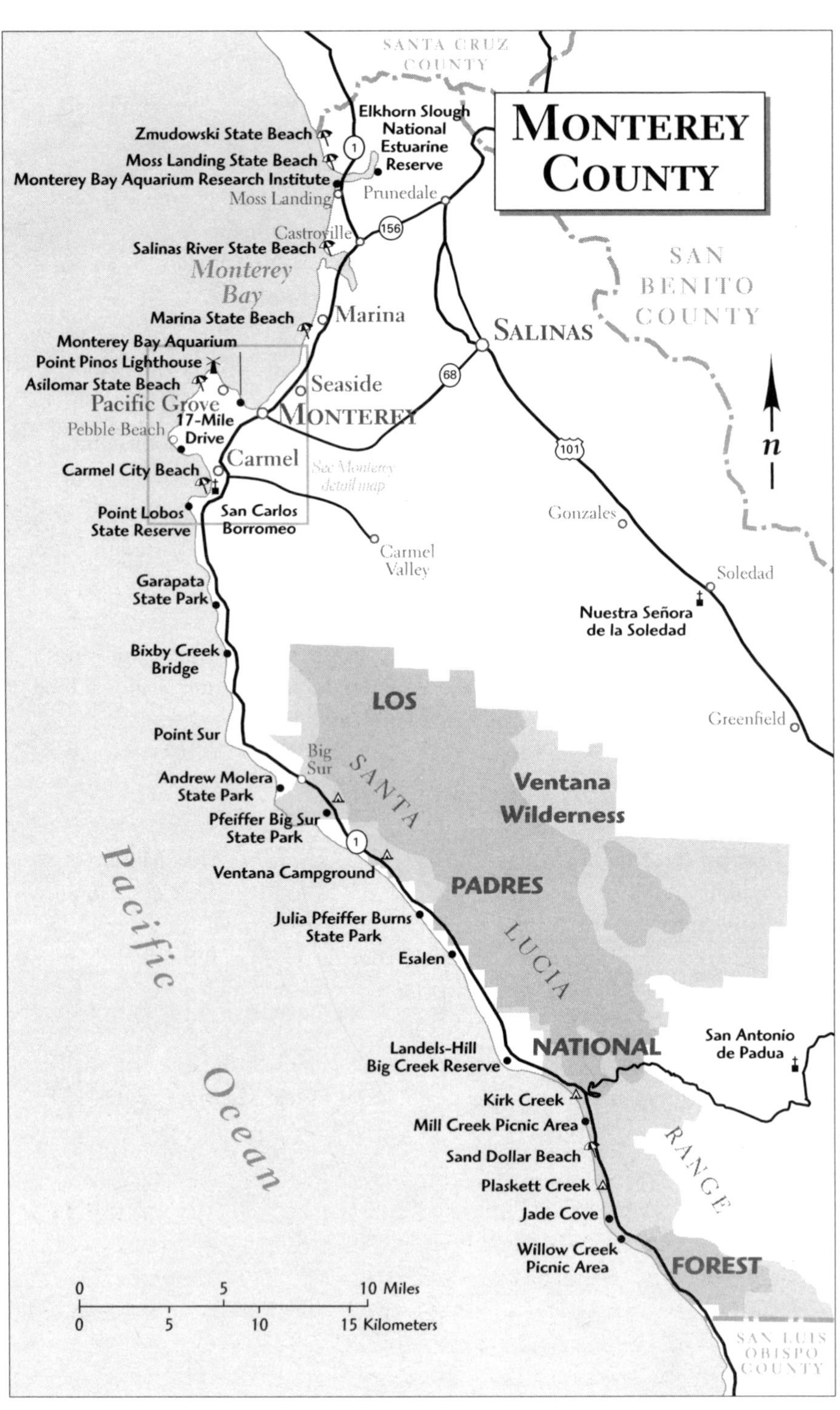

MONTEREY COUNTY
SANTA CRUZ COUNTY
SAN BENITO COUNTY
SAN LUIS OBISPO COUNTY
Zmudowski State Beach
Moss Landing State Beach
Monterey Bay Aquarium Research Institute
Moss Landing
Elkhorn Slough National Estuarine Reserve
Prunedale
Castroville
156
1
Salinas River State Beach
Monterey Bay
Marina State Beach
Marina
SALINAS
68
Monterey Bay Aquarium
Point Pinos Lighthouse
Asilomar State Beach
Pacific Grove
Seaside
MONTEREY
Pebble Beach
17-Mile Drive
Carmel
See Monterey detail map
Carmel City Beach
Point Lobos State Reserve
San Carlos Borromeo
Carmel Valley
101
Gonzales
Soledad
Nuestra Señora de la Soledad
Greenfield
Garapata State Park
Bixby Creek Bridge
Point Sur
Big Sur
Andrew Molera State Park
Pfeiffer Big Sur State Park
Ventana Campground
Julia Pfeiffer Burns State Park
Esalen
LOS PADRES NATIONAL FOREST
SANTA LUCIA RANGE
Ventana Wilderness
Pacific Ocean
Landels-Hill Big Creek Reserve
San Antonio de Padua
Kirk Creek
Mill Creek Picnic Area
Sand Dollar Beach
Plaskett Creek
Jade Cove
Willow Creek Picnic Area
n
0 5 10 Miles
0 5 10 15 Kilometers

CHAPTER SEVEN

Monterey County

MONTEREY COUNTY BEGINS just above San Simeon, near Salmon Creek. It is also the beginning of the Big Sur coastline, 64 miles of beautiful, undulating mountainside that falls in often steep cliffs to the shore. The Big Sur coast is the western shoulder of the Santa Lucia Mountains, the tallest section of the southern coastal range. Here the mountains reach 5000 feet, and more than 50 streams twist through valleys far below.

This is a wild area, much of it part of the Los Padres National Forest, which includes the Ventana Wilderness. Although there are pocket beaches in Big Sur—most of them near Point Sur itself—the typical coastline here consists of steep cliffs. Sections are composed of soft Franciscan rock and are prone to landslides. Road closures are common, as are traffic accidents. In winter, storms often contribute to the problems by washing rocks downhill onto the roads. The section between Crimes Point and McWay Canyon is particularly steep and prone to landslides—it should be driven with extreme caution.

Big Sur is also one of the most beautiful and most photographed sections of the California coast. The coast near Bixby Creek, with its headlands backed by the mountain range, with jagged offshore rocks . . . soaring Bixby Creek Bridge, which rises 717 feet and has a perfect central white arch . . . the coast with Point Sur rising out of the morning mist . . . the Big Sur Headlands, an endless series of bluffs and cliffs . . . the rock formations at Pfeiffer Beach . . . these are images that have been photographed by Ansel Adams and Cole Weston, William Garnett and Eliot Porter, and many others.

North of Point Lobos (a spectacular state preserve of 1276 acres of headlands, coves, beaches, and Monterey cypress) lies Carmel, a picture-perfect town of expensive bed & breakfasts, art stores, and boutiques. Just to the north of town is 17-Mile Drive, a scenic toll road with many beaches and excellent views.

The large southern curve of Monterey Bay begins beyond the Carmel Headland. Here is the historic city of Monterey, with Cannery Row and the Monterey Bay Aquarium. When Steinbeck made this area famous, it was in decline. Now, with the aquarium as a base, Monterey is alive with interesting, sometimes high-tech companies, mostly involved in one way or another with the ocean. With its pleasant beaches and attractions for children, this is an excellent area for a family vacation.

To the north of the city is the great sandy plain of Monterey Bay. The Salinas River and Elkhorn Slough empty into the sea here. The oceanfront dunes are young in this area, and still migrating inland, often drifting onto Highway 1. At the mouth of Elkhorn Slough is the Monterey Submarine Canyon, a cut in the ocean more than 3000 feet deep.

Beaches and Attractions

Note: Southern Monterey County's towns are few and far between, so although many listed sites are technically part of the town of Big Sur, mile markers along Highway 1—which hugs the coast nearly the entire length of the county—are sometimes used in addition to town names to give more precise locations. They start at 0 at the San Luis Obispo County border and go up as you head north, until they start again at 0 where Highway 1 meets Santa Cruz County.

IN BIG SUR ★

"At dawn, Big Sur's majesty is almost painful to behold. That same prehistoric look, the look of always. Nature smiling at herself in the mirror of eternity . . ."
—Henry Miller, *Big Sur and the Oranges of Hieronymus Bosch*

We recommend the **Big Sur Land Trust's** *unsurpassed* audio tour of Big Sur. Available in most local bookstores or directly from the trust (408-625-5523), it provides an excellent guide to Big Sur. (It's available in north- and southbound versions.) It is well produced and informative, and will add much to your drive along Highway 1. For travelers needing more detailed information on Big Sur, we also suggest *The Natural History of Big Sur*, by Paul Henson and Donald J. Usner (University of California Press, Berkeley, 1993). Serious hikers should get a copy of Jeffrey Schaeffer's excellent *Hiking the Big Sur Country*. It describes more than 300 miles of trails in the region. If you want a feel for the literary history of this stretch of coast, pick up some poetry by Robinson Jeffers, *Big Sur* by Jack Kerouac, or the later novels of Henry Miller.

Except for Ragged Point, Gorda, Lucia, and other way stations that offer gas and/or food, most of southern Big Sur is undeveloped and managed as part of the Los Padres National Forest. At **Redwood, Salmon, Willow, Plaskett,** and **Kirk Creeks** are scenic way stations and trailheads. Redwood Creek is the southernmost natural extent of redwood trees and provides trail access into the national forest. Salmon Creek's waterfall is dramatic. Camping is available at Plaskett and Kirk Creeks. Picnicking is excellent at Willow and Mill Creeks. Rest rooms are at Willow and Plaskett Creeks. For more information, call the **National Forest Ranger** at 408-385-5434.

Jade Cove Mile 29.9N (~12.4 miles south of Lucia). As the name implies, this is where hikers can walk down to a small beach and see large amounts of nephrite jade. (Incidentally, it is illegal to take nephrite jade from above the high-tide line; what's below that line technically is fair game, but we still don't recommend it.) There are no facilities. Parking is free along the shoulder of Highway 1; access is through fields and paths leading down to the ocean. For more information, call Los Padres National Forest at 805-385-5434.

Sand Dollar Picnic Area and Beach Mile 30.4N (~11 miles south of Lucia). Another good spot to eat, Sand Dollar's picnic tables are shaded by cypress trees. Paths lead through the bluffs above the crescent-shaped beach, down to a beach that was scoured of sand in 1995. The ocean may in time replace the sand, but for now it's mostly a rocky shore. This is also a popular landing area for hang gliders, many of which launch from nearby Plaskett Creek Campground, ¾ mile south of Sand Dollar. Access is via a free parking lot west of Highway 1; call 805-385-5434 for further information.

Mill Creek Picnic Ground Mile 35.2N (~5 miles south of Lucia). Also a popular hang-glider landing site, this is a small picnic area with a fairly rough, steep trail leading to an alternately sandy and rocky beach. Access is via a free parking lot west of Highway 1; call 408-385-5434 for further information.

Limekiln State Beach, Mile 37.6N (~2 miles south of Lucia). Part of Limekiln State Park, this is a dramatic place in which to camp and hike in several different settings. There are tent and RV sites, and visitors camp among redwoods or along the beach at the ocean outlet of Limekiln Creek. The area's name comes from the historic kilns scattered nearby. Access is via a parking lot off Highway 1; there is a fee for parking.

Big Creek ★ The most pristine portion of Big Sur is preserved at Big Creek as part of the **University of California Natural Reserve System**. Almost 4000 acres comprising most of Big Creek's watershed are used for research and environmental education. Although it burned in 1986, it still provides habitat for many rare and endangered animals and plants. The **Landels-Hill Big Creek Reserve** is open only for walks led by Nature Conservancy docents. For reservations call 415-777-0541

The Ventana Wilderness Area provides more than 235 miles of trails throughout its 164,500 acres. The gateway to these rugged valleys, ridges, and steep mountains is the Big Sur Ranger Station on Highway 1 just south of Pfeiffer Big Sur State Park. The Pine Ridge Trail leads to secluded campsites. Stop at the station first to register before going into the backcountry. Campfire permits are required during the fire season (May–October). Permits are also available at Pacific Valley Ranger Station, 33 miles south of Carmel, and at Bottcher's Gap on Palo Colorado Road off Highway 1 about 10 miles south of Carmel. For more information, call the District Ranger's Office in King City at 408-385-5434.

Esalen Institute 14.6 miles south of Pfeiffer Big Sur State Park. An early center for the "human potential" movement, Esalen still functions as a retreat that offers classes and workshops. After a day of hiking along the coast, though, Esalen's hot springs may be the bigger draw. Public hours are limited to between 1 and 5 AM, though (yes, that's one to five in the morning). Access is via a fee parking lot west of Highway 1; call 408-667-3000 for more information.

Julia Pfeiffer Burns State Park ★ Mile 52.7N (11 miles south of Big Sur State Park). One of the jewels of the state park system, this coastal beauty has it all: environmental campgrounds (read "minimal facilities"), picnic tables, steep hills, hiking trails up to 1500 feet, and a stream running through a redwood-bordered canyon. A paved path follows the stream to just above its outlet at the Pacific—and the only waterfall in California that flows directly into the ocean, a must-see for visitors. A trail leads to Partington Cove (Mile 54.5N), where you can see a 110-foot tunnel burrowed into the coastal cliffs by 19th-century pirates looking to stash their loot. This park encapsulates the drama of the California coast, all within hiking distance of the parking lot. Access is via lots east and west of Highway 1; there are parking and day-use fees. *Note*: This park provides no direct beach access.

Pfeiffer Beach Mile 63.2N (1 mile south of Big Sur State Park). This is a wide, sandy beach strewn with boulders. Offshore there are wave-battered rocks that the ocean has carved into gigantic sculptures, sometimes boring completely through to create a natural arch. You descend from the parking lot through sycamore trees, exiting the bluff to emerge onto the main beach, which is divided by a stream. There is a strong undertow and no lifeguard, so swimming is discouraged, but there is some nude sunbathing. Pfeiffer Beach has rest rooms but no other facilities. Access is via a winding 2-mile-long drive down Sycamore Canyon Road to the beach. For further information, call 408-667-2315.

Pfeiffer Big Sur State Park 26 miles south of Carmel, this is a beautiful 821-acre park located primarily within a flat section of the Big Sur River Valley. It's fairly well developed, with a gift shop, grocery store, and restaurant near the campsites, but visitors can quickly get away from it all by heading out on one of the park's numerous hiking trails. There are also opportunities for safe—although sometimes heart-stoppingly cold—swimming in the Big Sur River itself, which has a couple of deep sections suitable for jumping in. The park also features redwoods, the Pfeiffer Falls, and guided walks during summer months, as well as separate camping areas for bicyclists and groups. Pfeiffer Big Sur is a primary trailhead for the Ventana Wilderness, 150,000 acres mostly set back from the coast. The river is packed with trout and salmon and the campsites have fire pits, so dinner can be just a hook and line away for the patient angler. Access is via Highway 1; the park is well marked from the highway. Call 408-667-2315 for further information.

Ventana Campground at Highway 1, 2.5 miles south of Pfeiffer Big Sur State Park, offers full camping facilities as part of the resort of the same name. No reservations; arrive before 6 PM. Call 408-667-2331 for more information.

Henry Miller Memorial Library just north of Julia Pfeiffer Burns State Park. Operated by the Big Sur Land Trust, the museum offers an intriguing sculpture garden, bookstore, and research library on the famous bohemian writer. Miller lived on nearby Partington Ridge from 1944 to 1962. Hours are erratic but it's worth a stop, especially if you go to the restaurant Nepenthe, just a half mile to the north. Call 408-667-2574.

Big Sur Valley is the heart of the rural Big Sur community. Located along Highway 1 inland from the coast between the Ventana Inn and Andrew Molera State Park, the Valley offers information, most of the lodging options, and restaurants. **Pfeiffer Big Sur State Park** provides the most extensive visitor services and amenities. Three private campgrounds supplement the state facilities. **Fernwood Park Campground** (408-667-2422), **Riverside Campground** (408-667-2414), and **Big Sur Campground** (408-667-2322) are funky old-time resorts located on the Big Sur River.

Andrew Molera State Park Here visitors will find more than 4700 coastal acres—from the ocean to mountaintops 3400 feet high—with very little on them that's man-made. There are 16 miles of hiking trails, a sandy beach second only to Pfeiffer Beach (see above) in Monterey County, and a 60-site, tent-only campground. As with Pfeiffer, an undertow makes swimming hazardous, but hikers can enjoy the view from blufftops and alongside the Big Sur River, which empties into the Pacific within Molera's confines. Access is west of Highway 1 via the south end of Old Coast Road, about 3 miles north of the town of Big Sur. Parking is free; call 408-667-2315 for more information.

Old Coast Road For those who have time to get off the beaten track, this road is a must. Beginning just north of Andrew Molera State Park on Highway 1, its 11 miles of old-school dirt were once the primary means of travel along this stretch of the coast. Long since supplanted by Highway 1, it nonetheless features many spectacular vistas of the ocean and several of the Santa Lucia Mountains. It is extremely rutted and winding; don't let the breathtaking

Diane Clark—Big Sur Highway Patrol

■ "The road doesn't follow the rules," Diane Clark says, talking about the 64 miles of Highway 1 that go through the isolated Big Sur coast. In winter, the road may not even exist in places, because of landslides where the hill has been undermined by rain and erosion. At every turn—and there are turns everywhere—there's a chance you'll come upon a fallen tree or a jackknifed big rig, or maybe you'll become a member of the West of One Club—which means you've driven over the side of Highway 1 and managed to survive the fall. West of One isn't a big club—the cliffs along the Big Sur coast are too steep, too high, so don't try to qualify.

In the rest of the state, units of the highway patrol are doubled up after 10:30 PM, increasing the safety factor. But not on Highway 1 in Big Sur. There are only two highway patrol officers covering this stretch of highway. The two officers are pretty much on call all the time. Diane Clark is one of them. So far this month—which is only half over—Diane has worked 70 hours of overtime. Many weeks she doesn't have time to get to the store. Or get a haircut. Or do all the other things she needs to do. None of this bothers her; she happens to love her job.

In some parts of California the main duty of the Highway Patrol becomes "chasing taillights," but on the twisting, dangerous Big Sur coast, Diane and her partner are the only full-time law enforcement officers. Their job is varied and complex. They deal with domestic quarrels and campground incidents, traffic accidents and emergency medical services.

Rutted dirt driveways in Big Sur twist up through back canyons to reach out-of-the-way homesteads. To navigate these roads, Diane drives a four-wheel-drive Suburban. It's big enough to hold the chain saw, shovels, and temporary barricades she may need. The Suburban also has a winch on the front so that Diane can move a wreck off the road. Often alone and isolated, Diane and her partner carry H Bar rifles with scopes—big guns with heavier ammo than the standard Highway Patrol issue.

When she worked in Santa Barbara, Diane could keep her home life separate from the job. But here in Big Sur, she's deeply embedded in the community. What difference would it make to have an

views distract you from the road. Driving back down to the coast, you will rejoin Highway 1 at **Bixby Bridge**, another famous California coastal scene (see below).

Point Sur State Historic Park 5 miles north of Point Sur. Every Sunday morning, docents give a 2½-hour walking tour of this historic 1889 lighthouse, dramatically situated across a wide beach on a 360-foot volcanic rock outcropping. The station's light and foghorn still warn ships away from hazardous waters off Point Sur, and the complex is listed on the National Register of Historic Places. Access is via a parking lot on Highway 1 in front of the lighthouse station, and there is a fee for the tour. Dogs are not allowed on-site. Call 408-667-2315 for further information.

unlisted number when every member of the fire department is a volunteer and knows how to reach her day or night? She and her partner are also emergency medical technicians—they're not only the law enforcement agency but also often the ambulance of first resort, as well as the only tow truck around to get a car off the road before someone center-punches it rounding a blind turn. The local people of Big Sur see Diane and the Highway Patrol as essential members of the community, jacks-of-all-trades who solve a wide range of problems. They call them "our officers."

Diane likes working in the Big Sur area so much that she can see herself staying in the Highway Patrol for 20 years—when she'd be eligible for retirement—or even longer. (She's been in the Highway Patrol for 12 years so far.) Maybe she'll even be a 30-year officer, if she doesn't get injured, which is a constant possibility, particularly on a road like Highway 1 in Big Sur: narrow and twisting and often full of distracted tourists. The big danger for a Highway Patrol officer here isn't being gunned down; it's being mowed down by accident when she's out of her car trying to clean up the highway.

Inattention—looking at the beauty of the area instead of concentrating on the road—is one of two big problems here. The second is aggression, the angry desire to get around a slow-moving line of vehicles no matter the cost. A slow-driving tourist can stack up 20 cars behind him. The aggression builds—you're sure there's nothing around the bend, you haven't seen a car coming in the other direction for miles, you're going to pass this idiot . . . You swing out, step on the accelerator, and—if you're lucky—join the West of One Club. One of the last to join was a dog. Its master died in the crash, but the dog survived for five days alone on a beach at Big Sur before someone spotted it and called Diane.

Diane once flew in the Army and later in the National Guard. The Highway Patrol has an aviation wing, which she intended to join until she was posted to Big Sur. But Big Sur is so challenging—it calls on so many of her skills—that she's decided to stay on the road. ■

Bixby Creek Bridge 5.4 miles north of Point Sur. Built in 1932, Bixby is one of the largest concrete arch bridges in the world, and its location across a 260-foot-deep gorge makes it one of the most photogenic. It's impossible to miss. Access is along Highway 1 at Bixby Creek.

Garrapata State Park ★ about 12 miles south of Carmel. This is a broad, white-sand beach that also offers rocky tide pools and views of otters playing in the surf. There are paths from Turnout 13 to Whale Peak, which, as one might guess, is a prime whale-watching point. Visitors should note that Garrapata is quite popular as a clothing-optional beach. There is a 1.2-mile trail along the bluffs above the beach, which offers spectacular views of the ocean. The beach has only chemical toilets. Access is via free parking at Turnout 13 or Turnout 14 along Highway 1, 2 miles south of Malpaso Creek.

TOM MIKKELSEN

Bixby Creek Bridge, Big Sur

Bottcher's Gap National Forest Campground (408-385-5434), at the top of Palo Colorado Road. You'll pay a small fee at this oak and madrone campground with views of Pico Blanco and Ventana Double-Cone Mountains. *Note*: No drinking water is available, so bring in your own.

Point Lobos State Reserve ★ 3 miles south of Carmel. More than 1200 acres in size (both above and below water), Point Lobos is another diverse Monterey County park, with beaches, tide pools, cypress groves, hiking trails, and picnic areas. The park consists of a series of meadows on bluffs above the Pacific; otters, seals, and sea lions play offshore, while 250 bird species live or migrate through the park's lands and offshore rocks. Visitors can swim in cold water at China Cove. A 6-mile hike runs around the park's perimeter, from Bird Island to Granite Point. Another of the park's trails goes through one of the world's two remaining natural stands of Monterey cypress. Access is via fee parking lots along Riley Ranch Road off Highway 1; call Point Lobos State Reserve at 408-624-4909 for more information.

IN CARMEL

Carmel-by-the-Sea is an international destination for its "artist colony," majestic beach, and recreational shopping opportunities. Carmel, through many strict environmental regulations, has maintained its small-town, pedestrian-friendly atmosphere. The downtown area near the ocean is dedicated to trendy boutiques and excellent—often expensive—restaurants, while the outlying areas have a rustic beauty. The town's origin was as a turn-of-the-century retreat for a tight group of artists and writers. Jack London and Sinclair Lewis stayed here, and many other celebrities continue to enjoy the town. (Clint Eastwood was elected mayor in 1986.) The town has preserved the twisting streets, massive trees, and eclectic architecture, and contained commercial development. The **Ocean Avenue** shopping district offers myriad restaurants, art and photographic galleries, jewelry shops, local stores, and factory outlets.

Carmel River State Beach. Though Carmel River State Beach is upstaged by Point Lobos State Reserve to the south and Carmel City Beach to the north, it is a beauty in its own right. Set on both sides of the mouth of the Carmel River, this is 106 acres of alternately sandy and rocky beach. Swimming and surfing are somewhat hazardous here due to the rocks, but this is a popular diving spot because of the Carmel Bay Ecological Reserve just offshore. Along the river and associated marshes is a refuge where several different species of birds can be seen, including pelicans, kingfishers, and sandpipers. Dogs are not allowed on the beach. Access is along Scenic Road at Carmel Street; there are no parking or entrance fees. Access to the southernmost part of the beach, sometimes known as San Jose Creek Beach, is directly via Highway 1. Call 408-624-4909 for more information.

Mission San Carlos Borromeo del Rio Carmelo west of Highway 1 at Rio Road, was the second mission established in California by Padre Junípero Serra. After a century of disuse, it was restored in 1936 to feature a Moorish-inspired tower and large cemetery. For more information, call 408-624-3600.

Tor House located off Scenic Road at Ocean View Avenue and Stewart Way, was built out of local boulders by the poet Robinson Jeffers. His lyric poetry captured the people and land from Big Sur to Carmel.

Scenic Road provides fabulous views of Carmel Bay and other architectural attractions. **Walker House**, designed by Frank Lloyd Wright, and the **"Butterfly" House** are worth driving by.

Carmel City Beach. This is a beautiful, crescent-shaped, white-sand beach nestled in the heart of increasingly urban Carmel. It is spotless—

TOM MIKKELSEN

Offshore Point Lobos State Reserve

the sand is so clean it squeaks—and, given its proximity to Carmel's wealth of attractions, restaurants, and stores, an ideal family beach. Backed by blufftop houses and fronted by the two points of land that tip the beach's crescent, it is one of the most dramatic urban beaches you will find anywhere. Though the water is cold, the surf generally is gentle and safe for swimming. (There are no lifeguards, however.) There are volleyball nets and fire rings on the beach, and a ¾-mile trail runs along the bluff that cradles the beach. Otters play in the kelp beds just beyond the breakwater, and dolphins have been seen offshore as well. Access is via the end of Ocean Boulevard; there is metered street parking on perpendicular streets but no access fee.

IN PEBBLE BEACH/PACIFIC GROVE/MONTEREY

Pebble Beach features many upscale options for dining, shopping, and recreation. It is accessible only via scenic **17-Mile Drive.** Since 1919, the Del Monte Lodge and Pebble Beach Golf Links have been a mecca for golfers. Pebble Beach hosts many world-class golf tournaments; it is also home to tennis matches and the Concours d'Elegance, a prestigious classic auto showcase. Several newer golf courses add to the attractions. All links are open to the public, but the fees are very high. Driving, hiking, or biking 17-Mile Drive offers spectacular coastal views including the Lone Cypress, probably the most photographed site on the coast. A fee is charged for autos.

Seventeen-Mile Drive Access to this private community is via tollgates at five different points in Monterey; the signs for the drive are difficult to miss as you approach from Highway 1, or from Asilomar Boulevard in downtown Monterey. Call 408-624-3811 for more information. A great way to see 17-Mile Drive is via bicycle. Not only is entry to the drive free, but the shoulders are wide, paved, and well marked, and the ride itself is mostly flat and pleasant—not the grueling up-and-down of Big Sur by any stretch. It is worth the effort to leave your car in Carmel or Pacific Grove and surround yourself fully—at least for an afternoon—with the beauty of this stretch of coast.

Fanshell Beach. This is a small, white-sand cove beach with surfable waves. It is also a good site for picnicking and fishing, but has little else in the way of facilities. With seals and sea otters frequenting it, the beach is closed during the spring for seal pupping season, so it's a good idea to call ahead. Access is via Signal Hill Road at 17-Mile Drive; call the Pebble Beach Co. at 408-624-3811 for further information.

Spanish Bay Recreational Trail/SB Shoreline Pedestrian Trail Spanish Bay is a small, geographically shallow bay on the western edge of the Monterey Peninsula, between Point Joe and Asilomar State Beach (see below). Though accessed via 17-Mile Drive, the area contains several high-profile public facilities. Foremost for visitors is the beach itself, a half mile of white sand popular with surfers. Those looking to stay out of the water may want to try either the Spanish Bay Recreational Trail or the Spanish Bay Shoreline Pedestrian Trail. The former is a bicycle/pedestrian path running behind the Spanish Bay Hotel, and runs concurrently with 17-Mile Drive for part of its length. The latter is

TOM MIKKELSEN

Divers on Carmel River State Beach

TOM MIKKELSEN

Carmel Mission

slightly longer than a mile and runs from Point Joe to Spyglass Hill Road. The path is wheelchair accessible and takes visitors past beautiful views of Seal Rock and Bird Rock.

Access to the beach is along the **Spanish Bay Recreation Trail**, which itself is accessible via the Spanish Bay Hotel, at Sunset Drive and Asilomar Boulevard in Pacific Grove. Access to the **Spanish Bay Shoreline Pedestrian Trail** is at Spanish Bay Road and 17-Mile Drive. A fee is required for vehicle access to the drive (see above), but pedestrians and cyclists may enter for free. Call the Pebble Beach Co. at 408-624-3811 for more information.

Pacific Grove ★ is an unpretentious town on the Monterey Peninsula. Founded in 1875 as a Methodist summer retreat, it remains a hometown kind of place. "P.G." is also home to a thriving and well-protected colony of monarch butterflies. From November to March, millions of the monarchs roost in the town's trees. There is even a butterfly parade each fall. A walk through any of P.G.'s neighborhoods reveals a wealth of well-preserved Victorian houses.

Asilomar State Beach is a rugged bit of coast that forms the western edge of the town of Pacific Grove. There is some sandy beach, but Asilomar is primarily coarse sand and pebbles, tide pools, and white-sand dunes. Though strong currents make it a poor choice for swimming, there's plenty to explore from the land—tide pools with fish, shells, kelp, starfish, crabs, and, of course, spectacular views of the Pacific. The beach is large enough not to be crowded and is a Monterey must-see. Access is via Pico Avenue at Sunset Drive; call Asilomar State Beach at 408-372-4076 for more information.

Point Pinos Lighthouse Open to the public only Saturday and Sunday 1–4, this is the oldest continuously operating lighthouse on the West Coast. Visitors can take self-guided tours of the light and a small Coast Guard museum on the surrounding reservation. There are also spectacular views of the Monterey coast from the lighthouse.

Scenic Drive. Enjoy a slow drive along Sunset Drive and Ocean View Boulevard to see the protected shoreline on Pacific Grove.

Lighthouse Avenue ★ Around George Washington Park, about 10 blocks east of the lighthouse, visitors should be able to see thousands of migrating monarch butterflies descend on the town from about November 1 to March 1. They are beautiful and quite large, and should not be molested both for ethical reasons and because Pacific Grove hands out $1000 fines to those who do so. Access is via the end of Lighthouse Avenue, west of Asilomar Avenue; call 408-648-3116 for more information.

Lover's Point A great family spot, this is a grassy area atop bluffs that overlook the ocean and Monterey Bay, with views as far north as Santa Cruz. There is a small fishing pier, plus grills and picnic tables for cooking and eating the catch. There is also access to the Monterey Peninsula Pedestrian Trail, which allows biking as well as walking. Lover's Point is a popular diving and surfing spot, particularly the area west toward Point Pinos, which is nicknamed the Boneyard for its hazardous but exhilarating surf conditions. Access is via Ocean Boulevard at 17th Street. There is a free parking lot; call Pacific Grove's Parks Department at 408-648-3130 for more information.

Shoreline Park is the collective name for Berwick, Greenwood, and Andy Jacobsen Parks, all of which are small and dot the shoreline east of Lover's Point toward the Presidio of Monterey. They are somewhat set back from the bay and connected by the **Monterey Bay Recreational Trail.** There are several beaches accessible by steep paths or scrambles over riprap (boulder

Tom Moss—Restoring the California Coast

■ "Think like the wind," Tom Moss told the operator of the big yellow bulldozer. The operator was in his 70s, a builder of roads and foundations. He came from a local Monterey family that had been in construction for three generations, and he thought in terms of lines and right angles, everything laid out just as perfectly as he could make it.

Tom Moss was up on top of the bulldozer with the operator, directing him, trying to get him to feel the spirit of a sand dune. He wanted the operator to let go of everything he had ever learned about the machine, let go of everything he felt should be expected of him. "You're the wind with your 'dozer," Tom told the operator.

Tom was about to transform 107 acres of white sand beach at Asilomar, a state park and conference center on the Pacific Grove peninsula, one of the most beautiful sections of Monterey County. Hundreds of years ago, the area had been filled with dunes. Now it was just flat, lifeless beach.

Sand dunes, as distinct from beach, are about 40 percent vegetation. The native vegetation of a California sand dune is typically beach sagewort, mock heather, yellow bush lupine, beach aster, and perhaps 25 other species. (Ice plant, often found in great quantities on the state's beaches and along its highways, was imported into California.) Vegetation not only holds the dunes in place, it also creates areas where water can be held in the sand. Birds come to dunes because of the vegetation, as do animals such as the black legless lizard, a beautiful reptile that is protected by law.

When the plants colonizing a sand dune die out, it becomes beach. From the bulldozer, Tom Moss was looking at beach, acres and acres of clean white sand, broken by a few tiny spots of green. Out of all that sand he was going to create a great dune—plan it, mold it, plant it. If he did the work correctly, he hoped, the dune would be self-sustaining. Native vegetation would grow. With the vegetation in place, animals and birds would return. The beach would disappear and sand dunes would take its place once again.

The operator of the bulldozer was able to "think like the wind" when Tom was on the 'dozer with him. But when Tom left to do other jobs on the restoration project, sometimes the old mentality would return. Tom would come back and find that a beautiful "natural" sand dune had been transferred into a perfectly flat square.

The bulldozing and sculpting of the Asilomar dunes occurred in 1987. The previous two years had been spent preparing the people of Pacific Grove for the advent of the great yellow monster on their beach. Tom's employer, the State Park Service, was behind him, and so was the Asilomar Operating Corporation, a nonprofit company that manages the park and conference center. But many of the people of Pacific Grove did not understand that their beach had once been thriving sand dunes. Tom didn't want them to wake up one morning, see a bulldozer pushing sand around the beach, and think that some government official was at work destroying it.

For two years, he went to every meeting he could, describing the plans for the restoration of the sand dunes, preparing the community for what was to come.

Tom's plans also called for an intricate series of ground-level boardwalks threading their way through the sand dunes that he intended to sculpt with the bulldozers. These walks were crucial. None of the indigenous plants that Tom would establish are people-resistant; they are small, soft and fragile. And they would be destroyed if people trod on them (one of the very reasons the old sand dunes had been lost). But Tom didn't want signs directing people to stay on the path, or fences and walls to keep them there. All this would have defeated the idea of natural sand dunes.

Tom wanted paths that people would *want* to stay on. He tried to plan them to have a sense of mystery, to make the walker want to see what was around the next corner. Thus, he laid the paths and the dunes to avoid long, straight lines, or a clearly recognizable configuration. He hid switchbacks in the trails behind the dunes he built with the bulldozers. He wanted his paths to "pull you into the dunes," the way a great painting or photograph draws you in to its scene.

Tom had detailed plans, of course. But as he tried to shape the sand so that it seemed "formed by the wind" he often found himself designing on the spot, riding with the 'dozer operator. No one had ever tried to restore sand dunes before, let alone attempt to design them. He had few guidelines to follow. Tom was like an artist, working in a strange new medium—107 acres of white sand.

After the dunes were sculpted, the plants and wooden boardwalks went in. As the plants grew, the birds and insects came back. It was the "return of life," Tom says. The small black legless lizard appeared. Tom had sculpted out little valleys where plants flourished and enabled the sand in these depressions to hold water, making small ponds. Frogs somehow found out about the ponds and moved in. Over the next few years, a whole sand dune environment sprang into life. The Asilomar dune project became a model for other private and public dune restoration projects and provided work for a new generation of 'dozer operators who learned to "think like the wind."

You can explore Tom's dunes at the **Asilomar State Beach and Conference Grounds**, 800 Asilomar Avenue, Pacific Grove (408-372-8016). ■

---

placements that protect the shore from waves). The parks of Shoreline offer a great place from which to watch migrating whales. Access is via Ocean View Boulevard east of Lover's Point; call the Monterey Parks Department at 408-646-3866 for further information.

Monterey is the historical centerpiece of the California coast, comparable to Jamestown, Virginia; Plymouth, Massachusetts; and St. Augustine, Florida, on the East Coast. The Spanish, then Mexican Presidio rule was deposed by the gringos when they invented the California Republic here in 1849 at **Coulton Hall.** Monterey was the first capital of California. The adobes of the Spanish, Mexican, and US eras have been preserved in great measure due to a strong local commitment to historical preservation (and the fact that they often are expensive to demolish). The foot-thick walls offered protection from the elements as well as rapacious developers. Get a brochure and take the

TOM MIKKELSEN

Cannery Row

"Path of History" Walking Tour through downtown Monterey to see the historic heart of the city. The **Custom House Plaza** serves as a focus for the downtown attractions. Walk down Alvarado Street to see the Colonial and turn-of-the-century architectural sights. **Fisherman's Wharf** offers a wide variety of seafood restaurants and shops. Metered parking here is well signed and a convenient spot to leave a car to walk the town. Take the **Monterey Bay Recreational Trail** north to Monterey State Beach and toward Seaside. Or walk on this old railroad corridor, now converted to walking, biking, and in-line skating, to **Cannery Row** and the **Monterey Bay Aquarium**.

The Monterey Peninsula is undergoing an economic and cultural renaissance. The Monterey Bay Aquarium jump-started the change; it was the catalyst for tourist development of Cannery Row. The hotels, restaurants, and shops have all but obliterated the history of the row. An old saying in the area is that Cannery Row isn't like it used to be and probably never was. John Steinbeck started his novel about the legendary bon vivant marine biologist Doc Ricketts as follows: "Cannery Row in Monterey in California is a poem, a stink, a grating noise, a quality of light, a tone, a habit, a nostalgia, a dream." Vestiges of the real canneries have been converted into shopping centers and amusement halls, and most canneries have been replaced by hotels and restaurants. **Doc Ricketts's Lab** (two doors down the row from the Aquarium), after years as a private club, is now owned by the city of Monterey. The working seafood industry has mostly gone offshore. The ocean still supports some fishing industries in the harbor at **Municipal Wharf #2** and at **Moss Landing**.

A stroll along Cannery Row is a modern tourist experience shrouded in history. Walk along the street, then take the Recreational Trail for a view of the area from the old railroad right-of-way. The south end of the row, at the corner of Drake and Wave, is now San Carlos Park. Here scuba divers use the nearshore area to learn diving techniques. For information on diving opportunities in Monterey, pick up a copy of "Monterey Bay Marine Sanctuary Diver's Chart," available at **Monterey Bay Dive Center** (408-656-0454), 225 Canney Row, or other local dive shops. This block of Cannery Row retains the old functional industrial architecture. In 1953, Marilyn Monroe was filmed in the Enterprise Packers for *Clash by Night* (not her best film). The **Monterey Bay Plaza Hotel** provides visual and actual access to the shoreline. It stands on the site of a former mansion. Past Hoffman Avenue is McAbee Beach, the site of a former Chinese settlement. Built over the beach, the **Spindrift Hotel** also provides access to the beach below via staircases on both sides of the building. Avoid Steinbeck Plaza, at Prescott Avenue, where the wax museum tries in vain to resurrect the glory of the past in a commercialized atmosphere. Enjoy the views from the small park and the beach below. Just past the Plaza is the Monterey Canning Co. This historic building is a restored original example of the street crossover that carried sardines from the oceanside cannery to the streetside warehouse. On the street side are other sites from Steinbeck's books. The flophouse was at **Bruce Arliss Walkway. Kalisa's La Ida Cafe**, now a café, was one of the many houses of ill repute on the row. **Alicia's Place** in **Wing Chung's building** conjures up the old days. Across the row is the unmarked wood building, two doors from the aquarium, that was Ed "Doc" Ricketts's Pacific Biological Laboratory. Ricketts was a powerful influence on Steinbeck, and many others, as a friend and mentor. As a visionary marine biologist, he inspired generations of scientists through his book *Between Pacific Tides*. His holistic view of the marine environment is reflected in the design of the aquarium.

Moreover, the bay supports growing research, educational, and recreational industries, including the aquarium and its spin-offs. High-tech video production houses, hardware and software developers, ocean kayak and scuba-diving

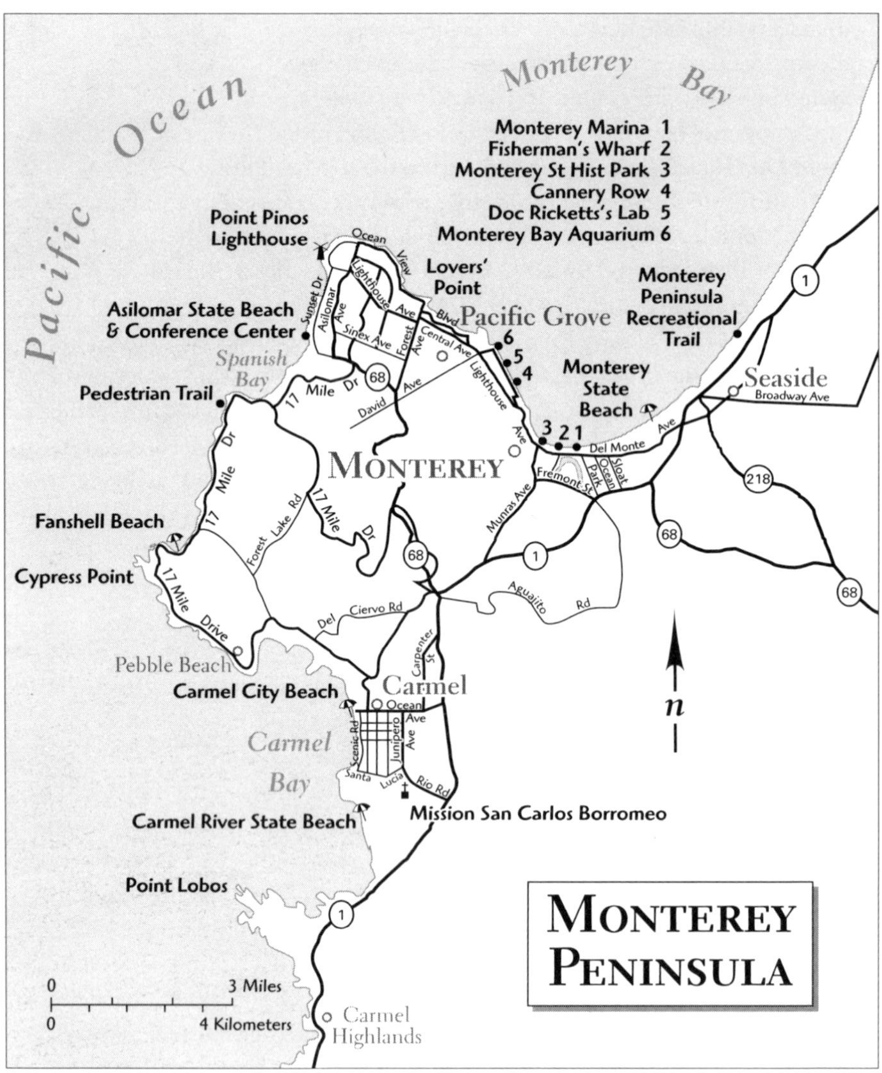

schools, and other ocean-related companies fill the nooks and crannies left by the tourism revitalization. Each year 1.7 million visitors flock to the aquarium; often the experience is more like crowd control than environmental education. However, the Monterey Bay Aquarium, featuring the coastal and offshore resources of the area, is the premier educational attraction of the California coast.

Just past the aquarium is the **American Tin Cannery**. This former can factory now houses outlet stores and the Pat Hathaway Collection of historical photos of this area. Across from the Tin Cannery is Stanford University's

Hopkins Marine Station. This is California's first marine research center, in operation on the Monterey Peninsula since 1892.

Offshore, Monterey offers the most intensely used diving area along the coast. For an exciting perspective on the shoreline, rent a kayak; try **Monterey Bay Kayaks** (693 Del Monte Avenue, 408-373-5357) or **Pete's Sports Supply and Service Co.** (408-655-6761).

Monterey Bay Aquarium Since its opening in 1984, this 2-ton whale of the water world has become one of the can't-miss destinations on the California coast. It gets high marks for combining spectacular presentation—like a three-story, glass-enclosed kelp forest—with endlessly interesting facts about the denizens of Monterey Bay, which plunges from the Pacific Coast into one of the deepest undersea canyons in the world. There are sharks and sea otters here, with thrice-daily feedings of the latter, as well as a touch pool for those who want to get closer to tidal invertebrates. There are

TOM MIKKELSEN

"Doc" Ricketts's Lab, Cannery Row

Sea Studios—Cannery Row

■ Of all the animals in the world, 99.9 percent are invertebrates—which means they don't have backbones. These are the jellyfish, crabs, mollusks, octopuses, barnacles, sea anemones, and squid, to name but a few (and to leave out the entire insect world, which also fits the category).

In Monterey, the squid is the most important invertebrate in the bay, a prime commodity in Japanese markets. Every night, boats are out "squidding." Squid are also very important to medical and scientific research because they have large cells, so large, in fact, that tiny instruments can be inserted inside them to report on how cells work and develop.

Despite the fact that invertebrates make up most of the inhabitants of the ocean—and most of the life along the California coast—they don't get much attention. Consider the sea otter, for example. Warm, cuddly, and incredibly cute, sea otters are stars of stage and screen. But they don't really have a big role in Monterey Bay—certainly nothing like the star of the show, the lowly squid, which keeps a whole harvesting industry in business and helps the high-tech medical companies out in the Silicon Valley.

Sea Studios started on Cannery Row in the early '80s. It was an outgrowth of the new aquarium. The big new aquarium wanted specimens, of course, but it also needed complex video displays to educate the public. Sea Studios was started to meet that need. But even an outfit as large as the aquarium wasn't big enough to keep Sea Studios going.

In the old days, ocean pioneers like Doc Ricketts, who was made famous by John Steinbeck, collected ocean specimens that were used in classrooms to study the sea. (Doc Ricketts's lab was called Pacific Biological Laboratories, and it was at 800 Cannery Row. The exterior of the building is the same as it was in the '40s. Steinbeck collaborated with Ricketts on *Sea of Cortez*; Ricketts appears as "Doc" in Steinbeck's books *Cannery Row* and *Sweet Thursday*.) Doc Ricketts specialized in the lowly, and crucially important, invertebrates. Sea Studios, well aware of its Cannery Row heritage—its place was right next to Doc Ricketts's old lab—wondered if it couldn't do the same thing. After all, there were plenty of people making videos and movies about sea otters, but how about an animal such as the jellyfish? How about an ocean studio that focused on the underpublicized, unusual, and unglamorous animals that make up most of the

---

tours and educational programs as well. It's well worth the fairly stiff cost of admission. Access is via Cannery Row at David Avenue; there are fee parking lots galore in the area. Call 408-648-4888 for more information.

Monterey State Historic Park This park is a collection of historic buildings that jointly display the heritage of Monterey Bay through successive incarnations: Native American land, Spanish colony, Mexican state, and US fishing town. Especially interesting is the **Maritime Museum of Monterey** at 5 Custom House Plaza; it's got a collection of ship models and an in-house

food chain in Monterey Bay, and in the rest of the world, for that matter?

Jellies took the cameras down deep, where the big jellyfish are, using a remotely operated vehicle that belonged to the aquarium. Many jellyfish have translucent bodies that glow in the dark. Against the black background of the ocean depths, the jellies looked like wondrous spaceships.

Seasons of the Squid followed, showing the great colonies of sea squid that inhabit Monterey Bay. Using tiny cameras, Sea Studios also followed tadpoles through a coastal estuary. One camera was so small and unobtrusive that the tadpoles tried to eat it. And for the St. Louis Zoo, Sea Studios made *Be a Bass*. It is about a smallmouth bass traveling downstream to spawn. On the way downstream, there are challenges to overcome, dangers to be faced. Using laser-disk technology, visitors to this exhibit pretended to be a bass, navigating downstream, making decisions, and sometimes being eaten.

Sea Studios also developed a business selling stock footage. When interesting things happen on the bay, Sea Studios is there. One day, a huge number of juvenile seals came into Monterey Bay. They were on a hunt for food, coming north from the Channel Islands. They rested on wharves and beaches, covering the bay. Staff members grabbed their cameras, jumped into their boats, and started filming. Another time pelagic crabs invaded the bay, turning it red, which is the color of their skin. (*Pelagic* means "open ocean"—these were ocean crabs, unlike the Dungeness crabs that are caught by fishermen up and down the coast of California. Tuna are "pelagic," too—that is, they live out in the sea.) When the crabs came in, Sea Studios went out again.

These days, Sea Studios is working on a multipart TV show about the world of animals. It will be hours long, but the part dealing with vertebrates—the animals and fishes we are all familiar with, such as humans and sea otters—will take up only about 20 minutes' time. The rest will be filled with invertebrates, because so much more of nature really is.

Note: Besides doing important research, Doc Ricketts also wrote a book called *Between Pacific Tides*—one of the finest books ever published about California's ocean biology. It is still in print, and is the best guide available to the marine life on the California coast. ■

---

model maker at work. Access is via the park headquarters at 20 Custom House Plaza; there is a free parking lot. Call 408-649-7118 for more information. Also on the square is the original **Custom House**. Once the only port of entry into California, this is the oldest government building in the state. It has been restored to its 1830s look.

Down Calle Principal from the Plaza are restored historic adobes including **Stevenson House** (where Robert Lewis Stevenson lived), **Coulton House** (site of first California Constitutional Convention), and the scenic **Cooper-Molena Adobe**.

Monterey Peninsula Recreational Trail This is a 3-mile-long paved bicycle and pedestrian trail running from the town of Seaside to the Monterey Bay Aquarium (see above). It is wheelchair accessible and has benches strategically placed at spectacular vistas of Monterey Bay. Access is all along the waterfront east of Monterey Bay Aquarium; call 408-646-3866 for more information.

Fort Ord, a little farther up the coast out of town, is a successful swords-into-plowshares conversion of a surplus Army base into an educational park. Along Highway 1, check out the farm stands for local artichokes.

Molera Road is a scenic detour toward the coast off Highway 1. Prosperous coastal agriculture can be seen on both sides of the road.

Castroville, "The Artichoke Capital of the World," is on Highway 1 at Highway 156 (a scenic shortcut to Highway 101). Here you will find more varieties of fresher, bigger, and maybe greasier artichokes to take home or eat than imaginable.

IN MARINA

Marina State Beach. This is 170 acres of sandy beach backed by dunes and bluffs, and a popular spot from which to launch hang gliders. It features a 2000-foot-long boardwalk running from near the parking lot to an observation platform and the beach; the platform is wheelchair accessible. Though it's a popular beach for surf-fishing, swimming and surfing are not recommended due to hazardous waves, wind, and currents. It can be crowded during the summer, when hordes of people flee the high temperatures of the inland valleys. Access is via the end of Reservation Road; there are free parking lots. Call 408-384-7695 for further information.

Elkhorn Slough National Estuarine Research Reserve ★ studies and protects the valuable wetland system. The visitors center, located at 1700 Elkhorn Road, is open Wednesday–Sunday 9 AM–5 PM and provides trail access and educational exhibits. Fee required. Take Dolan Road off Highway 1 to Elkhorn Road, then make a left and go approximately 2 miles to the reserve. Drive carefully during rainy season; roads here are subject to flooding and are often impassable. Pick up the map for access sites to the slough. Many species of plants and animals live in harmony with encroaching industrial and agricultural developments. Kayaks and pontoon boats are available in the yacht harbor from **Elkhorn Slough Safari** (408-633-5555) or **Kayak Connection** (408-724-5692).

IN MOSS LANDING

Moss Landing is a commercial fishing harbor in the shadow of the Bay's major industrial plants. **Pacific Gas and Electric's "Mighty Moss"** power plant is the second largest fossil-fueled generator in the world. The massive structure vibrates when it really gets going. **The National Refractory** next door is also an impressive industrial structure. Don't let these megaliths distract you from the harbor and the rich **Elkhorn Slough**, though. The fishing industry is struggling to survive here. On the island, derelict boats are strewn on the dunes. Fishing from the beach and marine research are thriving. The newly built **Monterey Bay Aquarium Research Institute** and the **Moss Landing Marine Laboratories** (scheduled to rebuild their earthquake-destroyed facilities soon) are both located on Sandholt Road on the island. Drive slowly, and yield to the first-arrived vehicle on the one-way bridge. The weekday nautical atmosphere is replaced by the weekend antiques shoppers. Over 20 antiques stores draw large crowds. On the last Saturday in July is an antiques street fair. Fun, but no bargains. Offshore is the deep Monterey Trench, a major feature of the bay. The upwelling from the deep feeds the rich marine life in these waters.

Salinas River State Beach. This beach is 246 acres of sand and sand dunes, and at its south end lies the Salinas River's ocean outlet. It's cold, windy, and quite unsafe for swimming, and these crowd-chasing conditions make it perfect for those seeking solitude. Hiking, fishing, and clamming are the main activities here; visitors should note that they may need a clamming permit before digging up dinner. Just south of the beach is the **Salinas River National Wildlife Refuge;** it features hiking trails and a separate parking lot. Access is via a parking lot on Molera Road at Monterey Dunes Way; there is a smaller lot at the end of Potrero Road off Highway 1. Call 408-384-7695 for further information.

Elkhorn Slough National Estuarine Research Reserve ★ This waterway runs inland from Moss Landing Harbor; it is 1400 acres of salt marshes and other wetlands. It provides a safe haven for several types of large, endangered birds like the peregrine falcon and golden eagle, and currently has 5 miles of hiking trails. There is a fee for access, although this is waived if visitors have a valid California fishing license. There is parking east of Highway 1; call 408-728-2822 for more information.

Moss Landing State Beach (aka Jetty Beach) is wide and windswept, backed by sand dunes and used primarily for surfing and clamming (although horses are allowed April 15–August 15). The view inland is of power-plant smokestacks, but the beach also provides access to Elkhorn Slough (see above). There are only chemical toilets available. Access is via Jetty Road at Highway 1; there is a fee parking lot. Call 408-384-7695 for more information.

Zmudowski State Beach The last beach as you head north to Santa Cruz County, Zmudowski boasts 177 acres of dunes and sand. You traverse a boardwalk to get to the beach, which, like its southern neighbors, is used mostly for clamming and surfing. The winds and waves can be unexpectedly strong, though, so exercise caution when getting into the water. Swimming definitely is not recommended. Access is via the end of Gilbertson Road from Highway 1, just north of Moss Landing, and there is no fee for use. Call Marina State Beach, which administers Zmudowski, at 408-384-7695 for more information.

Lodging

IN BIG SUR

Ragged Point Inn (805-927-4502), off Highway 1, 15 miles north of San Simeon. Moderate. The inn boasts 19 large, modern guest rooms. Enjoy spectacular southern Big Sur views from cliffside rooms. Each has TV, coffee, and full bath. A path leads to the beach below. A restaurant is planned.

Lucia Lodge (408-667-2391), 24 miles south of Pfeiffer Big Sur State Park. Expensive. Ten very rustic rooms sit on the edge of the ocean. The lodge features dark slatted wood walls and beamed ceilings. All rooms have fine-quality beds and showers. Units 7–10 offer fabulous views of Lucia Bay and the southern Big Sur coast. The Lucia store and restaurant are a short walk away.

Ventana Inn (408-667-2331; 1-800-628-6500) and the **Post Ranch Inn** (408-667-2200; 1-800-527-2200), just south of Big Sur Village, are two luxury resorts. Located 150 miles south of San Francisco and 300 miles north of Los Angeles, both offer exceptional accommodations and full services, pools, and prize-winning restaurants. They comprise a series of small buildings nestled into their sites on opposite sides of Highway 1. All rooms have ocean or mountain views. Set on its own 243-acre slice of the Santa Lucia Mountains, Ventana is the last word in getting away to it all. Its secluded location doesn't preclude amenities like in-room marble fireplaces, Japanese baths, saunas, two pools, a clothing-optional sun deck, and afternoon wine and cheese. Ventana is large enough to have its own hiking trails, and free coffee and pastries can be delivered to your room each morning.

The way the **Post Ranch Inn's** lodgepole construction, earth tones, and building sites fit into the landscape takes the ecohotel concept to the extreme. The "tree houses" are nestled into the redwoods without disturbing their ecology. The Ventana, with a 20-year head start on the Post Ranch, is above the highway on a brow of the ridge. Its many buildings are spread out, affording privacy and a feeling of decadence. Both are very expensive, but either is a worthwhile indulgence. Reservations are required at both resorts.

Ripplewood Resort (408-667-2242), Highway 1. Expensive. With its 16 spartan cabins clustered along a rugged section of the highway, Ripplewood Resort is the perfect place to go with a large group of friends. Try to book cabins 1–9, which are set on the river far below the road. During the summer the popular units are reserved 4 months in advance, so plan ahead.

Big Sur Campground and Cabins (408-667-2322), Highway 1. Moderate. The 17 "cabins" here range from fully equipped mobile homes to wooden A-frames with sleeping lofts and kitchens. Several of the units sit along the Big Sur River, and each has a private bath and fireplace. In the summer, four tent cabins are also rented—with beds and bedding provided—or you can bring your sleeping bag and rough it at one of the 80 year-round campsites set in a large redwood grove. Guests often while away the day swimming or fishing in the river (steelhead season runs November 16–February 28, on weekends, Wednesdays, and holidays only). Amenities include a store, laundry, playground, basketball courts, and inner-tube rentals.

Deetjen's Big Sur Inn (408-667-2377), Highway 1. Moderate to expensive. Built in the '30s by a Norwegian immigrant, this is a collection of about 20 cottages and cabins of different sizes and shapes. All the buildings are simple and have various idiosyncrasies, like throw rugs, fireplaces, and unfinished doors that may not quite fit. It's all part of the charm, though, as are solid beds with big, thick comforters and dinner by candlelight in the restaurant, which is Helmut Deetjen's original house.

Glen Oaks Motel (408-667-2105), Highway 1. Moderate. This basic 15-unit motel is friendly, clean, quiet, and comfortable.

IN CARMEL

Highlands Inn (408-624-3801; 1-800-682-4811), Highway 1, 4 miles south of Carmel. Expensive. High above the rocky coastline with breathtaking views of nearby Point Lobos, the Highlands Inn is a local favorite—so well landscaped and so oriented to the fabulous views that guests hardly notice that the 142 rooms and suites are really quite dull. All amenities.

Mission Ranch (408-624-6436), 26270 Dolores Street. Expensive. Owned by Clint Eastwood, this dairy ranch has been renovated into a 31-room resort. Relaxing setting and enjoyable grounds make this a good choice to get away from it all. Breakfast included.

Cypress Inn (408-624-3871; 1-800-443-7443), on Lincoln Street at 7th Avenue. Expensive. Doris Day owns this pleasant 33-room Mediterranean-style inn in the center of town. Attentive service makes up for the slightly shabby rooms.

San Antonio House (408-624-4334), on San Antonio Street between Ocean and 7th Avenues. Expensive. Built in the late 1920s, this four-room B&B is quite pleasant. It's also near the beach.

Carmel River Inn (408-624-1575); take Oliver Road off Highway 1 at the south end of Carmel River Bridge. Moderate. The Carmel River Inn's 24 cottages and 19 motel units offer basic but homey accommodations. There's a heated pool, and some rooms have kitchens and separate bedrooms, so this is a good spot for families.

Pine Inn (408-624-3851; 1-800-228-3851), Ocean between Lincoln and Monteverde. Expensive. This 100-year-old lodge is a favorite base for shopping in the vicinity. Recently renovated, there's an on-site restaurant and excellent service.

Coachman's Inn (408-624-6421; 1-800-336-6421), San Carlos Street near Ocean Avenue. Moderate. A slightly shabby but adequate motel, it still gives good value.

Colonial Terrace Inn (408-624-2741), San Antonio and 13th Avenues. Moderate. This seven-unit hotel is surprisingly inexpensive, considering that it's practically next to the beach in downtown Carmel. Rooms all have gas fireplaces, some face the ocean, and there's complimentary breakfast in the morning.

La Playa Hotel (408-624-6476; 1-800-582-8900), Camino Real and 8th Avenue. Expensive. This is a quiet place to stay very close to the beach—so close that the sounds of the Pacific come through the windows. Visitors can choose from rooms in the main building or detached bungalows, and there is also a swimming pool and extensive garden.

IN PEBBLE BEACH

The Inn at Spanish Bay (408-647-7500; 1-800-654-9300), 2700 17-Mile Drive. Expensive. The inn—newer, and marginally less expensive than the lodge up the road—is a luxurious, beachfront, 270-room golf resort. Included are tennis courts, a fitness club, swimming pool, and access to the magnificent beaches, hiking, and equestrian trails.

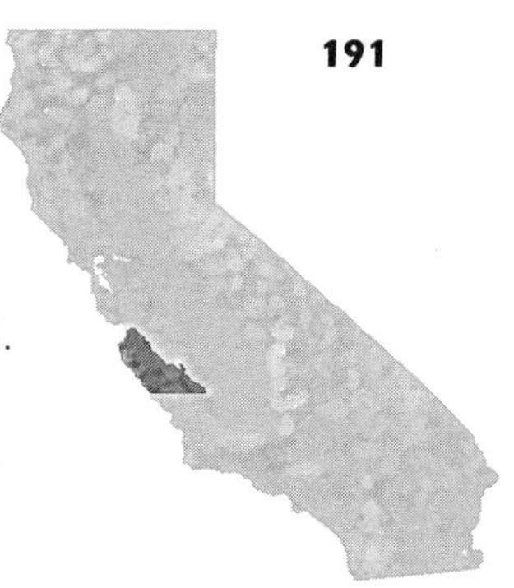

The Lodge at Pebble Beach (408-624-3811; 1-800-654-9300), 17-Mile Drive near Carmel Gate. Expensive. Greens fees of more than $200 do not deter golfers from these courses and this landmark hotel. Recently renovated, the 161 suites have top-of-the-line amenities, views, and service. Several restaurants offer a variety of dining options.

IN PACIFIC GROVE

Borg's "Ocean View" Motel (408-375-2406), 635 Ocean View Boulevard. Moderate. Borg's is the best buy for beachfront accommodations on the peninsula, clean, with good service, and convenient to all attractions. It often requires a 2-day stay on weekends for its 60 units.

Seven Gables Inn (408-732-4341), 555 Ocean View Boulevard. Expensive. A classic bed & breakfast built in 1886 with a magnificent view of Monterey Bay. Victorian styled throughout, the inn is managed informally and well. There are 14 varied rooms, and breakfast and afternoon tea are served in a formal dining room.

Gatehouse Inn (408-649-8436; 1-800-753-1881), 225 Central Avenue. Expensive. Built in 1884, it has nine Victorian rooms with all amenities and scenic ocean views.

Lighthouse Lodge and Suites (408-655-2111; 1-800-528-1234), 1150 and 1249 Lighthouse Avenue. Moderate. Of the 100 rooms, ask for one of the 30 newer suites. They are packed with amenities such as Jacuzzi, large TV, and plush furnishings.

The Asilomar Conference Center (408-372-8016), 800 Asilomar Boulevard. Moderate. Many of the original buildings at Asilomar were designed by famed Bay Area architect Julia Morgan. They were donated to the YWCA by Phoebe Apperson Hearst and are now owned by the State Parks system, operated by the Asilomar Corporation as a conference ground. However, individuals and small groups can rent rooms up to 60 days in advance on a space-available basis. The center's 105 acres of pines and dunes include a heated, Olympic-sized swimming pool, wooded trails, and a scenic stretch of beach. There are 315 units in the complex; the older rooms, designed by Morgan, are spartan, but they are also more charming. Breakfast is included; food is not Asilomar's strength.

Rosedale Inn (408-655-1000; 1-800-822-5606), 775 Asilomar Boulevard. Moderate. A more upscale motel, it's adequate if you can't get into Asilomar. The 19 rooms are large and comfortable.

IN MONTEREY

The Monterey Hotel (408-375-3184; 1-800-727-0960), 406 Alvarado Street. Moderate to expensive. In the heart of historic downtown Monterey, this restored turn-of-the-century hotel is a classy value.

Monterey Bay Inn (408-373-6242; 1-800-424-6242), 242 Cannery Row. Expensive. Most of the 47 rooms have dramatic views of the bay from private balconies.

Monterey Plaza Hotel (408-646-1700; outside California: 1-800-637-7200), 400 Cannery Row. Expensive. The luxury choice on the row, this elegant full-service hotel is suitable for extravagant romantic or family splurges.

Spindrift Inn (408-646-8900; 1-800-841-1879), 652 Cannery Row. Expensive. On the beach in the midst of the excitement of the Row, the Sprindrift offers pampering luxury, terrific views, and excellent service. Try for the corner rooms; they have the best views.

Del Monte Beach Inn (408-649-4410), 1110 Del Monte Avenue. Moderate. Across from Montery State Beach, just out of the downtown, is this European-style bed & breakfast. Most rooms don't have private bath, but the inn is clean and well managed, with guests from all over the world as well as diving groups. Generous breakfasts make this a special value. Only about 20 rooms, so reserve early.

Old Monterey Inn (408-375-8284), 500 Martin Street. Expensive. A Tudor-style bed & breakfast with 10 units, the inn is close to the attractions of downtown Monterey but set back from it all on a side street. The rooms all are different, and several have fireplace, sun deck, or library, and the inn will deliver the complimentary full breakfast to visitors on request.

Restaurants

IN BIG SUR

Lucia Lodge (408-667-2391), 24 miles south of Pfeiffer Big Sur State Park. Inexpensive. Great views from outdoor seating, fair food. Fresh fish selections, and a generous fish-and-chips basket. Meat and pasta also served. Lunch only.

Pacific Valley Cafe (408-927-8655), 32 miles south of Pfeiffer Big Sur State Park. Inexpensive. Choose indoor and outdoor seating in a meadow setting, or in a rustic café. Burgers, fresh fish, and good pies are on the menu. The café serves breakfast, lunch, and dinner.

Nepenthe (408-667-2345), Highway 1. Moderate. Here's a beautifully located place for lunch, 800 feet above sea level with a great view of the ocean, and a varied menu to boot: quiches, Ambrosiaburgers, and salads for lunch, more substantial meat and fish entrées for dinner. Or just come by for an afternoon drink at the bar; the view is worth it.

Ventana Restaurant (408-667-2331), Highway 1 (at the Ventana Inn, see **Lodging**). Expensive. Visitors will find this a deluxe restaurant suiting Ventana's deluxe accommodations. The menu changes constantly, but filet mignon, fresh pasta, fish and other seafood, salads, and rack of lamb all have been known to make an appearance. There is an enormous wine list.

Sierra Mar Restaurant (408-667-2800; 1-800-527-2200) at the Post Ranch Inn. Expensive. Also a fabulous setting. Dramatic architecture and sophisticated California cuisine are reasons to check out the newest resort on the Big Sur coast. Reservations recommended.

Deetjen's Restaurant (408-667-2378), about a mile south of Pfeiffer Big Sur State Park. Expensive. Day visitors are offered excellent meals at this inn's restaurant. Local produce and Continental cuisine combine in flavorful meals.

Big Sur Center Deli and Grocery (408-667-2225), in Big Sur Village. Inexpensive. Offers good sandwiches and food to go. Also in the village is the **Ripplewood Inn** (408-667-2242). Inexpensive. This is a good breakfast or lunch stop.

IN CARMEL

Rio Grill (408-625-5436), Crossroads Shopping Center at Highway 1 and Rio Road. Moderate. This is a busy grill filled with a loud crowd enjoying the barbecued ribs.

Hog's Breath (408-625-1044), San Carlos Street and Fifth Avenue. Moderate. This restaurant catapulted owner Clint Eastwood into Carmel's mayoral politics. The cinematic gumshoe, outraged that it was taking eight years to acquire a permit to expand Hog's Breath, made an end run around the system, winding up as mayor and slashing bureaucracy from the top rather than the bottom. Meanwhile, back at the restaurant, visitors will find Eastwood-themed burgers, steaks, and sausage sandwiches served among large crowds, especially in summer. A good choice for lunch, though Clint sightings are rare.

IN PACIFIC GROVE

A standard strip mall at 1184 Forest Avenue near Prescott has become a good, inexpensively priced food court. **Allegro** (408-373-5656) has the best pizza on the peninsula. **Pablo's** (408-646-8888) offers good, healthy Mexican food. The chef is rumored to have been Ansel Adams' cook. Candy, ice cream shops, and other restaurants are also located at this culinary gateway to the heart of Monterey Peninsula.

The Fishwife (408-375-7107), 1996½ Sunset Drive. Moderate. Lunch and dinner Wednesday–Monday, brunch Sunday. Local favorite, good with kids. Enjoy seafood with a Caribbean flavor. Recommendations include the chowder and Key lime pie. Standard pasta dishes are also served.

The Old Bath House (408-375-5195), 620 Ocean View Boulevard. Expensive. Dinner is served daily. Touristy, but excellent food matches the great views. Good service, a romantic treat.

Peppers Mexicali Cafe (408-373-6892), 170 Forest Avenue off Lighthouse. Inexpensive, but crowded with locals. Lunch Monday, Wednesday–Saturday; dinner Wednesday–Monday. Excellent home-made tamales, chiles rellenos, and seafood. Good beers, and the café has an extensive wine list.

IN MONTEREY

Franklin Street Bar & Grille 150 W. Franklin Street. Inexpensive. This is a good choice for lunch (think one step up from burgers and fries) or for an after-dinner beer, a comfortable "bar" bar where locals can go to get away from tourists.

Montrio (408-648-8880), 414 Calle Principal. Moderate. Sample innovative California cuisine with local produce and fish in the historic downtown.

Bay Books (408-375-1855), 316 Alvarado Street at Del Monte, is the best spot for local guidebooks, general literature, and good coffee and treats in downtown Monterey.

Fresh Cream (408-375-9798), Heritage Harbor across from Fisherman's Wharf at 99 Pacific Street near Scott Street. Expensive. When it's time to splurge on dinner, this may be the place to do it. Visitors will have a spectacular view of the bay through floor-to-ceiling windows and be plied with California interpretations of French cuisine, including lavishly prepared fishes, seafoods, and meats. A very romantic dining experience.

Gianni's Pizza (408-649-1500), 725 Lighthouse Avenue. Inexpensive. This is just what the name implies: a family-owned restaurant that serves solid Italian food like pizza, pasta, and garlic bread at bargain prices.

Trattoria Paradiso (408-375-4155), 654 Cannery Row. Inexpensive. A reliable seafood and Italian bistro, it has great views and reliable food. Try the calamari.

Monterey Fish House (408-373-4647), 2114 Del Monte Avenue. Moderate. One of the best seafood restaurants on the coast features excellent fish stews, oysters, and fresh daily catch from the bay. Friendly service; filled with locals, so make reservations.

IN MOSS LANDING

Phil's Fish Market and Eatery (408-633-2152), 7640 Sandholt Road. Inexpensive. Located next to the new research lab, Phil's specializes in fried local fish, to take out or eat on the deck. The market sells local catch and produce. A friendly place, it's good for kids and fronts the beach.

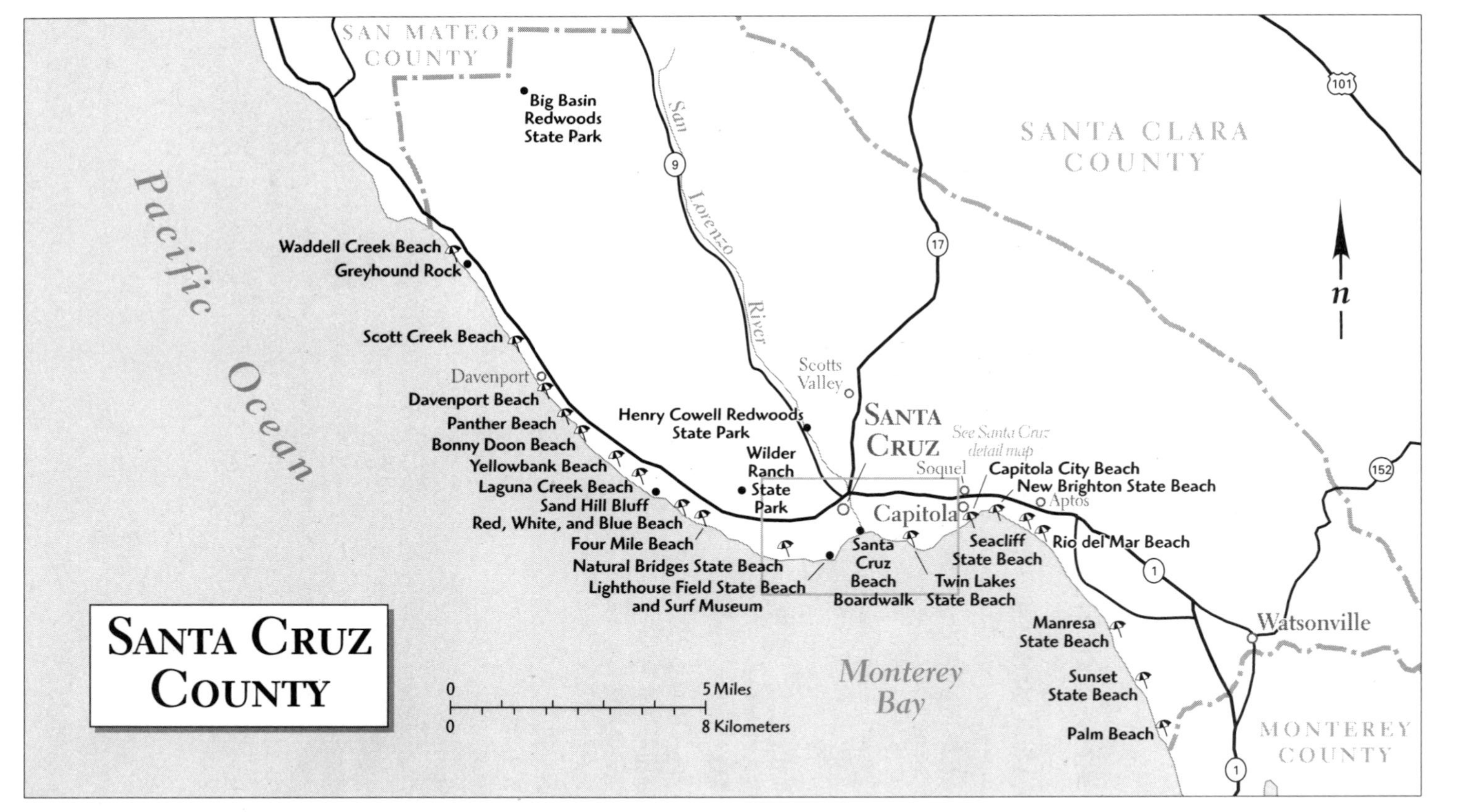
Santa Cruz County
San Mateo County
Santa Clara County
Monterey County
Pacific Ocean
Monterey Bay
n
Big Basin Redwoods State Park
San Lorenzo River
Scotts Valley
Santa Cruz
See Santa Cruz detail map
Soquel
Capitola
Aptos
Watsonville
Davenport
Waddell Creek Beach
Greyhound Rock
Scott Creek Beach
Davenport Beach
Panther Beach
Bonny Doon Beach
Yellowbank Beach
Laguna Creek Beach
Sand Hill Bluff
Red, White, and Blue Beach
Four Mile Beach
Natural Bridges State Beach
Lighthouse Field State Beach and Surf Museum
Henry Cowell Redwoods State Park
Wilder Ranch State Park
Santa Cruz Beach Boardwalk
Twin Lakes State Beach
Capitola City Beach
New Brighton State Beach
Seacliff State Beach
Rio del Mar Beach
Manresa State Beach
Sunset State Beach
Palm Beach
0
5 Miles
0
8 Kilometers
1
9
17
101
152

CHAPTER EIGHT

Santa Cruz County

THE SOUTHERN HALF OF SANTA CRUZ COUNTY is formed by Monterey Bay, which ends, in the middle of the county, at Point Santa Cruz. In this southern section, there are wide, sandy beaches, backed often by cliffs that sometimes reach 100 feet. Many of the pleasant beaches of this area—New Brighton, Seacliff, Manresa, and the Sunset beaches—have been set aside as state parks. In the far south of Santa Cruz, there is an area of sand dunes, the Pajaro.

North of Santa Cruz Point, the coast is defined by a ridge of mountains, the Santa Cruz. The main ridge of this range lies to the east. Along its eastern edge runs the San Andreas fault. Close to the northern Santa Cruz coastline are two western mountains of the Santa Cruz range, Bald Mountain in the south and Ben Lomand in the north. Around these two mountains, the coast bulges west in a soft curve; from their base, marine terraces slope gently to the beach. Below them is a string of pocket beaches, many of which are undeveloped and isolated and often beautiful. Just to the north is Big Basin Redwoods State Park, one of the loveliest parks in the state.

Between the main range of the Santa Cruz Mountains and the two western mountains of the coast, the San Lorenzo River flows through a long valley to the sea, which it reaches at Santa Cruz. This river, and the marine terraces through which it passes, form a striking backdrop for the city of Santa Cruz.

The Pajaro River forms the boundary between Santa Cruz and Monterey counties. From here north to New Brighton State Beach, the beaches are protected by Santa Cruz Point to the north, the upper edge of Monterey Bay. The coastline follows a gentle, smooth curve as it moves north. Of these beaches, 7-mile-long Sunset State Beach is perhaps the most beautiful.

New Brighton State Beach is large and sandy, with excellent views of Monterey Bay and nature trails. To the north of New Brighton, the suburbs of Santa Cruz begin with the city of Capitola, which may or may not be—as it claims—the "oldest resort on the Pacific Coast." The small city has interesting architectural features, including the "Venetian court" set along the beach. This is a condominium subdivision, built in the '20s, which mimics an ancient Mediterranean village. Art galleries, boutiques, a fishing pier, and a relaxed atmosphere are parts of what make the city a favorite destination point.

Near Capitola, the coast swings to the southeast as it moves toward the Santa Cruz headland. The beaches in this area are protected, often lovely, and more crowded than those to the south. As the coastline nears the city of Santa Cruz, there is a series of lagoons that are important breeding grounds for birds.

Santa Cruz has been a recreation destination for San Francisco residents for more than 100 years. The coastline here lies on a marine terrace and delta area that is often several miles wide. There is a long fishing wharf near the mouth of the San Lorenzo River. To the west, above Lighthouse Field State Beach, is the Santa Cruz Surfing Museum, which is located inside the old lighthouse. Santa Cruz is known as an excellent surfing area. One of the best breaks—the Steamer Lane—lies just offshore from the lighthouse. Lighthouse Field State Beach has excellent views—it's a good place for a picnic—but the cliffs are eroded and dangerous.

Santa Cruz is perhaps best known for its "boardwalk"—an old-time amusement park built on an excellent beachfront that begins at the western shore of the San Lorenzo River. This is a good beach for swimming, although it is often crowded. The boardwalk contains a terrifying wooden roller coaster, a rattling, ancient contraption that gives riders excellent views of the ocean before a steep vertical plunge. The only amusement park like it on the California coast, the boardwalk is a family destination that can be combined, over a weekend, with a trip to the Monterey Bay Aquarium as well as to the University of California at Santa Cruz, which has an architecturally significant campus area within the city.

North of Santa Cruz, the coastline is characterized by sandy beaches and low cliffs. The urban coastal corridor ends at Natural Bridges State Beach. This beach is noted for its monarch butterflies; it is the largest monarch wintering ground in the United States. Guided tours are offered of the excellent tide pools located here. From overlooks, there are good views of natural bridge rock formations. Just to the north is the Long Marine Laboratory, an important marine research institute.

Between Natural Bridges State Beach and Año Nuevo (in San Mateo County) the coast is formed of wide marine terraces used for agriculture, backed by mountainside. The northern section contains the western edge of a large—and beautiful—state park, Big Basin.

Davenport is the only real town in northern Santa Cruz. A series of often isolated, beautiful pocket beaches are found here between Red, White, and Blue Beach to the south and Davenport. These pocket beaches usually are found at the mouth of streams, as at Scott Creek and Waddell Creek Beach. Sometimes access, as at Scott Creek, is easy. At other pocket beaches, though, trails wind through the bluffs to the beach below.

Beaches and Attractions

IN SANTA CRUZ COUNTY

Palm Beach ★ Palm Beach is a unit of Sunset State Beach that provides access from the mouth of the Pajaro River north. Behind the dunes is a private development called Pajaro Dunes. The 9-mile **Pajaro River Bike Path** intersects the beach near here, running from the river mouth inland to Holohan Road and Highway 152. Access to the beach is off Highway 1 at Watsonville. Take the Highway 129 exit, then take Beach Road west to the parking lot. Rest rooms, picnic tables, and fire pits are available. The dunes and eucalyptus grove are delightful additions to the broad sandy beach. The slough at the mouth of the river provides rich habitat for many birds, including the brown pelican and least tern, both of which are endangered. For more information, call the State Parks Department at Sunset State Beach, 408-763-7063.

Sunset State Beach This destination beach provides almost 7 miles of broad, sandy shoreline somewhat marred by occasional residential development. Fishing and clamming are popular September–April. Bluffs provide scenic picnic areas amid meadows of lupines and poppies. The uplands and beach provide habitat for several endangered species, including the snowy plover and California least tern. Swimming is unsafe—sea otters often swim offshore, but the surf is hazardous for humans. Take the Mar Monte exit off Highway 1 to San Andreas Road, thence to Sunset Beach Road. Ninety campsites are available, in addition to some more primitive "en route" sites. Make reservations by calling 408-763-7063.

Manresa State Beach. The scenic dunes have been disturbed by past agricultural use, but they still afford good habitat for rare plants and birds. The surf offers good fishing, and you'll find salmon offshore in season. Pismo clams are taken September–April. Surfing is popular, but swimming is unsafe. The beach in front of La Selva is private, but visitors walking north in the wet sand can reach Lundborgh Beach, also called Trestle Beach. This is a popular surfing and fishing spot. Manresa Uplands offers 64 walk-in campsites at the end of Manresa Beach Road. To find this broad sandy continuation of state beaches, take the Mar Monte exit off Highway 1 to San Andres Road, continue south to Sand Dollar Drive, and park in the lot there. Access is also available through the adjacent condominium development, and is for pedestrians only. Minimal facilities include rest rooms and a stairway to the beach. *Warning!* There are 170 steps down to the beach from the scenic bluff. Make reservations by calling 1-800-444-7275. For more information, call 408-724-3750.

Rio Del Mar Beach. This southernmost unit of Seacliff State Beach is located at the end of Rio Del Mar Boulevard. Aptos Creek and Lagoon cross the beach and provide bird habitat including alders and bigleaf maples. A hiking and bike path leads to the main park. Rest rooms are available. Call State Parks at Seacliff for more information at 408-685-6442.

Seacliff State Beach/Seacliff Pier. Its 2 miles of sandy beach and uplands provide an enjoyable mix of facilities and activities. A 500-foot wooden fishing pier extends to the wreck of the *Palo Alto*, a World War I–vintage concrete supply ship. It was deliberately sunk here to serve as an amusement complex with pools, dance hall, café, and carnival booths. It is now reopened (after storm damage), and the pier is heavily used for fishing and promenading. There are also wheelchair-accessible rest rooms, a bait and sandwich shop, an interpretive center, and a large picnic area. This is the northern limit of the Pismo clam. It is common to see sea lions and other marine mammals offshore. There are 26 campsites with trailer hook-ups on the beach and some additional "en route" sites. Campsite reservations at 1-800-444-7275. This destination beach is located off Highway 1 at the end of State Park Drive, just south of Capitola. Take the exit marked APTOS-SEACLIFF. For more information, call 408-685-6442.

New Brighton State Beach provides 115 full-service campsites and some bike-camping facilities. Reservations at 1-800-444-7275. Interpretive nature trails and stairs take you down to the beach. On the bluffs are Monterey pines, which provide habitat for wildlife such as deer, raccoons, and opossum as well as a wintering site for monarch butterflies.

The trees shade the camping areas, and the beach—northeast of Capitola and protected by the Live Oak Area—is shielded from Monterey Bay's strong winds. There are lifeguards during the summer, and this beach also provides good surf-fishing. Exit Highway 1 at the Park Avenue exit to reach this scenic beach. For more information, call 408-464-6330.

Capitola City Beach Capitola's beach fronts the town south of the Esplanade and Monterey Avenue. It has been restored by a groin at the east end of the beach. The structure traps sand to compensate for the depletion caused by Santa Cruz Harbor's disruption of sand transport. The beach is popular with visitors to the town. The Soquel Creek and Lagoon empty into the bay here; beach and creek manage to sustain a rich habitat for various fish, including steelhead, as well as for frogs, birds, and other wildlife—in the midst of bars, restaurants, and shops. Volleyball nets, rest rooms, and benches are provided. This is a very popular swimming beach. **Hooper Beach** is a narrower beach north of the Pier.

Capitola claims to be the oldest beach resort in California. The village is almost entirely oriented to tourists. Traffic is horrible on summer weekends, so use the remote parking lots off Highway 1. The **Capitola Fishing Wharf**, built in 1856 as a commercial wharf, had a dynamic commercial life before the railroad came to town. Today it offers good fishing, food, a bait shop, and rest rooms. Call the bait shop for more information at 408-462-2208.

Live Oak Beaches. In the Live Oak Area, between Capitola and Santa Cruz, are many pocket beaches. They are the scene of some conflict between residents and visitors. Parking has been restricted on many streets, and local surfers tend to be proprietary, making the following beaches enjoyable but often difficult to reach. The Santa Cruz County Department of Parks, Open Space, and Cultural Services can provide more information at 408-462-8300.

Key Beach requires purchase of a key to open the gate at Opal Cliffs at 45th Avenue and Opal Cliffs Drive—the surfing is good, but not worth the hassle. At the end of 41st Avenue is the scenic Pleasure Point Overlook from which visitors can observe the intrepid surfers.

Pleasure Point Beach is located along East Cliff Drive between 34th and 36th Avenues. The stairway at 35th Avenue provides access to the intermittent beach below, where there's good surfing. At the end of Rockwood Drive and East Cliff Drive is another excellent spot from which to watch the surfers if you decide not to join them.

Moran Lake and Park offers parking and rest rooms at 27th Avenue and East Cliff Drive. The lake is a recently restored wildlife preserve with an interpretive trail. Across the road is a wide, pleasant beach. At East Cliff Drive and 27th Avenue is **Corcoran Lagoon Beach**, another pleasant beach with a rich wildlife habitat area. No facilities or parking.

Sunny Cove is located at East Cliff Drive and 17th Avenue, but visitors should note that public rights to this beach are unclear. It features interesting tide pools and a pocket beach.

Lincoln Beach stretches from 14th to 16th Avenues, off East Cliff Drive. The beach can be reached at the ends of 12th and 14th Avenues. Behind it is **Bonita Lagoon**, another freshwater lagoon providing limited wildlife habitat.

Santa Cruz Harbor Area offers vistas of recreational boats and some commercial craft. Boat rentals, sport-fishing charters, restaurants, and cafés form a real waterfront community. For more information on the harbor, call

408-475-6161. While you're there, don't miss **O'Neill's Surf Shop** (408-476-5200), 2222 East Cliff Drive. This is the classic surf shop. It offers the best and widest variety of water-oriented stuff—suits, boards, and services.

Twin Lakes State Beach ★ One of the twin lakes was dredged to become the harbor, the other remains as **Schwan Lake**, a rich, diverse marshlike habitat for many species of birds, plants, and small mammals. This popular beach extends from both sides of the Santa Cruz Yacht Harbor. It offers picnic areas, volleyball courts, and rest rooms. To the east is Seabright Beach, also called Castle Beach. Until the 1950s the castlelike Scholl Mar Hotel was located above the San Lorenzo River. Sandpipers, gulls, and the black-crowned night heron feed here. This unit of Twin Lakes Beach, which extends to San Lorenzo Point, can be reached from the end of Seabright Avenue. The main access is from 7th Avenue. No off-street parking is available. Call State Parks at 408-429-2850 for more information.

Santa Cruz City Museum (408-429-3773), 1305 East Cliff Drive. This local museum displays the region's natural history and cultural themes. Tours are offered Tuesday through Friday.

Santa Cruz (Main) Beach Few locals use this wide beach. It nearly always draws a crowd and is backed by the renowned boardwalk, the only large amusement park left on the California coast. While the other parks faded because of real-estate pressures combined with changes in public taste, here the beach and boardwalk thrive in a well-managed public-private partnership. The beach has many volleyball courts, which are used for championship competitions; it also is the site of beauty pageants and music and comedy specials that draw crowds on weekends. Rest rooms and lifeguards make this mile-long beach popular with swimmers and dry-land tourists alike. The beach itself is seaward of Beach Street, east of the Municipal Wharf; access is through the boardwalk via 10 stairs and from a landscaped path along the street. Call the Santa Cruz Department of Aquatic Services for more information at 408-429-3747.

Santa Cruz Beach Boardwalk The last of the great beachfront amusement parks. Great rides, especially the classic Big Dipper roller coaster. Located behind the Main Beach, east of the wharf on Beach Street, it is the site of many special events and concerts. Well maintained and patrolled, it is a survivor. It draws more visitors than any other California amusement park except Disneyland. Despite the crowds, kids of all ages can spend at least half a day mixing junk food with stomach-churning excitement. The indoor arcade is fun in any weather. For seasonal schedule and information, call 408-426-7433.

Roaring Camp and Big Trees Narrow-Gauge Railroad Connects the Beach Boardwalk to Roaring Camp (a center for antique steam trains) in the Santa Cruz Mountains, near Felton. A fun alternative to driving. Board the train for a ride into the redwoods or enjoy the main train attraction on Graham Hill Road in Felton. For more information, call 408-335-4400.

Santa Cruz Municipal Wharf. Over a half-mile long, this pier offers mostly mediocre, overpriced restaurants with excellent views of the city's shoreline, surfers, and marine mammals. Good fishing. Fee for parking. For information on boat rentals, call 408-423-1739. For ocean kayak rentals, call 408-425-8445.

Cowell Beach/Steamer Lane This is an alternately sandy and rocky shore that once hosted the Miss California pageant and still does a brisk trade in volleyball tournaments. There are lifeguards and rest rooms here, and, of course, volleyball nets. Just west, on the other side of the Municipal Wharf from the main Santa Cruz beach, is one of the most famous surfing spots in California, **Steamer Lane**. Offshore conditions and the orientation of the coast make for truly huge swells. This by itself would be enough to scare off most surfers, but the waves break in an area of exposed and submerged rocks that threaten to shish-kabob the unwary. It makes for a thrilling spectacle, however. Access to Cowell Beach is via West Cliff Drive and Bay Street. For more information, call 408-429-3747.

©JAMES BLANK

Santa Cruz beach boardwalk

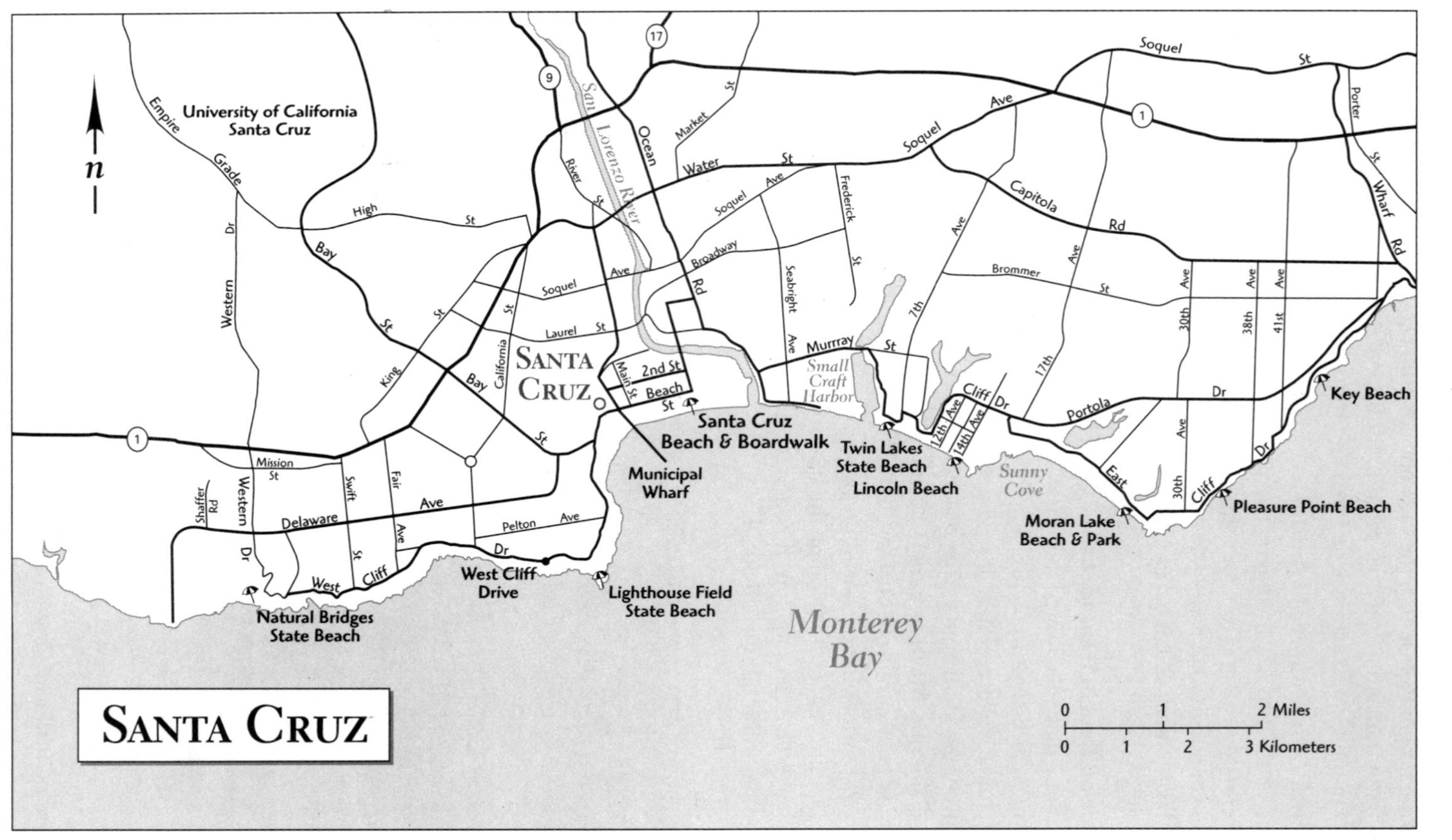

Santa Cruz
University of California Santa Cruz
Santa Cruz
Monterey Bay
Natural Bridges State Beach
West Cliff Drive
Lighthouse Field State Beach
Municipal Wharf
Santa Cruz Beach & Boardwalk
Twin Lakes State Beach
Lincoln Beach
Small Craft Harbor
Sunny Cove
Moran Lake Beach & Park
Pleasure Point Beach
Key Beach
San Lorenzo River
0 1 2 Miles
0 1 2 3 Kilometers

Neary's Lagoon City Park. A freshwater marsh, preserved by the city off California Street north of Bay Street. This is a vibrant wildlife sanctuary in the middle of residential development and adjacent to the sewer plant. Parking and rest rooms available.

Downtown Santa Cruz Santa Cruz was a sleepy resort and retirement town until the University of California built an expansive campus within its city limits in the '60s. Then came safety improvements to formerly treacherous Highway 17, and the town woke up. Now, current and former students, refugees from Silicon Valley over the hill, and hard-core hippies dominate the streets. **Pacific Garden Mall** and the commercial district have come back strong from the 1989 Loma Prieta earthquake. The mall is a very pleasant contrast to boring suburban shopping centers; over 250 shops and eateries are located in the downtown. Cafés, restaurants, movie theaters, shops, and two of the region's best bookstores (**Bookshop Santa Cruz**, 1520 Pacific Agenue, 408-423-0900; and **Logos**, 1117 Pacific Avenue, 408-427-5100) offer visitors excellent retail therapy and an alternative to the beach scene. On the mall, enjoy the **McPherson Center for Art and History** at 705 Front Street. They operate the **Octagon Building,** built in 1882. Somehow this brick building has survived all the area's earthquakes. It now shows local art and historical exhibits. The **San Lorenzo Riverfront** provides pleasant parkland and excellent hiking and biking trails on the levees from River Street to the beach. The **Bicycle Rental Center** is located at 415 Pacific Avenue (408-426-8687).

Mystery Spot. A weird optical illusion is located at 1953 Branciforte Drive, a fun diversion from the surf scene. For information and hours, call 408-423-8897. Admission fee.

Henry Cowell Redwood State Park. The Santa Cruz Mountains offer respite from too much sun and surf in several spectacular state parks. One of the best and most convenient is this one, just up Highway 9 from downtown Santa Cruz. This 1,800-acre park has over 20 miles of trails through cool tall trees and meadows. An easy hike is the Redwood Grove Trail, a scenic ¾-mile trail. Enjoy the interesting nature center. For more information, call 408-335-7077 or 408-335-4598.

Lighthouse Field State Beach. Located atop Point Santa Cruz, Lighthouse features about 40 acres of beach and blufftop, a scenic viewpoint, picnic tables, rest rooms, and a great location for fishing. Its centerpieces are a lighthouse and a surfing museum named for Mark Abbott, a local surfer who died offshore. The museum's bookstore is reputed to have the largest collection of

TOM MIKKELSEN

Lighthouse Point

surfing books and publications on the West Coast. Access is along West Cliff Drive at Point Santa Cruz. For more information about this museum, call 408-429-3429.

West Cliff Drive. West Cliff Drive links Lighthouse Field and Natural Bridges State Beaches. This scenic drive along the cliff shows how residential development can be compatible with shoreline protection. Only one house is located seaward of the road. Walking or biking on the shoreline path is recommended. Views are excellent and there is access to many pocket beaches. Use caution in climbing the cliffs. Stairs are located at 3rd Avenue and Monterey, Pelton, and Almar Streets. Some areas are used by nudists. Rest rooms are found at the state beaches only. Parking is tight on weekends.

Natural Bridges State Beach ★ Waves hitting offshore rock formations create the natural bridges that gave the beach its name; you can view these fascinating rock sculptures from shore. Also keep an eye peeled for sea lions, and, during fall and winter months, migrating monarch butterflies. You'll find tide pools along the sandy shore. For information call 408-423-4609.

Joseph M. Long Marine Laboratory and Aquarium ★ just west of Natural Bridges State Beach, has tanks packed with marine life, a shell collection, and even the skeleton of a blue whale. There is no fee, and docent tours are available, making this a great deal for families. The laboratory is a University of California research facility. For more information, call 408-423-4609.

Wilder Ranch State Park One of the newest California state parks, about a quarter of Wilder's 3600 acres are still under cultivation. The other three-quarters are open to the public and feature picnic tables, a visitors center around the original Wilder Ranch buildings, views of beaches, and 28 miles of hiking/biking/equestrian trails, most notably the Ohlone Bluff Trail, which leads to Wilder Beach. Access is via Highway 1, about 2 miles north of Santa Cruz. There is a fee for parking; for more information, call 408-423-9703.

Four Mile Beach. Part of Wilder State Beach, Four Mile's distinguishing feature is that it's clothing-optional. To reach the beach, hike about 10 minutes from roadside parking and cross some railroad tracks. It's a friendly spot during the day, but kids from town and the inland valleys make the place rather too lively for most visitors after dark.

Red, White, and Blue Beach This is a private clothing-optional beach 5 miles north of Santa Cruz. It gets high marks for providing a very safe family environment with plenty of sand. Red, White, and Blue requires beachgoers

DON NEUWIRTH

Natural Bridges State Beach

TOM MIKKELSEN

Windsurfers at Waddell Beach

to be 21, married, or with parents. The management, unfortunately, has been noted to be unfriendly toward non-nuclear families seeking to camp. There are fees for access. Look for a red, white, and blue mailbox about 5 miles north of town and turn down that road to get to the beach. For more information, call 408-423-6332.

Northern Santa Cruz County Beaches This is the blanket heading for a series of beaches north of Red, White, and Blue, including **Laguna Creek**, **Yellowbank**, **Bonny Doon**, **Panther**, **Davenport**, **Davenport Landing**, and **Scott Creek Beaches**. Most lack facilities, but have roadside parking adequate for all but the hottest weekend days. There is a new wheelchair-accessible ramp and rest room at Davenport Landing. Bonny Doon, Yellowbank, and Panther all are clothing-optional, with the former especially noted for its stunning amphitheater setting where you can roast at the base of a semicircle of cliffs and watch the gorgeous violence of waves crashing. Access is via various turnouts and roadside parking along Highway 1, 1–8 miles north of Red, White, and Blue Beach. Some are unmarked, so the intrepid traveler must look for strings of cars parked alongside the highway and investigate what's off-road. For more information, call the county Department of Parks, Open Space, and Cultural Services at 408-462-8300.

Scenic Drive. The officially designated Scenic Highway between Santa Cruz and Half Moon Bay is delightful, with agricultural valleys and ocean vistas to the east and west.

Davenport. Davenport is an old commercial center halfway between San Francisco and Monterey. This small town of just 200 folks does not have a gas station, but boasts the only traffic light between Santa Cruz and Half Moon Bay. It offers a dozen funky shops. The large building on the ocean side of the highway was briefly the headquarters of Odwalla Juices. If you have time, check out the Jail Museum and weather station; both are open most weekends. To the north is a large cement plant. Pick up the Street Map and Visitors Guide at any of the shops or restaurants.

Waddell Creek Beach/Big Basin Redwoods State Park ★ Waddell is a unit of Big Basin Redwoods State Park, a windy sand-and-dunes beach and the last in Santa Cruz County as visitors head north toward San Mateo County. The nearly constant blow makes it a popular spot for hang gliding and windsurfing, though, and anglers will find ample fishing for perch and cod. There are rest rooms but no lifeguards. Access is via a parking lot on Highway 1, one mile south of the San Mateo County line. There is a fee for parking. For more information, call 408-425-1218.

Big Basin ★ is 18,000 acres of second-growth pine, manzanita, and redwood forests and upland meadows, including 80 miles of hiking trails, 145 developed and 6 backpack-in campsites. The ecological variety within the park truly is astonishing; visitors will go from redwood forests to seeming high-desert viewpoints where manzanita dominates to nearly jungle settings in which waterfalls plunge over thick ferns and mossy rock. Access to Big Basin is primarily via Highway 9, 14 miles north of Santa Cruz. For more information, call 408-338-8860.

Lodging

IN WATSONVILLE

K.O.A. Cabins and Camping (408-722-0551), 1186 San Andres Road. Inexpensive. One- and two-bedroom log cabins share bathrooms and shower facilities with the 200-space campground. Only a mile from Manresa State Beach.

Gary Griggs and Living with the California Coast

■ In 1982, Gary Griggs was 39 and an assistant professor at the University of California at Santa Cruz. A professor at Duke University, Orrin Pilkey, who had started a series of books on the coastlines of America, came to Gary and asked him to write one on California.

Gary studied beach sand—where it comes from and where it goes. He was also interested in where waves come from, and how different types of waves and man-made structures—seawalls and bulkheads, jetties and breakwaters—shape the coast of California. He studied these problems on California's central coast, where he lived and worked.

Pilkey's proposal was exciting. Gary wanted to write Pilkey's book—he thought it was important to do a definitive, exhaustive study of the coast, one that detailed how the coast was changing as a result of erosion and new man-made structures. But Gary didn't know the north coast or the south coast nearly as well as he did the central coast, and his knowledge of San Francisco was spotty.

Guidebooks—like the one you are reading—can tell you a lot about the coast, but they tend to focus on accessible places where you might actually go. They also tend to favor the beautiful over the ugly, the exciting over the mundane. And for lots of practical reasons, they tend not to go into exquisite detail. Gary's assignment was different: to plot the entire coast of California in exacting detail—each distinct segment of coastline would receive individual attention. As there are more than 1100 miles of California coast, the assignment was to describe more than *8800 individual sections of coast*, a daunting task.

Gary had studied marine geology at the University of California at Santa Barbara, with Robert Norris. Norris had studied at the Scripps Institution of Oceanography with Francis Shepard. And now Gary was himself a professor, and he had graduate students studying with him. One of the best of them was Lauret Savoy, who was interested in the project as a thesis.

As Gary looked at the connections among these and other academicians of the California coast, he realized that they spanned the state. For the north coast, he knew Derek Rust at Humboldt State University. For the central coast, he had another graduate student, Kim Fulton, at UC Santa Cruz; as well as a colleague who worked with environmental studies professor Jim Pepper. Moving down the coast, he had contacts at the US Geological Survey in Menlo Park, at the Scripps Institution at La Jolla, at UC Santa Barbara, at the University of Southern California, at UC Los Angeles, and at San Diego State. There was a network of coastal study centers and coastal colleagues, and one way or another, Gary had connections to all of them.

What looked like an impossible task now began, suddenly, to seem doable. Gary began contacting these people, cajoling, begging, pleading—anything to get them to commit to take a section of the coast and a chapter of the book.

In 1983, Gary's colleagues fanned out all along the coast with cameras, maps, and aerial photographs and started to document exactly what was there. Their material began to arrive back in Gary's office, where the information was transferred to detailed, scaled maps that showed—for approximately each eighth of a mile of coastline—exactly what the coast was like: whether it was a coastal cliff, whether the cliff was protected by a beach, whether it was a sandy beach, whether the beach was safe or hazardous. Any special problems were noted—for example, where there was erosion and how fast it was proceeding.

In 1985, three years after the project was started, *Living with the California Coast* was published by Duke University Press, edited and co-authored by Gary Griggs and Lauret Savoy, Gary's graduate student. Four generations of students of the California coast were among the contributors, who were affiliated with nine different institutions.

On the front cover is a picture of a front-end loader piling rocks to build a temporary wall against the encroaching sea, and inside the book, pictures of houses built too close to the ocean and falling off eroding cliffs. There are pictures of riprap and seawall barricades destroyed by the constant movement of the waves, of undercut highways and unstable bluffs, of landslides and the remnants of piers blown out by storms. There are also interesting chapters on revetments, bulkheads, groins, jetties, and breakwaters; on eroding cliffs or bluffs; and on the difference in destruction among waves from the Aleutians and from Hawaii.

Living with the California Coast was a labor of love, dedication, and high intelligence, involving most of the important coastal universities in California. It contains unique maps that are an indispensable companion for anyone interested in the California coast. Gary's book is the single best description of what is *there* on the coast of California. Nothing before or since has even come close.

Nevertheless, it failed to catch on with the general public—think about the tractor on the cover—and is now out of print. Luckily, it is still possible to find copies in secondhand bookstores. They may even be marked down to a few dollars.

Gary Griggs is now a full professor at UC Santa Cruz, the director of its Institute of Marine Sciences, and the acknowledged expert on the flow of sand along the coast. At the moment, he's tracking the sand that flows into Monterey Bay. He knows it comes from San Francisco. He wants to document how it makes the trip south. ■

IN APTOS

Rio Sands Motel (408-688-3207), 116 Aptos Beach Drive. Moderate. Close to the beach just south of Santa Cruz, the Rio Sands is a comfortable spot to spend the night, owing to a selection of comfortable rooms and suites and an outdoor spa in the motel's courtyard.

Seascape Resort and Conference Center (408-688-6800; 1-800-929-7727), Seascape Boulevard and Sumner Avenue. Expensive. Full facilities, including golf privileges and a swim and tennis club, round out this newer resort setting for the studio and one-bedroom units. A restaurant is on the grounds; lots of ocean views from private balconies.

Bayview Hotel (408-688-8654), 8041 Soquel Drive at Trout Gulch Road. Expensive. Santa Cruz's oldest inn offers 11 atmospheric rooms harking back to its past as an 1878 mansion. A busy café is downstairs.

IN SOQUEL

The Blue Spruce Inn (408-464-1137; 1-800-559-1137), 2815 S. Main Street. Moderate to expensive, depending on the season. A six-room bed & breakfast in a 120-year-old house, the Blue Spruce offers guests breakfast wherever they'd like it and a hot tub, plus proximity to Soquel's many antiques shops and the nearby Capitola and Santa Cruz beaches.

IN CAPITOLA

The Inn at Depot Hill (408-462-3376), 250 Monterey Avenue near Park Avenue. Expensive. A relatively new hotel in a 90-year-old former train depot has designed each of its 12 rooms as a different world destination: Paris, Valencia, and Portofino, for example. All modern conveniences combine with excellent service to make this a fanciful luxury.

IN SANTA CRUZ

Harbor Inn (408-479-9731), 645 Seventh Avenue. Moderate to expensive. This is a 19-unit bed & breakfast with a wide range of accommodations to choose from, as well as a friendly staff.

The Babbling Brook Inn (408-427-2437; 1-800-866-1131), 1025 Laurel, near California. Expensive. Santa Cruz's oldest bed & breakfast offers a dozen rooms in a garden and waterfall setting. Each room is themed by a different French Impressionist. Modern facilities, excellent service, and a generous breakfast combine for a rustic experience in the center of town. This bed & breakfast really does have a babbling brook, set amid an acre of trees and gardens. Most of the rooms have their own fireplaces and decks, and there's a wine and cheese hour in the living room where guests can socialize if they like.

Carmelita Cottages (408-423-8304), 321 Main Street off Beach Street. Inexpensive. These Victorian cottages have been converted into a year-round hostel, just two blocks north of the wharf. Dorm rooms and a few family and couples rooms are available. A great bargain; reservations are needed in summer. Only AYH (American Youth Hostel) members accepted in peak season, so call ahead.

Cliff Crest Bed & Breakfast (408-427-2609), 407 Cliff Street. Expensive. Just two blocks from the wharf, this B&B keeps its 100-year-old Victorian feel.

Casa Blanca Inn (408-423-1570), 101 Main Street. Moderate to expensive. This is a 27-unit inn with views of the Santa Cruz boardwalk. Visitors will appreciate the inn's cozy feel and central location, and it's attached to a Moroccan-themed restaurant (the **Casablanca**) that serves a traditional continental menu of seafood and steak.

Sea and Sand Inn (408-427-3400), 201 W. Cliff Drive. Moderate. Its small, pleasant rooms all have views; it's unpretentious and convenient to everything.

IN DAVENPORT

New Davenport Bed & Breakfast Inn (408-425-1818; 1-800-870-1817). Moderate to expensive. Situated in a small coastal town above and beside the New Davenport Cash Store, a combination bakery, art gallery, and restaurant, this inn features comfortable accommodations in rooms with private bath, oak furniture, and homemade pottery.

Restaurants

IN APTOS/SOQUEL/WATSONVILLE

Jalisco (408-728-9080), 618 Main Street, Watsonville. Moderate. This is the place for mesquite grilled Mexican cuisine. Worth a detour to funky downtown Watsonville.

Cafe Sparrow (408-688-6238), 8042 Soquel Drive near Trout Gulch Road, Aptos. Moderate. This French bistro has good service and excellent meats and seafood. Lunches are modest. Desserts are worth the calories.

Theo's (408-462-3657), 3101 N. Main Street, Soquel. Moderate. A romantic, small, French-style restaurant, Theo's is good for a leisurely lunch or dinner. Greens are from its own garden. A local favorite.

IN CAPITOLA

Shadowbrook (408-475-1511), 1750 Wharf Road. Expensive. Nearly an entire world by itself, Shadowbrook is reached by descending in a red cable car from the parking lot above, then walking through extensive outdoor landscaping.

The menu includes seafood, prime rib, and a host of California cuisine specialties. Romantic setting on terraces facing the creek. Daily dinner and Sunday brunch only.

Gayle's Bakery and Roticeria (408-462-1200), 504 Bay Avenue. Inexpensive. Not so much a restaurant as an outstanding place for takeout, Gayle's is a super-deli where visitors can stock up on sandwiches, salads, pasta, cheeses, and desserts to take to the beach.

IN SANTA CRUZ

Crow's Nest (408-476-4560), 2218 E. Cliff Drive at the south side of the harbor entrance. Moderate. A local favorite for the bar and fresh seafood, chicken, and aged beef. Great views of the bay and harbor from the upstairs Oyster Bar; weekend entertainment and dancing.

Rosa's Rosticeria (408-479-3536), 493-B Lake Street off Murray. Inexpensive. This high-quality Caribbean and Mexican restaurant is disguised as a surfer joint. A very professional seafood kitchen produces excellent seafood and Mexican specialties. The seafood soup is wonderful.

Riva's (408-429-1223) Bldg. 31, Municipal Wharf. Inexpensive. Best seafood on the wharf. Specials are heavily sauced, but the charcoal-grilled fish is fresh and excellent. No credit cards.

Royal Taj (408-427-2400), 270 Soquel Avenue. Moderate. A very friendly Indian restaurant right next to downtown Santa Cruz. Visitors can choose from a wide range of appetizers, desserts, and tasty meat and vegetarian entrées. The service is outstanding and patrons can choose how hot they want their food, plus there's cold Indian beer to help put out the fire.

Zachary's (408-427-0646), 819 Pacific Avenue. Moderate. A longtime favorite for grilled meats, Zachary's is located on the lower end of the mall.

Restaurant Keffi (408-476-5571), 2-1245 E. Cliff Drive. Inexpensive. One of Santa Cruz's many vegetarian restaurants, this one prepares flavorful versions of classic American dishes for the seeds-and-nuts set.

India Joze (408-427-3554), 1001 Center Street at Union Street. Moderate. An eclectic, generous local favorite, it serves Asian, Middle Eastern, and American food in great combinations with rich sauces. Located in an arts center downtown; highly recommended.

O'Mei Restaurant (408-425-8458), 2316 Mission Street near King Street. Moderate. Great Pacific Rim food is served here at the north end of town. It's a good stop before leaving Santa Cruz. No weekend lunches.

Pontiac Grill (408-427-2290), 429 Front Street at Cathcart Street. Moderate. This is a great place for kids downtown. Auto themed and loud, it's a retro experience for parents, just fun for kids.

El Palomar (408-425-7575), 1336 Pacific Garden Mall. Moderate. Located in the center of Santa Cruz's downtown, this really is two restaurants in one. The El Palomar lets diners choose between more formal sit-down tables and barside beer-and-fish-taco grazing, with good results in either case.

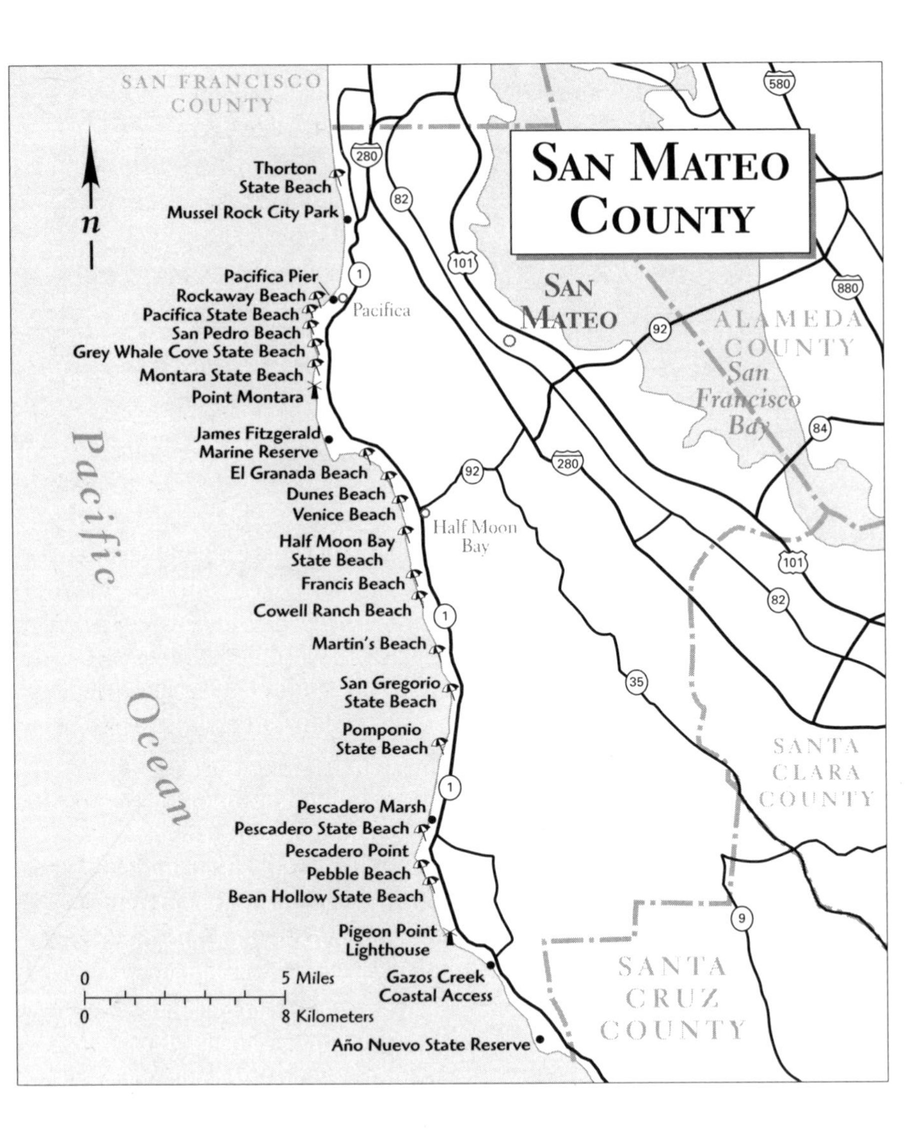
SAN MATEO COUNTY
SAN FRANCISCO COUNTY
n
Thorton State Beach
Mussel Rock City Park
Pacifica Pier
Rockaway Beach
Pacifica State Beach
San Pedro Beach
Grey Whale Cove State Beach
Montara State Beach
Point Montara
James Fitzgerald Marine Reserve
El Granada Beach
Dunes Beach
Venice Beach
Half Moon Bay State Beach
Francis Beach
Cowell Ranch Beach
Martin's Beach
San Gregorio State Beach
Pomponio State Beach
Pescadero Marsh
Pescadero State Beach
Pescadero Point
Pebble Beach
Bean Hollow State Beach
Pigeon Point Lighthouse
Gazos Creek Coastal Access
Año Nuevo State Reserve
Pacifica
Half Moon Bay
San Mateo
Alameda County
San Francisco Bay
Santa Clara County
Santa Cruz County
Pacific Ocean
0
5 Miles
0
8 Kilometers
580
280
82
101
1
880
92
84
35
9

CHAPTER NINE

San Mateo County

THE SAN MATEO COAST begins at Point Año Nuevo, an area of great dunes, and then swings softly west in the first of its gentle curves. At Pescadero, the second of these curves begins as the coast moves inland to the east. This arch terminates with Half Moon Bay and the great point just above it, Pillar. Now the coast moves west again. At Pacifica it straightens out and goes directly north, to Daly City, and beyond, to San Francisco.

The coastline of this county extends 56 miles and is intensely varied. There are at least nine distinct sections, each reflecting a particular mix of geology and wave action. The resistance of rock to erosion is perhaps the most important factor. Overall, the shoreline here is sand-deficient, although there are several beaches of great beauty.

Much of the coast here is agricultural, and the small towns along it are friendly and down-to-earth. Also found here are some of the best tide pools in all of California. At the southern end of the county, elephant seals come to breed at the Año Nuevo State Reserve from approximately the beginning of December to the end of April. Elephant sea lions can reach 15 feet in length and weight up to 3 tons. The active breeding grounds are restricted to guided walks by park rangers.

Above Año Nuevo, the shoreline—running from Franklin Point to the mouth of Pescadero Creek—has low cliffs and, here and there, pocket beaches. This 11-mile section of coast contains rocks resistant to erosion. It is also relatively unpopulated. The result is a part of the California coast that has not changed over the past 5000 years. Just below Pescadero Creek is Pebble Beach, whose elaborate rock formations and beautiful small stones are protected by law.

Just inland from Pescadero State Beach lies the town of Pescadero, a small, friendly farming community known for its excellent girls' softball team and the extraordinary pies at Duarte's, which uses locally grown fruits. Children love the place.

Six miles above Pescadero Creek is Tunitas Creek. This section of coast has tall, steep cliffs and towering bluffs. A few excellent pocket beaches exist in the shadow of the cliffs. At Pescadero and at San Gregorio, there are extensive tide pools.

TOM MIKKELSEN

South Coast Bluffs

On the 6 miles of coast between Tunitas and Miramontes Point, rocky headlands jut from tall sea cliffs. Here, streams have often cut ravines into the cliffs. The rocks here are soft. Waves cut deep caves and arches into the rocks and cliffs; offshore are sea stacks. The few pocket beaches are usually reached by stairs, as at Cowell Ranch Beach.

Above Miramontes Point, the coast of San Mateo changes yet again. Here is Half Moon Bay, which stretches from Miramontes Point to Pillar Point. Each of these points is a resistant headland. Between these points lie areas of soft rock. Waves have eroded the cliffs, producing a broad, 6-mile-long beach backed by a narrow coastal terrace. This sandy coastline contains numerous beaches. Here Highway 1 runs close to the shore; access to the beaches is uncomplicated.

The city of Half Moon Bay lies in the center of this area. Part commuter town for San Francisco, part agricultural center (flowers are a specialty), the town lacks coherence. Many of the motels and restaurants are gaudy and unattractive. Yet Half Moon Bay is also friendly and centrally located; it can be a good base camp for a weekend trip exploring the lower San Mateo coast.

Tucked in the lee of Pillar Point and protected by a man-made breakwater is Pillar Point Harbor, the only harbor between San Francisco and Santa Cruz.

Above Pillar, the coast swings gently westward. Going north, past the towns of Moss Beach and Montara, the coast is highly varied. There are small sections of broad sandy beach, as at Montara; elsewhere, irregular eroding cliff fronts fall to rocky shoreline, as at the coast south of Seal Cove; at other places, soft rolling hills lead to low sea cliffs with beach beneath, as just north of Pillar Point.

Above Pillar Point is San Pedro Mountain. Crossing the face is the most notorious section of Highway 1 in all of California. Here at Devil's Slide, debris chutes run down the face of the steep hillside. On the beach, wave erosion undercuts the base of the mountain. Landslides are common. The road is often closed and always dangerous to drive.

Just above Devil's Slide is Point San Pedro. Five miles separate it from Mussel Rock. Here the coastal suburbs of San Francisco begin, with Shelter Cove and Pacifica. This is a low, straight area of small coastal cliffs fronted by sandy beaches. Near Mussel Rock the San Andreas fault crosses into the ocean, to run inland again north of the Golden Gate Bridge at Point Reyes. North to the county line are numerous beaches backed by city suburbs.

Beaches and Attractions

Año Nuevo State Reserve ★ Punta del Año Nuevo was named by Spanish explorers to commemorate New Year's Day in 1603. Today it is preserved much as it was then. The reserve is a 4000-acre breeding ground for northern elephant seals, Steller's sea lions, and harbor seals. It is also a series of scenic beaches and cliffs, and has an excellent wheelchair-accessible viewing area. The active dune field provides good birding in spring and fall. Excellent whale-watching also is available in the winter. Offshore is Año Nuevo Island, prime habitat for numerous marine mammals and birds. Enter the main parking lot from Highway 1 at New Year's Creek Road. South of the point and north of Cascade Creek are two surfing sites with clean summer breaks but poor winter surf. While the elephant seals are breeding on the mainland, December 1–April 30 each year, the area south of Cascade Creek is open only to guided tours. The hikes are led by volunteer naturalists, covering 3 miles in about 2½ hours. Reservations are available by calling 1-800-444-7275. For additional information, call State Parks at 650-879-0227. An entrance fee and a tour fee are charged.

Gazos Creek State Beach. Enter the paved parking lot off Highway 1 just north of Gazos Creek Road. Good fishing for rainbow trout and salmon in the creek; surf-fishing for rockfish and surfperch. The path is wheelchair-accessible, as are the rest rooms. Walk south along the beach to reach **Franklin Point** to see tide pools and snowy plover nesting sites. Offshore are many marine mammals. No entrance fee.

Bean Hollow State Beach. Linked to Pebble Beach to the north, Bean Hollow offers a perspective on the rapidly eroding shoreline. An interpretive trail shows that the sandstone cliff can retreat more than 20 feet a year. The trail has been rerouted several times because it has been washed out by advancing waves. The surf is hazardous. Paved parking, rest rooms, and a picnic area are located at Bean Hollow Road. For more information, call State Parks at 650-879-2170.

Pebble Beach. Located west of Highway 1 between Hill Road and Artichoke Road, Pebble Beach is a small cove backed by high cliffs. The beach owes its name to the wave-crushed pieces of quartz that are polished and deposited at its shoreline. It is illegal to remove these pebbles. Picnic facilities and rest rooms are available. Fossils can be seen in the cliffs and tide pools are south of the beach. Wildflowers bloom on the bluffs. For more information, call State Parks at 650-879-2170.

Pescadero State Beach Enter the 1-mile-long beach at Pescadero Road or just north of the bridge over Pescadero Creek to enjoy this destination beach. A rocky shoreline, tide pools, offshore rocks, and sandy beaches combine to offer spectacular vistas and interesting walks. Picnic facilities are located along the bluffs; parking and rest rooms are on the cliffs. Pay an entrance fee at the northern parking lot. For more information, call State Parks at 650-879-2170.

Pescadero Marsh Natural Preserve ★ just inland, is a fascinating place and great for birding. An interpretive trail rings the marsh. For information on the marsh and tide-pool walk, call State Parks at 650-879-2170.

Pomponio State Beach. Pomponio State Beach is just off Highway 1 at Pomponio Creek. A parking lot, picnic area, and rest rooms are available. A day-use fee is charged. Good birding at the creek for egrets, plovers, and herons. There is an entrance fee. Less than a mile south of the main entrance is a nude beach. For more information, call State Parks at 650-879-2170.

San Gregorio State Beach San Gregorio is another destination beach. Located at Highway 1 at San Gregorio Road, the sweeping cove offers a scenic sandy beach, a freshwater marsh, and an estuary at the creek mouth. Excellent wildlife viewing, fishing, and hiking opportunities abound. Watch the surf for sleeper waves and rising tides. Prevent erosion by using only blufftop trails. This was an Ohlone village and the site of a camp of Portola's expedition in 1769. An entrance fee is required. One mile north is a longtime private nude beach called **San Gregorio Private Beach**. Farther north is **Tunitas Beach**, with interesting riparian habitat and the ruins of the Ocean Shore Railroad pilings. For more information, call State Parks at 650-879-2170.

Martin's Beach. This private beach with fishing, beachcombing, and wildlife observation is located about 1½ miles south of Half Moon Bay. A store offers minimal provisions and rents nets to catch surf smelt during the summer. Rest rooms and picnic tables are also available. Worth exploring inland is the ghost town of **Lobitos** and its creek. To the north, at Purisima Creek, is another ghost town. Only the cemetery remains of the once thriving agricultural town of **Purisima**. Entrance fee. For more information, call 650-712-8020.

Half Moon Bay State Beaches. About a half mile south of the Half Moon Bay city limits is **Cowell Ranch Beach**. This recently acquired unit of Half Moon Bay State Beach will, we hope, stop the otherwise inexorable sprawl of development south of Half Moon Bay. Facilities are limited to a steep staircase to the beach, a parking lot, and rest rooms. No fee yet. For more information, call State Parks at 650-726-8820.

Francis Beach The most popular of the region's state beaches is located at the end of Kelly Avenue west of downtown Half Moon Bay. Camping is available for tents and RVs in 51 sites. Day-use and overnight fees are charged. Rest rooms with showers and picnic facilities are on the bluff. Bathrooms and beach access are wheelchair accessible. Group camping is available for up to 50 people at **Sweetwater Group Camp**, a mile north. Tents only. For campsite reservations, call 1-800-444-7275.

Venice Beach, at the foot of Venice Boulevard, **Dunes Beach**, at the end of Young Avenue, and **Naples Beach**, at the end of Roosevelt Avenue, are all less crowded and easy to reach from Highway 1. Parking and rest rooms are available at each beach. An equestrian trail goes from Dunes Beach south to Francis Beach. Horse rentals are offered by two stables on Highway 1 between Venice and Young Avenues. Call 650-726-2362 for rental information; for other information, call State Parks at 650-726-8820.

El Granada Beach. Off Mirada Road and the East Breakwater of Pillar Point Harbor is El Granada Beach. It is a wide beach backed by eroding bluffs. To the immediate south is **Miramar Beach**, reached at the end of Magellan Avenue off Highway 1. And just to the north is **East Breakwater**, where there are RV camping sites and rest rooms. These three beaches are popular for water sports and fishing. The surf breaks all year, so it attracts surfers. Parking is tight on summer weekends; park on the shoulders of Highway 1. For more information, call the Half Moon Bay Parks Department at 650-726-8297.

Pillar Point Harbor An authentic working harbor offers the chance to watch the commercial fleet and fish-processing activities from Johnson Pier. Food and provisions are available. Hoists, short-term moorings, and a launching ramp are offered for boaters. Charter boats are available during the fishing season. Call 650-726-4382 for harbor information.

©JAMES BLANK

Pillar Point Harbor

Mavericks just offshore is a renowned surfing spot. Head toward the Tracking Station at Pillar Point, north of the outer breakwater, for a sandy beach and access to Mavericks. (See the essay about Bank Wright on page 82 for a discussion of the discovery of Mavericks.)

James Fitzgerald Marine Reserve ★ This rich, rocky shoreline offers a diverse intertidal shale reef with more than 50 different species of sea life, such as crabs, snails, barnacles, urchins, and anemones. Surf-fishing is allowed, but all tide-pool species are protected. (Abalone diving is prohibited here until May 19, 2007, in an effort to restore dangerously depleted colonies.) To the south, toward Pillar Point, the beach is building up as sand is trapped behind the north harbor breakwater. Picnic tables and rest rooms are in the cypress grove. The grassy bluffs offer safe hiking trails; the tide pools are slippery, so be careful. The northern section of the reserve, at Seal Cove, is a good example of earthquake faults and landslides. Native plants, such as Monterey cypress and coyote bush, provide habitat for numerous birds. Watch the tides; try to visit at low tide. Take California Avenue off

Highway 1 to N. Lake Street to reach the 3-mile-long marine reserve. For more information, call 650-728-3584.

Montara State Beach. At Highway 1 and 2nd Street in Montara is the parking lot for Montara State Beach. The public is allowed to use the lot at the Charthouse Restaurant, next door, for beach parking during daylight hours. Rest rooms are located at the southern end of the lot. Another parking area is at Martini Creek, about a half mile north. Call 650-726-8819 for more information.

Gray Whale Cove State Beach A half mile south of Devil's Slide is the inland parking lot for Gray Whale Cove State Beach. Although this is state owned, it is privately operated as a nude beach. No cameras, binoculars, or dogs allowed. Entrance fee. Rest rooms are at the beach. Drive carefully through Devil's Slide and do not park on shoulders or climb on hazardous cliffs. For more information, call 650-728-5336

San Pedro Beach (Pacifica State Beach) In Pacifica, just north of Devil's Slide, are a parking lot and rest room with showers servicing San Pedro Beach, now officially called Pacifica State Beach. Surfing is popular, and you'll find good fishing and clamming. Call 650-738-7381 for more information.

Rockaway Beach is located at the end of Rockaway Beach Avenue at San Marino Way, off Highway 1. There's good clamming and mussels, and it's also popular for surfing and fishing. Watch the tides.

Sharp Park Beach and Pier. Between Crespi Drive and Linda Mar Boulevard, off Highway 1, is Sharp Park Beach. A dreary gray beach offers good fishing from shore and the pier, which carries the sewage outfall past the surf zone (and can be smelly). Park along Beach Boulevard. There are concessions and rest rooms at the pier. For more information, call 650-738-7381.

Mussel Rock City Park. A restored dumpsite offers trails and a look at the San Andreas fault as it goes out to sea. The trail is the former railbed of the Ocean Shore Railroad. No facilities. To the north, along Northridge Drive, are **Palisades** and **Northridge Parks**, offering playgrounds and overlooks. Take Westline Drive, off Skyline Drive, to the parking lot for Mussel Rock City Park.

Thornton State Beach. The parking lot for Thornton Beach, at the end of Thornton Beach Road, has been closed since 1982 due to a landslide. It has been transferred to the Golden Gate National Recreational Area (GGNRA). Park on Highway 35 (Skyline Boulevard) by the gate at John Daly Boulevard and walk down the bluff. No facilities; use Burton Beach to the north. For more information, call Candlestick Point State Recreation Area at 415-671-0145.

TOM MIKKELSEN

Bluffs at Montara

Lodging

No commercial accommodations exist in San Mateo County south of Half Moon Bay. We can recommend several hotels in that town, though, and in nearby Pillar Point Harbor. However, the central coast offers a string of hostels for hardy travelers and bicyclists.

Pigeon Point Lighthouse Hostel (650-879-0633), west of Highway 1 at Pigeon Point Road. Inexpensive. Next to the second tallest lighthouse in the United States is a hostel providing 53 beds. It's a fabulous site, with minimal accommodations for members and the general public. The office is open for check-in 7:30–9:30 AM and 4:30–9:30 PM. Hostel closes 9:30 AM–4:30 PM; no smoking or alcohol. Bring your own bedding and food. Call for more information and reservations. Parking is on-site and along Pigeon Point Road. It's worth a visit to enjoy the scenery, even if you find the setup too spartan.

Rancho San Gregorio (650-747-0722), Route 84, about 5 miles inland from Highway 1. Expensive. Call for reservations. There are four large rooms in this charming bed & breakfast.

Old Thyme Inn (650-726-1616), 779 Main Street, Half Moon Bay. Expensive. At the southern end of town, this 1899 Victorian provides modern amenities such as hot tubs, VCRs, and hot breakfasts.

Zaballa House (650-726-9123), 324 Main Street, Half Moon Bay. Expensive. This bed & breakfast is the oldest house in Half Moon Bay, built in 1859. Nine tasteful rooms are rented daily. Some have hot tub and fireplace. Quiet and friendly.

Mill Rose Inn (650-726-9794), 615 Mill Street, Half Moon Bay. Expensive. One block from Main Street, this comfortable, English-style inn provides a romantic setting and good service. However, its six large rooms lack subtlety in decor.

San Benito House (650-726-3425), 356 Main Street, Half Moon Bay. Moderate. Another downtown choice, this one provides 12 rooms in a comfortable setting. Shared and private baths; sauna.

Pillar Point Inn (650-728-7377), 380 Capistrano Road, Princeton-by-the-Sea. Expensive. A faux Cape Cod bed & breakfast located at the harbor has 11 small rooms, with all the modern conveniences including videos and refrigerators, in a traditional setting. Fireplaces and deck.

Cypress Inn on Miramar Beach (650-726-6002; 1-800-83-beach), 407 Mirada Road, Half Moon Bay. Expensive. In a residential neighborhood, but all 12 rooms have ocean views. New rooms have all the amenities. Good breakfast, and a masseuse is on call.

Seal Cove Inn (650-728-4114), 221 Cypress Avenue, Moss Beach. Expensive. Ten rooms have all the B&B amenities such as flowers, antiques, fireplaces, hidden TVs, and lots of treats. Breakfasts are good.

Montara Lighthouse Hostel (650-728-7177), Highway 1 at 16th Street, Montara. Inexpensive. This 30-bed hostel provides minimal accommodations at rock-bottom prices at the historic Coast Guard Lighthouse. Scenic site and friendly atmosphere. Kitchens, hot tub, and family rooms are available. The hostel closes 9:30 AM–4:30 PM; no smoking or alcohol. Bring your own bedding and food. The office is open 7:30–9:30 AM and 4:30–9:30 PM.

Restaurants

Duarte's (650-879-0464), 202 Stage Road, Pescadero. Moderate. This wonderful family restaurant is 2 miles inland from Highway 1 at the corner of Stage and Pescadero. It is worth the trip. Park in its lot or on the street. Try the artichoke or green chili soup or get a combination of the two. It's their specialty, as are the pies. Ollallieberry, locally grown, is a favorite. Seafood and meats are the main fare. After your meal, explore the stores in the old town. It is still a genuine place, resisting development and serving tourists in a tasteful way. Reservations are suggested for weekends.

San Benito House (650-726-3425), 356 Main Street, Half Moon Bay. Expensive. This gourmet restaurant offers California cuisine in a turn-of-the-century setting. Local produce and fish are featured. Sunday brunch is popular.

Main Street Grill (650-726-5300), 435 Main Street, Half Moon Bay. Inexpensive. This funky greasy-spoon grill offers good lunches and large breakfasts. Burgers and beer for lunch, and we recommend the omelets or sourdough French toast for breakfast.

Flying Fish Grill (650-712-1125), Main Street and Highway 92, Half Moon Bay. Inexpensive. Best buy in downtown; try the fish tacos. Open only Wednesday–Sunday.

TOM MIKKELSEN

Pigeon Point Lighthouse

2 Fools Cafe and Market (650-712-1222), 408 Main Street, Half Moon Bay. Moderate. Healthy breakfasts and sandwiches are the fare here; eat in or take out to the beach. Dinners and lunch daily; breakfast on weekends only.

Barbara's Fish Trap (650-728-7049), 281 Capistrano Road, Princeton-by-the-Sea. Moderate. This fried-fish-and-beer joint is greasy, but worth the calories for the fantastic view.

Pasta Moon (650-726-5125), 315 Main Street, Half Moon Bay. Moderate. Great pasta is served here with lots of garlic and fresh ingredients. Seafood and desserts are also excellent.

Mezza Luna (650-712-9223), 3048 N. Cabrillo Highway next to the Ramada Inn, Half Moon Bay. Moderate. Authentic Italian food is what you'll get in a modest spot, up the road from the downtown.

Miramar Beach Restaurant (650-726-9053), 131 Mirada Road, Miramar. Expensive. This recently remodeled, expensive seafood restaurant offers views and decent food; music at night.

Moss Beach Distillery (650-728-5595), Beach Way and Ocean Boulevard, Moss Beach. Moderate to expensive. This romantic former speakeasy still provides seafood with an ocean view. It's rumored to be haunted, so watch for a female ghost. Good spot for a scenic drink.

The Foglifter (650-728-7905), 8455 Cabrillo Highway, Montara. Moderate. This small, funky restaurant has large portions of good seafood and Italian fare.

Ristorante Mare (650-355-5980), 404 San Pedro Avenue, Pacifica. Moderate. Decent Northern Italian food here tries to be healthy. The prime rib on weekend evenings is a better bet.

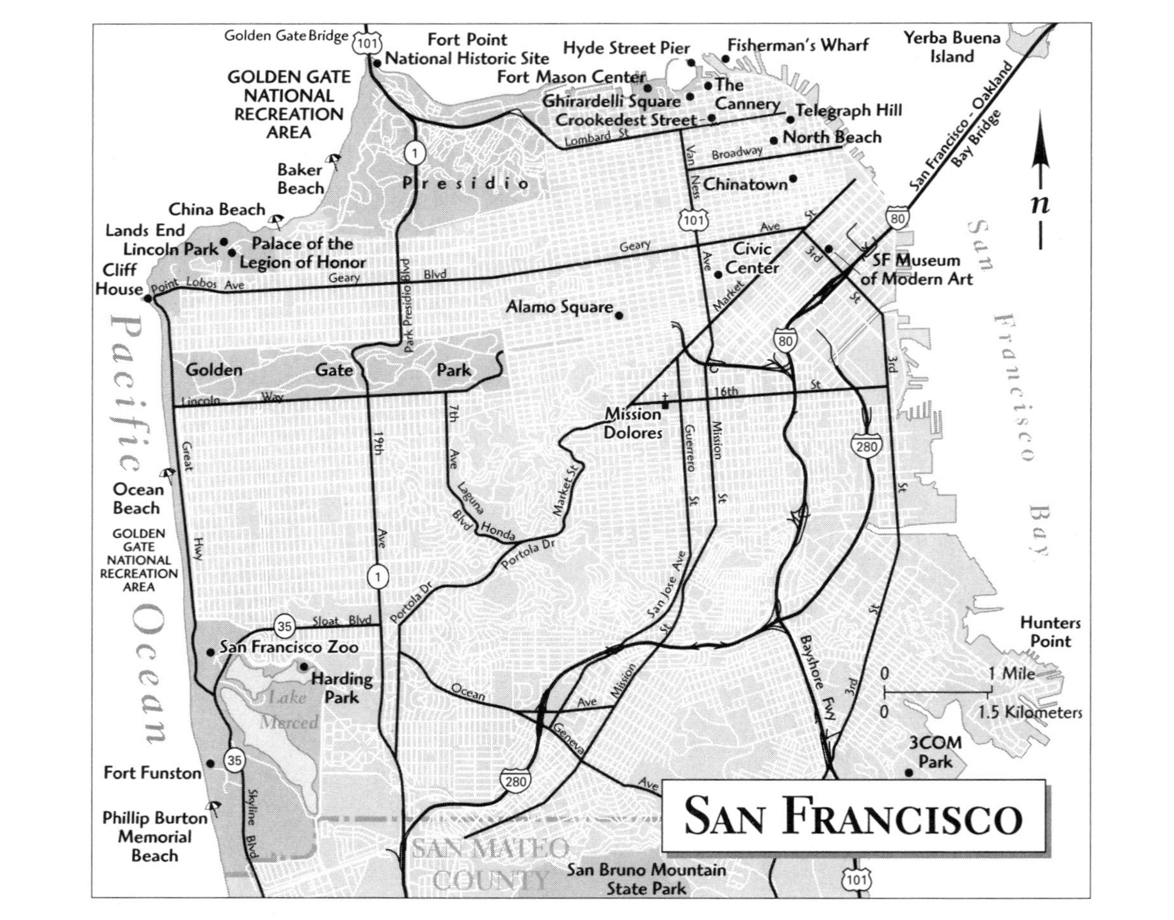
SAN FRANCISCO
Golden Gate Bridge
101
Fort Point National Historic Site
Hyde Street Pier
Fisherman's Wharf
Yerba Buena Island
GOLDEN GATE NATIONAL RECREATION AREA
Fort Mason Center
Ghirardelli Square
The Cannery
Crookedest Street
Telegraph Hill
North Beach
Lombard St
Broadway
Van Ness Ave
Chinatown
Baker Beach
Presidio
China Beach
Lands End
Lincoln Park
Palace of the Legion of Honor
Cliff House
Point Lobos Ave
Geary Blvd
Geary Ave
Park Presidio Blvd
Civic Center
SF Museum of Modern Art
San Francisco - Oakland Bay Bridge
80
n
San Francisco Bay
Alamo Square
Market St
3rd St
Pacific Ocean
Golden Gate Park
Lincoln Way
16th St
Mission Dolores
Guerrero St
Mission St
280
Great Hwy
7th Ave
19th Ave
Laguna Honda Blvd
Ocean Beach
GOLDEN GATE NATIONAL RECREATION AREA
Portola Dr
San Jose Ave
1
35
Sloat Blvd
San Francisco Zoo
Harding Park
Lake Merced
Ocean Ave
Mission St
Geneva Ave
Bayshore Fwy
Hunters Point
0
1 Mile
1.5 Kilometers
3COM Park
Fort Funston
Skyline Blvd
Phillip Burton Memorial Beach
SAN MATEO COUNTY
San Bruno Mountain State Park

CHAPTER TEN

San Francisco County

PEOPLE DO NOT COME TO SAN FRANCISCO for its ocean coastline. The beaches just to the north in Marin and to the south at Santa Cruz have better weather and a more beautiful shoreline. But San Francisco's coast offers a real sanctuary from city life. As distinct from the Bay, it is an ocean coastline, wild and isolated, with little development and exposed to large ocean waves. On the horizon, there will be freighters making for the Golden Gate. On the waves will be packs of surfers, warmly dressed in full-body wet suits. Above are hang gliders, sailing up from the south.

The coastline of San Francisco County extends 8 miles from the San Mateo County line to the south end of the Golden Gate Bridge. Most of the coastline is sandy beach, backed by either rolling dunes or cliffs. All this area is government land, state and federal; thus, the beaches are mostly undisturbed and wild in nature.

Ninety years ago, however, this was not the case. In 1885, Comstock millionaire Adolph Sutro bought the Cliff House, in those days a high-class bordello. Surrounding it, he built the Sutro Baths, an enormous pool and museum. He also created an amusement park above the baths. On the rock outcropping above the Cliff House, he built his estate, the grounds of which have always been open to the public.

To the south, amusement parks, buggy races, brothels, and gambling joints opened (and closed, depending on the whims of City Hall). Bootleggers braved the violent surf to service speakeasies with smuggled liquor.

Now all that is gone. The Cliff House was destroyed by fire and rebuilt several times. The amusement park was razed, and housing took its place. Work was done at the shoreline—sand dunes were stabilized by careful planting. Ocean Beach became wild once again.

Steep cliffs and bluffs begin at the San Mateo County line. This is the Phillip Burton Memorial Beach. Just to the north is Fort Funston, whose tall bluffs, overlooking the sandy beach below, generate thermal updrafts—perfect for hang-gliding. A large hang-gliding club is located here.

North of Fort Funston, Ocean Beach begins, running in a continuous ribbon north to the cliffs of the San Francisco headland. Close to the Golden Gate, an immense, ½-mile-long concrete seawall provides a buffer. Originally built in 1929, the seawall has been extended and reinforced. It contains an esplanade from which to watch surfers and freighters in the distance.

Ocean Beach is the outer edge of a huge sand dune area on which most of western San Francisco is built. The "Great Highway" that runs on the eastern edge of Ocean Beach has been landscaped with native beach grasses. Access to the beach is easy—there are parking areas at regular intervals. Parking is also available on the city streets just to the west of the Great Highway.

City attractions come down to the edge of the beach. The southern end of Ocean Beach is adjacent to Lake Merced, which has boating and fishing. Just to the north of Lake Merced is the San Francisco Zoo. There are numerous beach-related shops in the Sunset and Richmond communities to the north.

The northern edge of Ocean Beach runs next to Golden Gate Park. The southern area of the park, adjacent to the beach, is wilder and less used than the eastern section, which runs into the heart of the city. It contains a golf course—and miles of walking and riding trails. A restored windmill, a San Francisco landmark, sits at the western edge of the park.

Ocean Beach has excellent surf, particularly in winter. Local surfers, many of them middle aged, form a vibrant local mini-community.

North of Ocean Beach, between the Cliff House and the Golden Gate, lie rocky, and often dangerous, headlands. Largely serpentine, they have a greenish color, and are soft and prone to landslides. Set between cliffs and steep hillsides, a series of pocket beaches line this north-facing area. Of these, Baker Beach and China Beach are the safest and best for children. Both provide excellent views of the Golden Gate Bridge.

The Golden Gate is the end point of a huge river network, a drainage system that starts at the Sierra Nevadas on the eastern edge of California and winds through the central valley, principally by way of the Sacramento and San Joaquin Rivers, and then cuts through the coastal range at the gate. The sand dunes of the San Francisco coast were carried there by these rivers.

Beaches and Attractions

Coastal Trail The entire San Francisco ocean shoreline can be hiked via a patchwork of trails from the Golden Gate Bridge to Fort Funston. The trail begins above Fort Point National Historic Site on a dirt trail that goes under the Golden Gate Bridge at the toll plaza. Take the paved path around the west side of the bridge to the signed trailhead. The trail goes west along steep bluffs, passes along Lincoln Boulevard, past Baker Beach, to El Camino Del Mar (through the exclusive Sea Cliff neighborhood), past China Beach, through Lincoln Park, past the Palace of the Legion of Honor, to Lands End. To circle back, from the USS *San Francisco* Memorial take the stairway down to the lower trail, which follows the old right-of-way of the Ferries and Cliff House Railroad. Unfortunately, several portions of the trail are unsafe to all but the most agile hikers. The trail, built by Works Progress Administration (WPA) crews in the 1930s, was restored by the Youth Conservation Corps in the late 1970s. However, it has not been well maintained since then. On clear days, the vista spans the Marin Headlands; Mile Rock Lighthouse, with its siren; and the locales of many shipwrecks. On overcast days, the foghorns, wind, and fog combine to make the trail dramatic but even more treacherous.

From Lands End, the trail follows south along Ocean Beach to Fort Funston. Several options now exist. Obviously, you can walk along the shoreline. And the Promenade in front of Golden Gate Park leads to the dune trail just west of the Great Highway at Lincoln Way. Finally, the paved trail east of the Great Highway is easy and shared with bikers and skaters. South of Sloat Boulevard, follow the shoreline to the sand ladder at Fort Funston. The entire trail is of moderate difficulty; length is approximately 3 miles from the bridge to Lands End and 5 miles from there to Fort Funston. For more information, call 415-556-8371.

Phillip Burton Memorial Beach connects the closed Thorton State Beach to the San Francisco beaches. Burton was the local congressman responsible for the creation of the Golden Gate National Recreation Area (GGNRA). The beach is used by equestrians from the blufftop stables in Daly City. Fishing for striped bass and redtail surfperch is also popular.

Fort Funston The main portion of Fort Funston starts north of the Olympic Golf Course; this unit of the GGNRA is a former Nike missile base. Although no missiles ever took flight, now many hang gliders soar from the blufftop. The gliding season runs from early spring to early fall, and the site is considered of intermediate difficulty. Viewing is excellent from the wheelchair-accessible deck overlooking the launch area. Beach access is via a sand ladder just south of the hang-gliding observation platform. The ruins of the missile silos and support facilities of Battery Davis (the first 16-inch gun emplacement built on the coast) are visible from the paved ¾-mile-long, wheelchair-accessible Sunset Trail, north of the large parking lot. Access is from the Great Highway at Skyline Boulevard. Much of the bluffs is closed to public access to protect the endangered snowy plover. Rest rooms are adjacent to the parking lot. Excellent views of the coast can be had from the northern blufftop trails. Dune trails connect to Ocean Beach to the north. For more information, call 415-556-8371.

San Francisco Zoological Garden ★ More than 60 acres of exhibits are being modernized and expanded south of Sloat between Skyline Boulevard and the Great Highway. Latest plans include the incorporation of the massive sewage treatment plant's grounds and roof into the zoo's more natural habitats. More than 1000 animals, including many rare and endangered species, can be seen. Highlights are the snow leopard, the Primate Center, and Gorilla World. Park on Sloat and Zoo Road; admission fee. And bring a picnic lunch, rather than eat the expensive junk food on sale. For more information, call 415-753-7080.

Lake Merced/Harding Park. This lake was a brackish estuary prior to the 1906 earthquake. Today, it is a freshwater lake that provides an emergency backup water supply to the city while being used as a recreational lake. Joggers, walkers, and bikers lap the lake for their exercise. Boaters and anglers enjoy the lake. It is stocked with trout and largemouth bass. The 168-foot fishing pier is popular. Boat rentals, launches, and food are offered on the peninsula. The clubhouse has a popular bar with jazz at night. Call 415-566-0300 for more information.

Harding Park Golf Course is an inexpensive, well-regarded course adjacent to Lake Merced. For more information and reservations, call 415-664-4690.

Ocean Beach. West of the Great Highway from Fort Funston to the Cliff House are the remnants of the dunes that covered western San Francisco. Ocean Beach, a unit of the GGNRA, is a 4-mile strand backed by restored dunes, except for two seawalls. To prevent erosion, a hard-edged seawall topped with a promenade was built in the 1980s from Santego to Pacheco. A grand wall was built from the Cliff House to Lincoln Way to protect Golden Gate Park. This magnificent feat of engineering was completed in the 1920s by M.M. O'Shaughnessey, the builder of the Hetch Hetchy Water System. A popular promenade is located behind this wall. Park behind the promenade between Fulton Street and Lincoln Way. Parking is also available at Sloat Boulevard and the Great Highway; enter by heading west on Sloat, then turn left. There's a rest room and sand shower at the entrance to the lot. Other rest rooms are unreliable on the Lower Great Highway at Judah and Taraval.

A trail through the dunes is located just west of the Great Highway from Lincoln Way to Sloat Boulevard. Stay on the trail to protect the dune grasses. Safe access across the highway is limited to the traffic lights at Judah, Taraval, Noriega, and Wawona. Off Ortega Street, the wreck of the *King Philip* can still be seen. This is one of more than 20 shipwrecks off Ocean Beach. Scavenging souvenirs was once a popular pastime of the locals. Fishing is good for redtail surfperch and striped bass. Offshore run halibut and sea bass. In early September, a kite-flying contest is held on the beach.

Swimming is generally not recommended because of dangerous currents, riptides, and rough surf. However, many excellent surfing sites are on this stretch of shoreline. Especially in winter, surfers can be seen near Seal Rock, off Golden Gate Park, and in front of the zoo. The Bud Surfing Tour takes place at Ocean Beach during the second week of October. It is an important event for surfers and body-boarders. **Wise Surfboards**, 3149 Vicente (at 43 Avenue, 415-665-7745; for surf conditions, call 415-665-9473) supplies much of the surfing gear used at Ocean Beach and is an excellent place to check on local conditions and to get general information.

East of the Great Highway is a landscaped bike, skating, and jogging trail between Lincoln Way and Sloat Boulevard. Park on the lower Great Highway or on side streets. Check signs for parking restrictions. For GGNRA information, call 415-556-8371.

(Under the Great Highway is a 40-foot-square sewage transport box, which moves all the west side of San Francisco's wastewater to the new sewage plant in front of the zoo. The box holds storm water and sewage to prevent overflows into the ocean from several outfall structures located on the beach.)

Ocean Beach

TOM MIKKELSEN

Mural at Beach Chalet, Golden Gate Park

Golden Gate Park. In 1868, San Francisco bought 1013 acres of sand dunes and began converting them into an exotically planted pleasure field with a variety of recreational and cultural attractions. Inspired by William Hammond Hall, whose ideas were implemented by John McLaren for over 50 years, it is one of the great triumphs of urban park planning, now being renewed after years of neglect. The western edge of the park fronts the Great Highway from Fulton Street to Lincoln Way. This portion, suffering more from the harsh coastal winds, is in particular need of attention.

The Beach Chalet, long a rowdy VFW bar but closed for more than a decade, is a newly restored visitors center and brewery café. Its WPA murals, done by Lucien Labaudt, are excellent city scenes from the 1930s. The building, designed by famous local architect Willis Polk in 1925, also features tile mosaics and wood-carvings. New trails and landscaping will soften the transition from the beach into the park woodlands and improve access. The demolition of the Richmond-Sunset Sewage Plant will add a fifth soccer field. Other attractions are the restored Dutch Windmill and the soon-to-be-rehabilitated Murphy's Windmill. These landmarks used to pump water to irrigate the park. Inland excursions into the park will yield many scenic vistas, museums, playgrounds, formal gardens, and museums. For more information, call 415-831-2700.

Sutro Heights Gardens Adolph Sutro was a civic-minded mayor of San Francisco. Among his many legacies is the site of his mansion and gardens. Built in 1879, his gardens were opened to the public. Now a part of the GGNRA, the neglected ruins overlook the coast from the Marin Headlands to the San Mateo coast. The parapet offers the best views. Enjoy the statuary ruins, groves of fir, Monterey and Norfolk Island pine trees, and extensive pathways. Enter from 48th Avenue at Point Lobos Avenue and park across the street at Merrie Way. Just down the cliff to the south of the gardens was the famed Playland at the Beach. Replaced by condominium developments in the 1980s, Laughing Sal and the rides are only memories.

Cliff House Since 1863, five successive Cliff Houses have occupied this site. In the early days, tightrope walkers walked from the shore to Seal Rocks 400 feet offshore to draw thrill-seeking crowds. The first Cliff House was an exclusive casino for the wealthy. It was bought by Adolph Sutro in 1881. Sutro wanted this scenic resort to be more accessible to the public, so he built a steam railroad from downtown to his pleasure palace. He charged only a nickel per ride. After a fire in 1894, he rebuilt the roadhouse as a

TOM MIKKELSEN

Cliff House

sumptuous Victorian palace. It survived the Great Earthquake to be rebuilt in 1909, after another fire. The current structure has been remodeled several times to present a sober, boring facade, at odds with its exciting past. Today, it provides food and drink in opulent surroundings with excellent views of Seal Rock and the Golden Gate. Food is mediocre, but it's still worth a visit for drinks at sundown. Also in the complex are a **National Park Visitor Center**, with tourist and historical exhibits. Call 415-556-8642; open 10 AM–5 PM daily. Don't miss the camera obscura, a fabulous optical contraption providing a unique perspective of the scenery. A Musée Mechanique displays odd amusements including an unbelievable Mechanical Farm with suckling pigs. Both are on the oceanside lower level. Seal Rock, offshore, shelters California and Steller's sea lions as well as many shorebirds such as cormorants, gulls, and brown pelicans. There are no seals on Seal Rock. Parking is difficult by noon on summer weekends. Try the lot uphill at Merrie Way and walk.

Sutro Bath Ruins North of Cliff House are the water-filled ruins of the Sutro Baths. Also built by Adolph Sutro in 1890, they covered more than 3 acres with five saltwater swimming pools, a freshwater plunge, restaurants, some 500 private dressing rooms, and arcades. The structure was enclosed by 100,000 square feet of glass. At its peak, it was claimed that more than 25,000 people swam per day. After decades of decline, the facility was converted into an ice rink in 1937. In 1966, a fire destroyed all but the original foundations. The site is now part of the GGNRA and accessible by a trail from the parking lot at Merrie Way.

Lands End. The vista point off El Camino Del Mar provides a fabulous view of the Golden Gate and a panorama of 30 miles of coast. Parking is available near the USS *San Francisco* Memorial. Down the trails are several pocket beaches, best explored at low tide. These are listed as nude beaches in the most recent *SF Bay Guardian* survey. Behind the parking area is the West Fort Miley Batteries and Picnic area. Take the first road off El Camino Del Mar to the left for a scenic grassy picnic area among 100-year-old gun emplacements. Ranger Station: 415-556-8371.

California Palace of the Legion of Honor is located in Lincoln Park. Newly restored, expanded, and earthquake-proofed, this classical French palace is approached by car from Clement Street and 34th Avenue. Drive through Lincoln Park Golf Course till you see the palace on the knoll and the circular drive. Park there, or continue north to El Camino Del Mar to find a spot. The Coastal Trail passes here. Rodin's *The Thinker* in the courtyard sets the tone of the museum. Built originally in 1924 by the Francophile Spreckels family, the museum contains some excellent pieces of European art. Don't miss the Achenbach Foundation for Graphic Arts downstairs. It has a great collection of American and Japanese prints. For information, call 415-750-3600.

Holocaust Memorial Just past the California Palace of the Legion of Honor is the Holocaust Memorial. Sculpted by George Segal, this powerful statue of corpses and barbed wire with a perfect view of the Golden Gate makes the obvious contrast between the present and the horrible past. The Coastal Trail passes just downhill from the site.

China Beach. China Beach and Aquatic Park are the only areas certified by the National Park Service as safe to swim in San Francisco. Located at El Camino Del Mar and Sea Cliff Avenue, China Beach is a small protected cove with showers and changing rooms. Lifeguards are on duty April–October. A sun deck is on top of the lifeguard station. Parking is limited on the street; check signs for restrictions. A monument commemorates the early Chinese fishing settlement that preceded today's wealthy residents. For more information, call 415-556-8371.

TOM MIKKELSEN

Detail of Holocaust Memorial, Palace of Legion of Honor

For Mystery Lovers: Coastal Detectives

■ "Our living room has a picture window which looks south across the bay to Point Loma, the most westerly part of San Diego, and at night there is a long lighted coastline almost in our laps. A radio writer came down here to see me once and he sat down in front of this window and cried because it was so beautiful. But we live here, and the hell with it."

Raymond Chandler wrote this to Alex Barris, a correspondent for *New Liberty Magazine*, in 1949 (p. 27, *Raymond Chandler Speaking*, Houghton Mifflin, 1977).

Philip Marlowe, Chandler's detective, would weave up and down the California coast, from San Diego to Malibu. Often he was investigating Los Angeles, but in *The Long Goodbye*, Chandler's best book, Marlowe prowled through Santa Monica—Chandler's fictional Bay City. Bay City was "on the edge" of violence, the continent, and the language itself.

The coastal feeling of being "on the edge" was crucial to Chandler's novels. That was the hardboiled style: The coast of California was so beautiful that people cried. How did you deal with all the beauty? You said the hell with it and carried on.

But Marlowe was only the first in a long line of coastal detectives. Humphrey Bogart was Philip Marlowe in Chandler's *The Big Sleep*. Bogart was also Sam Spade in *The Maltese Falcon*, written by Chandler's older colleague, Dashiell Hammett. In the late '30s, the Maltese falcon came in through the Golden Gate—not under the Golden Gate Bridge; it hadn't been built—on the freighter *La Paloma*. The freighter docked on the Embarcadero. Its captain, named Jacobi, took the falcon to the office of Sam Spade. Jacobi got shot on the way and died in Spade's office and it wasn't the real falcon anyway, only Spade didn't know it until later. That was a tough break, but Spade said the hell with it and carried on. *The Maltese Falcon* was Dashiell Hammett's most famous book, wonderfully evocative of San Francisco, a great coastal city.

In the '50s, '60s, and up through the mid-'70s, the last great hardboiled coastal detective, Lew Archer, worked Santa Barbara—called Santa Teresa in the novels of Archer's creator, Ross Macdonald. Macdonald wrote great Oedipal stories in which the solution to a current mystery was necessary in order to solve another mystery long buried in the past. The one mystery echoed the other—fate repeated itself in intricate tracings.

Macdonald was a conservationist, a lover of the coast, the problems of which are echoed in many of his books, notably in *Sleeping Beauty*, set against the backdrop of an oil spill in the Santa Barbara channel: "It lay on the blue water off Pacific Point in a free-form slick that seemed miles wide and many miles long. An offshore oil platform stood up out of its windward end like the metal handle of a dagger that had stabbed the world and made it spill black blood" (p. 1). Macdonald's work created Archer within the classical tradition: As in Sophocles, a great plague or natural destruction signals an imbalance with nature, which in turn seems to lead inevitably to death and mayhem.

It was hard to see how the great coastal detective would evolve after the classic works of Macdonald—and indeed he did not. The hardboiled coastal detective slipped away in the fog of the past and became a legend.

A new detective took his place. She is a woman.

Abigail Padgett's heroine is Bo Bradley—a reworking of the name of Boo Radley, a character in Harper Lee's *To Kill a Mockingbird*. Bradley works the San Diego coast in interesting mysteries such as *Turtle Baby* (Mysterious Press). She's on medication for severe depression, but that doesn't inhibit her ability to solve a crime.

Marcia Muller's heroine, Sharon McCone, is a private investigator who explores the Sonoma coast in *Both Ends of the Night* (Mysterious Press) and San Francisco in *Till the Butchers Cut Him Down* (Warner Bros.). McCone started out working for a legal co-op, All Souls, but recently has gone out on her own.

Another good Bay-area detective is Diane Day's Fremont Jones, a woman who works the San Francisco of 1900. *The Bohemian Murder* opens with the earthquake of 1906 (Doubleday).

The private eye Jeri Howard, created by Janet Dawson, explores Monterey in *Don't Turn Your Back on the Ocean* (Fawcett). Jeri is spunky but levelheaded, like most of the new breed of woman detective, with the notable exception of Bradley.

In *Port Silva*, a book that takes place on the north coast, Meg Halloran is a high school teacher who moved there to start a new life. Created by Janet La Pierre, Meg finds that the north coast is full of trouble (Worldwide Mystery).

If you're looking for a private eye who works the coast and will amuse as well as connect you with a particular section of the area, it may pay to consult a pro. In San Francisco, Bruce Taylor at the San Francisco Mystery Bookstore can fill you in—he's an expert (415-282-7444; 4175 24th Street, San Francisco. Open Wednesday– Sunday 11:30–5:30). In the south, at the Mysterious Book Shop in Beverly Hills, the resident expert is Shelly McArthur. ■

Baker Beach. Located off Lincoln Boulevard northeast of 25th Avenue, this popular beach offers a wide strand, picnic facilities, and a restored working artillery battery and museum. The surf is unsafe for swimming, but good for fishing and birding. The northern section is listed as a nude beach by the *SF Bay Guardian*. At extreme low tide, it is possible to walk all the way to the Golden Gate Bridge. Be aware of the tides at all times.

Battery Chamberlin was built in 1903 to protect the harbor entrance with a "disappearing" 97,000-pound cannon. Rangers often demonstrate how the gun is cranked in and out of its camouflaged emplacement on the beach. The battery's military history is shown in an occasionally open museum. For more information, call 415-556-8371.

Lodging

There are only a few good hotels near Ocean Beach in San Francisco, mostly because the area is protected parkland. But the rest of San Francisco is full of wonderful hotels and restaurants. We list some of our favorites here. They are not the ones "tourists" typically stay in.

Triton (415-394-0500), 343 Grant Avenue (at Bush). Expensive. For one room with a full-sized bed, expect to pay about $160, up to $239 for a room with a king-sized bed or two double beds. At the gates of Chinatown, in the heart of the shopping district, the Triton is large. It has an "ecology floor," with water and air-filtration systems, and organically grown cotton furnishings. You can stay in the Carlos Santana suite, decorated by the musician's designers, or the Jerry Garcia suite. Another room has a 100-gallon tropical fish tank in the suite.

Inn at the Opera (415-863-8400; 1-800-325-2708; fax: 415-861-0821), 333 Fulton Street near the corner of Franklin. Expensive. Prices for rooms run about $160 to $200; suites are available for substantially more. This is one of the most pleasant bed & breakfast inns in San Francisco. As its name implies, it is near the refurbished Opera House, the excellent restaurant corridor at adjacent Hayes Street, and City Hall, the new library, and the ballet.

Hotel Griffon (415-495-2100; 1-800-321-2201), 155 Stewart Street, at the Embarcadero. Expensive. The hotel has 62 rooms: $185 a night for a regular room, $225 for a bay-view room, and $285 for a suite. With a room reservation, you get access to the YMCA. The hotel is near the ferry building and the rebuilt (and beautiful) Embarcadero bayshore path. A pleasant walk is south, along the Embarcadero, to the South Beach Marina, where there are several pleasant shorefront cafés.

Inn at Union Square (415-395-3510), 440 Post Street. Expensive. This is one of the most pleasant small hotels in San Francisco. Tucked unobtrusively into Post Street, very near Union Square and near several huge hotels, the inn is a pleasant alternative. Floors have tasteful nooks to enjoy breakfast and tea. The rooms themselves are very quiet—remarkable, considering the location. The interiors are subdued and tasteful. This is the hotel if shopping is your primary goal.

Dolores Park Inn (415-861-9335), 3641 17th Street in the Noe Valley section of San Francisco. Moderate. This is a true small bed & breakfast, in one of the most delightful residential areas of the city. The Noe Valley corridor along Church Street, between Dolores Street and Castro, is full of coffeehouses, used-book stores, and offbeat-clothing stores. Access to Union Square, the Embarcadero, and other San Francisco attractions is simple: The J Church branch of the Municipal Transit System, or MUNI, runs directly from the Noe Valley to Market Street and from there to the Embarcadero.

Stanyon Park Hotel (415-751-1000), 750 Stanyan Street. Moderate. A small, elegant hotel, the Stanyon Park is very near Golden Gate Park and within walking distance of the Haight, San Francisco's famous 1960s hippie neighborhood. This hotel is off the beaten track, but the proximity to Golden Gate Park makes it a good alternative to being "downtown." The Haight, although well past its glory and now for the most part a residential neighborhood, is still lively and interesting, with numerous quirky shops.

The Seal Rock Inn (415-386-6518), 545 Point Lobos Avenue. Moderate. An unassuming motel, this is allegedly where Hunter S. Thompson was ensconced with a case of Wild Turkey to finish several of his books. It is tolerant, well run, and quiet. The food in the coffee shop is good and very reasonable. A pool is available for hardy, fog-tolerant guests. Ask for an ocean-view room.

The San Francisco International Youth Hostel (415-771-7277), in Building 240 at Upper Fort Mason. Inexpensive. It is run by the American Youth Hostel Association. The site is reached through the entrance to Fort Mason at Franklin and Bay Streets. Head north past the Chapel and Park Headquarters; follow signs. The hostel serves 130 guests per night at rock-bottom prices; there's a discount for AYH members, but it's open to all. Good views of the Bay. Laundry facilities and snacks are available; friendly staff.

Roberts-at-the-Beach Motel (415-564-2610), 2828 Sloat Boulevard. Moderate. Just across from the zoo and only a block from the beach, it's cheap and relatively clean, with only a hint of mildew for atmosphere. Parking on-site. Noisy on party weekends.

Large San Francisco hotels: San Francisco, of course, has many large and famous hotels. Most are near Union Square, as are all of these. All are very expensive. **St. Francis** (415-397-7000), off Union Square, is a veritable city unto itself. **The Palace** (415-392-8600), on Market Street but near enough to Union Square to walk, has the Garden Court, a beautiful place for a Sunday tea or brunch. **Campton Place** (415-781-5555), another Union Square Hotel, is famous for its service. **Hotel Nikko** (415-394-1111), 222 Mason near Union Square, is also known for its service. Two legendary Nob Hill hotels are the **Fairmont** (415-772-5000) and the **Huntington** (415-474-5400), which has one of the best piano bars in town.

Restaurants

Here is a highly personal selection of our favorite San Francisco restaurants. We have chosen those that are reasonably priced.

Firecracker (415-642-3470), 1007 Valencia, is in the trendy Valencia/Mission district corridor, where the most innovative San Francisco eating places have emerged. Firecraker has inexpensive, imaginative Chinese-American food.

Greens (415-771-6222), located at Fort Mason, is a famous vegetarian San Francisco restaurant.

Mangiafuco (415-206-9881) on Guererro at 22nd Street, is a trendy but excellent Italian restaurant.

Mayflower (415-387-8338), 6255 Geary Street. Moderate. Chinese food, served "cloth table" (which means that it has tablecloths). The excellent quality of the food makes this place a great deal.

Slanted Door (415-861-8032), 584 Valencia at 17th Street. Moderate. This is another innovator. Slanted Door offers excellent, creative Vietnamese-Californian food. Often crowded, but several tables are kept for couples without reservations.

Uncle Vito's Pizzeria, (415-391-5008), 700 Bush Street. Moderate. Near Union Square and the heart of San Francisco, this is a classic San Francisco pizzeria, the best in the city. The pizza dough is made a day ahead so that it will have time to rise and breathe. (They treat it like fine wine.) Yet the place is relaxed, friendly, and not expensive (though not cheap either). This is the kind of place that tourists keep coming back to night after night and where the owners will notice and give them a listing of other restaurants they might enjoy.

South Park Cafe (415-495-7275), 108 South Park (which is a hidden square near the Moscone Convention Center). Expensive. This is a true French bistro, one of the most delightful restaurants in all of San Francisco. It is also a great favorite of the fashion industry. You will see the elegant, the strange, and the interesting. This is also a friendly place. You may be able to eat at the bar if you don't have a reservation, which is necessary if you wish a table. Highly recommended.

The Flying Saucer (415-641-9955), 1000 Guererro at 22nd Street. Moderate. Trendy, but not fancy, and very original. On a good night, this small restaurant ranks with the best in the world. On a bad day, it's still one of the best in San Francisco. We consider it the best buy in town if you're willing to spend $100 for dinner for two (including wine). Ask for a quiet table; it can be very noisy. Be prepared to go along with the flow: Unusual things happen here—let them.

Sam's Grill and Seafood Restaurant (415-421-0594), 374 Bush Street. Moderate. Downtown; business favorite for the best seafood in town. Worth the wait; wait longer to get a private booth. Closed weekends.

Hayes Street Bar and Grill (415-863-5545), 324 Hayes Street near the Opera and Symphony. Moderate. A San Francisco institution, Hayes serves wonderful seafood in a lively, bouncing atmosphere. The bar here is excellent.

Chez Panisse (510-548-5525), 1517 Shattuck Avenue at Ceder, in Berkeley, across the Bay but worth the trip (about a half-hour drive from downtown San Francisco). Expensive. This is Alice Waters's famous restaurant. Eat upstairs in the café rather than in the more formal restaurant. The café is not an expensive place, despite the reputation of the chef.

Leon's Bar B Que (415-681-3071), across from the zoo at 2800 Sloat Boulevard. Inexpensive. This hole-in-the-wall serves some of the best soul food in San Francisco. Eat in the small booths or take out a combination to the beach or the zoo. There's also run an upscale branch on Fillmore Street.

Java Beach Café (415-665-5282) 1396 La Playa. Inexpensive. Neighborhood café that has the best coffee near the beach. Friendly, food OK.

The Beach Chalet (415-386-8439), JFK Drive and the Great Highway. Moderate. This is a newly restored visitors center and brewery café where you can get fresh-brewed beer and fresh-caught fish. Loud, but fun; great views. Lots of parking in front. Don't miss the WPA murals downstairs in the visitors center.

The Cliff House (415-386-3330) offers the choice of several restaurants and bars. They are all popular with locals, who bring their out-of-town relatives and friends for a meal or drink at dusk. The view of Seal Rock, the surf, and shoreline is fabulous. Unfortunately, the food does not match the scenery. The downstairs restaurant offers mostly seafood in an art deco ambiance. Upstairs, pasta and American food supplement the seafood. Eating at the bar is best and less expensive.

Louis' Restaurant (415-387-6330), 902 Point Lobos Avenue. Inexpensive. Park uphill at the Merrie Way lot. Just up the hill from the Cliff House, overlooking the Sutro Bath ruins, its breakfast and lunch are large and tasty. The staff are rude in the pleasant way that keeps the tables flipping. Views and hearty food make this a better bet than the Cliff House. Closed for dinner.

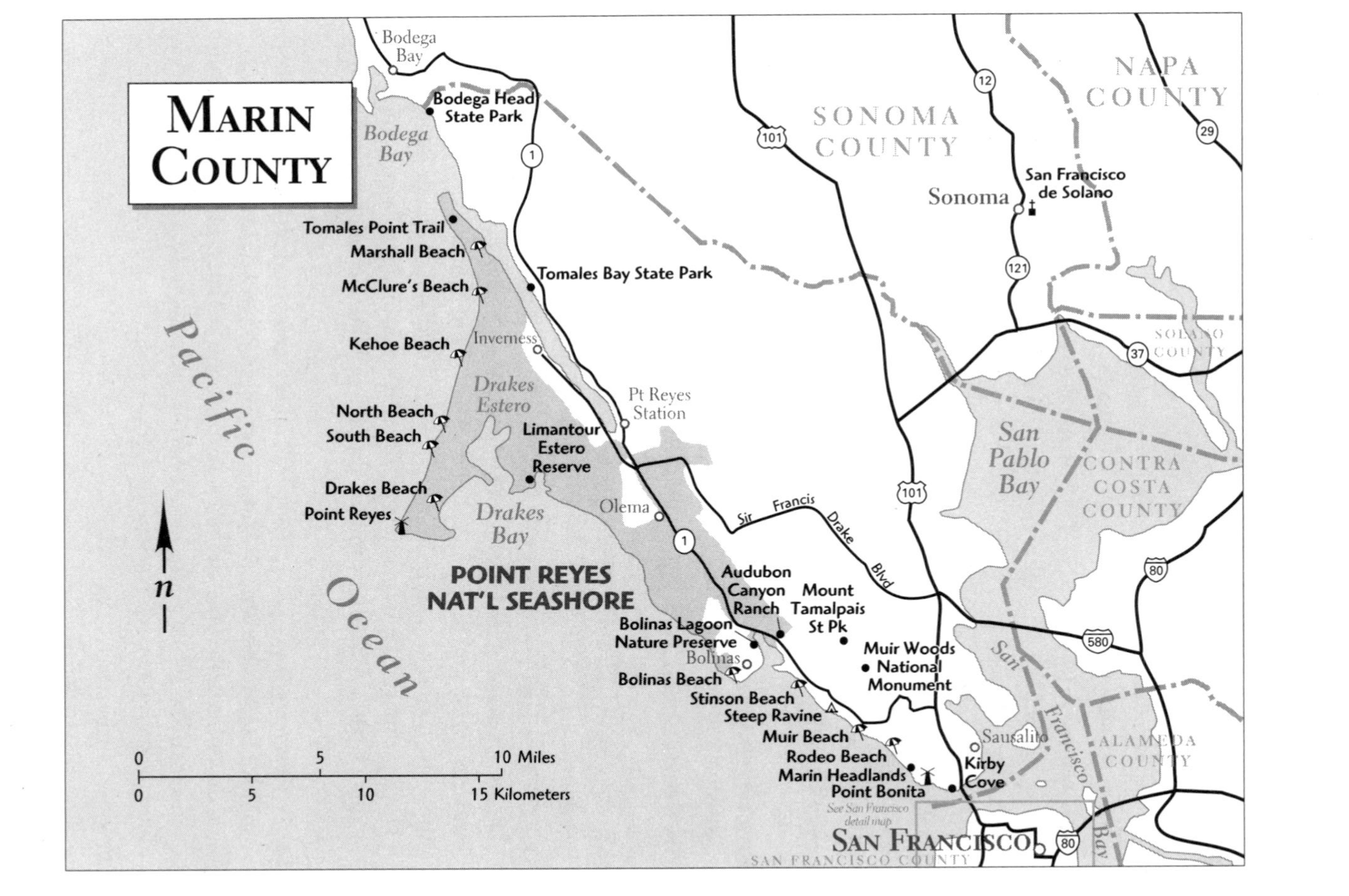

MARIN COUNTY
Bodega Bay
Bodega Head State Park
Bodega Bay
SONOMA COUNTY
NAPA COUNTY
Sonoma
San Francisco de Solano
Tomales Point Trail
Marshall Beach
Tomales Bay State Park
McClure's Beach
Kehoe Beach
Inverness
SOLANO COUNTY
Pacific
Drakes Estero
Pt Reyes Station
North Beach
South Beach
Limantour Estero Reserve
San Pablo Bay
CONTRA COSTA COUNTY
Drakes Beach
Point Reyes
Drakes Bay
Olema
Sir Francis Drake Blvd
POINT REYES NAT'L SEASHORE
n
Ocean
Audubon Canyon Ranch
Mount Tamalpais St Pk
Bolinas Lagoon Nature Preserve
Muir Woods National Monument
Bolinas
Bolinas Beach
Stinson Beach
Steep Ravine
Muir Beach
Rodeo Beach
Marin Headlands
Point Bonita
Sausalito
Kirby Cove
San Francisco Bay
ALAMEDA COUNTY
See San Francisco detail map
SAN FRANCISCO
SAN FRANCISCO COUNTY
0 5 10 Miles
0 5 10 15 Kilometers
1
12
29
37
80
101
121
580

CHAPTER ELEVEN

Marin County

THE SAN ANDREAS FAULT swings into the ocean in south San Francisco and returns inland again at Stinson Beach. East of the fault, between the Golden Gate Bridge and Stinson Beach, lie the Marin Headlands, one of the largest preserved natural areas in the United States located near a major city. To the north of the headlands is the Point Reyes Peninsula, another protected parkland, with one of the longest and most beautiful beaches in California, Limantour.

It is not by accident that this great beach resembles other great beaches far to the south. The entire Point Reyes Peninsula has, over millions of years, slid north along the San Andreas fault from the Santa Barbara area. Separating the Point Reyes Peninsula from the rest of Marin County is Tomales Bay, a long, thin estuary formed by the San Andreas fault, which runs beneath it. The northern end of that bay faces Bodega Bay and Sonoma County.

The Marin Headlands is an area of steep, oak-studded hills falling to the sea, with isolated, and infrequent, pocket beaches lying in valleys formed in the shoulders of these hills. It is part of the Golden Gate National Recreation Area, a large public trust that has kept the headlands in a wild state, a major public achievement.

Here, wherever there is a beach there is often a stream that has carried sand to the shore and cut a path to the sea. The beautiful but small beaches at Tennessee Valley and Muir Beach are examples. The first of these pocket beaches, Kirby Cove, provides excellent views of the Golden Gate Bridge and the San Francisco headlands to the south. Rodeo Beach, just to the south of Tennessee Valley, has the California Marine Mammals Center, among other ecological organizations, many of which provide educational programs.

To the north of these pocket beaches at Stinson Beach, the San Andreas fault swings inland again, running down the center of Bolinas Lagoon. The beach at Stinson is one of the widest and sandiest on the northern California coast, and excellent for children. The adjacent small town of Stinson has restaurants and shops. To the north, the exclusive gated community of Seadrift, built on a sand-dune spit on the San Andreas fault, is sure to be destroyed eventually by an earthquake.

To the north of Stinson is the Bolinas Peninsula, the southern end of the much larger Point Reyes Peninsula. Bolinas is an extended headland, a flat terrace whose edges falls in steep cliffs to the ocean below. At the tip of the Bolinas Headland is Duxbury Reef, more than a mile long, the largest exposed shale reef in all of California. It is a marine preserve.

Just to the north is the Point Reyes Peninsula. Part of the Point Reyes National Seashore is a series of adjacent parklands, including the Phillip Burton Wilderness Area and Samuel P. Taylor State Park. The peninsula is one of the great wild areas of the coast. Its form is that of a great triangle whose eastern edge is Tomales Bay. From the southern edge at Bolinas, the coastline moves out in a grand curve to form Drakes Bay. Along this curve, moving west to Drakes Estero, a large saltwater lagoon, is the massive, wide, sandy beach of Limantour, the greatest beach in northern California.

To the west of Drakes Estero is Point Reyes, the tip of this great peninsula, on which is a lighthouse with a fine view of passing whales. Here the third side of the Point Reyes triangle begins, as the coast swings east in a straight line ending at Tomales Point. Along this coast are several beautiful beaches—South and North Beaches, Kehoe Beach, and McClures Beach—and Abbott's Lagoon, a bird sanctuary. From Tomales Point it is possible to see Bodega Head in the north. Tomales Lagoon, narrow and shallow, is warm enough for swimming.

Within an easy morning drive from San Francisco, the Point Reyes Peninsula is a true wildlife area. There are whales at sea, seals on the beaches, and, at Sea Lion Cove, frolicking sea lions. Inland there are several kinds of deer, fox, Tule elk, and, occasionally, mountain lion. In the air there are marsh and redtail hawks, puffins, cormorants, and kites. In April and May, sections of the peninsula are covered with wildflowers—iris, Indian paintbrush, lupines, bluebells, and poppies. Miles of hiking trails crisscross the peninsula. At the park headquarters, on Bear Valley Road, the extensive displays include a Miwok Indian village. Park headquarters is also the starting point of more than 100 miles of trails, many leading to beaches. With excellent camping facilities on the point itself, and secluded bed & breakfast inns in the towns of Inverness and Point Reyes, this is one of the best coastal family destination areas in all of California.

Beaches and Attractions

Golden Gate National Recreation Area (GGNRA). Created in 1972 by the legislative vision of Phil Burton, one of California's most farsighted congressmen, the GGNRA preserves in perpetuity one of the most stunning stretches of the state's coast, a series of hills, groves, and beaches ranging from San Francisco nearly to Sonoma County. Some of these beaches are not incorporated as parts of municipalities and may be listed by name only. Note that the ocean in this area generally is not warmer than 62 degrees, and usually is much cooler than that. The Golden Gate has notoriously strong and fast tides—the tidal current near the Golden Gate can reach 5 knots, the speed of a fast-moving sailboat, and three times faster than any person can swim. The beaches' steepness creates violent, fast-breaking waves; there are no lifeguards, and plenty of sharks offshore. Much thought should be given before swimming or surfing at most Marin County beaches. The beaches in the GGNRA tend to be clothing-optional, or at least to have clothing-optional areas, but this generally is low-key and rangers cite only people engaged in what is delicately called "inappropriate touching."

Kirby Cove/Bonita Cove These two tiny pocket beaches are just west of the Golden Gate Bridge. Both involve scrambling down trails, so visitors should exercise caution. What makes them worth the effort is that they are beautiful, peaceful, have "black" volcanic sand, and feature extraordinary views of the bridge and the San Francisco coast. Both are clothing-optional, but the effort involved in getting to them filters out gawkers (unlike Baker Beach in San Francisco); this makes them good beaches for beginning nudists. Access is via high, winding Conzelman Road, which visitors can pick up by making a left turn after getting off Highway 101 at the Alexander Avenue exit. Kirby is accessed by a gated fire road that drops sharply off to the left as you climb to the level of the bridge, while Bonita is a little farther along toward Point Bonita, reachable via a hiking trail from World War II–era Battery Alexander. Look for cars parked on the side of the road for no apparent reason. *Note*: Enforcement of government rules on this beach is strict. Dogs are not allowed. The park service hands out tickets and listens to no excuses. There is no access fee; parking is along winding roadsides. For more information, call the GGNRA at 415-561-4304.

Rodeo Beach/Tennessee Cove ★ Just over the first set of hills from the Golden Gate lies Tennessee Valley, a protected area crisscrossed with hiking trails from which patient visitors can see foxes and, increasingly, small wild cats and feral pigs. Rodeo Beach is at the seaward side of Rodeo Lagoon, a small inlet that plays host to migrating waterfowl. The sand at Rodeo is coarse but the scenery beautiful, and there are small coves at the southern end of the beach that provide a measure of privacy. This southern end also has a certain amount of nudity, but is isolated from the larger portion of Rodeo Beach by rocks and won't be apparent unless visitors are looking for it. The Rodeo Lagoon area has an extensive network of trails. When through sun-worshipping or hiking, visitors may want to try the **Marine Mammals Center**, which rescues and rehabilitates injured sea mammals. Access to Rodeo is via the Alexander Road exit from Highway 101; head to the end of Bunker Road. For Tennessee Cove, take the Highway 1 exit off Highway 101 and turn west shortly thereafter onto Tennessee Valley Road. Follow this until it ends at a parking lot. Reaching Tennessee Cove requires a hike of 2 miles along the headlands from that point. There is a pond near the beach that also is frequented by waterfowl, but there are no facilities. Tennessee Cove is clothing-optional. For more information, call 415-331-1540.

Point Bonita Lighthouse This lighthouse has kept ships on track for the Golden Gate since 1877, and is open to visitors Saturday and Sunday 12:30–3:30. There are also full-moon and sunset walks around the lighthouse and grounds. There are great views of the Gate and San Francisco as far as Lands End. Access is via the end of **Conzelman Road,** at the southwestern corner of the headlands, a beautiful scenic drive. There is parking; for more information, call 415-331-1540.

IN MUIR BEACH

Muir Beach This is a small, sandy beach that sits below the southwest arm of Mount Tamalpais. It is striking for being framed by the mountain, the headlands, the ocean, and farms directly inland. Though frequently windy and/or foggy, it is a beautiful place to go with the family, and there are picnic tables, parking, and rest rooms. It also sits very close to the highly recommended Pelican Inn (see **Lodging**). There is no fee. Access is via Highway 1 from Highway 101. For more information, call 415-331-1422.

Muir Woods National Monument ★ Heavily visited, this monument to the naturalist John Muir is the sole remaining stand of old-growth redwood trees anywhere near San Francisco, and as such is a national treasure. Its beauty loses nothing for the throngs that visit it each year; all you need to do to get away from the crowds is take one of several trails out of the valley, and soon you are up, out, and into redwood solitude on all but the heaviest weekend days. The main valley is paved, level, and quite wheelchair accessible. At the entrance there are rest rooms, a ranger station, and a gift shop. Admission fees have recently been implemented. Access is via Muir Woods Road, 3 miles from where it leaves Highway 1 on the way out of Mill Valley. There is free lot and roadside parking. For more information, call 415-388-2596.

IN MILL VALLEY

Highway 1 leaves 101 in Mill Valley. It is a scenic wonder for its entire length to Rockport in Mendocino County. Drive carefully!

Mount Tamalpais State Park Framed on the south and west by the GGNRA and on the north by the Marin Municipal Water District's no-build watershed, Mount Tam, as it's known, is the crown jewel of the Marin County coast. It is nearly 2600 feet high and girdled by several well-developed trails that range from "quite easy" (the Old Railroad Grade) to "quite a workout" (the Dipsea). The park as a whole contains 6200 wooded and grassy acres. It's a hiker's and biker's paradise (mountain biking was invented on Mount Tam) and the view from the top is unparalleled, sweeping from the Pacific to the Sierras. There are various fee parking lots near trailheads and some free roadside parking on narrow shoulders. *Note*: Water generally is available only at ranger stations and at the rest rooms near the East Summit; bring your own for hikes of any duration. Access is via various points along Panoramic Highway, Ridgecrest Road, Muir Woods Road, and Pan Toll Road. For more information, call 415-388-2070.

IN STINSON BEACH

Steep Ravine Environmental Camp/Steep Ravine Beach. This is a set of 10 cabins and 6 environmental campsites at the bottom of a steep, paved road. They are on a rocky outcrop right above the Pacific, and due to their rugged, beautiful location they are much sought after; reservations are required (call 1-800-444-7275). One attraction here is Steep Ravine Beach, an

TOM MIKKELSEN

Muir Woods National Monument

alternately sandy and rocky pocket beach that has hot springs right on the ocean. These are accessible at low tide and can be crowded at the oddest times of day or night, as those with tidal charts flock to the hot water. Visitors should note that Steep Ravine is the one exception to the state's rule that a campsite *must* be provided for those arriving on bike or on foot, as we found to our chagrin late one afternoon a few years ago. Access is via a gated parking lot (if camping or cabin-ing) or free roadside parking (if going down to the beach) along Highway 1, 2 miles south of Stinson Beach. For more information, call 415-388-2070.

Red Rock Beach. This is an informal, clothing-optional beach at the foot of a steep cliff. It can be rocky, but generally has a wide enough strip of sand to lie on or throw a Frisbee. It's a very popular place on hot days, but the fog can come in quickly. The trail to the beach is extremely steep. Access is via a trail on the west side of Highway 1, near roadside parking about 1.5 miles south of Stinson Beach.

Stinson Beach This is a very wide, sandy beach in front of the town of the same name. As this is the first really full-service beach north of Santa Cruz, you can count on it to be crowded with families fleeing inland Marin's heat on sunny days. Visitors can swim and surf in the ocean—in fact, the surfing is

TOM MIKKELSEN

Stinson Beach

moderate. This is a beach break that changes often. However, given the moderate waves, it is an excellent place for the beginning surfer, and there are lifeguards watching over the scene. Near the beach's southern end there are sand dunes that help cut the wind for sunbathers. Even on foggy days, the beach has a certain windswept beauty, lying as it does at the base of the western arms of Mount Tamalpais. There is also a great deal of surf-fishing, and there are picnic tables, grills, rest rooms, and a snack bar. Particularly during the week, Stinson is an excellent family beach, and it has a free parking lot. Access is west of Highway 1 in downtown Stinson Beach. For more information, call the Stinson Beach rangers at 415-868-0942.

Audubon Canyon Ranch ★ A mile or so north of Stinson Beach on Highway 1 are large colonies of great blue herons and great egrets. This ranch is run by the Audubon Society as a reserve for these fabulous birds. It is open March–mid-July on weekends and holidays. The redwoods provide the habitat and are well protected. Trails and overlooks, a visitors center, historic house, and bookstore are provided. Call 415-868-9244 for more information or for group reservations during the week.

IN BOLINAS

Bolinas Beach/Bolinas Lagoon Nature Preserve ★ This is a low-tide, sand-and-pebble beach at the southern end of the town of Bolinas. It hosts a small park with tennis courts and rest rooms, and provides sweeping views of Stinson Beach and Bolinas Lagoon. There is no day-use fee. Access is via the end of Wharf Road in Bolinas. For more information on Bolinas Lagoon, call 415-499-6387. The lagoon is home to several species of waterfowl and the occasional sea lion. Access to it is via paths along the shore or by non-motorized boats (rowboats, kayaks, canoes), which must be kept away from the sea lions.

Agate Beach/Duxbury Reef ★ This alternately sandy and rocky beach lies on the western end of Bolinas's peninsula. Though bluffs and narrowness keep it from being the sunbather's first choice, Agate can't be beat for its beachcombing and tide-pooling opportunities. The beach is surrounded by Duxbury Reef Marine Reserve, a wide shelf of rock that is alternately covered and uncovered by tides, making it possible for cautious visitors to see a large variety of tide-pool life at close range. Access is via a trail down the bluffs, from the parking lot at the end of Elm Road in Bolinas. For more information on Agate Beach, call 415-499-6387.

IN POINT REYES/INVERNESS

Point Reyes Bird Observatory ★ This ornithological lab is open to the public, so you can watch researchers banding birds or go on a self-guided nature tour. There is a small visitors center. There is no access fee, but a nominal donation is requested. The observatory is open every day April–November, but only on Wednesday and weekends December–March. Access is via Mesa Road, about 4.5 miles north of Bolinas. For more information, call 415-868-1221.

Limantour Beach (a destination beach) This is a long, sandy beach at the southern end of the Point Reyes Peninsula, backed by the 500-acre Limantour Estero Reserve. There are lightly vegetated dunes behind the beach (less vegetated since the 1995 wildfires), and deer, elk, shorebirds, and whales can be seen in abundance. *Note*: Part of this beach is clothing-optional. There are rest rooms and access to the hiking trails that crisscross Point Reyes Peninsula. Access is via Limantour Road, west of Highway 1 about 4 miles south of Olema, or via the Coast Trail from the south end of Point Reyes National Seashore. There are parking lots and no fees. For more information, call 415-663-1092.

Drakes Estero/Drakes Beach Drakes Beach is the most popular at Point Reyes, owing to ease of access from Sir Francis Drake Boulevard and the extensive visitors center, which features displays about the coast and its history.

TOM MIKKELSEN

Drake's Bay, Point Reyes National Seashore

The beach itself is fairly wide and sandy, backed by cliffs, and reasonably swimmable. Near the beach are rest rooms, showers, a snack bar, and picnic tables, helping make this an excellent spot to bring the family. Access is via Drakes Beach Road, off Sir Francis Drake Boulevard within Point Reyes National Seashore. There is parking, and no fee for access. For more information, call 415-669-1250.

Point Reyes Headlands/Point Reyes Lighthouse Here is the very southern tip of the Point Reyes Peninsula, and as such it has spectacular views of the ocean and is a prime whale-watching spot. The lighthouse dates back to the 19th century and still helps illuminate one of the foggiest points on the California coast. There is a ½-mile-long paved path from a large parking lot to a stairway, which leads down some distance to the lighthouse proper. Rangers lead interpretive walks in the lighthouse, but be aware that the stairway is sometimes closed during adverse weather. There are no day-use fees. Access is via the end of Sir Francis Drake Boulevard. For more information, call 415-663-1092.

South Beach/North Beach. This pair of contiguous beaches make up the western border of the Point Reyes Peninsula. They are sandy and scenic, partially backed by bluffs, uncrowded, and beautiful for long oceanside walks.

TOM MIKKELSEN

Point Reyes lighthouse, Point Reyes National Seashore

Phil Arnot—Point Reyes and Secret Beaches

■ In Marin as in most parts of the California coast, there are secret beaches, places unknown to the general tourist. And then there are *really* secret beaches, like the ones Phil Arnot writes about in *Point Reyes: Secret Places and Magic Moments*. Really secret beaches are unknown to *everyone*.

The first time Phil Arnot went hiking, he was 3 years old. His grandmother took him. It was 1927. He hiked through the Marin Headlands, up to Kent Lake. By the time Phil was 9, in 1933, his grandmother was taking him hiking through Bear Valley, on the wild Point Reyes Peninsula. Point Reyes Peninsula wasn't a national park then. Phil's grandmother would walk up to the farm houses and ask permission to hike. She must have been a persuasive woman, because she was never refused.

When Phil grew up, he became a high school teacher. He continued hiking every chance he could get, in the Sierras, in Oregon, and still on the Point Reyes Peninsula, often taking kids with him.

One day, poking around on McClures Beach, at the north end of Point Reyes, he walked toward a massive rock at the far south end of the beach. He noticed a small slit between the rock and the headland, and slithered through. There was a small beach beyond. At the south end of this beach, he climbed and traversed a slippery rock protrusion, then waded through tide pools, then onto a small rocky beach under sheer cliffs. A little farther on, he discovered the mouth of a huge cave. The ceiling was 30 feet high at the entrance, but the roof tapered to 4 feet at the other end, where there was a hole leading to an opening. Phil climbed through the 4-foot hole and made his way 20 feet down a rock face onto the beach below.

He had found a *really* secret beach. He had found part of what he would later explore and call the Unknown Coast.

Another time, Phil was hiking on Kelham Beach, near Point Resistance, on a day when there was a *minus* tide, that is, one much lower than an ordinary low tide. Because the tide was so low, Phil was able to get past a truncated rock promontory to some terraced arches, where he discovered the mouth of another cave, this one about 12 feet long. Once again, the entrance was high, but tapered down. He climbed through. On the other side was a perfect 150-foot semicircle of a beach.

This beach he called *Real* Secret Beach, to distinguish it from another beach, designated by the Park Service as Secret Beach, which runs north of Point Resistance to Sculptured Beach along Drake's Bay.

Phil retired from teaching in the '70s and began devoting himself full time to leading hikes—expeditions, really—that went into the Sierras and other mountain ranges for weeks at a time. He also led day trips to continue his exploration of Point

Reyes. With more time, and more hiking, he found more secret Point Reyes places. He found Secret Cave, Phantom Falls, Sculptured Beach, and the Sea Tunnel. It wasn't that no one had ever been to these secret places before. Maybe they had. But these places weren't marked on the hiking maps you could buy at the ranger station in Bear Valley. They were difficult and sometimes dangerous to get to. They took effort and planning.

Eventually, Phil wrote a book about his special places—*Point Reyes: Secret Places and Magic Moments*. It contained *really* secret beaches like the ones described here.

After Phil's book was published, the park service had to rescue two kids stranded at one of these beaches at high tide. It was a section of the Unknown Coast south of Elephant Rock. It was so difficult to get to that the rangers had to use a helicopter to make the rescue. When the rangers found them, the kids were waving a copy of Phil's book to attract help.

Phil's book is being sold at the Point Reyes Park store again, but it now contains a specific warning about the Unknown Coast. "Only for very experienced hikers," says the added text. "When the tide begins to turn there comes a time when the only way to turn the promontories, which are becoming inundated, is to traverse their steep cliffs six to fifteen feet above the water and this is NOT RECOMMENDED."

Phil's book has many warnings now and they are good advice on any beach: Always take a tide book, and study the tide to make sure you can get back from a secret beach . . . If the waves are big, do not continue . . . Always stop to study a questionable situation before moving on . . . Never turn your back on the waves because a large sneaker wave could be coming. This is advice every California beachgoer should consider.

Despite the many disclaimers in his book, there are actually some secret beaches in Point Reyes that Phil left out for safety's sake or because he hadn't had the time to fully explore them yet. One he calls the Impassable Coast and another the Coast of Despair. These places, and others, are waiting for the intrepid explorer to discover them on her own.

We asked Phil for a magic place in beautiful Point Reyes that wasn't too demanding to get to, a secret beach that wasn't necessarily so secret after all. He suggested the Tomales Peninsula, flanked by the beach of Tomales Bay, in May. The route is in Phil's book, and in the other guidebooks available at the ranger station, and on page 257. In May, Phil says, the last mile of the hike to the beach takes you through a "sea of yellow lupine, sometimes four to seven feet in height."

Phil is 73 now and still leading hikes through the Point Reyes National Seashore and extended backpacking trips in the Sierras. He says he "goes to the wilderness to be re-created." You can reach him at Arnot Explorations, PO Box 181, Lagunitas, CA 94938. Or call him at 415-488-4452. You can order his book through Wide World Publishing, PO Box 476, San Carlos, CA 94070; 415-593-2839. ■

TOM MIKKELSEN

Point Reyes Beaches, Point Reyes National Seashore

Swimming and surfing are not recommended, however, as tidal conditions and visibility can and do change rapidly. There are free parking lots and wheelchair-accessible rest rooms at both beaches. Access is via marked turnoffs from Sir Francis Drake Boulevard on the way to Point Reyes Lighthouse from Highway 1. For more information, call Point Reyes National Seashore at 415-663-1092.

Kehoe Beach This is a nearly empty extension of the beaches that run up the western side of the Point Reyes Peninsula. Getting here requires a ½-mile hike from the trailhead, which is at a free parking lot. The beach is sandy and backed by sand dunes, bluffs, and wetlands. It is frequented by the many locals who appreciate its beauty and off-the-beaten-track feel. Access is via Pierce Point Road, which is a right turn off Sir Francis Drake Boulevard north of Inverness. There is no day-use fee, and dogs are allowed. For more information, call 415-663-1092.

McClures Beach The last beach on the peninsula's west coast, it is also the most isolated and, some might say, the most beautiful. It is sandy, backed by dunes, and fronted by numerous tide pools and mounds of driftwood. There are shorebirds everywhere, and you may also spot seals. As McClures is somewhat narrow, visitors should take care not to be nailed by so-called sleeper waves, which can rise rather suddenly from calm surf. Don't let this warning deter you from fully enjoying this stretch of coast. Access is via the end of

Pierce Point Road (see also Kehoe Beach, above). There is a parking lot, and no day-use fee. For more information, call 415-663-1092.

Tomales Bay State Park This 1800-acre park is the main shore access point for Tomales Bay, running alongside the eastern slope of Inverness Ridge. Visitors will find a network of hiking trails on the western side of the bay, with views of the oyster-farming operations below. There is safe swimming from the beaches within the bay (Heart's Desire Beach, Indian Beach, Pelican Beach), and the water here is up to 20 degrees warmer than it is in the ocean. There are also showers, rest rooms, parking, and hiker/bicyclist campsites available. There are day-use and camping fees. Access is via Pierce Point Road, about 2 miles north of the town of Inverness. For more information, call 415-669-1140.

Marshall Beach. Technically part of Point Reyes National Seashore, this beach is a 1½-mile walk down a trail that leads to Tomales Bay. It is sandy and also has wetlands, and is a relatively safe, warm swimming beach. Access is via a parking lot off L Ranch Road, which itself is off Pierce Point Road. There is no day-use fee. For more information, call 415-663-1092.

TOM MIKKELSEN

Kehoe Beach, Point Reyes National Seashore

Lodging

IN MARIN HEADLANDS

Golden Gate Hostel (415-331-2777), off Bunker Road east of Rodeo Lagoon. Inexpensive. Operated by American Youth Hostels, this simple 60-bed facility welcomes AYH members and nonmembers alike. There is bicycle storage, and both dorm and family accommodations are available. *Note*: Reservations are highly recommended during the summer.

IN MILL VALLEY

Mountain Home Inn (415-381-9000), 810 Panoramic Highway. Expensive. Located on a ridge that looks west and sharply down into Muir Woods, this beautiful 10-room inn sports views of either the headlands or Richardson and San Francisco Bays from every room. There is also a quiet public restaurant and bar in the lobby, and the staff will pack a lunch for guests before they set out to hike Mount Tam.

IN MUIR BEACH

The Pelican Inn (415-383-6000), 10 Pacific Way. Moderate. This English Tudor inn and pub is a cozy place to stop for a beer or spend the night, with the caveat that it can be noisy sometimes.

IN STINSON BEACH

Steep Ravine Environmental Cabins (1-800-444-7275), Highway 1, about 1 mile south of Stinson Beach. Inexpensive. Located at the bottom of Steep Ravine Canyon and just about on the ocean, these hostel-type cabins are some of the great bargains on the Pacific Coast. Sleeping bags and pads are a must, and there's no electricity, but the location absolutely cannot be beat.

Casa del Mar (415-868-2124), 37 Belvedere Avenue. Expensive. This five-room bed & breakfast is set on the hills above Stinson Beach, and has trails out its back door that lead directly up Mount Tam. It's a friendly place that serves a big breakfast, all just a short walk from Stinson Beach proper.

Stinson Beach Motel (415-868-1712), 3416 Highway 1. Moderate. An informal motel in the downtown area, its six studios and apartments are a bargain, considering the motel's central location.

IN BOLINAS

Smiley's Schooner Saloon and Hotel (415-868-1311), 41 Wharf Road. Moderate. Located in downtown Bolinas, Smiley's features clean, sparsely furnished rooms in one of the quieter towns on the coast. Plus, it's just across the street from the Bolinas Bay Bakery & Cafe (see **Restaurants**).

Thomas' White House Inn (415-868-0279), 118 Kale Road. Moderate. With only two guest rooms but an enormous lawn, Thomas' offers quaint accommodations and sweeping views of the coast from Marin to Half Moon Bay.

IN OLEMA

Roundstone Farm (415-663-1020), 9940 Sir Francis Drake Boulevard. Expensive. Centered on a passive-solar house that's just 10 years old, this inn has five rooms, each with private bath, on 10 acres of ranchland with views of Point Reyes National Seashore. The price includes a full breakfast.

Point Reyes Seashore Lodge (415-663-9000; 1-800-404-5634), 10021 Highway 1. Expensive. A good alternative place to stay, this three-story inn has 21 modern rooms, most with their own fireplace, telephone, and garden view. The one drawback is a certain amount of noise from Highway 1 and a nearby restaurant.

Bear Valley Inn (415-663-1777), 88 Bear Valley Road. Moderate. Although sometimes noisy, this inn is a great place from which to start exploring the Point Reyes area. There are just three guest rooms, and a living room with woodstove and overstuffed chairs is a welcoming place to rest after a long day of sight-seeing.

IN INVERNESS

Ten Inverness Way (415-669-1648), 10 Inverness Way. Expensive. This bed & breakfast has five units, all located near the middle of Inverness, offering guests good access to Point Reyes National Seashore and Tomales Bay. It also has a piano, games, and a small but interesting library.

IN POINT REYES STATION

Holly Tree Inn (415-663-1554), 3 Silverhills Road. Expensive. One author's favorite inn in Marin County, this is a quiet yet funky bed & breakfast with four cozy rooms. There is also a large living room where guests can lounge in comfy chairs near a fireplace. A separate two-room cottage is available for complete privacy.

Point Reyes Hostel (415-663-8811), off Limantour Road (call for directions). Inexpensive. This hostel features a family room and two common rooms heated by woodstoves, plus a fully equipped kitchen and a patio.

Restaurants

IN MUIR BEACH

Pelican Inn (415-383-6000), 10 Pacific Way. Moderate to expensive. This woody Tudor-looking pub and inn has a bar that's generally packed with friendly people—locals and visitors alike—who want to have a beer after a hard day of work or play. There's fish-and-chips and bangers and mash for the hungry, and the Pelican also serves a Sunday brunch (call ahead for times). A civilized spot to relax.

IN STINSON BEACH

Sand Dollar Restaurant (415-868-0434), 3458 Highway 1. Moderate. An inexpensive, informal place to get burgers and several different kinds of seafood. There are good microbrewed beers, and sunny patio seating for when the weather cooperates.

Stinson Beach Grill (415-868-2002), 3465 Highway 1. Moderate. A great place to go for breakfast or lunch, both for proximity to the beach and for large portions of omelets, huevos rancheros, and pancakes. There also are pasta, seafood, and burgers for later in the day.

IN BOLINAS

Bolinas Bay Bakery & Cafe (415-868-0211), 20 Wharf Road. Moderate. Pretty much the last word in healthy eating on this part of the coast, here visitors will find delicious salads, sandwiches, pizzas, pastas, and even burgers made from locally grown beef.

IN INVERNESS

Vladimir's Czechoslovakian Restaurant (415-669-1021), 12785 Sir Francis Drake Boulevard. Moderate. Founded by Vladimir himself, who fled the Communist takeover of his native country, this restaurant specializes in

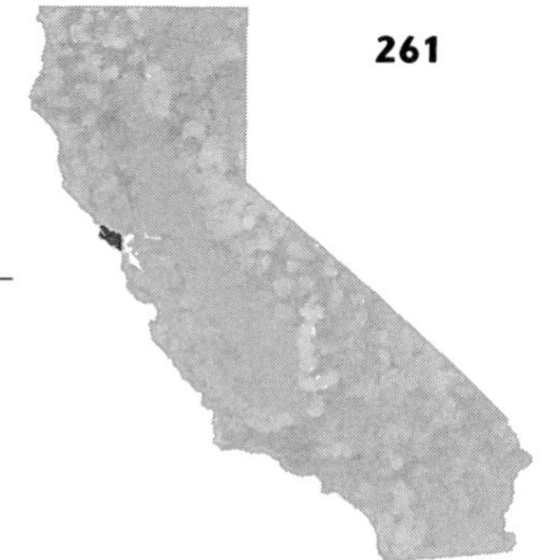

Eastern European and Continental dishes, especially meat. Vladimir's jodhpurs, riding whip, and free-range English make him quite a character—though the food's good, it's worth a visit just to say you've been here.

IN POINT REYES STATION

Station House Cafe (415-663-1515), 11180 State Route One (Highway 1). Moderate. This restaurant specializes in seafood, especially oysters raised just up the road in Tomales Bay, but doesn't skimp on chicken, steak, and fish. Also, it serves three meals a day and so is always ready for the weary traveler.

Point Reyes Roadhouse & Oyster Bar (415-663-1277), Highway 1 at the south end of Point Reyes Station. Inexpensive. A good choice for lunch or dinner, with the fairly standard menu of burgers, salads, and sandwiches augmented by barbecued short ribs or oysters—and chocolate malts for dessert.

Taqueria La Quinta (415-663-8868), 11285 Highway 1, Inexpensive. A large menu of classic Mexican-American dishes, prepared fresh and costing little.

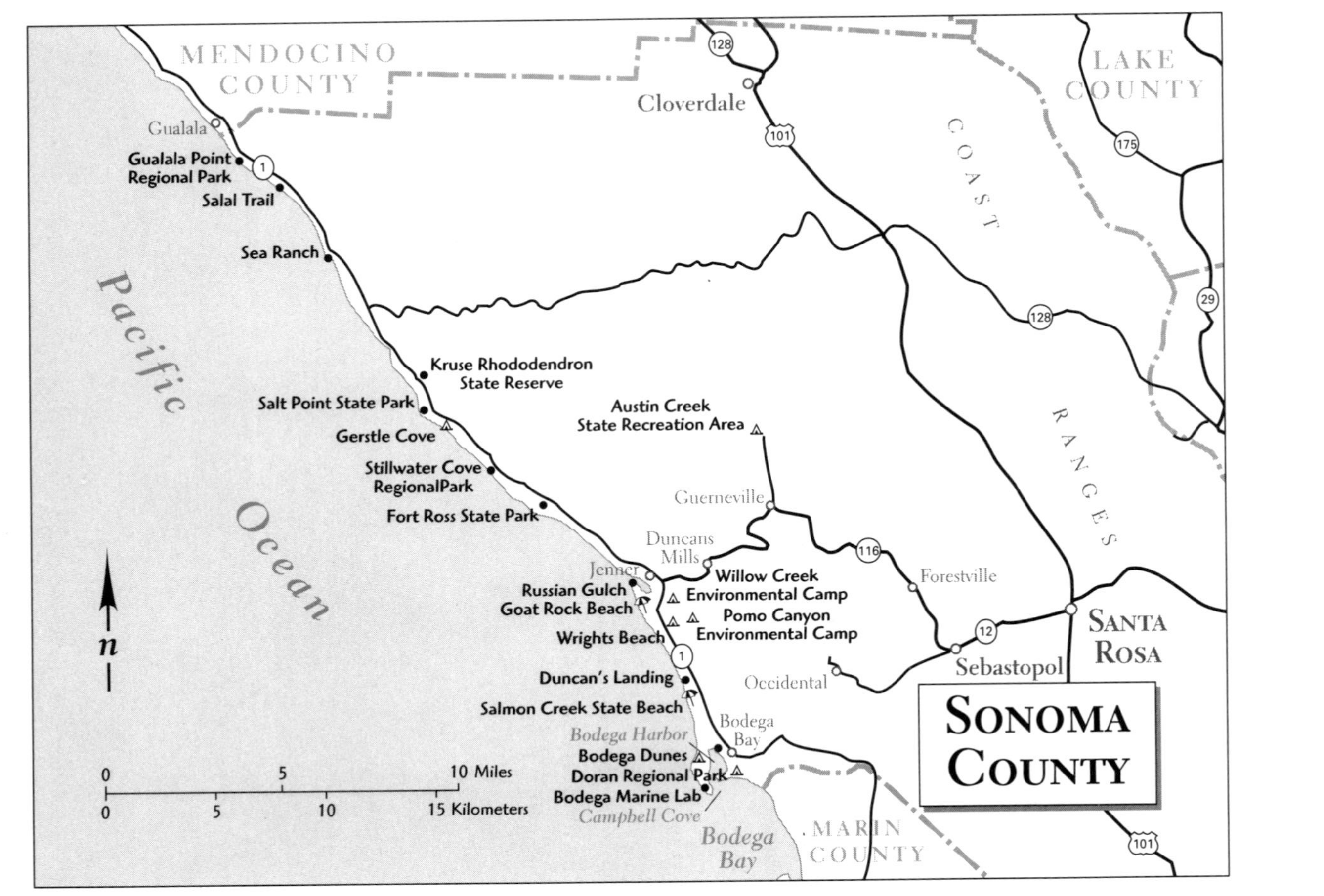
Sonoma County
Mendocino County
Lake County
Marin County
Coast Ranges
Pacific Ocean
Cloverdale
Gualala
Gualala Point Regional Park
Salal Trail
Sea Ranch
Kruse Rhododendron State Reserve
Salt Point State Park
Gerstle Cove
Stillwater Cove RegionalPark
Fort Ross State Park
Austin Creek State Recreation Area
Guerneville
Duncans Mills
Jenner
Russian Gulch
Goat Rock Beach
Willow Creek Environmental Camp
Pomo Canyon Environmental Camp
Wrights Beach
Duncan's Landing
Salmon Creek State Beach
Bodega Harbor
Bodega Dunes
Doran Regional Park
Bodega Marine Lab
Campbell Cove
Bodega Bay
Occidental
Forestville
Sebastopol
Santa Rosa
1
12
29
101
116
128
175
n
0 5 10 Miles
0 5 10 15 Kilometers

CHAPTER TWELVE

Sonoma County

THE SAN ANDREAS FAULT spills into Bodega Bay from Tomales Bay to the south, then rolls back along the coast, leaving Bodega Head to the west. It dips back into the sea going north past Bodega, then, near Fort Ross, comes inland again, paralleling the coast, going north toward Point Arena. Here the fault is only a few miles inland, and has formed a valley. The Gualala and Garcia Rivers flow through this depression before finally turning to the sea. In this area, between Fort Ross and Point Arena, Route 1 travels on the Salinian Block.

Here, the block is not granite—as at Point Reyes to the south—but rather softer rock carried north from Santa Barbara. The coastline is softer and there are many extended areas of marine terraces.

At the southern end of Sonoma, Bodega Bay is the largest coastal town, an interesting mixture of fishing port and resort. Above Bodega there is a great swath of state beaches running to the Russian River. Many are isolated and charming, as are the beaches at Goat Rock, though the trails down the face of the cliffs can be difficult. Often, as at Salmon Creek, these beaches are wide and sandy and access is easy—the beaches are more crowded.

North of the Russian River, cliffs mark the coast, and access down to the beach is difficult. The road clings to the hillside. Then, just north of Timber Gulch, the San Andreas fault moves inland, forming the valley. Now, running north to the Mendocino line, the marine terraces return, and the coast is forgiving and accessible. Once again there is a procession of parks and public beaches, until the Sea Ranch development just north of Stewarts Point.

There are public access ways through this large, private development of interesting, beautiful homes, but you may feel like a trespasser nevertheless. To appreciate Sea Ranch, it is probably best to rent a house here—which can be easily arranged, and often at an attractive price.

The Gualala River marks the boundary line between Sonoma and Mendocino. The park here is beautiful, with a riverside campground sited in redwood groves. The adjacent beach has sand dunes, hiking trails, and excellent vista points. There is a visitors center in the park, where information can be obtained.

Beaches and Attractions

IN BODEGA BAY

Doran Beach Regional Park This park, located on the broad, sandy, east–west spit that forms Bodega Bay's southern border, features more than 100 campsites, picnic tables, rest rooms, an ocean pier visitors can fish from, and a fish-cleaning station. The beach has excellent views south of Tomales Point. There are both day-use and camping fees. Access is via Doran Park Road, off Highway 1 near the Best Western. For more information, call 707-875-3540.

Bodega Harbor. A series of full-service commercial and pleasure boat marinas. Restrooms, scenic views. For information call 707-875-3422.

Bodega Head/Campbell Cove Bodega Head is the tip of the peninsula that protects the western half of Bodega Bay. Here you'll find a boat-launch area, hiking trails that cross the peninsula, and sandy pocket beaches backed by granite cliffs. There are good vantage points for winter whale-watching, and a hiking trail that you can take to walk up the coast, past Mussel Point to Salmon Creek Beach (see below). Amazingly, this outcropping of granite, just 2 miles from the highly unstable San Andreas fault, was once considered to be a prime location for a nuclear power plant. (Bodega Head, part of the so-called Salinian Block, is drifting slowly north and in a few hundred million years will pull alongside the Gulf of Alaska.)

TOM MIKKELSEN

Rocky southern Sonoma coast

Campbell Cove is on the interior of the peninsula and boasts a small, sandy beach; there is also a boardwalk that leads to an observation deck, as well as picnic tables and rest rooms. There are entrance fees for both Bodega Head and Campbell Cove. Access is via the end of Westside Road, which runs down the western edge of the bay. For more information, call 707-865-2391 or 707-875-3483.

Bodega Marine Laboratory ★ This is a University of California lab that is open to the public on Friday afternoons. It features displays of the lab's ongoing aquaculture program. Access is via Westside Road. For more information, call 707-875-2211.

Salmon Creek Beach/Bodega Dunes Campground Here visitors will find a wide, sandy beach and enormous vegetated dunes flanking Salmon Creek's ocean outlet. It's a wild stretch of coast and swimming definitely is not recommended, due to cold water and rough waves. Here, as at other Sonoma County beaches, there are no lifeguards, so extra care must be taken even when wading. There is camping behind one set of dunes (thus the name Bodega Dunes); fees apply, but for the money you'll get beautiful, peaceful sites beneath pine and cypress trees, rest rooms, hot showers, and RV hookups. Plus, the campsites are less than a mile north of town. Access is via Highway 1; the main entrance to Salmon Creek Beach is 2.5 miles north of Bodega Bay, while the entrance for Bodega Dunes is just a half mile north of town. For more information, call 707-875-3483.

Duncan's Landing. Used in the 1860s and 1870s for loading local timber onto ships, this point now sports the nickname Death Rock for the number of drownings that take place here. Visitors take heed; there is a small beach, but doing anything in the water is out of the question. There is free parking and rest rooms, and the fishing is reputed to be good. Access is via Highway 1, 5 miles north of Bodega Bay. For more information, call 707-875-2391.

Goat Rock Beach/Russian River mouth This beach is on the peninsula formed by the Russian River's abrupt northern swing as it approaches its Pacific outlet. It's a big grassy area with great views of the ocean and the lower Russian River Valley, as well as picnic tables, rest rooms, and fire pits. The Kortum Trail follows 2.6 miles of blufftops south to Shell Beach. There is a parking lot and no fee; access is via the end of Goat Rock Road, off Highway 1 south of the Russian River. For more information, call 707-865-2391 or 707-875-3483.

Willow Creek/Pomo Canyon Campground. Pomo Canyon is the scene of a small number of beautiful primitive campgrounds, including 21 sites that are within a redwood grove. There are toilets, fire rings, and picnic tables, but you'll have to provide your own water. An alternative is to purify water obtained from a stream that passes by a beautiful hiking trail from the Willow Creek sites to Shell Beach. The trail dips into redwood forest with an exposed walk through grassy hills, and visitors will enjoy spectacular views of the Russian River Valley and the ocean beyond. Access is via Willow Creek Road, the very last right turn before the Russian River Bridge—just before the restaurant—as you drive north on Highway 1; this is a dirt access road that leads to roadside parking. For more information, call 707-875-3483.

Other state beaches south of the Russian River There are several small state beaches on the coast between Bodega Bay and the Russian River. They are immediately accessible from Highway 1, and tend to have few facilities other than a parking lot. Here they are listed with mileage north of Bodega Bay in parentheses. From south to north: **Miwok Beach** (2.5), **Coleman Beach** (3.0), **Arched Rock Beach** (3.2), **Schoolhouse Beach** (4.0), **Portuguese Beach** (4.2), **Gleason Beach** (4.7), and **Wright's Beach** (6.0).

IN JENNER

Russian Gulch North of the Russian River, the San Andreas fault continues running close to the coast, building up steep cliffs above Highway 1 and allowing for only tiny beaches. Russian Gulch is one of these, a small, alternately sandy and rocky crescent nestled beneath unstable bluffs. As with all Sonoma County beaches, swimming is not recommended, but visitors can enjoy some majestic solitude on land. Access is via a parking lot off Highway 1, 2.5 miles north of Jenner. There is no fee for access. For more information, call 707-865-2391 or 707-875-3483.

IN FORT ROSS

Fort Ross State Historic Park This is a museum commemorating the time when the Russians were not just coming but actually here. The czar's fur traders were the first European settlers of this part of the coast, and conducted a thriving business on Fort Ross's 1100 acres in the 19th century. Volunteers help portray the lives of these early colonists, and a museum and several restored buildings help re-create the period. Other facilities include hiking trails, an alternately sandy and rocky beach, and picnic tables. There is a fee for the museum. Within the park is Fort Ross Cove, a small beach that sees a lot of shell collectors, as well as picnickers who come for the garden planted here. Offshore is an underwater park called Fort Ross Reef. Access is via Highway 1, 11 miles north of Jenner. For more information, call 707-847-3286.

Stillwater Cove Regional Park Situated at the mouth of Stockhoff Creek, this park features about two dozen campsites as well as a stairway to aid in making the steep descent to a sometimes sandy, sometimes rocky shore. Visitors can also hike along any of several trails and there are abalone to be taken offshore. Other facilities here include picnic tables and rest rooms. Access is via Highway 1, 3 miles north of Fort Ross. For more information, call 707-847-3245.

Salt Point State Park (including Stump Beach and Fisk Mill Cove) This is a popular abalone-diving spot, but visitors here can take advantage of nearly every activity a coastal park can offer. Sitting on 4300 acres, Salt Point offers miles of hiking trails both high and low, equestrian trails, picnic tables, and several small beaches. There are whale-watching lectures given on weekend days each January. There are specialized camping sites for groups, hikers and bicyclists, and walk-ins. Fisk Mill Cove, Gerstle Cove, and North Horseshoe Cove all are part of Salt Point State Park. **Gerstle Cove,** particularly, is recommended for its diving and tide-pooling possibilities. Access is via various parking lots directly off Highway 1; the main entrance for Salt Point State Park is 20 miles north of Jenner. Fees are charged for day use and camping. For more information, call 707-847-3221.

TOM MIKKELSEN

Fort Ross

TOM MIKKELSEN

Sea Ranch condominium

Kruse Rhododendron State Reserve ★ From April to June, this area inland from Salt Point State Park is ablaze with rhododendrons. Originally planted to take the place of trees destroyed in a forest fire, the reserve is now a noted stop for visitors driving up Highway 1. It covers 300 acres and features 5 miles of hiking trails through redwood and rhododendron. Other facilities include rest rooms and a parking lot. There is no access fee. Access is via Kruse Ranch Road, east off Highway 1. For more information, call 707-847-3221.

Sea Ranch access Sea Ranch is an exclusive housing development that extends along the northernmost 10 miles of Sonoma County's coast. It is unusual in the degree of its control over these 10 miles. Following a series of court cases, the public now may use any of several beaches within Sea Ranch's domain. The most prominent of these are **Black Point Beach**, **Pebble Beach**, **Walk-On Beach**, **Stengel Beach**, and **Shell Beach** (the last not to be confused with the other Shell Beach, just south of the Russian River; see above). Visitors walk ¼ mile over grassy blufftops to reach alternately sandy and rocky cove beaches, which sport spectacular views of the Pacific and the majestic, wave-beaten rocks just offshore. Access is via marked public parking lots between mileposts 50 and 56. There is a fee for access. For more information, call the Sea Ranch Association at 707-785-2444.

Gualala Point Regional Park This park is on a peninsula at the ocean outlet of the Gualala River, facing the eponymous town across the water in

Mendocino County. It covers 75 acres and has hiking trails, a broad sandy beach that changes with each year's storms, and campsites along the east side of Highway 1. There also are picnic tables and rest rooms. Volunteers staff a visitors center containing exhibits and objects from Gualala's past as a logging port; it is open weekends between Memorial Day and Labor Day. Access is via a parking lot 1 mile south of the Gualala River along the west side of Highway 1. There is a fee for access to the park. For more information, call 707-785-2377.

Lodging

IN BODEGA BAY

Bodega Harbor Inn (707-875-3594), 1345 Bodega Avenue. Moderate. Older than the Bodega Bay Lodge and Inn at the Tides, and much more to scale at only 14 rooms and 7 houses and cottages, this is the best place to stay in Bodega Bay.

The Inn at the Tides (707-875-2751; 1-800-541-7788), 800 Pacific Coast Highway. Expensive. This is a resort with 86 rooms, all of which face Bodega Bay and the Pacific beyond. The rooms are spread among a dozen buildings, and guests walk to the main lodge for a complimentary breakfast.

Bay Hill Mansion (707-875-3577; 1-800-526-5927), 3919 Bay Hill Road. Moderate to expensive. Located on a hill above the village, this large white mansion has six rooms, a spacious parlor with great sunset views, and serves a full breakfast each morning.

Bodega Bay Lodge (707-875-3525; 1-800-368-2468), 103 Highway 1. Expensive. A nice but very large place to stay, all of its 78 units have recently been remodeled. Rooms have private balconies with great views of Bodega Bay, and there are lovely flower gardens backing an outdoor spa. On a recent visit, however, the fitness center was closed.

IN JENNER

Fort Ross Lodge (707-847-3333), 20705 Highway 1. Moderate to expensive. With a total of 22 units above the ocean and its own path leading down to tide pools, this inn is made to order for those who can't get enough of the Pacific. Some rooms have a private deck with barbecue, and there is a glassed-in hot tub with great views of Pacific sunsets.

Murphy's Jenner Inn (707-865-2377), 10400 Highway 1. Moderate to expensive. Although the decor could use some updating, Murphy's offers a wide range of accommodations, from bed & breakfast-style rooms to rentals of entire houses. Their river- and beachfront location makes them a good deal for the money, and there is also a restaurant on the premises (see **Restaurants**). This bed & breakfast features 13 guest rooms split among seven cottages, all with private entrance and bath, and all overlooking the ocean or the scenic Russian River Valley. Guests get a continental breakfast at the main lodge. Murphy's also rents out six vacation homes along the river, in Jenner Canyon, or overlooking the ocean, and these are not to be missed for those who want even more privacy.

Timber Cove Campground and Boat Landing (707-847-3278), 21350 Highway 1. Inexpensive. Bring your tent or RV here if the state park campgrounds are full. Funky but fun.

Timber Cove Inn (707-847-3231), 21780 N. Coast Highway 1. Expensive. Located 15 miles north of Jenner, this hotel emphasizes exposed wood and rock in its architecture. Its 49 rooms are simply furnished, and many have decks with hot tubs that give guests great views of the ocean and surrounding mountains. On the grounds is the sculptor Benny Bufano's *Peace* statue, an impressive work well sited on the headland.

Stillwater Cove Ranch (707-847-3227), 22555 Highway 1. Moderate. This former boys' school has a collection of buildings with different types of accommodations, from a bunkhouse to private cottages. *Note:* No meals are served here, and guests may have to drive to Gualala (to the north) or back south into Jenner for food.

Salt Point Lodge (707-847-3234), 23255 Highway 1. Moderate. This modern motel, with good amenities, is recommended for kids. The restaurant serves three decent meals a day.

Ocean Cove (707-847-3422), across from Salt Point Lodge on Highway 1. Moderate. Ocean Cove has a private beach and bluff for camping, diving, and fishing.

Sea Ranch Lodge (707-785-2371; 1-800-732-7262), 60 Sea Walk Drive. Expensive. The public lodging at the Sea Ranch development, this is a famous piece of architecture in a dramatic coastal setting.

Restaurants

IN VALLEY FORD

Dinucci's, (707-876-3260), Highway 1 in Valley Ford. Moderate. It's a classic Italian eatery road stop: The food isn't great, but the atmosphere compensates.

IN BODEGA BAY

Lucas Wharf (707-875-3522), 595 Highway 1. Moderate. The location is scenic, the food is mostly mediocre, but the fish stews are good. Fishing-dock atmosphere; takeout is available.

Tides Wharf Restaurant (707-875-3652), 835 Highway 1. Expensive. Specializing in fresh seafood, the Tides is a good place to try a famed northern California specialty, the Hangtown Fry: oysters fried up with bacon, eggs, and potatoes. The restaurant is part of a large resort that has pretentions.

IN JENNER

River's End (707-865-2484), 11048 Highway 1. Expensive. This restaurant is situated just above the mouth of the Russian River and offers expansive views to go with its excellent food. The dinner menu tends toward game and seafood dishes made with locally grown ingredients. River's End features a simpler and cheaper lunch menu, too. Many tables have ocean views, and there is a small deck outside as well.

Salt Point Bar and Grill (707-847-3234), 23255 Highway 1. Expensive. Serving breakfast, lunch, and dinner, this is a good choice because of a wide-ranging menu featuring seafood, steak, chicken, salads, and sandwiches.

Murphy's Jenner by the Sea (707-865-2377), 10400 Highway 1. Expensive. Attached to the inn (see **Lodging**), this restaurant offers beef, seafood, and vegetable dishes, as well as a full bar.

IN FORT ROSS AND NORTH

Fort Ross Lodge (707-847-3333), 20705 Highway 1. Moderate to expensive. Ocean views and a wide price range.

Timber Cove Inn (707-847-3231), 21780 N. Highway 1, 15 miles north of Jenner. Expensive. Dine on decent seafood and Continental cuisine in a well-designed resort. Check out the Benny Bufano sculpture on the headland.

Sea Ranch Lodge (707-785-2371), 60 Sea Walk Drive, Sea Ranch. Expensive. The Sunday brunch is the best choice here.

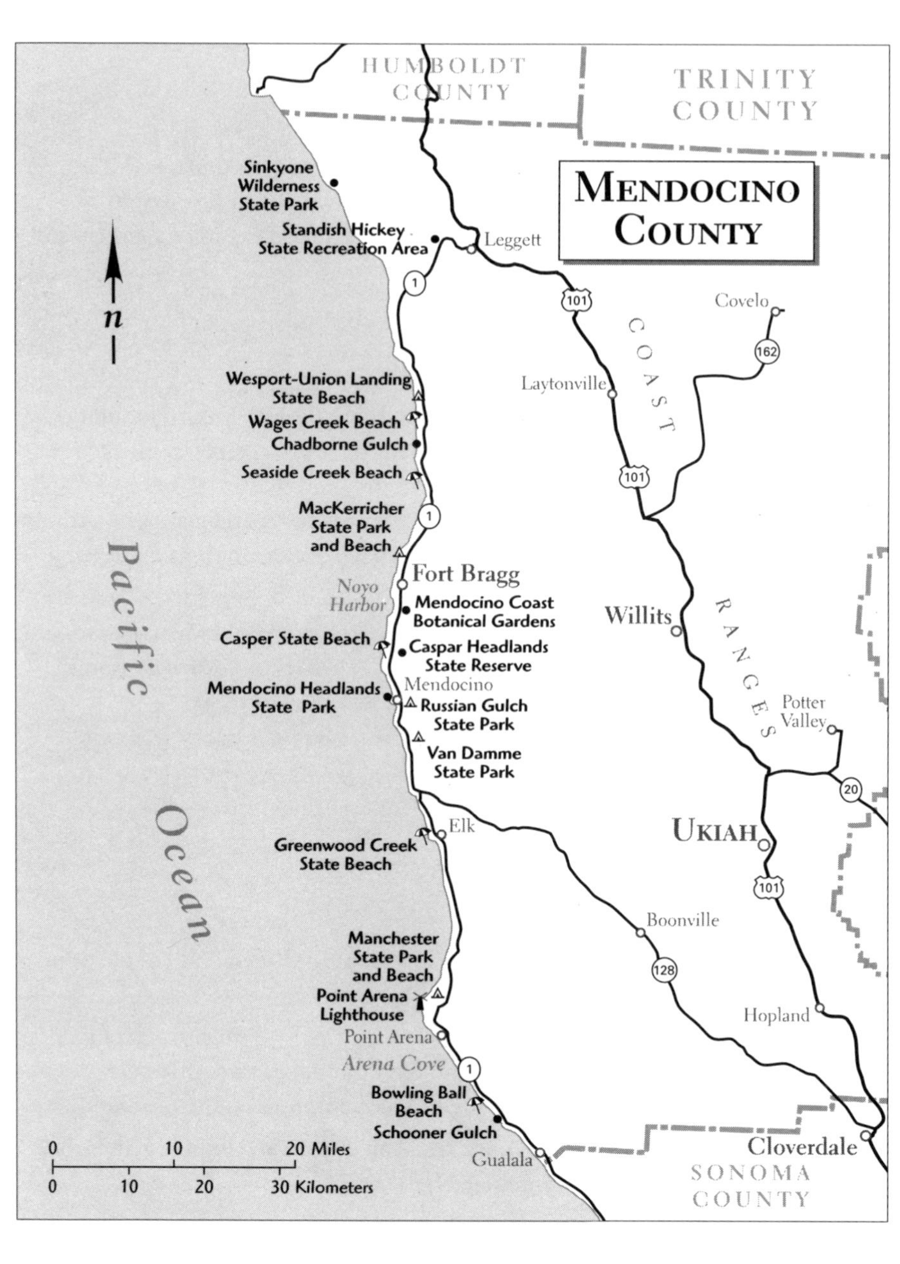

HUMBOLDT COUNTY
TRINITY COUNTY
MENDOCINO COUNTY
Sinkyone Wilderness State Park
Standish Hickey State Recreation Area
Leggett
n
Covelo
COAST
Laytonville
Wesport-Union Landing State Beach
Wages Creek Beach
Chadborne Gulch
Seaside Creek Beach
MacKerricher State Park and Beach
Pacific
Fort Bragg
Noyo Harbor
Mendocino Coast Botanical Gardens
Willits
RANGES
Casper State Beach
Caspar Headlands State Reserve
Mendocino Headlands State Park
Mendocino
Russian Gulch State Park
Potter Valley
Van Damme State Park
Ocean
Elk
Greenwood Creek State Beach
UKIAH
Boonville
Manchester State Park and Beach
Point Arena Lighthouse
Hopland
Point Arena
Arena Cove
Bowling Ball Beach
Schooner Gulch
Cloverdale
Gualala
SONOMA COUNTY
0 10 20 Miles
0 10 20 30 Kilometers

CHAPTER THIRTEEN

Mendocino County

THE GEOLOGISTS DAVID ALT AND DONALD HYNDHAM in their excellent book *Roadside Geology of Northern California* refer to the distinctive headlands of the Mendocino coast as "emergent marine terraces." These are the spectacular, softly sloping, grass-covered high fields. Often, as in the town of Mendocino, which is built on one of the most beautiful of these terraces, each side of the wide shelf is cut by rivers or streams—in the case of the Mendocino Headland, by Big River in the south and Russian Gulch to the north. These headlands end in eroded cliffs, below which lies the beach. Alt and Hyndam tell us that these terraces are "old beaches planed to their present shape by wave action and then raised above sea level by uplift of the coastal range" (p. 53).

In the spring these coastal fields, full of wildflowers, meet the shades of blue corresponding with the ocean's depth. It is a sight lovely to behold. Carefully preserved towns such as Mendocino—small, meticulously maintained western Victorians, brightly colored shops, weathered water towers, shady front porches —nestle into these headlands as if they were made for each other.

The many rivers of Mendocino are another important feature of this celebrated section of the California coast. Pudding Creek, Noyo, Big, and Little Rivers; Navarro, Casper, Mitchel, Jug Handle, and Albion Creeks; and a hundred more smaller streams have cut their way through the mountain wall. The result is beautiful fingers of land extending out to the sea, rivers or streams on either side. Several of these streams—Big River below the town of Mendocino is the best example—are waterways that can carry you upstream, where ducks and geese abound. Lower downstream, toward the mouth, there will be hawks.

Over the rivers, the highway is often suspended on arched bridges, or is left to the east as it hugs the mountainside. The extended fingers of land may end in intricately carved rock formations—caves and tunnels carved into isolated, small rock islands full of birds.

The Mendocino coast has some of the best—and most famous—bed & breakfast establishments in all of California. They range from architecturally designed re-creations of a Victorian village to wonderfully idiosyncratic homes in the process of restoration. They cling to clifftops and lie by winding rivers that snake through soft foothills to the sea. Mendocino is also home to many of the most beautiful and carefully planned state parks, such as the varied MacKerricher in the north.

Mendocino is also renowned as a place for artists, and they have served it well in fighting to preserve its coastline. You will find their art not just in town, but also in bed & breakfasts as well as in galleries at Fort Bragg.

Mendocino County begins at the Gualala River, which runs parallel to the coastline for several miles before finding an opening to the ocean. Between the river and Point Arena the beaches are mostly rocky, as at Bowling Ball Beach and Arena Cove.

The Point Arena Headland juts to the northwest in a peninsula that has been cut from the shoreline by the Garcia River. At the end of the peninsula is Point Arena Lighthouse. Built in 1870, its powerful light is still functioning. There are tours of the lighthouse and the adjacent museum, and the former keeper's houses nearby can be rented.

Just north of Point Arena is Manchester State Beach, one of the largest sandy beaches in the county. It has an adjacent campground. Offshore lies the Point Arena Underwater State Reserve, a protected diving park.

The Navarro River is 10 miles to the north. There is a broad, sandy beach on its south bank. Just to the north is the Albion River, which has carved out one of the most beautiful bays of the Mendocino coast.

Above the Albion River, the coastline is cut frequently by rivers and streams. There are many pocket coves, some with sandy beaches, as at Caspar State Beach and Van Damme State Park. The headlands in this area also contain many scenic overlooks. This is an area of spectacular beauty.

Just past Van Damme State Park is Mendocino Bay, formed by the Big River, which flows into it. This bay, large for the serrated Mendocino coast, is one of the most beautiful in the state. This is one of the prime destination points in all the California coast.

The Mendocino Headlands continue to the north. Just below Noyo Harbor you'll find the Mendocino Coast Botanical Gardens, where informative trails lead through lovely gardens that explain the plants and flowers of the area. The docents here are extremely helpful. (This is where horticulturists retire.) There is a sandy beach with many facilities to the north at Noyo Harbor. Above Noyo is the largest city on the Mendocino coast, Fort Bragg. The industrial bases of this town—lumber and fishing—are part of its allure. The Skunk Railroad, which winds through the eastern mountains on daylong outings, is beloved by children. Hotel accommodations are unlimited, lining the road in and out of town.

Above Fort Bragg lies one of the greatest of all the California state parks, MacKerricher. Campsites have been tastefully arranged for privacy. (The ones to the north, near the dunes, are best.) Activities are incredibly varied. There is fresh-water fishing in the small lake, tide pooling, boardwalk nature walks with wonderful protected viewing areas, horseback riding, and, to the north, a large area of sand dunes to explore. There is even an offshore park for divers. Although heavily used, MacKerricher never seems crowded.

Above Fort Bragg there are several very small towns, each with a grocery store whose owner will provide information. Bed & breakfasts pop up around each turn in the headlands.

Above Cape Vizcaino, Highway 1 swings east away from the coast in order to avoid the Lost Coast to the north. This is an area of steep coastal mountains, impassable roads—and excellent hiking. For almost all visitors, this section of the coast is inaccessible.

Beaches and Attractions

IN GUALALA

Gualala River/Gualala beaches The Gualala River parallels the ocean behind a wide sand spit for roughly 2 miles from the Sonoma County border. Access to this beach is either by backtracking south to Gualala Point Regional Park and hiking north, or via kayak or canoe.

The nearest public beach access from Mendocino County is at **Fish Rock Beach**, reachable through privately run Anchor Bay Campground, 0.2 miles north of Anchor Bay. (The town is itself 4 miles north of Gualala.) Here visitors will find an alternately sandy and rocky ¾-mile-long beach backed by the campground, which has picnic tables, rest rooms, showers, and fish-cleaning tables. The beach is used primarily for fishing and abalone diving. There is a small day-use fee and parking. Access is via Highway 1 in Anchor Bay. For more information, call Anchor Bay Campground at 707-884-4222.

IN POINT ARENA

Schooner Gulch/Bowling Ball Beach Connected at low tide, these two beaches are reached from the same trailhead. Getting to either beach will take you across blufftops and through ravines (forested with redwoods, in Bowling Ball's case) to sandy pocket beaches. Both offer rugged isolation, tide pools, and driftwood; Bowling Ball's name comes from the wave-carved, spherical rock formations that lie on its shore. Both these beaches become notably smaller at high tide, so packing a tide chart is a good idea. Neither beach has any facilities besides roadside parking. Access is via the west side of Highway 1 at Schooner Gulch Road, about 3.5 miles south of Point Arena. There is no day-use fee.

Arena Cove Beach This is a small, rocky beach with good waves for surfing, marred by very shallow offshore reefs that make navigation a hazard; still, it's surfed by experts during the winter. There is a new pier here that features fish-cleaning tables, outdoor showers, and rest rooms. Perch and flounder are good bets for the angler, and there is also a boat-launch facility and parking. Access is via the west end of Port Road in Point Arena.

Point Arena Lighthouse Built in 1870, the Point Arena lighthouse sits just south of both the outlet of the Garcia River and the point where the San Andreas fault dives for good into the Pacific; from here north, visitors are solidly on North America. The lighthouse itself is 115 feet high, and tours of it are offered by docents. There are rest rooms, and a fee is charged for access to the lighthouse and a small museum. There are three houses on the site, which are rented out to visitors. Access is via the end of Lighthouse Road, a little over 1 mile south of Point Arena. For more information, call 707-882-2777.

Manchester State Beach ★ This 3½-mile-long sand-and-dunes beach lies on nearly 1000 acres of state land. Though it can be cold and desolate in the fog, there are enough giant driftwood logs ashore that finding a windbreak is no problem. Offshore is the Point Arena Underwater State Reserve, so the beach is heavily used by divers and birders as well. There is a campground with 46 sites about 15 minutes' walk upland from the beach; it has rest rooms and hiking trails. Access is via three different roads from Highway 1, which has signs to direct visitors. The access roads are Stoneboro, Kinney, and Alder Creek Roads, and there is parking at each entrance. A day-use fee is charged; for more information, call 707-937-5804.

IN ELK

Greenwood Creek State Beach. Located in the small town of Elk, this is a mile-long, alternately sandy and rocky beach that features big driftwood and "sea stacks," offshore rock formations dramatically carved into pillars by wave action. There are picnic tables and fire rings at the beach, surf-fishing is popular, and ocean kayaks can be rented in Elk for use here. Tidal, rock, and surf conditions make swimming dangerous, however. Access is via a trail west of the parking lot, just across the street from the Elk Store in town.

IN LITTLE RIVER

Van Damme State Park This park is built around the original 40-acre bequest of a logger who wanted to preserve the area's forest for the future. It has since grown quite a bit, to 2000 acres, and now backs up a small, sandy beach and a great deal of upland redwood and pine forest. There is a "pygmy" forest here where, owing to poor soil conditions, visitors can see pine trees that are fully grown at anywhere from 6 inches to 8 feet. There are hiking trails and a nature trail, including one wheelchair-accessible walk through a redwood forest. Offshore is what's reputed to be the best abalone diving on the north coast. All in all, there's something for nearly everyone at Van Damme. Fees are charged for forest day-use and camping, but there is no fee for beach day-use. The parking lot is free. Access is via Highway 1 at Little River; visitors will see signs for areas on either side of the highway. For more information, call 707-937-5804.

MENDOCINO

During the summer, it is a good idea to get a reservation at one of the many bed & breakfast inns, but it is not absolutely necessary. Fort Bragg, 10 miles to the north, is loaded with relatively cheap, if not ideal, motels, that can be used as a backup—there will be a room here. Indeed, despite the warnings about overcrowding, there are so many bed & breakfasts, and so many tourists change their plans, that it is very possible to land a wonderful room in a charming B&B with no advance work. For peace and quiet, try a bed & breakfast to the south of Mendocino, in Albion or in Little River. (**The Heritage House** in Little River and the **Albion River Inn** are good places to start. If they are full, stop by **Rachel's Inn** and the large, 65-room **Little River Inn and Golf and Tennis Resort**. Or be picky: By 6 o'clock, every bed & breakfast is eager to show you all the rooms it has available and will probably cut a deal on the price as well.)

When you have a room, drive on to Mendocino itself. Park where you can find a place on Main Street, and follow the map to the **Ford House Visitor Center**, also on Main. There are public bathrooms here, historical displays, and incredibly helpful guides—many of them retired couples from southern California who spend their summers in Mendocino, volunteering with the Park Service. They will go out of their way to help you out and load you up with more brochures than you want to carry.

The kids (if you have them and brought them) will want some exercise, so take them down to the beautiful beach to the south of Ford House and rummage for driftwood. Then go back into town for lunch at **Mendo Burger**, a hole-in-the-wall on Lansing Street with a friendly red chow guarding the door. In the afternoon, visit the **Mendocino Art Center** on Little Lake Street for its galleries and attractive grounds. On the way back to your inn, stop by **Catch a Canoe**, located on the other side of the south bridge, on Big River, and reserve a boat for a slow

TOM MIKKELSEN

Mendocino headlands

morning's paddle up the river in one of its unique "outriggers"—unlike a kayak, you can't tip these over and you get to sit upright in a real seat.

You'll get an excellent breakfast included in your lodging fee wherever you stay. Dinner plans depend on how much money you want to spend. **Cafe Beaujolais** on Ukiah Street is the recognized gold standard—the north coast's Chez Panisse—but will be unfriendly toward exuberant children. (They have been known to suddenly dust off a "dress code" when faced with a 10-year-old complaining about the slow service.) The Albion River Inn's dining room is also excellent, as well as less crowded and more tolerant. So is the **Moose Cafe**, on Kasten, where you can eat in the garden on a warm evening. **The Bay View Cafe** on Main is much less expensive than either of them and has outstanding views of Mendocino Bay. If the children are feeling boisterous, try **Patterson's Pub**, on Lansing, where they will fit right in. Or just wander through town, poke around, and find a place on your own that feels right for you. There are many choices—see **Restaurants** in this chapter.

In the afternoon, you can fish from the dock at the campground on Albion Creek, or take a hike in **Russian Gulch State Park**, which has miles of winding trails, a waterfall, and a striking picnic ground at the beautiful cove. (The park also has excellent campsites, but they are often booked months ahead. A camping family will do better in **MacKerricher State Park**, just to the north of Fort Bragg, one of the largest and most sensibly planned parks in all of California.) The park contains an incredible number of great family activities, including tide pools, a trout pond, boardwalks exploring the headlands, bird-watching, and excellent hiking trails. It can serve as a home base for a week of north coast exploration on a budget.

Mendocino Headlands State Park This park at the mouth of the Big River has 2 miles of sea cliffs fronting the town of Mendocino. Visitors can walk the tops of grassy bluffs for spectacular views of waves and wave-carved rocks, or take a stairway to the narrow beaches below. There is a small, sandy beach at the mouth of the Big River, and canoes can be rented to use in exploring the river's long inland estuary. Access to the headlands is via the seaward (generally, west) side of the town of Mendocino; access to the beach is via N. Big River Road, just south of the Big River. For more information, call 707-937-5804.

Russian Gulch State Park. Like Mendocino Headlands, this park centers on the outlet of a river, in this case Russian Gulch Creek. It features 12 miles of hiking trails, some of which lead north to Jackson State Forest. There is also a 2½-mile paved trail accessible to wheelchairs and bicyclists. Blufftop trails take visitors past a large collapsed sea cave through which inbound waves crash, shooting occasional geysers into the air. Visitors can also fish, as well as skin-dive, at an underwater park offshore, but note that here as elsewhere on the Mendocino coast, swimming is not recommended. The park has about 30 creekside campsites slightly inland, many of which lie beneath redwoods and

TOM MIKKELSEN

View down Lansing Street, town of Mendocino

Mae Laver—Wild Flower

■ When Mae Laver was a young girl, her parents would drive from their farm in Ukiah to a little place they had on the Mendocino coast. Sitting in the touring car, Mae could tell when they were near the coast by the smell of the wild azaleas and rhododendrons, even though she wasn't tall enough to see out the car window.

Even when she was just a little girl, Mae knew all about flowers. She also sewed well enough to make her own clothes, and grew her own vegetables. Her personal garden was a quarter of an acre.

Mae's grandfather was a stagecoach driver—when she thinks of driving with her family from Ukiah to the coast, she thinks of him, too. He was driving the last stage to be robbed in California—a passenger was killed on that trip. The passenger was working for a timber company and carrying its payroll. Mae's great-grandfather, a farmer, came to California from England in 1854—he introduced licorice and walnuts to the Sacramento Valley.

Mae joined the 4-H club when she was 7, in 1928. You were supposed to be 10 years old to become a member, but Mae's mother was the head of her group, so Mae got a special dispensation. She was the first child anywhere around to earn the honor of 4-H All Star, for her garden and her sewing.

After Mae got married, her aunt gave her a small greenhouse. Coincidentally, a friend presented Mae with a single orchid. Soon Mae was a collector of *Oncidium* orchids—prize-winning ones—which filled a second greenhouse, and then a third.

Mae and her husband did what Mae's parents had done—they lived in the central valley but kept a little place in Mendocino. When Mae and her husband retired, they moved to Mendocino permanently. There was a rhododendron nursery there that Mae had her eye on. It was the oldest one on the coast, and when it came up for sale, Mae bought it.

"Retired" Mae was now growing 12,000 rhododendron plants all by herself. People often stopped at the nursery after driving Highway 20, which goes through prime wild rhododendron dales, which in April are covered in bloom. They asked

pines. Reservations are a good idea for summer visits; call 1-800-444-7275 to make them. There is parking, and day-use and camping fees apply. Access is west of Highway 1 at Russian Gulch.

Caspar State Beach/Caspar Headlands State Reserve. Caspar is a small, sandy beach at the mouth of Doyle Creek. It has parking but no other facilities, though it's used for fishing. The state reserve mixes several acres of beautiful public and private blufftops, but, unfortunately, a permit is required to visit here. Permits are available at the State Park District Office, 3 miles south at Russian Gulch State Park (see above). Beach access is via Point Cabrillo Road, also known as Old Highway 1. Headlands access is via the end of Headlands Drive, off S. Caspar Drive, which in turn is off Highway 1. For more information, call 707-937-5804.

Mae who planted all those rhododendrons and she would patiently explain that they were wildflowers, native to California, and so were the irises they admired and the azaleas and lots of the other beautiful flowers that grew on the coast. She would tell them how the birds had planted them by spreading their seeds. She would advise her visitors to walk out on the bluffs by the ocean and look carefully at all the tiny wildflowers right under their feet. May through June, they could see California • buttercups, baby-blue-eyes, and tidy-tips—all growing among the native grasses.

When Mae finally sold the nursery, the new owners couldn't do the work that Mae had done all by herself and had to hire help.

Mae's mother was a gardener, too—a master of the iris. Seeing Mae without garden or nursery, she said, "Mae, you better do something." So Mae went to work at the Mendocino Coast Botanical Gardens, specializing in irises.

Like the azaleas and the rhododendrons that Mae loved to smell in her youth, the Pacific Coast irises are native plants. Mae particularly loves the *Douglasiana* variety, which comes in white, cream, yellow, and sometimes lavender blue. April is the best month for them. She sees them all over the coast—some are still blooming even in July.

When Mae goes home after working at the botanical gardens, she looks out her window at calla lilies. They aren't native, but they're so well established now that she wonders what the difference is. White ones, like the ones she sees outside her window, have spread up and down the coast. Mae thinks the gophers have helped with this work—propagating the plants every time they carry a choice piece of the roots home to eat.

Mae's five children and her seven grandchildren all come to visit her regularly. They always take home a plant when they leave. ■

IN FORT BRAGG

Mendocino Coast Botanical Gardens ★ Located 2 miles south of Fort Bragg (at 18220 N. Highway 1), this is 47 acres of gardens sporting 2 miles' worth of walks. Visitors will move through carefully planted stands of ivy, ferns, rhododendrons, dwarf pines, and other species, all along coastal bluffs that have outstanding views of the coast around Fort Bragg. There is parking, and an entrance fee is charged. Access is via Highway 1 south of Fort Bragg. For more information, call 707-964-4352.

Fort Bragg. Mendocino's real coastal city, the business center with a working commercial fishing port at Noyo Harbor.

MacKerricher State Park This park runs along the coast north of Fort Bragg and consists of about 6 miles of sandy beach and dunes, much of which

TOM MIKKELSEN

Coast Guard housing, Point Cabrillo lighthouse

is backed by an old logging railway that's being undercut by wave action. There are more than 140 campsites beneath pine trees here, several of which are reserved for those arriving on foot or by bike. The park features nearly every kind of terrain: beach, dunes, forests, grasslands, lake, and tide pools. The beach here totals 8 miles long and has astonishingly beautiful views of the coast; visitors can sit on the edges of small bluffs and imagine they are in a giant amphitheater formed by the curvy beginnings of the Lost Coast to the north. A paved path leads from MacKerricher to downtown Fort Bragg about 3 miles south, and trails curve in and out over tide pools. There are picnic tables, barbecue grills, rest rooms, and showers, as well as plenty of parking. A fee is charged for day use and camping. Access is via Highway 1, three miles north of Fort Bragg. For more information, call 707-937-5804.

Northern Mendocino beaches This category includes the following beaches, accessible along Highway 1 in Mendocino County in the roughly 15-mile stretch between Inglenook and Rockport: **Seaside Creek Beach**, **Chadbourne Gulch**, **Wages Creek Beach**, and **Westport-Union Landing State Beach**.

Seaside Creek Beach is sandy, entirely undeveloped, and accessed directly via Highway 1. **Chadbourne Gulch** is slightly friendlier, being a mile long and peppered with surfers, harbor seals, and fishermen; there is parking along the shoulder of Highway 1 about 2 miles south of Westport, and no fees for access. **Wages Creek Beach** is an alternately sandy and rocky beach accessed via the private Wages Creek Campground; it has campsites, showers, and rest rooms, and the campground rents surf nets. **Westport-Union Landing State Beach** is a 2-mile strip of bluffs with about 130 campsites on them; stairs and trails lead down to a sandy beach. There are fees for access to these two beaches.

Sinkyone Wilderness State Park ★ This is the southern extremity of the Lost Coast, by far the largest area of California coast left undeveloped. With good reason: The mountains rear up out of the Pacific north of Rockport and quickly attain heights of 4000 feet. Even Highway 1 has to detour around this series of sheer rock fortresses, turning inland to join up with Highway 101 at Leggett. The park itself consists of about 7300 beautiful acres of beaches, mountains, and second-growth forest that is recovering nicely after being heavily logged. There are no paved roads through the area, and the roads that are here are impassable during the winter—say, November to March. There are many trails and gravel fire roads to be hiked, however,

TOM MIKKELSEN

Noyo Harbor, Fort Bragg

Sally and Sunny Grigg—Howard Creek Ranch

■ In 1974, Sally and Sunny Grigg bought a run-down, beautiful, tiny lumber ranch on the coast of northern Mendocino. The old ranch was just outside Westport, 10 miles south of the inaccessible Lost Coast. There were outbuildings of all kinds: the old ranch house, a carriage house that was like a big barn, and the remains of a small logging railroad that led up into the forests to the east. There was even an old boat that had gotten itself stuck up Howard Creek. The creek wandered out of the hills, down through the property, into the sand dunes, under a tall cement bridge and out to the beach. There were sea stacks on the beach, and birds everywhere.

When Sunny got time off from his job dismantling buildings, he worked on fixing the foundation of the ranch house. The house was made of old-growth redwood milled at the farm, and it was very strong and still in good shape. Sunny wanted to build balconies around the house and it seemed a pity to use any other kind of wood, so he bought a portable lumber mill to make boards from redwood trees he cut himself right there at the ranch.

Sally was also working to pay for the ranch, but in her spare moments, she went to work on a garden on the south side of the house. There had been chicken coops and pigpens there, so the soil was well fertilized. Sally went into Fort Bragg, where there is a heritage rose garden, to get old roses that would match the period of the house, 1871. She also worked with Sunny restoring the outbuildings—Sunny shoring them up, Sally fixing the inside. At night, Sally read gardening books to get ideas on what to plant. The garden became the love of her life.

In the old days, the ranch was a working sawmill. Loggers cut the trees back in the forest and hauled them by oxen to the little railroad, which ran them down to the carriage house, where they were milled. Then they took them to the beach and off-loaded them to coastal schooners. In the 1900s, lumber to build San Francisco had been the only business on the Mendocino coast; now, almost 100 years later, the business of Mendocino was vacationers. Sunny and Sally decided to open a bed & breakfast inn. An inn was different from logging, of course, but many things at the ranch were just the same—at the old mill, they were self-sufficient, and at the new ranch they were, too, milling their lumber, growing their food.

By 1978, Sunny and Sally had made much progress fixing up the ranch, so Sunny's mother, Katherine, who collected

antiques, gave them some pieces to help furnish the B&B. The first room Sally decorated looked out on the garden she had built. In 1978 they opened the Howard Creek Ranch to guests.

By the mid-'80s they had done most of the work on the little outbuildings, turning them into individual houses for guests. They had built the "beach house" almost from scratch; it is a larger cabin down the creek that has skylights, a whirlpool bath, and a view of the beach.

Now Sunny was working on the first version of the swimming pool—he would decide to build a better one later on—and he was carving intricate redwood pieces—sconces, really—to surround the lights on the porches that he'd built almost 10 years before. He could afford to do these finishing touches because Howard Creek was paying for itself now—he could give it his full attention.

He left the old boat where it was next to the stream and built a redwood cabin around it. It is a private place with its own fireplace, refrigerator, and microwave. Sunny also fixed up a room in the carriage house, on the second floor. In his mind, this room is a kind of extension of the boat, with a wall of windows that look out at the trees. He called it the Captain's Quarters.

Now it was the middle '90s—Sunny and Sally had been working on the ranch for more than 20 years, but they still weren't done. They weren't even *close* to being done. Sunny was rebuilding the swimming pool and making a salmon-rearing pond in the field behind the house. He also decided that the carriage house ought to have balconies like the farmhouse. Sally decided to raise bulls, and that required fences. So did the sheep and the llama. (It is a "watch llama" that guards the sheep. When once a mountain lion came, the llama barked like a dog. Then Sally woke up and ran out to scare away the lion by banging on a gong she'd bought in South America.) Sunny decided they also needed cabins up on the mountain, and he moved the portable sawmill up there so that he could mill more redwoods to build them.

Guests at the Howard Creek Ranch always ask Sally and Sunny questions about all the projects—questions like, "When are you going to finish those cabins on the hill, Sunny?" Sally and Sunny don't try to answer. For the couple, all the projects have blended into one project. That project is the ranch itself, and they know it isn't ever going to be finished. ■

---

including the 16.7-mile Lost Coast Trail, as well as 10 primitive campgrounds sprinkled throughout the park. Interestingly, surfers have been known to strap their boards to their backpacks and bushwhack in to catch the most uncrowded waves of all. *Note:* Camping here is a fairly serious business; water and firewood must be packed in, and a Wilderness Permit is required before setting off into the woods. It's all worth it, though, for those who want to get away from the crowds with a vengeance.

Lodging

IN GUALALA

Gualala Hotel (707-884-3441), Highway 1 (in town, on the right heading north). Moderate. This hotel was built in the 1900s and still reflects an earlier, wilder time on the Mendocino coast. Though the rooms can be small, they are comfortable, and there is a parlor/library on the second floor to relax in. There is a bar off the lobby, and a restaurant on the other side with a prix fixe dinner that has defeated even the most famished coastal bicyclist. A holdover from Gualala's logging past, this hotel features clean rooms but is noisy on occasion.

St. Orres (707-884-3303), 36601 Highway 1. Moderate to expensive. St. Orres has eight rooms and a dozen cottages perched on 42 wooded acres above Highway 1; its octagonal turret—actually the main dining room—is impossible to miss approaching from downtown Gualala. St. Orres has its own access to an extremely isolated stretch of beach. It's comfortable and rooms are quite private; all have shared baths. This Russian-style inn offers a choice of rooms at a central lodge or in cottages. It is easy, however, to drop a lot of money at the restaurant and leave unsatisfied.

Seacliff (707-884-1213; 1-800-400-5053), 39140 S. Highway 1. Expensive. This recently built lodge has 16 private rooms.

Serenisea Ocean Cabins (707-884-3836; 1-800-331-3836), 36100 S. Highway 1. Moderate to expensive. Serenisea consists of 4 cottages and 23 full-sized houses, with dramatic views and a close-to-nature feel.

Surf Motel (707-884-3571), S. Highway 1 (in "downtown" Gualala). Moderate to expensive. Newly remodeled out of a drab past, the Surf is a clean alternative to some of the pricier B&Bs in the area.

IN POINT ARENA

Coast Guard House Historic Inn (707-882-2442; 1-800-524-9320), 695 Arena Cove. Moderate to expensive. This is six rooms and one cabin located at a historic Coast Guard station.

Sea Shell Inn (707-882-2000; 1-800-982-4298), 135 Main Street. Moderate. The Sea Shell is an inexpensive place to stay in the heart of Point Arena.

IN ELK

Harbor House (707-877-3203), 5600 S. Highway 1. Expensive. This all-redwood inn features 10 rooms, its own restaurant, wonderful ocean views, and a private beach.

Sandpiper House Inn (707-877-3587; 1-800-894-9016), 5520 S. Highway 1. Expensive. Sited on an ocean bluff, the Sandpiper offers five rooms with great views and serves a full breakfast.

Greenwood Pier Inn (707-877-9997), 5926 S. Highway 1. Expensive. This is a beautiful 11-room inn with gardens, located just on the edge of the ocean.

Elk Cove Inn (707-877-3321; 1-800-275-2967). Moderate to expensive. Perched on a bluff above the Pacific, this is an expensive but very private 14-room inn featuring gourmet breakfasts.

IN ALBION

The Wool Loft (707-937-0377), 32571 Navarro Ridge Road. Moderate to expensive. This quiet, relaxed bed & breakfast offers spectacular views of the Navarro River's outlet to the Pacific. Full breakfast is served.

Albion River Inn (707-937-1919), 3790 Highway 1. Expensive. This is a series of clifftop modern yet romantic cottages directly above the Albion River's outlet to the Pacific. The cottages have decks and sliding glass doors from each bedroom, allowing breathtaking views of the meeting of waters. Visitors will find a fire laid in the fireplace as well as a bottle of wine and two glasses, making this a great romantic getaway.

IN LITTLE RIVER

Heritage House (707-937-5885; 1-800-235-5885), 5200 N. Highway 1. Expensive. An enormous, 66-room inn is on cliffs overlooking the Pacific. Guests will find 37 acres to relax on, as well as a nursery for the little ones.

Blanchard House (707-937-1627), 8141 Pacific Coast Highway. Expensive. If you want complete isolation, this is the place for you—one room in a Victorian home overlooking the ocean.

Rachel's Inn (707-937-0088), 8200 N. Highway 1. Moderate to expensive. This inn has nine rooms set amid gardens and meadows adjacent to Van Damme State Park, with easy access to the park's hiking trails.

Little River Inn & Golf & Tennis Resort (707-937-5942; 1-888-466-5683), 7750 N. Highway 1. Moderate to expensive. This full-blown resort features 65 rooms and a host of family-friendly facilities, as well as a golf course, lounge, and restaurant.

The Inn at Schoolhouse Creek (707-937-5525), 7051 N. Highway 1. Moderate to expensive. This quiet, clean inn has 13 rooms and cottages with spectacular ocean views and walks to the ocean or forest.

Andiron Lodge (707-937-1543), 6051 N. Highway 1. Moderate to expensive. There are five cottages and two rooms here, with each cottage sited on its own acre of land for maximum privacy.

IN MENDOCINO

Mendocino Hotel (707-937-0511), 45080 Main Street. Moderate to expensive. This is a 19th-century, false-front hotel with small rooms but big public areas, including a bar, large parlor off the lobby, and full restaurant. It retains much of its antique heritage in its wood paneling and overstuffed furnishings; many rooms face the ocean and the hotel is centrally located downtown.

Joshua Grindle Inn (707-937-4143), 44800 Little Lake Road. Expensive. Just a short walk from downtown Mendocino, this two-story bed & breakfast sports comfortable rooms and a full, hot breakfast.

Stanford Inn by the Sea/Big River Lodge (707-937-5615; 1-800-331-8884), Highway 1 and Comptche-Ukiah Road. Expensive. A large (33-room) lodge fronted by meadows and the Pacific. The inn features a full breakfast and rents kayaks, canoes, and bicycles for local explorations.

Headlands Inn (707-937-4431), Howard and Albion Streets. Expensive. A six-room Victorian with a beautiful garden and ocean views, full breakfast, and fireplaces in each room.

Agate Cove Inn (707-937-0551; 1-800-527-3111), 11201 Lansing Street. Moderate to expensive. This inn consists of 10 romantic cottages sited amid a series of gardens. Full breakfast is served, and guests can mingle in a living room in the main house.

Mendocino Farmhouse (707-937-0241), 43410 Comptche-Ukiah Road. Moderate to expensive. Somewhat off the beaten track, this five-room inn is surrounded by gardens and redwood forest, making it a good place to get away from it all.

Blair House (707-937-1800), 45110 Little Lake Street. Moderate to expensive. TV-watchers will recognize this Victorian as the fictional residence of Jessica Fletcher of *Murder, She Wrote*. In reality, it's a pretty, quiet four-room inn with full breakfast and ocean views.

Pine Beach Inn (707-964-5603), Highway 1, 2 miles south of Fort Bragg. Moderate to expensive. This 51-room inn is set on 12 acres near the sea, and features

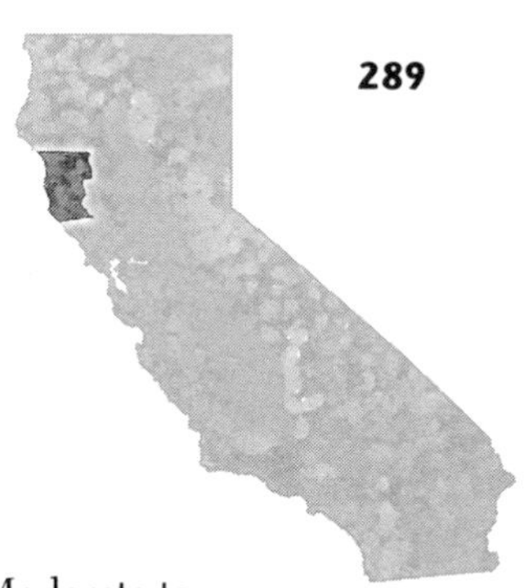

nine two-room suites good for families. Guests can play tennis and enjoy either a full (April–October) or continental (November–March) breakfast, depending on the season.

IN FORT BRAGG

Grey Whale Inn (707-964-0640), 615 N. Main Street. Moderate to expensive. In the distant past a regional hospital, the Grey Whale became the grandfather of Fort Bragg bed & breakfasts. It has 14 large rooms and is located in the northern part of town, away from the tacky shopping strip that greets visitors arriving from Mendocino.

Annie's Jughandle Beach B&B Inn (707-964-1415), 32980 Gibney Lane at Highway 1. Moderate to expensive. This small, quiet bed & breakfast is a comfortable place in which to relax or start hikes to the ocean or Jughandle State Reserve.

Beachcomber Motel (707-964-2402; 1-800-400-7873), 1111 N. Main Street. Moderate to expensive. This 27-room motel is adjacent to beautiful MacKerricher State Park, and redwood decks, ocean views, and some private hot tubs await guests returning after a long day of sight-seeing.

Colonial Inn (707-964-9298), 533 E. Fir Street. Moderate. This eight-room inn is located on a side street in downtown Fort Bragg. It's quiet, friendly, and a good place to take kids.

Avalon House (707-964-5555; 1-800-964-5556), 561 Stewart Street. Moderate to expensive. This house is in a quiet part of town and has six rooms, all with fireplace, whirlpool bath, ocean views, and down comforters.

IN CLEONE

Cleone Lodge Inn & Beach House (707-964-2788; 1-800-400-2189), 24600 N. Highway 1. Moderate to expensive. This resort offers a variety of accommodations, including rooms, suites, a cottage, and a full beach house.

IN WESTPORT

Dehaven Valley Farm Country Inn & Restaurant (707-961-1660), 39247 N. Highway 1. Moderate to expensive. This eight-room inn has a new owner and is somewhat in transition, but nonetheless features a full breakfast, hot tub, fireplaces, and ocean views.

TOM MIKKELSEN

Point Arena Harbor

Howard Creek Ranch (707-964-6725), 40501 N. Highway 1. Moderate to expensive. This is the best bed & breakfast in Mendocino County. Set on 40 acres, it is a work still in progress after 25 years of the owners' adding on fireplaces, gardens, skylights, and even a footbridge over Howard Creek. Definitely worth pulling out all the stops to stay here.

Westport Inn (707-964-5135), North Highway 1. Moderate. This is a cheap, clean, basic motel, just a few minutes' walk from the ocean.

IN LEGGETT

Eel River Redwoods Hostel (707-925-6425), 70400 Highway 101. Inexpensive. This is a great hostel with rooms for couples and families, an Indian tepee, a 24-hour sauna and hot tub, full kitchen, on-site pub, 24-hour access to rooms, and even a swimming hole in the Eel River. A great, low-budget place to take the kids.

Restaurants

IN GUALALA

St. Orres (707-884-3303), 36601 S. Highway 1. Expensive. A dinner-only restaurant with a prix fixe menu that seemed to us a little too pricey for the amount and quality of food served. The setting, in a three-story octagonal dining room, is stunning, though.

Gualala Hotel (707-884-3441), 39301 S. Highway 1. Inexpensive. Large portions of generally solid Italian and American dishes served either prix fixe or à la carte. Like the hotel, sometimes noisy but with a certain charm.

The Food Company (707-884-1800), Highway 1 at Robinson Reef. Inexpensive. A great deal for those looking to grab a quick bite or find something to take on the road, TFC offers fresh, locally made foods.

Gualala Bakery (707-884-9247), 39225 S. Highway 1 (in Sundstrom Mall). Inexpensive. Good fresh breads and cakes are baked here.

IN POINT ARENA

Pangaea (707-882-3001), 250 Main Street. Inexpensive. A fresh, diverse menu emphasizes vegetarian and fish dishes, all at low prices. Highly recommended.

Pirate's Cove (707-882-2360), 405 School Street. Inexpensive. Enjoy fast food and meet some of Point Arena's inhabitants.

IN ELK

Roadhouse Cafe (707-877-3285), 6061 Highway 1. Inexpensive. A good choice for fueling up with a basic American breakfast or lunch: you can get pancakes, egg dishes, sandwiches, and burgers.

Harbor House Inn (707-877-3203), 5600 S. Highway 1. Moderate to expensive. Tasty local specialties head the prix fixe breakfast and dinner menus here.

Bridget Dolan's (707-877-1820), 5910 S. Highway 1. Moderate. This Irish pub is family-friendly and has a menu of reasonably priced pub food.

Greenwood Pier Cafe (707-877-9997), 5926 S. Highway 1. Expensive. A relative newcomer on the coast, this restaurant's menu of lighter, California-style dishes changes daily. An excellent country restaurant, it uses fresh, local ingredients.

Elk Store (707-877-3411), 6101 S. Highway 1. Inexpensive. This is one of the better small stores, featuring a full-service deli and a wide selection of cheeses and seasonal produce.

IN ALBION

Ledford House (707-937-0282), 3000 N. Highway 1. Inexpensive to moderate. Southern French cuisine is served in a dining room that has large windows on the Pacific—a good deal with great views.

Albion River Inn (707-937-1919), 3790 N. Highway 1. Moderate to expensive. Marvel at beautiful clifftop views of the ocean in a spacious dining room; call ahead to reserve a window table.

IN LITTLE RIVER

Little River Restaurant (707-937-4945), 7751 N. Highway 1. Moderate to expensive. This small restaurant is highly recommended for its classical French cuisine that makes good use of local ingredients. Best for breakfast and Sunday champagne brunch.

IN MENDOCINO

Cafe Beaujolais (707-937-5614), 961 Ukiah Street. Expensive. This French restaurant's menu has a host of influences, and dishes are made with organic produce and free-range meats when possible. Great crabcakes. Highly recommended for its ambiance and innovative cuisine.

The Moose Cafe (707-937-4323), 390 Kasten Street. Inexpensive to moderate. Guests at this restaurant will enjoy delicious dishes served—weather permitting—in a garden setting.

MacCallum House Restaurant/Grey Whale Bar & Cafe (707-937-5763), 45020 Albion Street. Moderate to expensive. Patrons here can choose from three dining areas: sun porch, parlor, or white-linen dining room. The food's good and the menu emphasizes fresh, local produce and seafood.

Mendocino Cafe (707-937-2422), 10451 Lansing Street. Inexpensive to moderate. This restaurant serves Pacific Rim dishes with an emphasis on organic ingredients, and it's a good place to take the kids as well.

Bay View Cafe (707-937-4197), 45040 Main Street. Inexpensive to moderate. This is a very affordable café overlooking Mendocino Headlands State Park. Bring the kids.

Mendo Burgers (707-937-1111), 10483 Lansing Street. Inexpensive. Like the name says, this is the best place to get excellent hamburgers, as well as vegetarian and chicken burgers.

Tote Fete Carry-Out & Bakery (707-937-3383), 10450 Lansing Street. Inexpensive. This take-out deli and bakery is a good place to get picnic foods before heading out for a day of hiking or sight-seeing.

IN FORT BRAGG

Wharf Restaurant & Lounge (707-964-4283), 780 N. Harbor Drive. Moderate to expensive. This restaurant features terrific food that kids will love and is popular with locals as well.

The Restaurant (707-964-9800), 418 N. Main Street. Inexpensive to expensive. The menu here changes frequently, but guests are pretty sure to get a good lunch, dinner, or Sunday brunch.

North Coast Brewing Co. (707-964-3400), 444 N. Main Street. Inexpensive to moderate. While the terrific beer made on the premises is the primary draw, hungry travelers also will appreciate a menu that features a range of seafood, pasta, and fish-and-chips.

Viraporn's Thai Cafe (707-964-7931), Chestnut and Main Streets. Inexpensive to moderate. A refreshing change from the meat and potatoes that dominate Fort Bragg, this Thai restaurant serves vegetarian, seafood, and meat dishes with flair.

D'Aurelio's & Sons (707-964-4227), 438 S. Franklin Street. Moderate. A family restaurant that serves good pizzas and pastas.

Claire's Pies & Desserts (707-964-0092), 636-A S. Franklin Street. Inexpensive. Kids will love Claire's for dessert: They can get cream and berry pies, as well as the marquee Peanut Butter Pie. Grab a slice to take back to the campsite or your room. Closes early.

IN CLEONE

Purple Rose Mexican Restaurant (707-964-6507), 24300 N. Highway 1. Inexpensive. Stop by for good Mexican food, including soups, chile rellenos, and chimichangas, as well as a solid margarita.

IN WESTPORT

Westport Community Store & Deli (707-964-2872), 24980 Abalone. Inexpensive. This deli features a wide range of delicious sandwiches, and is pretty much the last food stop for northbound travelers until Humboldt County. Also, the owner knows everywhere and everyone, and is a friendly source of information about the area.

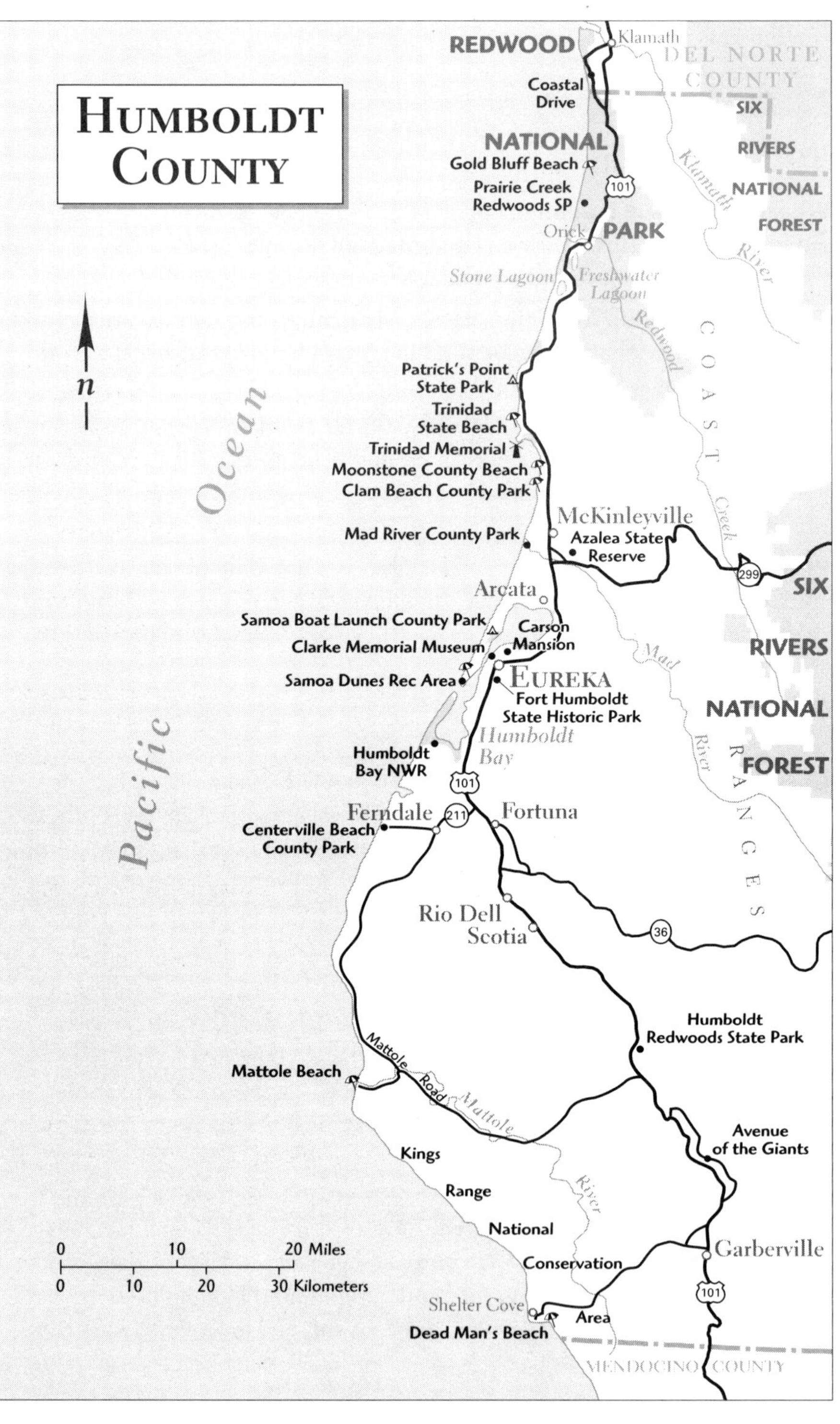

HUMBOLDT COUNTY
REDWOOD
NATIONAL
PARK
Klamath
DEL NORTE COUNTY
Coastal Drive
SIX RIVERS NATIONAL FOREST
Gold Bluff Beach
101
Prairie Creek Redwoods SP
Orick
Klamath River
Stone Lagoon
Freshwater Lagoon
Redwood
COAST
RANGES
n
Ocean
Pacific
Patrick's Point State Park
Trinidad State Beach
Trinidad Memorial
Moonstone County Beach
Clam Beach County Park
McKinleyville
Azalea State Reserve
Mad River County Park
Creek
299
Arcata
Samoa Boat Launch County Park
Carson Mansion
Clarke Memorial Museum
Samoa Dunes Rec Area
EUREKA
Fort Humboldt State Historic Park
Mad River
Humboldt Bay
Humboldt Bay NWR
101
Ferndale
211
Fortuna
Centerville Beach County Park
Rio Dell
Scotia
36
Humboldt Redwoods State Park
Mattole Road
Mattole Beach
Mattole River
Avenue of the Giants
Kings Range National Conservation Area
Garberville
0 10 20 Miles
0 10 20 30 Kilometers
Shelter Cove
101
Dead Man's Beach
MENDOCINO COUNTY

CHAPTER FOURTEEN

Humboldt County

IN SOUTHERN HUMBOLDT COUNTY, the coastline bends west, following the line of the San Andreas fault. This is a forbidding, wild, and intensely beautiful section known as the Lost Coast. The King Range National Conservation Area is located here, a region of rugged coastal mountains crisscrossed with hiking trails but with few roads. Local residents rarely try to drive here—a four-wheel-drive vehicle is necessary at all times of the year. In winter, even this may not be enough to get through safely. This is an area for dedicated, knowledgeable, and adventurous hikers planning multiday trips.

Above Punta Gorda, the San Andreas fault dissolves at the Mendocino Fracture, an unstable geological area from which many small faults lead. Then the coast swings east at Cape Mendocino and changes dramatically as it enters the large Eel River basin. The basin is bounded by two lesser faults, Russ fault in the south and Fresh Water fault in the north. Russ runs on an east–west line, hitting the coast near False Cape. Fresh Water trends north–south, nearing the coast north of Arcata.

Between these faults is the big fan of the Eel River basin, formed by the Eel, Elk, Salmon Creek, and Mad Rivers. (To the north and inland, the great Klamath River flows into Del North County, and then enters the ocean at Requa.) This basin, with its rivers, is one of the prime fishing areas of the coast.

The mouths of the Humboldt rivers have moved over time, leaving behind great bays, Humboldt and Arcata, and several freshwater lagoons. Huge deposits of sand have been carried down, creating enormous coastal sand dunes and large sand spits that form the entrance to Humboldt and Arcata Bays.

The city of Eureka lies between Humboldt and Arcata, on the eastern shore. Recently, a section of the city lying along the bay has been restored. Beautiful Victorian houses have been brought back to life. Sidewalks have been enlarged. Excellent—and expensive—bed & breakfast inns have opened, as well as fine restaurants. This part of the city is one of the most pleasant urban areas along the entire coast, but much of the rest of Eureka is economically depressed. Highway 101 cuts through the center of the city, past aging shopping malls, run-down hotels, and boarded-up storefronts. Just south of Eureka is Ferndale, a preserved Victorian town of great beauty.

North of Arcata, the Humboldt coast changes again. Here is Redwood National Park, with numerous hiking and camping opportunities. This is the southern end of the great redwood forest of the coast that extends up into Del Norte County. Now the trees flow down coastal ridges to the edge of the sea. (Redwoods need lots of water and an average temperature of about 63 degrees to thrive. This is the environment of northern Humboldt and Del Norte Counties.)

Beaches and Attractions

ON THE LOST COAST

King Range National Conservation Area ★ This is a massive parcel, more than 62,000 acres, with practically no human development on it. The main exception is Shelter Cove, a former sheep ranch near the southern end of King Range; it is reachable only by a winding, 24-mile-long road that sometimes takes an hour to negotiate. The rest of the area is largely untouched since its logging heyday in the 19th century, and the forests here have grown back to spectacular effect. It is an extremely wet area, averaging around 100 inches of rain per year, which certainly must help.

You can hike the entire north–south length of King Range if you like, and much of the hiking is along rocky and sandy beaches; in fact, you can hike along stable beaches for 24 solid miles, from Shelter Cove to the Mattole River and Punta Gorda, often without seeing anyone. There are also trails that follow the King Range ridgeline, for those seeking a little more altitude—in some cases a jump of 4000 feet in just 3 crow-flying miles.

The federal Bureau of Land Management maintains four campgrounds within King Range. They are hike-in, and primitive; backpackers must bring everything they will need except water. There are no fees and, remarkably, no wilderness permit is required, although visitors are encouraged to sign in at trailheads before setting off. Access to Shelter Cove, the main starting point for many trips, is via Shelter Cove Road, off Briceland Thorne Road, which in turn is off Highway 101 in Garberville. Much more could be said about the beauty of King Range and the practical aspects of visiting; for more information, call the Bureau of Land Management at 707-825-2300.

IN PETROLIA

Mattole River/Mattole River Beach This is the northernmost outlet of the 24-mile beach hike described above. It features a semideveloped campsite with rest rooms behind a sand-and-dunes beach. It is possible to walk along the beach 3 miles south to the abandoned lighthouse at Punta

Gorda. Access is via the end of Lighthouse Road in Petrolia. There is parking, and no fee for access. For more information, call 707-825-2300.

Mattole Road beaches The drive west from Petrolia along Mattole Road is highly recommended; it's an authentic country road that takes visitors past Cape Mendocino, the second westernmost point in the contiguous states and the site of countless shipwrecks. A lighthouse here is currently off-limits to the public, but nonetheless is a majestic sight. Offshore are sea stacks so large that they are called islands, and visitors will see plentiful waterfowl and sea lions on the rocks here.

There are numerous undeveloped pocket beaches along Mattole Road, but access is by walking through gates across private lands. Visitors should ask permission before doing so, but it's worth any loss of time that this entails, as the coastal views from these beaches are breathtaking. Access is by taking Mattole Road west from Petrolia, rather than east toward Humboldt Redwoods State Park. For more information, call 707-825-2300.

Ferndale Sixteen miles south of Eureka and just off Highway 101 is Ferndale, a preserved Victorian village that has been designated a State Historical Landmark. Many of the houses here are now excellent bed & breakfast inns (see **Lodging**). Ferndale is well worth a morning's visit. The **Ferndale Museum** (707-786-4466), at 3rd and Shaw, is the place to start a tour. It provides an intelligent insight into the nature of Victorian family life. The Ferndale Chamber of Commerce office, on Main Street, provides a map and self-guided tour of the city (707-786-4477). The Victorian buildings along Main Street provide excellent shopping, especially art galleries.

Centerville Beach County Park This is a very lightly used sand-and-dunes beach about 5 miles west of Ferndale. It's a good beach for fishing, birding, and long walks—there's practically no one around most of the time—but very rough conditions make swimming and surfing out of the question. Access is via the end of Centerville Road, west from Ferndale. There is parking and no fee for use. For more information, call 707-445-7651.

South Spit and Jetty. This is the lower "jaw" of Humboldt Bay, a long, relatively narrow spit of sand, riprap, and dunes that protects Eureka's southern flank and Highway 101. You'll find good fishing but, as usual in this area, swimming is a bad idea. There are no other facilities. Visitors should note that the RV parking at the end of S. Jetty Road appears to be in use as a homeless encampment. Access is via S. Jetty Road, off Table Bluff Road west of Highway 101.

Eureka. Highway 101 sweeps through the Eel River delta into Humbolt Bay and the heart of downtown Eureka, where it becomes Broadway and, later,

JOHN OSBORN

Natural bridge, southern Humboldt coast

5th Street. The city has been trying to climb out of a recession for more than a decade. Much of what you'll see as you drive into town is dilapidated and depressing. Fifth Street, however, goes through Historic Downtown and is adjacent to Old Town. Here, for a few blocks, Victorian houses have been restored and the streets made more friendly to walkers.

A family can have a pleasant night and day's stay in Eureka: Let the city serve as a base camp for exploring the Eel River basin and several attractive coastal areas to the north and south. Stop at the **Eureka/Humboldt County Convention and Visitor's Bureau**, 1034 2nd Street, 707-443-5097, for maps and information. Eureka is a gateway to prime fly-fishing territory, and the **Eureka Fly Shop**, 505 H Street, is a good source for information, not just about fly-fishing but also about the outdoors in general. See our listings for less expensive bed & breakfasts. (One of the more expensive, and best, is the Carter House Inn, which is located in Old Town. The Carter House has two separate institutions across the street from each other. The Hotel Carter, where breakfasts are served, has 23 rooms in a hotel atmosphere; the inn, across the street, is quieter and more interesting.) It is not necessary, however, to spend a lot of money in Eureka; you will pass all the well-known chain motels just by following Highway 101 through the center of town.

Fort Humboldt State Historic Park Visitors here will find a pair of buildings left from the fort's past as an outpost during the Indian conflicts of the 1850s. The main point of interest here is that Ulysses S. Grant, the future president of the United States, served briefly as the commander of the outpost. Today the fort, located on the eastern edge of Humboldt Bay, is mainly a museum with displays relating to logging; parking and rest rooms are available, and no fee is charged. Access is via Highland Avenue in Eureka. For more information, call 707-445-6567.

Samoa Dunes Recreation Area/North Spit/North Jetty. This is the upper "jaw" of Humboldt Bay. Samoa Dunes is one of the state's few off-road-vehicle recreation areas (like Pismo Beach in San Luis Obispo County). Here you can finally take your 4x4 off the road and wheel around, taking care not to get stuck in the sand. The area has picnic tables and a short nature trail.

North Spit is like South Spit, only wider and a little less civilized; it shields part of Humboldt Bay and all of Arcata Bay. **North Jetty** is an artificial extension that has picnic tables, cypress trees, and grills on it, and is a good mile-long walk. Large waves sometimes crash up onto it, adding to the excitement of watching surfers and surf-kayakers below. A Coast Guard station is at the end of New Navy Base Road. There is plenty of parking for all three areas, and no fees are collected. Access is via New Navy Base Road from Highway 255, off Highway 101. For more information, call 707-825-2300.

IN ARCATA

Mad River Beach County Park This is a sand-and-dunes beach, a scene of beautiful desolation at the mouth of the Mad River. It is another good fishing and walking beach, but undertows rule out swimming. There are rest rooms and a picnic area, parking lots, and no fee for use. Access to Mad River Beach is via the Janes Road exit from Highway 101; take a right on Heindon Road, left on Iverson, and finally right on Mad River Road. For more information, call 707-445-7651.

Mad River Slough and Dunes Cooperative Management Area, just to the south of Mad River Beach, is a jointly managed area that features the collision of a large number of river, ocean, and marsh ecosystems. As this book goes to press, however, there is no public access to this area. For information, visitors should call the Bureau of Land Management office in Arcata (707-825-2300) to find out where access is possible.

IN MCKINLEYVILLE

Clam Beach County Park/Little River State Beach. These two parks are both wide, sand-and-dunes beaches west of Highway 101. The primary difference between them is that Clam Beach has developed campsites with rest rooms and picnic areas, while Little River has none. Still, they are essentially swaths of the same beach that happen to be under different management. The beaches are covered in driftwood at points, and you can dig for razor clams. Access to Clam Beach is via the exit of the same name off Highway 101, 3.5 miles north of Arcata; for more information, call 707-445-7651. Access to Little River State Beach is via a turnout from Highway 101, 4 miles south of Trinidad and just south of the Little River. For more information, call 707-445-6547.

Moonstone County Beach This is a wide, sandy beach that gets fairly heavy use for this area. Located at the mouth of the Little River, it sees a lot of surfing and clamming, as well as families who come to picnic in the windshadows of the large rocks that dot the shore. There is even an opportunity to swim in the Little River (except in winter months), as the water is warmer and calmer than the ocean. The sand near the water generally is hard packed and

EMILIE OSBORN

Fishing from Eureka breakwater

good for walking. Access is west of Scenic Drive, about 3 miles south of Trinidad. No fees are collected, and there is a small parking lot. For more information, call 707-445-7651.

Trinidad State Beach. This is a wide, sandy, day-use beach that features picnic tables, rest rooms, and barbecue grills. There are trails leading to the beach and to **Humboldt State University's Marine Laboratory**, which has a small aquarium and exhibits (it's open weekdays). There is also a trail leading to **College Cove**, a popular clothing-optional beach. Access is via Trinity Street, north of Main Street in Trinidad. For more information about the HSU aquarium, call 707-677-3671. For more information about the beaches, call 707-488-2041 or 707-445-6547.

Patrick's Point State Park This park sports more than 600 acres of forest, beaches, trails, and rocky shoreline, including some giant sea stacks that are attached to the land and eminently climbable. Patrick's has 123 campsites, including hiker and bicyclist sites that are perched almost on clifftops. There is a re-created Yurok Indian village, with plenty of picnic tables and grills, grassy meadows to relax in, hot showers, and a nature trail. There are plenty of birds here, and whales can be seen from the cliffs. Trails wind up and down the coast and into forests of Sitka spruce. This park is another beauty that has something to suit almost every taste. Access is via a turnout from Highway 101, 5 miles north of Trinidad. There is parking, and day-use and camping fees are collected. For more information, call 707-488-2041 or 707-445-6547.

Humboldt lagoons In this depression before the steep hills leading up to the Klamath River Valley lie several lagoons, including Big Lagoon County Park, Dry Lagoon State Park, Stone Lagoon, and Freshwater Lagoon. All but Freshwater have direct ocean access, and their various facilities include fishing, boating, swimming, camping, and surf-fishing. Access is via a number of turnouts off Highway 101 north of Patrick's Point but south of Bald Hills Road. There is a fee for use of Big Lagoon and Stone Lagoon; for more information, call 707-445-7651.

IN ORICK

Prairie Creek Redwoods State Park This 14,500-acre park is completely surrounded by the larger Redwood National Park, but features access to various unique beaches and hiking trails. The most notable beach here is Gold Bluffs, a wide, long, lonely, dark-sand beauty backed by cliffs thick with Sitka spruce and a herd of Roosevelt elk. Visitors can camp at any of three sites: Elk Prairie, Gold

Shekky Bowen—A Native American of the Coast

■ On the Point Reyes peninsula, on Bear Valley Road, there is a re-creation of a Miwok village. The Miwoks were one of more than 50 coastal Native American groups that lived along the California coast. Built in a glade near the park headquarters, the informative exhibit at Point Reyes seems lifeless, as if it were an ancient archeological site that had been picked clean. In guidebooks and at exhibits we read a familiar tale: "The establishment of missions resulted in the introduction of European diseases and a displacement of Native American culture; Euro-American influences virtually exterminated the Native American population along much of coastal California by the early 1900s." We are left with the impression that the Native American people of the coast simply disappeared without a trace.

Six miles north of Trinidad in Humboldt County is Patricks Point State Park, set on a wonderful headland of meadow and forest. Trails lead up to the crests of hills such as Ceremonial Rock, Lookout Rock, and Wedding Rock. From these hills are spectacular views of the Pacific Ocean—and often of whales migrating past the point.

Here, as at Point Reyes, there is a traditional Native American village, this one of the Yurok group. The village has a sweat lodge, family houses, and a dance pit. It is used by the thriving Yurok tribe for ceremonial dances, which are open to the public. The site has a vibrant feeling even when the Yurok are not dancing. It seems lived in, as if the original inhabitants will be returning any moment to their seasoning coastal fishing village.

When Shekky Bowen was in the third grade growing up in Crescent City, in Del Norte County, his mother took him to his first Tolowa dance. Later his grandmother made sure he went to the ceremonial dances of the Yurok as well as the Tolowa, because Shekky is descended from both tribes.

The Yurok are river people; their main villages were set in a chain along the Klamath River. They built the roofs of their houses with three sides, two sides sloping up to meet a flat section in the middle. The Tolowa are people of the shore. Their villages were in and near what is now Crescent City. The roofs of their traditional houses had two sides. From carbon dating, we know that these two groups have lived along the coast of California from at least A.D. 1310, but it is thought that the California coast was inhabited as early as 9000 B.C. by Native American peoples, and it still is. According to the Yurok tribal office, there are more than 3500 members of the Yurok tribe living in Del Norte and Humboldt Counties.

Shekky participated in his first dance when he was in the seventh grade. He tried to forget about the people watching and to concentrate on what he was dancing for, but he was nervous. Shekky's first dance was not an exhibition dance, but a "reason" dance to heal a sick child. Anthropologists call this dance the brush dance, but its real name is the *May-loh*. When a child is sick and must be made well by the Medicine Woman, the *May-loh* is held. The complicated healing ceremony begins on a Thursday and ends Sunday morning. On Saturday, the ritual dancing lasts all night long.

When Shekky was in high school, he didn't dance much because he played almost every sport offered by his school. (His Tolowa name is One Who Runs.)

But for his language requirement, he studied Tolowa, which he believes is the hardest Native American language to learn. There are four Native American languages spoken in Del Norte and Humboldt Counties: Tolowa, Yurok, Hupa, and Karuk. Later, when Shekky transferred to another school, he continued his studies and now speaks Tolowa fluently.

Today Shekky dances with both Tolowa and Yurok tribes. Sometimes he does the *May-loh* in an abridged version designed to educate people about the customs of the Tolowa and Yurok. Native Americans bring their children to watch Shekky dance so that they will learn the traditions. Sometimes Shekky does demonstration dances at local schools. Often he dances with members of his extended family, which includes 42 cousins. Shekky dances wearing a bearskin hide and an abalone necklace. He carries arrows. His face is painted in the traditional way of the Tolowa and Yurok. His dress is simple. Others have elaborate clothing, of incredible complexity and beauty, all of it made from objects found in the natural world—from abalone shells, furs, pine nuts, dried juniper berries. Much of the ceremonial clothing has been passed down from generation to generation, but some of it has been newly made.

Shekky says he lives in two worlds, his "society world" and his "culture world." When Shekky graduated from high school a year ago, he joined AmeriCorps as part of a crew that has built hiking trails along the coast, repaired flood-damaged areas along the Klamath River, buried dead seals, planted native trees along the coast, and cleaned up trash on the beach. Now he is working as an assistant physical education teacher at the Crescent City Elk Middle School. He is also the coach of the girls basketball team. The school is in in the same town where Shekky's family has lived for 2,000 years.

On weekends or after work, Shekky will visit his culture world by hanging out with his cousins, or by visiting friends on one of the nearby rancherias, small reservations near Crescent City.

In August, the Yurok tribe holds the Salmon Festival in Klamath. You can call the tribe at 707-444-0433 for information. In June, Village Day is held at the Yurok village at Patrick's Point. Information can be obtained through the park (707-677-3570). An excellent source for traditional and contemporary Native American art and crafts, including works by both Yurok and Tolowa, can be found at the American Indian Art and Gift Shop (707-445-8451) 241 F Street, Old Town Eureka. ■

Bluffs Beach, and Butler Creek Backpack Camp. Visitors can also check out 50-foot-deep Fern Canyon, picnic at tables at Lost Man Creek, and maybe see a Pacific giant salamander—a 10-inch mini-dragon noted for its voracious appetite. There is parking, and a fee is collected for day-use. Access is west of Highway 101, about 6.5 miles north of Orick. For more information, call 707-464-6101 x5301 or 707-445-6547.

Redwood National Park This is an umbrella name for a giant park that takes up 40 miles of coastline from Orick to Crescent City, a sprawling collection of 106,000 acres of second-growth redwood forests straddling Humboldt and Del Norte Counties. Driving Highway 101 through this area, visitors can't help but stumble across groves of giant *Sequoia sempervirens*, as plentiful here as office buildings in a city, or even people on a crowded street. The park features miles of hiking trails and access to numerous pocket beaches, such as Redwood Creek Beach, 2 miles south of Orick. The visitors center is located at Freshwater Lagoon, 3 miles south of Orick. Here you'll find all the information you'll need to enjoy the drive north into Del Norte County, where the bulk of the park's attractions lie. It's a good idea to pick up maps here and chat with the rangers, who generally are very helpful. There are camping fees for some sites. Access to the park's sites is via numerous well-marked turnouts and side roads along Highway 101, the only major road that goes through this area. For more information, call the park headquarters in Arcata at 707-822-7611.

Lodging

IN GARBERVILLE

Benbow Inn (707-923-2124), 445 Lake Benbow Drive. Expensive. This 55-room inn is a luxurious establishment somewhat inland from the coast—but it's the route travelers have to take as Highways 1 and 101 swing inland from the Lost Coast. Amenities include afternoon tea and a dining room with a large Continental-cuisine menu. Herbert Hoover once slept in this elegant setting. There is excellent trout fishing in nearby rivers and streams; the Benbow is used by fishermen as a home base.

IN FERNDALE

Gingerbread Mansion (707-786-4000), 400 Berding Street. Moderate to expensive. A small Victorian bed & breakfast, the morning meal is served in a dining room overlooking the garden, while afternoon tea takes place in any of five—count 'em, five—parlors. This is one of the most photographed buildings in California.

The Shaw Bed and Breakfast Inn (707-786-9958; 1-800-557-7429), 703 Main Street. Expensive. This 1850s-era house is a good place to stay, and features six rooms packed with antiques, books, and photos. Each room has a different theme, and a full homemade breakfast is served.

Grandmother's House (707-786-9704), 861 Howard Street. Moderate. A pleasant, cozy, friendly inn that welcomes children.

IN EUREKA

Eureka Inn (707-442-6441), 7th and F Streets. Moderate to expensive. This giant, Tudor-style building houses more than 100 fairly spacious rooms, as well as a big fireplace in the lobby and a sauna, pool, and Jacuzzi. It is well maintained and registered as a National Historic Landmark.

Carter House Inn and Hotel Carter (707-444-8062; 1-800-404-1390), 301 L Street. Expensive. Carter House is a four-story, five-room Victorian reproduction in the heart of Eureka; the Hotel Carter is a larger, 23-room hotel located right across the street. While under the same ownership, the former is very cozy, and, in our opinion, just edges out the latter, which has a more contemporary feel and is a bit noisier. Amenities vary from room to room in both, but guests are sure to find accommodations to satisfy them. An outstanding full breakfast is served.

An Elegant Victorian Mansion (707-444-3144), 1406 C Street. Moderate. A restored 1880s Victorian with four rooms, each with a different and highly distinctive theme. The Governor's Suite in particular is great for guests who have a child. The owners dabble in early-20th-century music, saunas, and antique autos, and will be happy to help you find your way around Humboldt County.

Bayview Motel (707-442-1673), 2844 Fairfield Street. Inexpensive to moderate. A very clean 14-room motel with a carefully maintained lawn and garden. Each room has a private bath and queen-sized bed. A great choice for the budget-conscious.

IN ARCATA

Hotel Arcata (707-826-0217), 708 9th Street. Moderate. This hotel, a showpiece when it first opened in 1915, recently has been fully restored. Visitors will appreciate its hot tubs, swimming pool, and central location near downtown Arcata's shops, brewpubs, and restaurants.

The Lady Anne (707-822-2797), 902 14th Street. Moderate. Partly owned by a former mayor of Arcata, this very pretty, restored Queen Anne house has five guest rooms chock-full of antiques and Oriental rugs. The Cinnamon Bear room is a great choice for families, with a king-sized bed for the parents and trundle beds for the kids, and the inn's two parlors have several games and a piano.

Fairwinds Motel (707-822-4824), 1674 G Street. Inexpensive to moderate. The only budget accommodation in Arcata, the Fairwinds features 27 remodeled rooms, all with phone and cable TV and close by Humboldt State University.

IN TRINIDAD

The Lost Whale Bed and Breakfast Inn (707-677-3425), 3452 Patrick's Point Drive. Moderate to expensive. How often do travelers find an inn with its own private beach? This is a fine family inn with a "great room" filled with storybooks, games, and puzzles, and the owners are delighted to show visitors where to pick berries in season. There are eight rooms, all of which are soundproof, and excellent access to scenic Patrick's Point State Park. The full breakfast is quite large. The owners love kids—there's a playground and a menagerie with goats, ducks, and rabbits. Two rooms actually have separate lofts that provide the younger ones with their own space. *Note*: There is a minimum 2-night stay June–September.

Trinidad Bay Bed and Breakfast (707-677-0840), 560 Edwards Street. Expensive. This Cape Cod–style inn has four rooms, with the best option being either of the two suites. These feature large beds, spectacular views of Trinidad Bay and its fishing harbor, and private entrances. Breakfasts include homemade breads and locally produced cheeses.

Restaurants

IN FERNDALE

Victorian Village Inn (707-786-4949), 400 Ocean Avenue. Moderate. *Big* is the word here, as in the dining room and the portions of seafood, chicken, and steak served within it. There's also an inn here, in case visitors are too stuffed to make it to the car.

IN EUREKA

Restaurant 301 (707-444-8062), 301 L Street. Expensive. Formerly the Carter House Restaurant, this is a good place to eat when you're inclined to a certain amount of pomp—and expense—with dinner. Order from a large French and California-cuisine menu, and be sure to give the Humboldt County wines a try.

Samoa Cookhouse (707-442-1659), Cookhouse Lane, Samoa Peninsula (call for directions). Inexpensive. This Eureka standby is a living relic of the bygone days of lumber-camp cookhouses, and still serves portions massive enough for the hungriest lumberjack. Kids will love it for breakfast or dinner, and it's a great spot to meet the locals who pack the place nearly every night. A tradition since the 1940s, Samoa is also open for breakfast; families will appreciate this place.

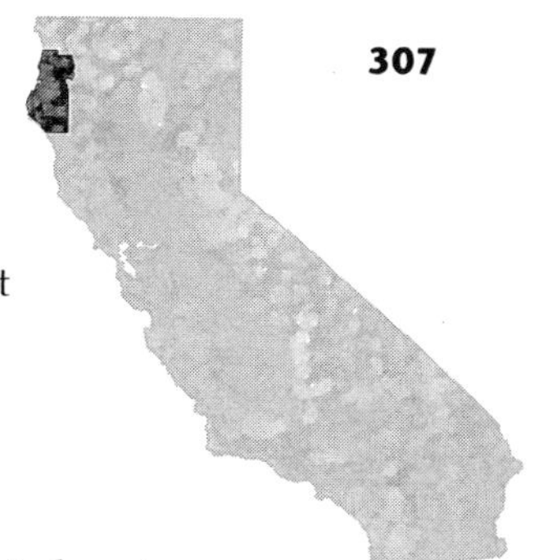

Bracco's (707-443-9717), 327 2nd Street. Moderate. Like Samoa Cookhouse, Lazio's is a big restaurant that's been around forever; it focuses on locally caught fish and seafood rather than meats.

IN ARCATA

Abruzzi (707-826-2345), 791 8th Street (on Arcata Plaza), downtown Arcata. Moderate to expensive. This restaurant specializes in Italian dishes, especially fresh pasta, fish, and seafood. The chocolate desserts are recommended.

Folie Douce (707-822-1042), 1551 G Street. Moderate. A very good gourmet pizza restaurant with specialty toppings like spicy shrimp and Brie. While the kids are busy with pizza, Mom and Dad can go upscale, if they wish, for dishes like filet mignon and chicken. Reservations are strongly recommended.

IN TRINIDAD

Larrupin' Cafe (707-677-0230), 1658 Patrick's Point Drive. Moderate. This popular restaurant features local seafood dishes and is also famed for barbecued pork ribs, hearty salads, and fresh breads. Diners can eat out on the patio during the summer, and it's a good thing there's that extra space, because Larrupin' is almost always crowded.

IN ORICK

Rolf's Park Cafe (707-488-3841), Davison Road and Highway 101. Moderate. A nice place to go for German-influenced fare like bratwurst and Wiener schnitzel, as well as game dishes like wild boar, elk, and buffalo. Chef Rolf Rheinschmidt piles on the portions, and you might also want to consider returning for breakfast and the massive German Farmer Omelet.

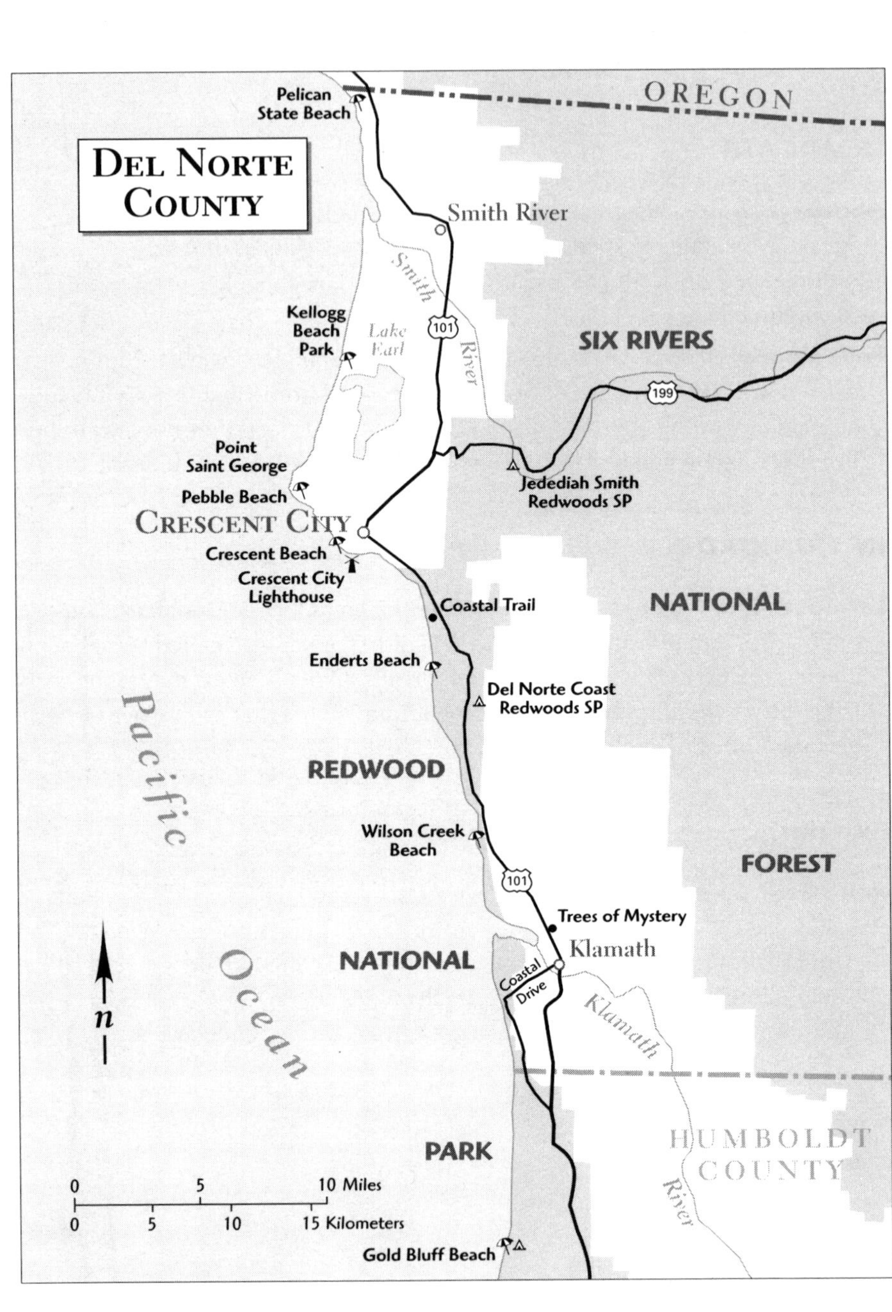

Del Norte County
Oregon
Pelican State Beach
Smith River
Smith River
Kellogg Beach Park
Lake Earl
101
Six Rivers
199
Point Saint George
Pebble Beach
Crescent City
Jedediah Smith Redwoods SP
Crescent Beach
Crescent City Lighthouse
Coastal Trail
National
Enderts Beach
Del Norte Coast Redwoods SP
Pacific
Redwood
Wilson Creek Beach
Forest
101
Trees of Mystery
Klamath
National
Coastal Drive
Ocean
n
Klamath River
Park
Humboldt County
0 5 10 Miles
0 5 10 15 Kilometers
Gold Bluff Beach

CHAPTER FIFTEEN

Del Norte County

DEL NORTE MARKS THE END of the Coast Ranges. Inland lie the Klamath Mountains. There are few marine terraces here; for the most part, hills fall directly into the sea. They are deeply forested; California's tallest trees are found on this section of the coast.

Large rivers—the Klamath in the south, the Smith in the north—cut through the coastal range. Between them lie several lagoons, the mouths of former rivers where sandbars have formed, cutting them off from the sea.

Point St. George lies just north of Crescent City. From here to the Oregon state line, the coastline is more forgiving. The Smith River delta has some of the best fishing in California. Numerous outfitters, both in Crescent City and in the small town of Smith River, provide guide services. In this area lies the Lake Earl Wildlife Area, where huge freshwater lagoons create a thriving habitat for birds and fish.

South of St. George Point, Crescent City has one of the finest harbors of the California coast and contains one of the most active commercial fishing fleets. Sportfishing is excellent here as well. Crescent City can serve as the launching point for varied outdoor activities: hiking, camping, fishing, birding. It is the only city of size in the county, and centrally located near Point St. George.

Below Crescent City, Redwood National Park, which extends into Humboldt County, contains striking stands of immense redwood trees. Often the area is covered with fog; in winter there is heavy rain. You'll find excellent camping and hiking in the area—it's wild and rugged and crisscrossed with a network of interesting trails.

Beaches and Attractions

IN KLAMATH

Alder Camp Road/High Bluff Beach Also known simply as Coastal Drive, Alder Camp Road is a side street that used to be Highway 101 before cliff erosion forced planners to move the route inland. It still exists as a turnout visitors can take from the present Highway 101, just south of the Del Norte/ Humboldt border. Over 8 rough, gravelly miles it winds past some spectacular coastal scenery that people whizzing by on the main highway will miss, including High Bluffs Overlook and High Bluff Beach below.

High Bluff Beach is reached by a half-mile hike and scramble, but once there visitors will find a brown-sand cove beach that's surrounded by steep, forested cliffs. It's completely undeveloped and tides tend to erase all traces of previous visitors, making High Bluff Beach one of those maybe-I'm-the-last-person-on-earth settings not to be missed.

Visitors also will be able to eyeball the mouth of the Klamath River, the second largest river in California, from Coastal Drive. The ocean and river are thick with life here; the whole area is popular for fishing, with campgrounds,

JOHN OSBORN

Logging truck on highway 101

motels, and restaurants too numerous to name between here and Requa, on the river's north side. There is no fee for use of Coastal Drive. Visitors should note that trailers and any other sort of large vehicles are not recommended for this winding, occasionally unpaved road. Access is via an exit off Highway 101 south of the Del Norte County line.

Wilson Creek Beach. This is a wide, sandy beach with tide pools and a freshwater lagoon nearby. There also are picnic tables, rest rooms, and a fire pit. Visitors will see the occasional hardy surfer here, but the beach's main use is for fishing and walking. There is parking, and no fee for use. Access is west of Highway 101 via Wilson Creek Road, about 5.5 miles north of Klamath. Those staying at Mill Creek Campground nearby can hike 6 miles to Wilson Creek Beach.

Trees of Mystery Perhaps the premier attraction in Del Norte County is the 49-foot-high Paul Bunyan and his 35-foot-high companion, Babe the Blue Ox. At 15500 Highway 101, they mark the entrance to Trees of Mystery, a 120-acre private park. Most interesting is the End of Trail Native American Museum in the gift shop. The exhibits are first-rate specimens and the collection is well presented. Worth a stop; ignore the tacky facade.

IN CRESCENT CITY

Redwood National Park Headquarters. Located at 1111 2nd Street, this office can provide information on every aspect of the park in Del Norte and Humboldt Counties. For more information, call 707-464-6101.

Enderts Beach This is a quarter-mile-long volcanic-sand beach, accessed via a half-mile trail from a parking lot at the end of Enderts Beach Road, south of Crescent City. The fairly strenuous walk makes this a peaceful and secluded place in which to relax. There are primitive campsites here, along with picnic tables and barbecue grills. Rangers sometimes lead interpretive walks among the tide pools during low tides. There is a parking lot, and no fee for day use. For further information, call 707-464-7230.

Crescent Beach. More accessible than Enderts, this wide, sandy beach practically touches Crescent City. It is covered with driftwood and has slightly larger numbers of people, but still seems uncrowded. It has rest rooms, fire pits, and picnic tables, some of which are modified to be wheelchair accessible. There is a parking lot, and no fee is charged for day use. Access is via Enderts Beach Road, about 2 miles south of town. For more information, call 707-464-7230.

©JAMES BLANK

Mouth of Klamath river

Crescent City Harbor. An important commercial fishing port and processing center. The full service marina also offers sport fishing and restaurants.

Crescent City Beaches. This heading includes **Pebble Beach**, **Point St. George (aka Radio Beach)**, and **Kellogg Beach**. All are long, wide, sandy, and somewhat underused—there's just too much beach per capita here to have anything resembling a crowd. Pebble and Kellogg have picnic tables, and Radio has three different types of clams for the taking (with the appropriate permit, of course). There is plenty of parking, and no fees are charged for day use. Access to Pebble Beach is west of Pebble Beach Drive; for more information, call 707-464-7230. Access to Point St. George (Radio) is west of Radio Road; for more information, call 707-464-7230. Access to Kellogg is via the west end of Kellogg Road, about 10 miles north of Crescent City; for more information, call 707-464-7230 or 707-464-7237.

Battery Point Lighthouse. The coast's only offshore lighthouse; it is reachable only at low tide. For tours, call 707-464-3089.

Smith River/Tillas Slough The Smith is designated a Wild and Scenic River, and lives up to its reputation by winding through miles of Del Norte redwood forest to Tillas Slough. It has several species of game fish, and anglers will have a field day year-round. Visitors may want to drive up Highway 199, which follows the Smith, and spend a day at **Jedediah Smith Redwoods State Park,** which has a series of campsites along the river and provides safe—albeit chilly—swimming in its long, level stretches. There is parking, and a fee is charged for use of the Smith River Fishing Access. There is no fee for day use of Jedediah Smith. Fishing access is via Fred Haight Drive, about 2 miles west of Highway 101. Jedediah Smith Park is accessed via Highway 199, east of Highway 101. For more information, call Jedediah Smith Redwoods State Park at 707-458-3310.

Pelican State Beach. This unremarkable collection of sand and dunes is California's final beach; the next stop is Oregon. It features about 5 acres of undeveloped, driftwood-laden coastline backed by lightly vegetated dunes; there are no other facilities. There is parking, though, and no fees are charged for day use. Access is just west of coast-hugging Highway 101, half a mile south of the Oregon border.

Lodging

IN KLAMATH

Redwood Hostel, Redwood National Park (707-482-8265), 14480 Highway 101. Inexpensive. Basic hostel accommodations are offered for both singles and couples in a 19th-century ranch house near Wilson Creek Beach.

Motel Trees (707-482-3152), 1549 Highway 101 S. Inexpensive to moderate. This 23-unit motel is quiet and clean, with a restaurant attached (see **Restaurants**). It's across from Trees of Mystery.

TOM MIKKELSEN

Redwoods, Redwood National Park

John Brunsing—North Coast Fisherman

■ In 1972, John Brunsing bought *Big Thomas*. The fishing boat was 28 feet long, not big for a fishing boat on the California coast, but it was cheap, *very* cheap. He became a salmon fisherman, working out of the harbor at Crescent City.

Tucked up in the far north, and quite small, Crescent City lacked the cultural institutions of other fishing ports, like Eureka. Later the state would build a huge prison at Crescent City, adding 300 guards to the town population and changing the flavor of the small port in ways some fishermen didn't like. But even with these limitations, Crescent City was the place John Brunsing wanted for his home.

That was because Crescent City had one thing outweighing everything else: *a harbor without a river*. Almost all the good harbors on the California coast—San Francisco, Morrow Bay, Moss Landing, Eureka—were formed by rivers. The rivers wash sand down to the mouths of these bays, creating sandbars. These sandbars would "close off"—waves meeting the bars would shoal, the shallow water at the sandbar turning ripples into giant waves, breaking at the narrow harbor entrance. Couple this with a high tide, and perhaps a storm, and getting out of these harbors is impossible.

Crescent City has no river, so the harbor never had a bar. John could get out to sea in almost any kind of weather, unless there was a tsunami, like the one that hit Crescent City in 1964 and flattened the downtown, drowning 10 people. (Luckily, tsunamis are rare.)

By 1977, John saw that salmon fishing, regulated by the federal government, was under pressure. He was scared the salmon fishing would be so restricted that he'd go broke. Maybe he should become a crabber, going after Dungeness crabs. Crabbing wasn't regulated by the federal government, but on the other hand, it was regulated by the state. Of course, if he went after crabs, he would need a different kind of boat, one with a wide stern that could hold crab pots. Crab pots are round steel traps, 3 feet in diameter and a foot high. They weigh 100 pounds. The new boat would also have to be bigger than the *Big Thomas* and have a hold that could be flooded so that John could keep the crabs alive.

Or maybe he should become a shrimper. That would take a different kind of boat, too, one equipped with big rollers to hold the nets he would use off the stern. What kind of boat, what kind of fisherman—these were difficult decisions, and for a fisherman like John, with a family, they were crucially important.

In 1982, John saw the *Mary Lou*.

She was a big boat, 50 tons and 58 feet, big enough to go 1200 miles offshore and fish for tuna, but still small enough to use for salmon. With a wide stern, she could hold nets to fish for shrimp. She also had a big "fish hole"—a large waterproof box on the deck. It could be flooded and used like an aquarium to keep crabs alive, holding 25,000 crabs, with another 15,000 in storage on deck. The hole could also be pumped dry and used as an icebox.

The *Mary Lou* was also large enough to hold three crew in comfort. She had a stateroom, bunkhouse, pilot room. She had space for all the electronics, including John's two computers. But she was also small enough that John could get by with only two crew in the summer. And she wasn't such a big boat that John would be strapped paying for maintenance and fuel. The *Mary Lou* had flexibility.

John built a big gear shed near the harbor, where he could store crab pots, nets, and other equipment so that he could adapt *Mary Lou* for whatever the ocean happened to be tossing his way. In a couple of hours, *Mary Lou* could change from a crab boat to a shrimp boat to a tuna boat—or a boat fishing for "channel rock" destined for the Japanese market.

Usually, the fish were found in certain areas where there were predictable, concentrated upwellings of food. But during El Niño years, warm water would stream into the northern California area, dispersing the fish and making fishing much harder. But *Mary Lou* even had a huge fuel tank. It could chase the fish all over the ocean, wherever they were.

When John found the *Mary Lou*, he knew this was his boat—the one he'd keep. Other fishermen bought big expensive rigs when times were good, and couldn't pay for them when times were bad. John put money away when times were good, and used it to cover *Mary Lou*'s expenses when times were bad. ■

IN REQUA

Requa Inn (707-482-8205), 451 Requa Road. Moderate. This 10-room riverside inn is an okay place to stay, near plenty of Redwood National Park's outdoor activities. It features a parlor furnished with overstuffed chairs and a woodstove; eight of the rooms have private baths, and four have views of the Klamath River.

IN CRESCENT CITY

Crescent Beach Motel (707-464-5436), 1455 Highway 101 South. Inexpensive to moderate. A modern motel, this one is unremarkable except for sweeping views of the Pacific and the coast.

Fernbrook Inn (707-458-3202), 4650 N. Bank Road. Moderate. With only two rooms, but very pleasant and clean, the inn is comfortably nestled in the redwoods.

Curly Redwood Lodge (707-464-2137), 701 Redwood Highway South. Inexpensive to moderate. This inn is notable mainly for having been constructed from exactly one 18-foot-diameter redwood tree.

Bayview Inn (707-465-2050), 310 Highway 101 South. Inexpensive to moderate. This three-story inn offers great views of Crescent City's bay.

Restaurants

IN KLAMATH

Babe's Iron Tender (707-482-3152), 1549 Highway 101 South. Inexpensive. Located at Motel Trees, this is a seafood-and-steak restaurant that also serves big lunches and dinners. Across from Trees of Mystery.

IN REQUA

Requa Inn (707-482-8205), 451 Requa Road. Inexpensive to moderate. A good place to enjoy the area's abundant seafood, this restaurant also features steak and chicken dishes.

IN CRESCENT CITY

Good Harvest Cafe (707-465-6028), 700 Northcrest. Inexpensive. This is a good place to break from the seafood-and-meat diet that's prominent on the north coast. Good Harvest features veggie sandwiches and salads, as well as brunch.

Chart Room (707-464-5993), 130 Anchor Way. Inexpensive to moderate. Everything at this family-style seafood restaurant seems freshly caught or picked.

Harbor View Grotto (707-464-3815), 150 Starfish Way. Moderate. Located right on the harbor and sporting ocean views, this is another reasonably priced seafood restaurant with family ambience.

IN SMITH RIVER

Best Western Ship Ashore (707-487-3141), Highway 1. Moderate. This is the last stop for seafood in California, here served fresh with views of the slough.

PART III

The Coasts of California

TOM MIKKELSEN

Exploring the Many Coasts of California

LOOK FOR SOMETHING, and you'll find it on the varied coast of California. The coast offers so many opportunities, for so many different activities, that deciding what you want to do or see is often the most difficult part of planning a trip.

Once you've decided what to do, the next problem becomes finding the best place to do it. That's where this section of the book comes in: to give you a quick reference that will help in discovering specific areas of interest.

What follows is a series of lists of places we highly recommend, organized around the six basic themes of this guide (all represented by a special symbol): the Family Coast, the Quiet Coast, the Cultural Coast, the Living Coast, the Sporting Coast, and the Urban Coast, where art galleries, shopping plazas, and theaters line the beach.

Each entry includes a reference to the page where the entry is discussed in detail.

I. The Family Coast

BEST TOUR IN THE SOUTH

Stay in one of the many accommodations in or near Mission Bay, San Diego, and enjoy the bay and nearby ocean attractions. Sea World will take most of a day. Rent bikes or boats on the bay. Enjoy the remnants of the Belmont Park amusement park. A stroll along the Mission Beach Boardwalk yields shopping, playgrounds, fishing, food, and, of course, the popular beach.

BEST TOUR IN THE NORTH

Santa Cruz is the best northern California family beach town—maybe because it's so much like a southern California beach town. Enjoy the Beach Boardwalk, surfing and volleyball scenes, some excellent restaurants, and the Wharf. Excursions to Capitola, the state parks in the Santa Cruz Mountains, and the northern

Santa Cruz beaches will make fun-filled long weekends. Recreational shopping for all ages is great at the bustling Downtown Mall, now fully recovered from the '89 earthquake. Better yet, miss the crowds; go in May, midweek during the summer, or after Labor Day.

DESTINATIONS

Here is a list of places that might interest a family with children, along with the safest beaches and most sheltered coves. They range from user-friendly camping areas to more traditional recreation areas, such as the Santa Cruz Beach Boardwalk. Destinations are listed from south to north, with a page reference for more information.

A. The Safe Coast

SAN DIEGO COUNTY

- ☐ Silver Strand State Beach 8
- ☐ Mission Bay beaches 12

ORANGE COUNTY

- ☐ Salt Creek Beach Park 34
- ☐ Crystal Cove State Park 35
- ☐ Balboa Beach/Balboa Pier 37

LOS ANGELES COUNTY

- ☐ Mother's Beach, Naples 60
- ☐ Seaside Lagoon, Redondo Beach 71–72
- ☐ Mother's Beach (aka Marina del Rey Public Swimming Beach) 75
- ☐ Malibu Creek State Park 85
- ☐ Zuma Beach County Park 86–87

VENTURA COUNTY

- ☐ Point Mugu State Park 97
- ☐ San Buenaventura State Beach 105

SANTA BARBARA COUNTY

- ☐ Carpinteria State Beach 117–118
- ☐ Arroyo Burro Beach County Park 122
- ☐ Goleta Beach County Park 122–123
- ☐ Gaviota State Park 125
- ☐ Jalama Beach County Park 125–126

SAN LUIS OBISPO COUNTY

- ☐ Montana de Oro State Park 147–148
- ☐ Morro Bay State Park 148
- ☐ Atascadero State Beach (aka Morro Strand State Beach, South) 151
- ☐ San Simeon State Beach 153–154

MONTEREY COUNTY

- ☐ Lover's Point 177

SANTA CRUZ COUNTY

- ☐ Sunset State Beach 199
- ☐ New Brighton State Beach 200
- ☐ Capitola City Beach 200–201
- ☐ Santa Cruz (Main) Beach 202

SAN MATEO COUNTY

- ☐ Año Nuevo State Reserve 219
- ☐ San Gregorio State Beach 220
- ☐ Francis Beach, Half Moon Bay 221

MARIN COUNTY

- ☐ Muir Beach 248
- ☐ Stinson Beach 250–251
- ☐ Limantour Beach, Point Reyes 252
- ☐ Drakes Estero/Drakes Beach, Point Reyes 252–253
- ☐ Tomales Bay State Park 257

SONOMA COUNTY

- ☐ Doran Beach Regional Park 264
- ☐ Salt Point State Park 267
- ☐ Gualala Point Regional Park 268–269

MENDOCINO COUNTY

- ☐ Manchester State Beach 276
- ☐ Van Damme State Park 276–277
- ☐ MacKerricher State Park 281–282

HUMBOLDT COUNTY

- ☐ Moonstone County Beach 300–301
- ☐ Patrick's Point State Park 301

B. Fun and Learning on the Coast

SAN DIEGO COUNTY

- ☐ Mission Bay area in San Diego, especially shoreline boardwalks and amusement areas at Belmont Park at Mission Beach 12
- ☐ Ocean Beach Park, San Diego 11–12
- ☐ Sea World, San Diego 12

ORANGE COUNTY

- ☐ Balboa Fun Zone on Balboa Island 37

LOS ANGELES COUNTY

- ☐ Santa Catalina Island 53–58
- ☐ *Queen Mary*, Long Beach 61
- ☐ Cabrillo Marine Aquarium, San Pedro 65
- ☐ Ports o' Call and Whalers' Wharf, San Pedro 63–64
- ☐ Fisherman's Village, Marina del Rey 74
- ☐ Santa Monica Municipal Pier, Santa Monica 77

VENTURA COUNTY

- ☐ Gulls Wings Children's Museum, Oxnard 103

SANTA BARBARA COUNTY

- ☐ A. Childs Estate Zoo, Santa Barbara 119

SAN LUIS OBISPO COUNTY

- ☐ Hearst San Simeon State Historical Monument (Hearst Castle), San Simeon 154–155

MONTEREY COUNTY

- ☐ Pfeiffer Big Sur State Park, Big Sur 168
- ☐ Camping at Andrew Molera State Park, Big Sur 169
- ☐ Point Lobos State Reserve 172–173
- ☐ Monterey Bay Aquarium, Monterey 183–184
- ☐ Maritime Museum of Monterey 185

SANTA CRUZ COUNTY

- ☐ Santa Cruz Beach Boardwalk 202

SAN MATEO COUNTY

- ☐ Año Nuevo State Reserve 219

SAN FRANCISCO COUNTY

- ☐ Cliff House, San Francisco 235–236

MARIN COUNTY

- ☐ Muir Woods National Monument 248
- ☐ Mount Tamalpais State Park 249
- ☐ Audubon Canyon Ranch 251

SONOMA COUNTY

- ☐ Fort Ross State Historic Park 266

MENDOCINO COUNTY

- ☐ Camping at MacKerricher State Park, near Fort Bragg 281–282

HUMBOLDT COUNTY

- ☐ Fort Humboldt State Historic Park, Eureka 299
- ☐ Samoa Cookhouse, Eureka 306–307
- ☐ Camping at Prairie Creek Redwoods State Park, Orick 301, 303
- ☐ Redwood National Park, Humboldt and Del Norte Counties 304

II. The Quiet Coast

BEST TOUR IN THE SOUTH

Western Malibu is about as quiet as southern California gets these days. Follow the tradition of the Chumash Native Americans by camping at Sycamore Canyon Campground. The canyon is beautiful, despite State Parks shoehorning a few too many campsites into the region. Scenic trails up into the Santa Monica Mountains and a glorious beach just across Highway 1 make this a spectacular area. Restaurants are available within a short drive, as are many other scenic beaches. Make reservations early, and crowds are easily avoided by planning ahead. Solitude is available just a short hike or bike ride away.

BEST TOUR IN THE NORTH

Kehoe Beach is a gem of the fabulous Point Reyes National Seashore. A short walk through the dunes is rewarded by a wild, empty beach. The vistas are beautiful, as are the other nearby natural attractions. Don't miss the lighthouse and McClure and Limantour Beaches. Food and lodging are available in Inverness and in Point Reyes Station.

DESTINATIONS

This list contains possibilities for those want to get away from it all in places of great beauty, whether hidden beaches, quiet hotels, or a combination of both. We have also included romantic spots and inspirational places. Destinations are listed from south to north, with a page reference for more information.

A. Secluded Beaches

SAN DIEGO COUNTY

- ☐ Border Field State Park, Imperial Beach 7
- ☐ Sunset Cliffs Park, Ocean Beach 11
- ☐ Torrey Pines City Beach, La Jolla 14

LOS ANGELES COUNTY

- ☐ Paradise Cove, Malibu 86
- ☐ La Piedra State Beach, Malibu 87
- ☐ El Pescador State Beach, Malibu 87
- ☐ Leo Carrillo State Beach, Malibu 87

VENTURA COUNTY

- ☐ Point Mugu State Park 97
- ☐ Rincon Parkway South beaches 107

SANTA BARBARA COUNTY

- ☐ Loon Point 119
- ☐ Vandenberg Air Force Base Beach 126
- ☐ Ocean Beach County Park 126–127
- ☐ Point Sal State Beach 127–128
- ☐ Guadalupe-Nipomo Dunes Preserve 128

SAN LUIS OBISPO COUNTY

- ☐ Pecho Memorial Coast Trail 142
- ☐ Leffingwell Landing, Cambria Pines 153

MONTEREY COUNTY

- ☐ Jade Cove, Big Sur 167
- ☐ Sand Dollar Beach, Big Sur 167
- ☐ Mill Creek Picnic Ground, Big Sur 167
- ☐ Pfeiffer Beach, Big Sur 168
- ☐ Garrapata State Park, Big Sur 171–172
- ☐ Salinas River State Beach, Moss Landing 187

- ☐ Zmudoski State Beach, Moss Landing 188

SANTA CRUZ COUNTY

- ☐ Palm Beach, Santa Cruz 199
- ☐ Wilder Ranch State Park 207
- ☐ Laguna Creek, Yellowbank, Bonny Doon, Panther, and Scott Creek Beaches 208–209

SAN MATEO COUNTY

- ☐ Año Nuevo State Reserve 219
- ☐ Tunitas Beach 220
- ☐ Cowell Ranch Beach, Half Moon Bay State Beaches 221

MARIN COUNTY

- ☐ Kirby Cove 247
- ☐ Limantour Beach, Point Reyes 252
- ☐ Kehoe Beach, Point Reyes 256
- ☐ McClures Beach, Point Reyes 256–257
- ☐ Tomales Bay State Park 257

SONOMA COUNTY

- ☐ Trail from Bodega Head to Salmon Creek Beach 264
- ☐ Stillwater Cove Regional Park 267

MENDOCINO COUNTY

- ☐ Manchester State Beach 276
- ☐ Sinkyone Wilderness State Park, Mendocino 283–284
- ☐ Northern Mendocino beaches 282–283

HUMBOLDT COUNTY

- ☐ King Range National Conservation Area 296
- ☐ Mattole River/Mattole River Beach 296–297
- ☐ Mattole Road beaches 297
- ☐ Mad River Beach County Park 299
- ☐ Humboldt lagoons 301
- ☐ Prairie Creek Redwoods State Park 301, 303

DEL NORTE COUNTY

- ☐ Redwood National Park 311
- ☐ Enderts Beach 311

B. Romantic Getaways

SAN DIEGO COUNTY

- ☐ Coronado Hotel Beach 8–9
- ☐ La Jolla 13–15, 26–27, 29

ORANGE COUNTY

- ☐ Laguna Beach 34–36, 44, 47–48
- ☐ Balboa Island, Balboa 37

LOS ANGELES COUNTY

- ☐ Santa Catalina Island 53–58
- ☐ Self-Realization Friendship Lake Shrine, Los Angeles 81
- ☐ Santa Monica Mountains National Recreation Area 81
- ☐ Malibu Creek State Park 85

VENTURA COUNTY

- ☐ Ojai 111

SANTA BARBARA COUNTY

- ☐ Montecito 119, 129
- ☐ Four Seasons Biltmore Hotel 129

SAN LUIS OBISPO COUNTY

- ☐ San Simeon 153, 161, 163

MONTEREY COUNTY

- ☐ Landels-Hill Big Creek Reserve, Big Sur 167
- ☐ Ventana Wilderness Area, Big Sur 167–168
- ☐ Esalen Institute, Big Sur 168
- ☐ Ventana Inn, Big Sur 188
- ☐ Post Ranch Inn, Big Sur 188–189

SAN MATEO COUNTY

- ☐ Pescadero State Beach 220

SAN FRANCISCO COUNTY

- ☐ Baker Beach, San Francisco 239–240

MARIN COUNTY

- ☐ Muir Beach 248
- ☐ Steep Ravine 249

- ☐ Point Reyes 252–258

SONOMA COUNTY

- ☐ Sonoma County state beaches 264–269
- ☐ Timber Cove Inn, Sonoma 270
- ☐ Sea Ranch, Sonoma 268, 270

MENDOCINO COUNTY

- ☐ Elk 276, 286–287, 291
- ☐ Mendocino 277–279, 288–289, 292–293
- ☐ Mendocino Coast Botanical Gardens, Fort Bragg 281
- ☐ Albion River Inn, Albion 287, 292

HUMBOLDT COUNTY

- ☐ Patrick's Point State Park 301
- ☐ Redwood National Park, Humboldt and Del Norte Counties 304
- ☐ Ferndale 304–305, 306
- ☐ Trinidad Bay B&B, Trinidad 306

C. Backpacking

LOS ANGELES COUNTY

- ☐ Malibu Creek State Park 85

VENTURA COUNTY

- ☐ Sycamore Canyon Campground, Point Mugu State Park 97

SAN LUIS OBISPO COUNTY

- ☐ Los Osos Oaks State Preserve 146–147
- ☐ Montana de Oro State Park 147–148
- ☐ Morro Bay State Park 148–149

MONTEREY COUNTY

- ☐ Plaskett Creek Campground, Big Sur 166
- ☐ Kirk Creek Campground, Big Sur 166
- ☐ Environmental campsites at Julia Pfeiffer Burns State Park, Big Sur 168
- ☐ Ventana Campgound, Big Sur 169
- ☐ Andrew Molera State Park, Big Sur 169

SANTA CRUZ COUNTY

- ☐ Manresa State Beach, Santa Cruz 199–200

SONOMA COUNTY

- ☐ Salt Point State Park, Sonoma 267
- ☐ MacKerricher State Park, near Fort Bragg 281–282

HUMBOLDT COUNTY

- ☐ Prairie Creek Redwoods State Park, Orick 301, 303

D. Vistas

SAN DIEGO COUNTY

- ☐ Cabrillo National Monument, Point Loma 11
- ☐ Sunset Cliffs Park, Ocean Beach 11
- ☐ Windansea Beach, La Jolla 14
- ☐ Vista Point off San Diego Freeway (CA 5) at Cardiff-by-the-Sea 16

ORANGE COUNTY

- ☐ Crescent Bay Point Park, Laguna Beach 35

LOS ANGELES COUNTY

- ☐ Bluff Cove overlook, Palos Verdes Estates 69
- ☐ Point Dume Whale-Watch, Malibu 86

SANTA BARBARA COUNTY

- ☐ Plaza Del Mar, 122
- ☐ Gaviota State Park, Santa Barbara 125

MONTEREY COUNTY

- ☐ Bixby Creek Bridge, Big Sur 171

SANTA CRUZ COUNTY

- ☐ Pleasure Point Beach, Santa Cruz 201
- ☐ Lighthouse Field State Beach, Santa Cruz 206

SAN MATEO COUNTY

- ☐ San Gregorio State Beach 220

SAN FRANCISCO COUNTY

- ☐ Hang Glider Observation Platform, Fort Funston 231–232
- ☐ Sutro Heights, San Francisco 235

MARIN COUNTY

- ☐ Muir Beach Overlook 248
- ☐ Mount Tamalpais 249

SONOMA COUNTY

- ☐ Bodega Head 264
- ☐ Goat Rock Beach/Russian River mouth 265
- ☐ Russian Gulch 266

MENDOCINO COUNTY

- ☐ Mendocino Headlands 279

E. Lighthouses

- ☐ Old Point Loma Lighthouse, San Diego County 11
- ☐ Piedras Blancas Lighthouse, San Luis Obispo County 155
- ☐ Point Sur Lighthouse, Monterey County 170
- ☐ Point Pinos Lighthouse, Monterey County 177
- ☐ Point Santa Cruz Lighthouse, Santa Cruz 206
- ☐ Pigeon Point Lighthouse, San Mateo 224
- ☐ Point Reyes Lighthouse, Marin County 253
- ☐ Point Arena Lighthouse, Mendocino County 276
- ☐ Battery Point Lighthouse, Del Norte County 312

F. Scenic Roads

LOS ANGELES COUNTY

Palos Verdes Peninsula Drive. Take the Harbor Freeway to the end, then go right on Gaffey Street to Palos Verdes Drive South. The road hugs the shoreline as it winds through the scenic Palos Verdes Peninsula. Point Vicente, with its excellent views, lies along this road.

SAN LUIS OBISPO COUNTY

Prefumo Canyon Road between Avila and Los Osos Valley. Exit Highway 101 on Avila Road, then go right onto See Canyon Road, which becomes Prefumo Canyon Road. This twisting road has spectacular vistas of the hills above Diablo Canyon and Montana de Oro State Park. Be forewarned that this road is challenging. Turn left onto Los Osos Valley Road, then right onto South Bay Boulevard and back to Highway 1.

MONTEREY COUNTY

Old Coast Highway, Big Sur. Leave Highway 1 just north of Andrew Molera State Park. The road returns to Highway 1 at Bixby Bridge. Along these 11 miles of dirt road are many excellent vista points with views of the Santa Lucia Mountains. The road is challenging in places.

Scenic Road, Carmel. Take Rio Road west from Highway 1. Turn left at Santa Lucia Avenue and then right onto Antonio Avenue. After 9 blocks, turn left on Ocean Avenue, and in one block, left onto Scenic Road, which parallels Carmel Beach City Park with its notable white sand beach. At the end of Scenic Road you will have returned to Santa Lucia Avenue.

Seventeen-Mile Drive, Monterey. Enter the Drive at one of the 5 gates, the most prominent of which is the Highway 1 gate at the exit onto Route 68. There is a $7 fee. Seventeen-Mile Drive winds through the famous golf courses of Pebble Beach and Spyglass Hill. It also provides striking vistas of offshore rock formations and glimpses of marine life.

Sunset Drive/Ocean View Boulevard, Pacific Grove. From Highway 1, Route 68 winds through the Monterey Peninsula to Sunset Drive, which goes through the Asilomar Conference Grounds with its famous dunes, and then along the coast past Point Pinos, after which it becomes Ocean View Boulevard. At Point Cabrillo, Ocean View goes through the heart of Old Monterey and Cannery Row. Turn left on Del Monte Avenue to rejoin Highway 1.

SANTA CRUZ COUNTY

Highway 1 between Santa Cruz and Half Moon Bay. Take Swanton Road just north of Davenport. It rejoins Highway 1 after 4 miles of twisting, beautiful road that passes through old ranch lands, dotted with rustic Victorian houses.

SAN FRANCISCO COUNTY

Great Highway and 49-Mile Drive, San Francisco. The Great Highway runs along San Francisco's Ocean Beach. Access points are numerous from the Sunset and Richmond Districts, or by driving west through Golden Gate Park. There are numerous parking places along the route, and there is also parking on the adjacent neigborhood streets. The Great Highway is part of 49-Mile Drive, a route that covers most of San Francisco's scenic spots.

MARIN COUNTY

Conzelman Road. Take the second right after exiting the Golden Gate Bridge into Marin. Turn left, under Highway 101, onto Cozelman Road. This winding road takes you through scenic headlands and an old army base, complete with gun emplacements. Conzelman Road leads to Bunder Road, which returns to Highway 101.

Shoreline Highway/Panoramic Highway. Exit 101 just north of Sausalito and follow the signs. You will wind up the shoulders of Mount Tamalpais to its ridgeline, where you'll find spectacular views of the coastal mountains and the sea. At the ridge there are numerous choices, but the adventurous one is to continue to Stinson Beach and Bolinas.

MENDOCINO COUNTY

Highway 1 from Marin through Rockport in Mendocino. The most efficient way to drive to Mendocino is by traveling north on Highway 101, then going to the coast by way of Route 128, which reaches the coast at Albion; or by taking Route 20, which reaches the coast at Fort Bragg. The longer, slower drive north from Bodega Bay through Sonoma is very rewarding, given the beautiful headlands and marine plateaus that line this section of the coast.

HUMBOLDT COUNTY

Highway 101 from McKinleyville to Crescent City. This is one of the loveliest sections of the California coast. There are redwood stands, lagoons, and breathtaking sights along the rugged northern shore.

Coast Drive in Prairie Creek Redwoods State Park. Go left on Alder Camp Road. This is an 8-mile route that runs through redwood forests with beautiful views of the ocean beyond.

DEL NORTE COUNTY

Pebble Beach Drive in Crescent City. Fifth, 7th, or 9th Streets will take you west to Pebble Beach Drive, which follows a scenic shoreline with pocket beaches, a dramatic breakwater, and a lighthouse. Washington Boulevard, at the north end of the drive, takes you back to Highway 101.

Smith River/Tillas Slough. Take Route 199 off Highway 101 and follow it to Route 197. Turn left on Route 197 and drive along the Smith River. This route takes you through part of California's Wild and Scenic River System. There are redwood groves, good fishing, and numerous picnic spots along this beautiful waterway.

G. The Agricultural Coast (pick-your-own produce, farmer's markets, rural scenery)

- ☐ Northern San Diego County
- ☐ Oxnard Plain, Ventura County
- ☐ Southern Santa Barbara County
- ☐ Northern Monterey County
- ☐ Southern and northern Santa Cruz County

- ☐ Southern San Mateo County
- ☐ Western Marin County
- ☐ Southern Mendocino County
- ☐ Eel River Delta, Humboldt County

H. The Redwood Forest Coast

- ☐ Big Sur 167–173, 188–189, 192–193
- ☐ Mendocino County 273–293
- ☐ Humboldt County 295–307
- ☐ Del Norte County 309–316

I. The Clothing-Optional Coast

- ☐ Black's Beach at Torrey Pines City Beach, San Diego 14
- ☐ Red, White, and Blue Beach, just north of Santa Cruz 208
- ☐ Northern Santa Cruz County beaches 208–209
- ☐ San Gregorio Beach, northern section, San Mateo County 220
- ☐ Gray Whale Cove State Beach, Devil's Slide, San Mateo County 223

III. The Living Coast ★

BEST TOUR IN THE SOUTH

As incongruous as it may seem, the best natural experience in southern California is right next to Los Angeles Harbor. At Cabrillo Beach, just after high tides from March through August, you can observe the grunion run. These weird little fish spawn here, near the massive industrial port. Interpretive programs are run by the Cabrillo Marine Aquarium, which is worth a visit any time of year. Accommodations and food are to be found in San Pedro, Long Beach, and Redondo Beach.

BEST TOUR IN THE NORTH

Monterey Bay is the most diverse natural environment in northern California. Using the Monterey Bay Aquarium as a base, explore the natural wonders of the bay from the beach uplands to the deep offshore Monterey Trench. Elkhorn Slough and its environs are a rich, well-preserved natural treasure. Also, don't miss Point Lobos State Preserve. Eat and stay on the Monterey Peninsula or in southern Santa Cruz.

DESTINATIONS

The California coast contains excellent nature preserves, native gardens, and protected ocean habitat. Tide pools, for example, might be listed under the Family Coast as well as the Living Coast, since children enjoy them so much. Destinations are listed from south to north, with a page reference for more information.

SAN DIEGO COUNTY

- ☐ National Estuarine Research Reserve, San Diego 7
- ☐ Sweetwater Marsh National Wildlife Refuge, National City 9
- ☐ Point Loma Ecological Reserve, Point Loma 11
- ☐ Sea World, Mission Bay 12
- ☐ Scripps Institution of Oceanography, La Jolla 14
- ☐ Torrey Pines State Reserve/Torrey Pines State Reserve Extension, La Jolla 14–15

ORANGE COUNTY

- ☐ Upper Newport Bay State Ecological Reserve, Newport Beach 38
- ☐ Bolsa Chica Ecological Reserve, Huntington Beach 40
- ☐ Seal Beach National Wildlife Refuge, Seal Beach 41

LOS ANGELES COUNTY

- ☐ Santa Catalina Island 53–58
- ☐ Cabrillo Marine Aquarium, San Pedro 65
- ☐ Point Fermin Park/Point Fermin National Wildlife Refuge, San Pedro 65
- ☐ Palos Verdes Estates Shoreline Preserve, Palos Verdes 69
- ☐ Roundhouse Marine Studies Lab, Mahattan Beach 72–73
- ☐ Point Dume Whale-Watch, Malibu 86

VENTURA COUNTY

- ☐ Santa Clara Estuary Natural Preserve, Oxnard 103
- ☐ Channel Islands 108–110

SANTA BARBARA COUNTY

- ☐ Andree Clark Bird Refuge/Zoo/Dwight Murphy Field, Santa Barbara 119
- ☐ Ocean Beach County Park, Santa Barbara 126–127
- ☐ Guadalupe-Nipomo Dunes Preserve, Santa Barbara and San Luis Obispo Counties 128

SAN LUIS OBISPO COUNTY

- ☐ Oso Flaco Lake Natural Area, Oso Flaco 139
- ☐ Los Osos Oaks State Preserve, Los Osos 146–147
- ☐ Morro Dunes Natural Preserve, Morro Bay 148
- ☐ Morro Rock Ecological Preserve, Morro Bay 151

MONTEREY COUNTY

- ☐ Landels-Hill Big Creek Reserve, Big Sur 167
- ☐ Julia Pfeiffer Burns State Park, Big Sur 168
- ☐ Point Lobos State Reserve 172–173
- ☐ Monterey Bay Aquarium, Monterey 183–184
- ☐ Elkhorn Slough National Estuarine Research Reserve, Moss Landing 186

SANTA CRUZ COUNTY

- ☐ Joseph M. Long Marine Laboratory, Santa Cuz 207
- ☐ Big Basin, Santa Cruz 209

SAN MATEO COUNTY

- ☐ Año Nuevo State Reserve 219
- ☐ James Fitzgerald Marine Reserve 222–223

MARIN COUNTY

- ☐ Muir Woods National Monument, Muir Beach 248
- ☐ Audubon Canyon Ranch, Stinson Beach 251
- ☐ Bolinas Beach/Bolinas Lagoon Nature Preserve, Bolinas 251
- ☐ Agate Beach/Duxbury Reef, Bolinas 251
- ☐ Point Reyes Bird Observatory, Point Reyes/Inverness 252

SONOMA COUNTY

- ☐ Bodega Marine Laboratory, Bodega 265
- ☐ Kruse Rhododendron State Reserve, Sonoma County 268

MENDOCINO COUNTY

- ☐ Mendocino Coast Botanical Gardens, Mendocino 281

IV. The Sporting Coast

BEST TOUR IN THE SOUTH

Things really haven't changed much at Windansea Beach in La Jolla since Tom Wolfe wrote *The Pump House Gang* 30 years ago. Check out the scene: The music is different, but the surfing, volleyball, and buff young crowd are still there. Accommodations and food abound in La Jolla and the Mission Bay vicinity. Snorkeling is great at nearby La Jolla Cove.

BEST TOUR IN THE NORTH

San Francisco and Marin are blessed with many beaches that are part of the Golden Gate National Recreation Area. This is an unlikely but real sports mecca. Hang gliding at Fort Funston, surfing at Ocean Beach, windsurfing just inside the Golden Gate, and hiking and biking everywhere make this shoreline a year-round place to burn calories. Excellent and varied food and lodging are available in San Francisco and Marin County.

DESTINATIONS

The range of opportunities for sports along the coast is huge. Many beaches—particularly in the Los Angeles area—host volleyball, surfing, swimming, sailing, and bicycling. Most of the beaches listed here are especially good for surfing. Destinations are listed from south to north, with a page reference for more information. (Also see **Backpacking** under the **Quiet Coast.**)

SAN DIEGO COUNTY

- ☐ Tourmaline Surfing Park, La Jolla 13
- ☐ La Jolla Strand Park/Windansea Beach/Marine Street Beach, La Jolla 14
- ☐ Swami's, Encinitas 16–17
- ☐ South Oceanside Beach, Oceanside 19

ORANGE COUNTY

- ☐ Capistrano Beach Park, San Juan Capistrano 33
- ☐ Doheny State Beach, San Juan Capistrano 33
- ☐ Main Beach, Laguna Beach 34–35
- ☐ Huntington State and City Beaches, Huntington Beach 39

LOS ANGELES COUNTY

- ☐ Mega-Bungee, *Queen Mary* complex, Long Beach 62
- ☐ International Surf Festival, Redondo Beach 71
- ☐ Hermosa City Beach, Hermosa Beach 72
- ☐ Zuma Beach County Park, Malibu 86

VENTURA COUNTY

- ☐ Point Mugu Beach, Ventura County 99
- ☐ Surfer's Point, Ventura County 106
- ☐ Rincon Parkway beaches, Ventura County 107–109

SANTA BARBARA COUNTY

- ☐ Leadbetter Beach, Santa Barbara 122
- ☐ Mesa Lane Stairs, Santa Barbara 122
- ☐ El Capitan State Beach, Santa Barbara 123–124
- ☐ Refugio State Beach, Santa Barbara 124

SANTA CRUZ COUNTY

- ☐ Pleasure Point Beach, Santa Cruz 201
- ☐ Cowell Beach/Steamer Lane, Santa Cruz 203
- ☐ Waddell Creek Beach/Big Basin Redwoods State Park, Santa Cruz 209

SAN MATEO COUNTY

- ☐ Mavericks, San Mateo County 222
- ☐ Rockaway Beach, Pacifica 223

SAN FRANCISCO COUNTY

- ☐ Fort Funston, San Francisco 231–232

MENDOCINO COUNTY

- ☐ Arena Cove Beach, Point Arena 276
- ☐ Van Damme State Park, Little River 276–277

V. The Cultural Coast

BEST TOUR IN THE SOUTH

The heralded new Getty Center, off Mullholland Road in Bentwood, will be worth a visit. More than a single museum, the new Getty Center is a complex of six buildings, situated high on a ridge in the Santa Monica hills. It's large enough and houses a vast enough collection of art to take an entire day to explore. Nearby, check out Will Rogers State Historical Park for a more down-home historical perspective.

BEST TOUR IN THE NORTH

Hearst Castle and southern Big Sur offer high art, campy pretense, and literary ghosts. The many tours of the castle show the eclectic taste of William Hearst and the talents of his remarkable architect, Julia Morgan. Politics, journalism, and glamour of the past are preserved in the well-managed facility. A trip up Big Sur to Partington Ridge is a good counterpoint to this establishment history; tread the same territory as bohemian writers and artists from Henry Miller to Jack Kerouac and Allan Ginsberg to Ansel Adams and Edward Weston. The Henry Miller Memorial Library, just a half mile south of Nepenthe, is a good base for learning about bohemia-by-the-sea.

DESTINATIONS

Here we list places of literary, historical, and general cultural interest. We are not parochial in our tastes. We include New Age retreats such as Esalen in Big Sur, as well as those places that explain the native Californian peoples. Destinations are listed from south to north, with a page reference for more information.

LOS ANGELES COUNTY

VENTURA COUNTY

- ☐ Ventura County Maritime Museum, Oxnard 101
- ☐ Carnegie Art Museum, Oxnard 102
- ☐ Olivas Adobe Historical Park, Ventura 104–105
- ☐ Ventura County Museum of History and Art, Ventura 106
- ☐ San Buenaventura Mission, Ventura 107

SAN LUIS OBISPO COUNTY

- ☐ Mission San Luis Obispo de Tolosa, San Luis Obispo 143, 146
- ☐ Hearst San Simeon State Historical Monument (Hearst Castle), San Simeon 154–155

MONTEREY COUNTY

- ☐ Esalen Institute, Big Sur 168
- ☐ Henry Miller Memorial Library, Big Sur 169
- ☐ Point Sur State Historic Park, Big Sur 170
- ☐ Mission San Carlos Borromeo del Rio, Carmel 173
- ☐ Tor House, Carmel 173
- ☐ Monterey State Historic Park, Monterey 184–186

SAN FRANCISCO COUNTY

- ☐ Sutro Heights area of San Francisco 235

SONOMA COUNTY

- ☐ Fort Ross State Historic Park, Fort Ross 266

HUMBOLDT COUNTY

- ☐ Fort Humboldt State Historic Park 299

DEL NORTE COUNTY

- ☐ Trees of Mystery, Klamath 311

VI. The Urban Coast

BEST TOUR IN THE SOUTH

Venice and Santa Monica offer fabulous diversity and excitement along the shoreline. Ocean Front Walk in Venice is a wild urban sideshow; fire-eaters, fortune tellers, weight lifters, and chainsaw jugglers are regulars on the weekends. Main Street in Santa Monica is a daily upscale shopping and eating experience.

The revived Third Street Mall and Santa Monica Place shopping center also are recreational shopping and eating meccas. Bikes and in-line skates can be rented so you can see more of the scene. But a stroll will capture the essence of L.A.'s oddball and yuppie cultures. Lots of food options; accommodations are varied in Santa Monica.

BEST TOUR IN THE NORTH

San Francisco's shoreline is more diverse than any other city's. From the gritty Ocean Beach, where streetcars bring everyone to the shore, to Seacliff, an elite neighborhood overlooking the Golden Gate, one can see anything and anybody at any time. Nude beaches, the ruins of a visionary mayor's dreams at Sutro Heights and Baths, trails, museums, and parks punctuate a vital coast. Only the cool, foggy weather keeps the crowds manageable. Golden Gate Park is the city's centerpiece, leading to many other attractions. Food and hotel options are limited along the coast, but downtown San Francisco has unlimited possibilities.

DESTINATIONS

Some sections of the California coast are closely tied to urban areas. Often these places offer unique experiences of their own, as at Venice, in Los Angeles County. Shopping, people-watching, and art galleries are all part of the urban coastal experience. We list the best of these areas below. Destinations are listed from south to north, with a page reference for more information.

A. The Gold Coast: Opulence on the Shoreline

- ☐ Orange County Coast 31–49
- ☐ Palos Verdes 67–70
- ☐ Pacific Palisades 79–81
- ☐ Malibu 81–87, 90, 93
- ☐ Montecito 119, 129
- ☐ Santa Barbara 121–123
- ☐ Big Sur 166–173, 188–189, 193–194
- ☐ Carmel 173–174, 189–190, 193
- ☐ 17-Mile Drive, Monterey County 174–175
- ☐ Inverness 259, 260–261
- ☐ Elk 276, 286–287, 291
- ☐ Ferndale 304–305, 306
- ☐ Trinidad 306, 307

B. Harbors and Ports

- ☐ San Diego 10
- ☐ Long Beach 59–60
- ☐ Port of Los Angeles 62–63
- ☐ Marina Del Rey Harbor, Marina Del Rey 74
- ☐ Channel Islands Harbor, Oxnard 100–101
- ☐ Ventura Harbor 103–104
- ☐ Santa Cruz Harbor 201–202
- ☐ Pillar Point Harbor, Half Moon Bay 221

C. Shopping

- ☐ Laguna Beach 34–36
- ☐ Newport Beach 37–39
- ☐ Belmont Shore in Long Beach 59
- ☐ Ports o' Call Village and Whalers Wharf, Los Angeles Harbor 63–64
- ☐ Western Avenue, Los Angeles 66–67
- ☐ Catalina Avenue, Redondo Beach 68
- ☐ Fisherman's Village, Marina del Rey 74
- ☐ Ocean Front Walk, Venice 76
- ☐ Main Street, Santa Monica 77
- ☐ Santa Monica Place, Santa Monica 78
- ☐ Carmel 173–174
- ☐ Cannery Row, Monterey 179–183
- ☐ Pacific Garden Mall, Santa Cruz 205
- ☐ Mendocino 277–279

Appendix A

The Coastal Code

What do you need to know to enjoy the coast without fear of breaking the law or risk of harm? Many of these "rules" are spelled out in the regulations of parks and municipalities, public beaches, and resource agencies. The following "Coastal Code" is modeled after Britain's Countryside Commission's "Country Code," developed as a comprehensive guide for tourists visiting its countryside. Such codes do not have the force of law. They are common sense guides to enjoying and safeguarding valuable resources.

- Respect coastal wildlife and plants.
- Safeguard all water quality.
- Protect agricultural and forest lands.
- Comply with all fishing regulations.
- Stay on trails and paths.
- Guard against fire.
- Respect private property.
- Leave no litter.
- Swim only under lifeguard supervision.
- Watch the waves and tides.
- Observe all boating rules.
- Keep small children under adult supervision.
- Keep dogs under proper control.
- Drive carefully.
- Be prepared.

Appendix B

Coastal Reading List

American Automobile Association. *TourBook: California/Nevada.* Heathrow, FL: American Automobile Association, 1997.

Bell, Stephanie C., and Elizabeth Janda. *The Best Places to Kiss in Northern California.* Seattle: Beginning Press, 1990.

Brada, Deborah, and Caroline O'Connell. *The Best Places to Kiss in Southern California: A Romantic Travel Guide.* Seattle: Beginning Press, 1990.

Bristow, Linda Kay. *Bed & Breakfast California.* San Francisco: Chronicle Books, 1994.

California Coastal Commission. *California Coastal Access Guide.* Berkeley: University of California Press, 5th ed. 1997.

California Coastal Commission. *California Coastal Resource Guide.* Berkeley: University of California Press, 1987.

Engbeck, Joseph H., and Drury, Aubrey, eds. *Point Lobos: Interpretation of a Primitive Landscape.* Berkeley: University of California, 1975.

Evens, Jules G. *The Natural History of the Point Reyes Peninsula.* Point Reyes, CA: Point Reyes National Seashore Association, 1993.

Femling, Jean. *Great Piers of Northern California: A Guided Tour.* Santa Barbara: Capra Press, 1984.

Franks, Jonathan. *Exploring the North Coast: The California Coast from the Golden Gate to the Oregon Border.* San Francisco: Chronicle Books, 1996.

Gebhard, David, and Robert Winter. *Architecture in Los Angeles and Southern California.* Santa Barbara: Peregrine Smith, Inc., 1977.

Griggs, Gary, and Lauret Savoy, eds. *Living with the California Coast.* Durham, NC: Duke University Press, 1985.

Harris, Eleanor. *Quick Escapes in Southern California: 21 Weekend Trips from Los Angeles and San Diego*. Old Saybrook, CT: The Globe Pequot Press, 1993.

Henson, Paul, and Usner, Donald J. *The Natural History of Big Sur*. Berkeley: University of California Press, 1993.

Holing, Dwight. *California Wild Lands: A Guide to The Nature Conservancy Preserves*. San Francisco: Chronicle Books, 1988.

Jaconet, Lucinda. *Monterey Bay and Beyond*. San Francisco: Chronicle Press, 1994.

Killeen, Jacqueline. *Country Inns of California*. San Ramon, CA: 101 Productions, 1987.

Kuhn, Gerald G., and Francis P. Shepard. *Sea Cliffs, Beaches, and Coastal Valleys of San Diego County: Some Amazing Histories and Some Horrifying Implications*. Berkeley: University of California Press, 1984.

Lorentzen, Bob. *The Mendocino Coast Glove Box Guide*. Mendocino, CA: Bored Feet Productions, 1995.

Mai, Bill. *The Best in Tent Camping: Southern California*. Birmingham, AL: Menasha Ridge Press, Inc., 1996.

Mallan, Chicki. *Guide to Catalina and California's Channel Islands*. Chico, CA: Moon Publications Inc., 1990.

McConnaughey, Bayard H. and Evelyn. *The Audubon Society Nature Guides: Pacific Coast*. New York: Alfred A. Knopf, 1997.

McFarlane, Marilyn. *Best Places to Stay In California*. New York: Houghton Mifflin Company, 1994.

McKinney, John. *Coast Walks: One Hundred Adventures along the California Coast*. Santa Barbara: Olympus Press, 1988.

——. *Walking the Central California Coast: A Day Hiker's Guide*. San Francisco: HarperSanFrancisco, 1996.

Moore, Charles, Peter Peter, and Regula Campbell. *The City Observed: Los Angeles*. New York: Vintage Books, 1984.

Phillips, Meredith. *The Child's Peninsula*. Menlo Park, CA: Perseverence Press, 1979.

Pierson, Robert John. *The Beach Towns: A Walker's Guide to L.A.'s Beach Communities*. San Francisco: Chronicle Books, 1985.

Poole, Matthew R. *Northern California Coast Best Places*. Seattle: Sasquatch Books, 1996.

Puterbaugh, Parke, and Alan Bisbort. *California Beaches: The Complete Guide to More Than 400 Beaches and 1,200 Miles of Coastline.* San Francisco: Foghorn Press, 1996.

Riegert, Ray. *Hidden Coast of California: The Adventurer's Guide.* Berkeley: Ulysses Press, 1988.

Thompson, Bob, ed. *Sunset Beachcombers' Guide to the Pacific Coast.* Menlo Park, CA: Lane Books, 1966.

White, Michael. *Best Beach Vacations: California.* New York: Macmillian, 1995.

Wilmer, Thomas C. *California Coast Getaways.* Ashland, OR: White Cloud Press, 1994.

Wolfe, Tom. *The Pump House Gang.* New York, Bantam Books, 1968.

Works Progress Administration. *California: A Guide to the Golden State.* New York: Hastings House, 1939.

Wright, Bank. *Surfing California.* Redondo Beach, CA: Mañana Publishing, 1973.

Wurman, Richard Saul. *LA/Access.* Los Angeles: Access Press Inc., 1980.

Appendix C

Useful Phone Numbers and Information

STATEWIDE INFORMATION

For any emergency, just call 911 and a local dispatcher will provide help. On the freeways, use the yellow phone boxes for roadside assistance.

TOURIST INFORMATION

California Department of Tourism, PO Box 1499, Sacramento, CA 95812-1499 (916-863-2543)

STATE PARKS

California State Park System, PO Box 942896, Sacramento, CA 94296-0001 (916-653-6995; 1-800-444-7275 for reservations)

NATIONAL FORESTS

US Forest Service, Pacific-Southwest Region, 630 Sansome Street, Room 527, San Francisco, CA 94111 (415-705-2874; 1-800-280-CAMP for reservations)

FISHING AND HUNTING REGULATIONS

Department of Fish and Game, 1416 9th Street, Sacramento, CA 95814 (916-653-7664)

County Information

SAN DIEGO COUNTY

San Diego Convention and Visitors Bureau, 1200 3rd Avenue, Suite 824, San Diego, CA 92101 (619-232-3101)

ORANGE COUNTY

San Clemente Chamber of Commerce, 1100 N- El Camino Real, San Clemente, CA 92672

Dana Point Chamber of Commerce, 24681 La Plaza , Suite 120, Dana Point, CA 92629 (714-496-1555)

Laguna Beach Chamber of Commerce, PO Box 396, San Juan Capistrano, CA 92652 (714-494-1018)

Newport Beach Conference and Visitors Bureau, 366 San Miguel Drive, Suite 200, Newport Beach, CA 92660 (714-644-1190)

Huntington Beach Chamber of Commerce, Seacliff Village, 2213 Main Street, #32, Huntington Beach, CA 92648 (714-536-8888)

LOS ANGELES COUNTY

Greater Los Angeles Visitors and Convention Bureau, Visitor Information Center, 505 S. Flower Street, Los Angeles, CA 90071 (213-624-7300)

VENTURA COUNTY

Oxnard Chamber of Commerce, 228 S. "A" Street, Oxnard, CA (805-385-8860)

Greater Ventura Chamber of Commerce, 785 South Seaward Avenue, Ventura, CA 93003 (805-648-2875)

SANTA BARBARA COUNTY

Carpinteria Chamber of Commerce, PO Box 956, Carpinteria, CA 93013 (805-684-5479)

Santa Barbara City Chamber of Commerce, PO Box 299, Santa Barbara, CA 93102 (805-965-3021)

SAN LUIS OBISPO COUNTY

Pismo Beach Chamber of Commerce, 581 Dolliver Street, Pismo Beach, CA 93449 (805-773-4382)

Cayucos Chamber of Commerce, PO Box 141, Cayucos, CA 93430 (805-773-4382)

MONTEREY COUNTY

Carmel Business Association, PO Box 4444, Carmel, CA 93921 (408-624-2522)

Pacific Grove Chamber of Commerce, PO Box 167B, Pacific Grove, CA 93950 (408-373-3304)

Monterey Peninsula Chamber of Commerce, PO Box 1770, Monterey, CA 93940 (408-649-1770)

SANTA CRUZ COUNTY

Capitola Chamber of Commerce, 410 Capitola Avenue, Capitola, CA 95010 (408-475-6522)

Santa Cruz County Conference and Visitors Council, 710 Front Street, Santa Cruz, CA 95060 (408-425-1234)

SAN MATEO COUNTY

Half Moon Bay Chamber of Commerce, 520 Kelly Avenue, Half Moon Bay, CA 94019 (650-726-5202)

Pacifica Chamber of Commerce, 450 Donde Way, Suite 2, Pacifica, CA 94044 (650-355-4122)

SAN FRANCISCO COUNTY

Convention and Visitors Bureau, 201 3rd Street, Suite 900, San Francisco, CA 94103 (415-391-2000)

MARIN COUNTY

Marin County Chamber of Commerce and Visitors Bureau, Marin Center, Avenue of the Flags, San Rafael, CA 94903 (415-472-7470)

West Marin Chamber of Commerce, PO Box 1045, Point Reyes Station, CA 94956 (415-663-9232)

SONOMA COUNTY

Bodega Bay Chamber of Commerce, PO Box 146, Bodega Bay, CA 94923 (707-875-3422)

Sonoma County Convention and Visitors Bureau, 5000 Roberts Lake Road, Suite A Rohnert Park, CA 94928 (707-586-8100)

MENDOCINO COUNTY

Mendocino Coast Chamber of Commerce, PO Box 1141, Fort Bragg, CA 95437 (707-964-3153)

HUMBOLDT COUNTY

Eureka/Humboldt County Convention and Visitors Bureau, 123 F Street, Eureka, CA 95501 (707-443-5097)

DEL NORTE COUNTY

Del Norte Chamber of Commerce, 1001 Front Street, Crescent City, CA 95531 (707-464-3174)

Lodging Index

General Index

Travel Guides from The Countryman Press

The alternative to mass-market guides with their homogenized listings, *Explorer's Guides* focus on independently owned inns, motels, and restaurants, and on family and cultural activities reflecting the character and unique qualities of the area. Planning a trip to the Northeast? Look for the following titles:

Cape Cod: An Explorer's Guide
Connecticut: An Explorer's Guide
The Hudson Valley and Catskill Mountains: An Explorer's Guide
Maine: An Explorer's Guide
Massachusetts: An Explorer's Guide
New Hampshire: An Explorer's Guide
Rhode Island: An Explorer's Guide
Vermont: An Explorer's Guide

Praise for our *Explorer's Guides* series:

"A terrific resource." —*Los Angeles Times*

"Many guides claim to be 'insider' takes on travel, but few deliver truly out-of-the-ordinary info. This one does . . . many listings will surprise even natives." —*New York Daily News*

"The most encyclopedic and useful guide to the state . . ." —*Travel & Leisure*

"Why can't we find books like these on all our travel destinations? All the standard tourist concerns are covered . . . very extensive details about restaurants, places to stay, and recreation. . . . More listings and more details on each listing than in other books." —*San Diego Union-Tribune*